(Post-)Colonial Archipelagos

(Post-)Colonial Archipelagos

Comparing the Legacies of Spanish Colonialism in Cuba, Puerto Rico, and the Philippines

EDITED BY HANS-JÜRGEN BURCHARDT
AND JOHANNA LEINIUS

UNIVERSITY OF MICHIGAN PRESS

ANN ARBOR

Published in the United States of America by the
University of Michigan Press
Manufactured in the United States of America
Printed on acid-free paper
First published February 2022

A CIP catalog record for this book is available from the British Library.

Library of Congress Cataloging-in-Publication data has been applied for.

ISBN 978-0-472-13316-1 (hardcover : alk. paper)
ISBN 978-0-472-03884-8 (paper : alk. paper)
ISBN 978-0-472-90260-6 (OA)

DOI: https://doi.org/10.3998/mpub.11747103

We gratefully acknowledge the Fritz-Thyssen Foundation and CALAS for supporting the publication of this volume.

Fritz Thyssen Stiftung für Wissenschaftsförderung

CALAS Center for Advanced Latin American Studies

Cover image: Carlos Celdran, *Sueño de Manila*, 2017, Mixed Media/Collage and Acrylic on Wood, 4 x 8 ft, Archivo 1984 Gallery. Image by Pioneer Studios 2021.

Contents

Digital materials related to this title can be found on the Fulcrum platform via the following citable URL: https://doi.org/10.3998/mpub.11747103

Figures and Tables

Figures

Tables

Acknowledgments

A book of this scope is a collective endeavor; what can be read on its pages is the culmination of many years of conversations, provocations, and teamwork across continents and lifeworlds. It is based on an enormous amount of work from everyone involved. Indeed, if we would have known of the challenges that a project of this size and scope would bring when we first met to discuss the idea of bringing together scholars from three continents to work on unraveling the colonial legacies of three island societies that, in our opinion, were more similar than usually assumed, we might not have begun this endeavor at all. The journey was long and riddled with unforeseen difficulties, but the book that you hold in your hands has been worth the effort.

We would not have been able to finish this project without the support of many people, of whom we can only name some:

First, we thank everyone who made it possible to have both an English and a Spanish version of the book, making its content available to a broad audience and overcoming the anglophone borders of academic publishing: Alicia Aguilar and Rachel Rarber, who translated several of the chapters from Spanish to English; Loida Frometa Castillo and Angela Ponce de León, who translated other chapters from English to Spanish; and Philip Fehling, who was tasked with keeping an overview of the various translation tasks and made sure everyone was paid. For providing financial resources for translating the chapters, as well as administrative and personal support, we thank the Centro de Estudios Latinoamericanos and the Centro de Estudios Avanzados Latinoamericanos. We especially thank Thomas Suermann from the Thyssen Foundation for the generous support and patience.

Without the support and critical comments of a great many people, the book would have been of lesser quality. We would like to thank Rebeca Ramos Padrón for making possible a first conference held in Havanna in 2017, which opened the conversation on the concept of this book; Hannes Warnecke-Berger and the participants of the workshop on comparison held at the University of Kassel in August 2019 for their feedback; and Sophia Zeh for the final proofreading of all chapters and especially the unthankful task of converting the numerous tables into the right format. We would like to thank everyone at the University of Michigan Press for their support in publishing the volume, especially Anne Taylor and Kevin Rennells for their meticulous copy-editing. We are grateful to Charles Watkinson and everyone involved at the University of Michigan Press for making the ebook available as open access.

Tesa Celdran, the widow of Manila-based artist Carlos Celdran, gracefully allowed us to feature his painting *Sueño de Manila* on the cover of the volume. We would like to thank her for trusting us with representing Carlos's artistic vision and politics to an audience largely unfamiliar with his work. We also would like to commemorate the passion of the late Carlos Celdran for interweaving the past and present of the city of Manila.

We especially thank all the authors, who kept their commitment to the project, notwithstanding the numerous challenges that arose throughout the years—from hurricanes to a global pandemic that kept many without internet access, printers, and other very material necessities of academic work. We really appreciate your determination to see this book published!

PART I

An Archipelagic View on (Post-)Colonial Legacies

CHAPTER 1

Of Archipelagic Connections and Postcolonial Divides

Johanna Leinius and Hans-Jürgen Burchardt

The Puerto Rican debt crisis, the challenges of societal transition in Cuba, and the populist politics of Duterte in the Philippines: these topics are typically seen as disparate experiences of social reality, discussed in distinct academic branches, connected to different societal genealogies, and examined with different conceptual frameworks. Though these three countries were colonized by the same two colonial powers—the Spanish Empire and, after 1898, the United States—research in history and the social sciences in general, and postcolonial studies in particular, rarely draws links between the three contexts.

One reason, certainly, has been the predominance of area studies as the discipline empirically analyzing formerly colonized societies. Area studies tends to separate countries according to their belonging to a specific region, predetermined by geographical, cultural, or (geo-)political aspects as well as histories of colonization. And the colonial trajectories of the three contexts diverged rapidly: Cuba was, from the very beginning, a settlement colony, center of trade, and important harbor on the Spanish shipping routes to and from the colonies. Puerto Rico, located on the rim of the Spanish Empire and in direct vicinity to territories claimed by other colonizing powers, gained military significance as an outpost tasked with defending the borders of the Spanish Empire (Rodríguez-Silva 2012, 22). The Philippines, in turn, served the Spanish Crown as a trading post with China and Japan; its enormous distance to Spain and New Mexico, to which it formally belonged, shaped Spanish colonialism on the Pacific archipelago (Liria Rodríguez 2014). Colonialism was also shaped differently depending on the period of Spanish colonialism. From the beginning of the 16th to the end of the 17th century, the Spanish Empire was characterized by its mercantilist orientation, meaning that it was geared toward economic self-sufficiency through the accumulation of wealth in the form of precious metals, privileging the land-owning classes as well as merchants holding exclusive trade rights on central goods (Burkholder and Johnson 2008, 32). With the advent of the Bourbon monarchy during the 18th century, however, reforms liberalized the political economy and introduced some level of competitiveness—though social stratification and restrictions on trade persisted. The crisis of the colonial system that this change engendered was felt most strongly in the colonies most heavily involved in colonial trading regimes, including the islands of Cuba, Puerto Rico, and the Philippines, as well as the mining economies of the Andes and Mexico (Lauria-Santiago 2008, 265).

While studying these contexts with conceptual frameworks focused on the common histories of (de-)colonization within Latin America, the Caribbean, and Southeast Asia, respectively, has yielded important insights, recent interventions have posited the need for transregional studies (Bentley, Bridenthal, and Yang 2005). These interventions underline the need to overcome methodological regionalism and, by drawing unfamiliar comparisons, to unearth new aspects of historical and contemporary constellations. Archipelagic American Studies, for example, proposes to bring the continental United States and its (formerly) colonized territories together in one analytic framework to scrutinize their mutual influences in one interconnected landscape. Tracing the genesis of the term "archipelago," Brian Roberts and Michelle Stephens, the editors of the volume *Archipelagic American Studies* (2017), argue that though the term was, in the 13th century, first used to describe the Aegean as a body of water, it soon became commonplace to use it for the set of islands located in this ocean (7). When traveling to other parts of the globe, seafarers and colonizers ceased to use the term to describe only a specific set of islands; by comparing the landscapes they saw to those they knew, they generalized the term to describe insular constellations interconnected in some way or other. As a term stemming from comparisons made in the wake of colonial endeavors, it seems a fitting analytic for examining interconnected (post-)colonial histories—especially those that, at first glance, do not seem to be interconnected but yet, much like archipelagos, might be linked by subterranean networks not easily visible from the surface and yet vital for their functioning.

Roberts and Stephens maintain that Archipelagic American Studies "exist in productive and generative tension with postcolonial and world-systems frameworks that center on core-periphery topologies" (2017, 18). We similarly argue that *postcolonial studies*, when based on an empirically anchored comparative sensitivity, can provide a productive context for probing the (post-)colonial archipelagos of Puerto Rico, Cuba, and the Philippines. Dedicated to the analysis of the continuing influence of colonial power relations on current societal relations, postcolonial studies deal with the long-term material, political, social, cultural, epistemic, and psychological effects of colonialism. Located in various academic disciplines such as literary studies, history, cultural studies, and social sciences, postcolonial approaches are as thematically wide-ranging as they are polyphonic (Loomba et al. 2005). What they have in common is their aim to critically reflect on models of thought and practices of European provenance, arguing strongly for local and historical contextualization: They reject and deconstruct Eurocentric assumptions of the superiority and universality of European modernity, showcasing the interconnected (re-)production of the Global North and South, and critique the (re-)production of colonial/imperial ways of thinking and practices. Within postcolonial studies, generally, scientific and political aims are intertwined, as, for example, at the academic level, the postcolonial project strives for analytical shifts in perspective that have repercussions also for the way knowledge is produced, disseminated, and taught. Topics range from the political non-representability of subaltern subjects and the incommensurability of their experiences to the demand to include authors and concepts beyond the Global North in the disciplinary canons of knowledge and text (Ashcroft 2009). Arguably, however, postcolonial studies have not succeeded in bringing their criticisms, creativity, and innovations into the empirical social sciences in a way that has gained broader methodological-analytical influence. In many cases, they are referred to in introductory paragraphs and when examining the current state of the art in research, but this acknowledgment does not always lead to an adjustment of methodologies and analytical perspectives and is often met with resistance and resentment (Loomba et al. 2005, 29; Ziai, Bendix, and Müller 2020, 2–5).

Apart from the difficulties in challenging hegemonic knowledge regimes, this disjointed reception can, among other things, also be traced back to the specific outlook of postcolonial studies. Composed of highly heterogeneous approaches, the various strands of postcolonial studies work with different analytical categories: Postcolonial theory, stemming from literary studies, often has only little empirical underpinning, which makes it difficult for social scientists to link its overarching claims back to social reality and anchor them in a rigorous methodological framework. Postcolonial approaches in cultural studies and the humanities often do not meet the expectations of social scientists concerning precision, operationalization, and validity of the concepts used. Even proponents of postcolonial studies argue that postcolonial approaches tend to work with a level of abstraction that is difficult to ground empirically and, at worst, that some work with absolute explanations (such as colonialism) that cannot do justice to the complexities of social change (Ziai 2012, 294; San Juan 1998; Rao 2006; Santos 2010).

In sum, postcolonial approaches have not yet offered a methodological framework that is open enough to capture the relevant particularities of different world regions but at the same time has sufficient consistency to justify decentralized research that allows for general statements and systematic comparisons—a project that some would also deliberately reject. As long as this line of study is not advanced, however, a stronger anchoring of postcolonial knowledge in the empirical social sciences is unlikely. The ability to carry out specific, thematically precise, and empirically saturated analyses should be fostered, we hold, so that the lack of context sensitivity of research on the Global South can be critically reflected while the further development of postcolonial studies' own research instruments can be stimulated. Our proposal is, therefore, that postcolonial studies should foster inductive category formation. This implies systematic comparisons as well as the combination—when useful—of quantitative methods with qualitative approaches. In a constructive linkage, it would be possible to underpin qualitative studies with quantitative data and, for quantitative surveys, to sharpen the variables or indicators in the direction of greater historical and contextual sensitivity. It also implies taking into account the positionality of those undertaking research, abandoning the notion of objective knowledge and, instead, acknowledging the situatedness of knowledge and the politics of knowledge production.

This volume makes a concrete proposal in this respect. We argue that an interdisciplinary comparative framework containing both a synchronic and a diachronic perspective can be a fruitful approach for the empirical analysis of colonial legacies. Our approach centers on the in-depth analysis of the past and present of the political economy and the dynamics of social differentiation in three (post-)colonial contexts. To tease out the potential but also the pitfalls of our approach, we analyze the effects of one colonial influence in differing spatial, cultural, and socioeconomic contexts: Cuba, Puerto Rico, and the Philippines. The analyses are undertaken by scholars intimately familiar with and, in many cases, embedded in the contexts they analyze. This has implied fostering a dialogue between historians and social scientists as well as between scholars located in the Global North and in the Global South. The challenges of translating between these different positionalities to make a conversation possible should not be underestimated. For us, they are a central part of the complexities of postcolonial theory production. Working at the borders of different knowledge regimes—be they disciplinary or regional—has shown us the importance of acknowledging the politics of knowledge production both concerning the content and the material and epistemic context of the analyses presented in this volume. In our analytical framework, the cases are compared only after the inductive analyses, so that the picture of colonial legacies that the comparative analyses paint can be troubled by the local specificities and historical genealogies presented in the case studies.

With this approach, we challenge the accepted narrative on the colonial legacies of Cuba, Puerto Rico, and the Philippines on several fronts. On the one hand, by focusing on the legacies of Spanish colonization, we unearth historical trajectories that are usually obscured by the more recent interventions and the ongoing influence of the United States in the three contexts. On the other hand, by bringing together three places whose comparability is not self-evident, we question narratives of statehood and development, tracing the interconnections but also the divergences of the paths these three former colonies of the Spanish Empire took.[1]

In the remainder of the introduction, we first show how and why postcolonial studies provide not only the background but also the target of our methodological and conceptual intervention. Then, we present the argument of the volume in more detail and give an overview of the chapters, which together provide a comprehensive picture of the past and present of the (post-)colonial archipelago under study.

Studying (Post-)Colonial Legacies

In historical research on Latin America, the persistence of colonial relations has been at the center of scrutiny, to the point of it having become a master narrative (Adelman 1999, xi). The continuing social inequalities within societies, the ubiquity of social conflict, the malfunctioning of democratic institutions, and the rule of corrupt elites have all been traced back to colonialism. As one of the early interventions putting forward a comparative view, the "Black Legend" purported to explain the differences between Spanish and British colonialism. Originally a campaign launched by the British to discredit the Spanish Crown in their competition over the colonial world, it created a myth that has reappeared in more recent writings and has served as underlying discourse for various other explanatory approaches to the colonial legacies of the Spanish Empire (Adelman 1999, 6–10; see Hartz 1964; Véliz 1994). Within the political economy, dependency theory has shown how unequal terms of trade have shaped the economies of Latin American countries to their detriment and to the advantage of the former colonizing countries (Frank 1969; Prebisch 1971; Dos Santos 2002).

More contemporary analyses offer a more nuanced evaluation of colonial legacies. Though colonialism certainly shaped colonized societies, it has been shown that it cannot be perceived as a uniform force flattening out local particularities and patterns (see Lauria-Santiago 2008). The legacies of colonialism, it is argued, can be seen as a result of the interaction of local and global forces (Mignolo 2005). Historically grounded analyses, therefore, need to take seriously the complexities of the specific trajectories of (de-)colonialization, or in the words of Anne McClintock: "The inscription of history around a single 'continuity of preoccupations' and 'a common past,' runs the risk of a fetishistic disavowal of crucial international distinctions that are barely understood and inadequately theorized" (1995, 12).

More than two decades after McClintock's call for historically more diligent analyses, there exists ample research on the colonial legacies of formerly colonized as well as colonizing states in the social sciences and humanities. This research was invigorated by the advent of postcolonial studies during the 1980s in the context of conceptual and political shifts in the humanities and social sciences in favor of poststructuralist perspectives, following in the wake of the French theoretical tradition of Michel Foucault and Jaques Derrida. Inspired by these currents and based on the work of the anti-colonial writers Frantz Fanon, Aimé Césaire, Albert Memmi, and Steven Biko, among others, the literary scholars Edward Said, Gayatri Chakravorty, Spivak and Homi Bhabha began to focus their research on matters of representation and identity formation in colonial discourses (see Go 2015). In a political context in which it became increasingly obvious that formal decolonization did not go hand in hand with a change in global relations of power, they strove to uncover the cultural and epistemic constellations that continued to subjugate non-Western peoples and knowledges by reexamining colonial discourses. In doing so, they initiated a paradigm shift that radically challenged Europe's central position and the associated Western notion of progress and development as a unilinear process. Within critical historical analyses, it was the Subaltern Studies Group that strove to provide a counterpoint to established historical narratives by studying the underprivileged more systematically (Guha 2001).

But in their analyses, Said (1978) and later Spivak (1988), among others, not only examined subject and identity formation but also discussed the material macrostructures in which these dynamics were embedded. Spivak's discussion of the role of political (self-)representation, for example, not only takes into account the positioning of specific actors but also emphasizes the role of institutions in legitimizing particular structures of power and authority. She understands subalternity as positionality without identity, troubling Marxist notions of class struggle as well as the Subaltern Studies Group's aim to uncover peasant insurgencies by rereading the colonial archives. She furthermore shows that social hierarchies (re-)produce themselves along different categories such as race, gender, or class.[2]

The focus on discourses and the deconstruction of epistemological axioms, however, eventually gained predominance. Stuart Hall (1992) and Dipesh Chakrabarty (2000) questioned the great "narrative" of European modernity, Arturo Escobar (1995) scourged the Western paradigms of development, and Bhabha (1994) emphasized that the (asymmetrical) interdependencies and breaks in colonial discourses lead to hybridity as an unintended side effect of colonial power, in which the potential of subversion is always already inscribed.

Apart from macro-level theorizing, recent approaches also increasingly refer to the knowledges and practices of ethnic and indigenous minorities. Following the example of the Subaltern Studies Group, socially marginalized subjects and movements have become the focal point of colonial (discourse) analysis, and often race or indigeneity are positioned as important markers for potential subalternity or oppression. Ideas on the "alternatives to development" (Acosta 2013) or the "pluriversalization" of concepts (Suárez-Krabbe 2014; Reiter 2018) have contributed to amplifying thinking from the exteriority of modernity and helped marginalized voices from the Global South to be heard more loudly. But the emphasis on "cultural difference" has also led, some argue, to describing all other differences and, above all, social inequalities as cultural constructions and thus ontologizing culture itself (Benhabib 2002). Thus, the focus of postcolonial studies on structures, institutions, and material relations has become less pronounced. This tendency was noticed and criticized from the onset, leading to a rich internal debate concerning the relative balance between the materialist underpinning of postcolonial studies and its poststructuralist view on discourse and identity formation. The dictum of Christine Sylvester (1999, 703) is certainly emblematic in this context: "Development studies does not tend to listen to subalterns and postcolonial studies does not tend to concern itself with whether the subaltern is eating."

Reacting to this debate, but also to the specific historical and material context of Latin America, the scholars of the modernity/coloniality approach have theorized modernity as a structural relationship emerging from colonial expansion accompanied by its darker side, coloniality. With recourse to the world-system approach and dependency theory, European colonialism is assessed as constitutive for Western modernity, since it guaranteed the political economy for the development of the colonial and capitalist expansion in the 16th century (Quijano 2000). Modernity, capitalism, racism, and patriarchy are seen as co-constitutive (Restrepo and Rojas 2010, 17; Krishnaswamy and Hawley 2008, 6). The Peruvian sociologist Aníbal Quijano holds that contemporary patterns of rule can be traced back to the colonization of the Americas, when the "coloniality of power" was constituted by two intertwined axes. First, world capitalism emerged as a new structure for organizing labor, production, and trade on a global scale based on the exploitation of large parts of the population. Second, the parts of the population subjected to exploitation were identified by racialized categories emerging for the first time to naturalize the domination of the conquering over the conquered populations (Quijano 2000, 216). This "dark side of modernity" (Mignolo 2008) can only be dismantled through decolonization, that is, the overcoming of continuing (colonial) power relations. Decolonial approaches based on this analytic take political-economic constellations into account but presuppose the dominance of capitalist relations. Material practices and relations fade to the background of many of their analyses as well, as their focus is either on the struggles of the marginalized and their proposals for decolonization or on the colonizing effects of broader discursive and cultural structures.

In our volume, we take inspiration from historical approaches, postcolonial studies, and the modernity/coloniality approach but scrutinize whether the hypothesis that colonial structures have persisted can be upheld in the face of a diligent historical and transregional comparison.

Usually, Cuba, Puerto Rico, and the Philippines do not figure prominently when sweeping claims are made about the countries formerly colonized by Spain. The transregional comparisons offered in the volume therefore problematize the narratives about the legacies of (Spanish) colonialism and provide a more complex reading from the margins of the Spanish Empire.

Doing Postcolonial Comparisons: The Colonial Legacies of Cuba, Puerto Rico, and the Philippines

Comparison is one of the central methodologies in both the social sciences and history. The scientific practice of doing comparisons, however, has been problematized not only in historical research. Cultural, literary, and global studies have engaged in critical reflections on how to compare, especially when inspired by postcolonial perspectives (Duara, Murthy, and Sartori 2014; Manning 2014). What these discussions show is that the implicit assumptions on which comparisons rest are problematic. On the one hand, comparative analyses start with the assumption of the comparability, and therefore of the commensurability, of the entities compared. On the other hand, European norms and developments are usually taken as comparative measurement sticks for analysis, which do not necessarily reflect local realities adequately (Midell 2014; Stoler 2001; Radhakrishnan 2009; Epple and Erhart 2015). In this context, Laura Ann Stoler (2001, 864) argues that postcolonial studies need "to do better comparisons, to pursue the politics and history of comparison, or to reach for connections that go beyond comparison altogether."

Stoler proposes that comparisons need to be historicized in order to avoid an overly mechanical reading of postcolonial processes in the sense of either assuming the determining influence of colonial histories on contemporary structures or denying the persistence of any colonial structures altogether. Comparative analyses of the Spanish colonies, however, tend to follow the lines criticized by Stoler and others: They often focus exclusively on Central and Latin American countries and exclude those constellations that would trouble their comparative framework instead of centering on these cases in particular. In James Mahoney's systematic comparative analysis of the postcolonial legacies for levels of development, for example, Cuba, Panama, and the Dominican Republic are excluded from analysis because they are not easily contained in the usual narrative of independence and sovereignty, as the author readily admits (2010, 33). Puerto Rico and the Philippines are not even mentioned. When Cuba, Puerto Rico, and the Philippines have been compared, the focus has been either on the way US imperialism played out after 1898 (Go 2006; Thompson 2010) or on presenting empirically rich historical analyses without a link to broader questions that would enable comparability (Naranjo, Puig-Samper, and García Mora 1995).

Johanna Leinius expands on this postcolonial debate on the comparability of the distinct historical trajectories of formerly colonized countries. She discusses the politics of comparison that the volume undertakes and critically evaluates its analytical framework. To further postcolonial studies' engagement with the comparative method, she proposes multivocal comparisons based on collective knowledge production as well as a focus on analyzing paradoxes. A deeper insight into the legacies of colonialism as well as ongoing patterns of coloniality can be gained, she argues, when the empirical debris of comparative analyses that cannot be easily subsumed under deductive logics is taken as a starting point for a deeper engagement with the historically anchored social realities under scrutiny.

The chapter by **Josep M. Fradera** focuses on the intensive transformation experienced by the three colonies after the breakdown of the Greater Spanish Empire at the end of the 18th century. From marginal outposts, Cuba, Puerto Rico, and the Philippines became important enclaves for the production of raw material. In the Caribbean, slavery became the main force to produce impressive exports of sugar and coffee; in the Philippines, exports of tobacco, sugar, and indigo were mainly reached through taxation and drafted labor. The economic transformation spearheaded by these changes, Fradera argues, was the basis for Spanish rule until the Spanish-American War of 1898.

The case studies that follow pick up one of the dimensions that existing research has identified as a central aspect of colonial legacies (see Adelman 1999, 7; Morse 1964): political economy and authority.

Antonio Santamaría García analyzes the elements that made up the Hispanic colonial regime in Cuba. He shows how the change in the Spanish Empire's economic outlook, which Fradera describes in detail in his chapter, promoting export agriculture and the slave trade, coincided with the interests of the island's producing elites. However, his chapter shows that as Spain lacked a market for the supply of the Greater Antilles, the system in fact facilitated an unparalleled economic expansion into English domains. Over time, he argues, the harmony of Hispanic-Cuban interests was weakened by the crisis of slavery and the concentration of colonial trade in the United States. Examining the contemporary political economy of Cuba, **Jacqueline Laguardia Martínez** traces the socioeconomic structures from the colonial era until the present day. She shows how Cuba's economy and society underwent dramatic changes after the 1960s but how, nonetheless, the country exhibits a mixed scenario of rupture and continuity with the colonial past. Colonial footprints are visible in territorial disparities and social divides, in spite of the significant reduction of racial and gender inequalities. The central role of the state as economic actor persists, as does the structural weakness of the economy due to its high vulnerability to exogenous events and dependence on imports and remittances, which limits economic diversification and facilitates technological lags and low productivity. **Emilio Pantojas-García** examines Puerto Rico's colonial legacies from the empires of Spain and the United States. He traces the contemporary socioeconomic regime, consisting of metropolitan citizenship, social welfare programs, constitutional guarantees, and, until recently, economic protectionism and subsidies, to its roots in the colonial experience, arguing that Puerto Rico has never been decolonized. **Ian Seda Irizarry** and **Argeo Quiñones** concur with Pantojas-García, analyzing in depth the institutional structure that has characterized the economic model of development of Puerto Rico to better understand the economic depression, the fiscal crisis, and the political economy of the island. They argue that an important aspect often neglected in discussions pertaining to the dismal performance of the economy is the relationship among the local private sector, foreign capital, and the local government. By placing this issue at the forefront and tying it to the general contours of the economic model, they trouble the prevalent explanations that offer a narrow analysis based on the politico-juridical relationship between the United States and Puerto Rico.

Turning the gaze to the Philippines, **Alvin A. Camba** and **Maria Isabel B. Aguilar** assess the political economy of the Philippines during the Spanish colonial regime. They argue that from the 16th to the 18th century, the Philippines' position in the Spanish colonial economy was unique, inasmuch as it departed from the conventional mercantilist relations that governed much of Spain's empire—thus providing a counterpoint to the overarching narrative of the Spanish Empire's economic policies. However, at the end of the 18th century, they state, the Philippines was eventually subsumed within the British world empire, converging to become an emerging cash crop exporter and thus following the path of other colonized societies. These patterns of continuity and change are picked up by **Teresa R. Melgar**, who uses the democratic transition in the Philippines as a reference point to examine the dynamics of political and economic power following the demise of authoritarian rule. She underscores how historically salient factors such as the control over economic resources, a prestigious political lineage, and high social status have continued to structure access to the state. Through their control over national policy-making processes, economic-political elites have hindered greater equity and democratization, even as civil society groups and their state allies have occasionally achieved key policy reforms. She concludes by showing how the rise to power of Philippine President Rodrigo Duterte has supplemented this dynamic with the growing suppression of democratic rights.

Another dimension of the colonial legacies includes the organization of labor and the interconnected marking and hierarchization of difference, especially "race," religion, and gender. By examining how the inequalities produced by specific labor regimes have been articulated culturally, socially, and politically, this dimension connects to existing research that has singled out the persistence of inequality as a characteristic of Latin American societies that can be traced back to the conquest (Munck 2013, 182; Hall and Patrinos 2006).

Javiher Gutiérrez Forte and **Janet Iglesias Cruz** turn to the colonial period in Cuba and show how a profoundly unequal society based on skin color, place of origin, gender, and appropriation of wealth has been consolidated. Legitimized by the political culture and political administration and sustained by a network of social relations based on a centralized structure and the disproportionate dominance of a small group, social inequalities predominantly based on "race," they argue, have been perpetuated. Their conclusion—that it is these cultural legacies, turned into "popular knowledge," that have survived colonialism and its institutions—is expanded on by **Jenny Morín Nenoff**, who examines the relationship between racial and social inequality in Cuban society since colonial times to the current socioeconomic transformation process. Although the Cuban government has banned institutionalized racism since 1959 and created an egalitarian society through comprehensive social policies, she shows that it has failed to overcome deeply rooted racial prejudices and discriminatory informal practices. In the wake of the economic reforms in the 1990s, her chapter shows, mulatto and black Cuban citizens cannot take equal advantage of economic reforms, because they do not have the same positive structural conditions as their "white" counterparts.

Milagros Denis-Rosario discusses the question of the continuing legacies of colonial hierarchization in Puerto Rico. She reviews the historical roots of the Spanish colonial system and the impact it has had on Puerto

Rican society, particularly among Puerto Ricans of African descent. She argues that the colonial infrastructure is closely linked to the perpetuation of inequalities of class, race, and gender, juxtaposing the contemporary oil painting *Plaza del Quinto Centenario* by the Afro–Puerto Rican artist Ramón Bulerín with the discussions in the wake of the construction of this space as part of the celebrations in 1992 of the fifth centenary of the discovery of the Americas. Her chapter resonates deeply with the work of artist and cultural activist Carlos Celdran, whose painting *Sueño de Manila* is featured on the cover of this volume. His guided walks of the Intramuros district in Manila, where the Spanish colonial administration was located, were aptly called "If These Walls Could Talk," as he pointed out how Manila's colonial history has been inscribed into the cityscape. Celdran experienced the enduring legacy of Spanish colonization when a law originating in the Spanish colonial era was used to sentence him for "offending religious feelings" in the wake of an artistic intervention in 2010 in which he protested the influence of the Catholic Church on Philippine politics. Forced into exile to Madrid in 2018, Celdran died in October 2019.

Miguel A. Rivera-Quiñones narrows down on how the governance of inequality has played an important role in the reproduction of colonial rule in Puerto Rico. He argues that the poor and the working classes have been economically incorporated in the colonial project through US economic transfers, migration, and consumerism, which together normalize the existing socioeconomic inequalities in Puerto Rico. **María Dolores Elizalde** turns to the Philippines and analyses, first, the different political models and economic regimes established in the Philippines during the time when the archipelago was part of the Spanish Empire. Second, she studies the social structure and population groups that defined Philippine society, concluding with a reflection on the legacies of the Spanish colonial regime and its influence on the subsequent development of the islands. **Cristina Cielo** follows the trajectories opened by Elizalde into present-day Philippines, examining the stark social inequalities there and arguing that contemporary configurations of economic and political power are marked by legacies of colonial hierarchies of elite dominance and land control. Postcolonial liberalization has combined with familial political structures to weaken the political power of a globally dependent and socially stratified workforce. The privatization of public decisions, policies, and services reinforces these differences, she argues, pointing to Duterte's politics that promise inclusion and a shared future through the definition and elimination of a vilified Other as a contemporary case of Othering rooted in colonial logics.

In the first of the comparative chapters, **Michael Zeuske** provides a historically detailed analysis of one specific aspect of Spanish (post-)colonial legacies: the impact of slavery. He traces the contemporary understanding of the legacies of Spanish colonialism and juxtaposes it with the historical debates on the legacies of slavery led during its abolition around 1880. He argues that of enduring importance has been the culture of Afrodescendants in Caribbean societies and structural patterns such as land ownership. He puts Cuba at the center of his analysis, with comparisons drawn to Puerto Rico and the Dominican Republic. **Jochen Kemner** picks up Zeuske's argument but, by slightly turning the focus of analysis, reveals another layer concerning the continuing legacies of slavery and forced labor. He shows how, during the colonial period, a regime of social stratification that created a close correlation between the means used to acquire income and wealth and social status emerged. He argues that this regime still characterizes to a considerable degree the social conditions of today's societies. Mechanisms that established economic privileges and exclusions became solidified in societal notions that led to a devaluation of manual work. The availability and control of the labor force became a mark of social distinction and created an antagonism that permeated the abolition of slavery and the end of colonial rule. **Hans-Jürgen Burchardt** systematizes the case studies and two preceding comparative chapters to provide a holistic comparison of the legacies of Spanish colonialism and develops suggestions for the further conceptual and methodological development of postcolonial studies. He proposes a material turn and, based on the results of the comparative analysis, suggests the engagement with rentier societies as a particularly productive venue for further research.

NOTES

1. Guam, the fourth of the last Spanish colonies, is not part of our framework. Colonized by the Spanish in 1565, it was ceded to the United States in 1989, constituting an unincorporated territory with limited citizenship rights for its inhabitants until this day (Perez 2005, 572). Scrutinizing the trajectory of Guam might have added important insights, as its history is rarely taken into account in debates in the social sciences and history. Its inclusion might, for example, have allowed for a deeper reflection on the role of indigeneity in processes of colonization and struggles for decolonization. The invisibility of Guam in academic debate in our respective fields, however, provided an insurmountable challenge when we intended to form a sufficiently large knowledge base from which to start our comparative endeavor.

2. Spivak (2003) has repeatedly pointed out that any struggle against cultural

discrimination is also a struggle for social advancement. Her stance provides an example of how intersectional analysis and postcolonial studies are linked. For an evaluation of the links between intersectionality research and postcolonial theories, see Wallaschek (2015).

REFERENCES

Acosta, Alberto. 2013. *El buen vivir: Sumak Kawsay, una Oportunidad Para Imaginar Otro Mundo*. Barcelona: Icaria.

Adelman, Jeremy, ed. 1999. *Colonial Legacies: The Problem of Persistence in Latin American History*. New York: Routledge.

Ashcroft, Bill. 2009. "Alternative Modernities: Globalization and the Post-Colonial." *Ariel* 40 (1): 81–105.

Benhabib, Seyla. 2002. *The Claims of Culture: Equality and Diversity in the Global Era*. Princeton: Princeton University Press.

Bentley, Jerry H., Renate Bridenthal, and Anand A. Yang, eds. 2005. *Interactions: Transregional Perspectives on World History*. Honolulu: University of Hawai'i Press.

Bhabha, Homi K. 1994. *The Location of Culture*. New York: Routledge.

Burkholder, Mark A., and Lyman L. Johnson. 2008. *Colonial Latin America*. New York: Oxford University Press.

Chakrabarty, Dipesh. 2000. *Provincializing Europe: Postcolonial Thought and Historical Difference*. Princeton: Princeton University Press.

Dos Santos, Theotônio. 2002. *La Teoría de la Dependencia: Balance y Perspectivas*. Buenos Aires: Plaza & Janes.

Duara, Prasenjit, Viren Murthy, and Andrew Sartori, eds. 2014. *A Companion to Global Historical Thought*. Malden: Wiley Blackwell.

Epple, Angelika, and Walter Erhart. 2015. "Die Welt Beobachten—Praktiken des Vergleichens." In *Die Welt Beobachten—Praktiken des Vergleichens*, edited by Angelika Epple and Walter Erhart, 7–34. Frankfurt: Campus.

Escobar, A. 1995. *Encountering Development: The Making and Unmaking of the Third World*. Princeton: Princeton University Press.

Frank, Andre Gunder. 1969. *Capitalism and Underdevelopment in Latin America: Historical Studies of Chile and Brazil*. New York: Modern Reader.

Go, Julian. 2006. "Imperial Power and Its Limits: America's Colonial Empire." In *Lessons of Empire: Imperial Histories and American Power*, edited by Craig Calhoun, Frederick Cooper, and Kevin W. Moore, 201–16. New York: Social Science Research Council.

Go, Julian. 2015. "Introduction: Entangling Postcoloniality and Sociological Thought." *Postcolonial Sociology* 24:3–31. https://doi.org/10.1108/S0198-8719(2013)0000024007

Guha, Ranajit. 2001. "Subaltern Studies: Projects for Our Time and Their Convergence." In *The Latin American Subaltern Studies Reader*, edited by Ileana Rodríguez, 35–46. Durham: Duke University Press.

Hall, Gillette, and Harry Anthony Patrinos. 2006. *Indigenous Peoples, Poverty and Human Development in Latin America*. New York: Palgrave Macmillan.

Hall, Stuart. 1992. "The West and the Rest: Discourse and Power." In *Formations of Modernity*, edited by Stuart Hall and Bram Gieben, 275–320. Cambridge: Polity.

Hartz, Luois. 1964. *The Founding of New Societies: Studies in the History of the United States, Latin America, South Africa, Canada and Australia*. New York: Harcourt.

Krishnaswamy, Revathi, and John C. Hawley. 2008. "Postcolonial and Globalization Studies: Connections, Conflicts, Complicities." In *The Postcolonial and the Global*, edited by Revathi Krishnaswamy and John C. Hawley, 2–21. Minneapolis: University of Minnesota Press.

Lauria-Santiago, Aldo A. 2008. "Land, Labor, Production, and Trade: Nineteenth-Century Economic and Social Patterns." In *A Companion to Latin American History*, edited by Thomas Holloway, 264–84. Malden: Blackwell.

Liria Rodríguez, Jorge A. 2014. *Filipinas y el Ultimo Colonialismo Español en el Pacífico*. Madrid: Mercurio Editorial.

Loomba, Ania, Suvir Kaul, Matti Bunzl, Antoinette Burton, and Jed Esty, eds. 2005. *Postcolonial Studies and Beyond*. Durham: Duke University Press.

Mahoney, James. 2010. *Colonialism and Postcolonial Development: Spanish America in a Comparative Perspective*. New York: Cambridge University Press.

Manning, Patrick. 2014. "Global Studies: A Historical Approach." In *Potentials and Challenges of Global Studies for the 21st Century*, edited by Madeleine Herren, Patrick Manning, Philip C. McCarthy, Matthias Middell, and Eric Vanhaute, 50–59. Basel: Institute for European Global Studies.

McClintock, Anne. 1995. *Imperial Leather: Race, Gender, and Sexuality in the Colonial Contest*. New York: Routledge.

Midell, Matthias. 2014. "What Is Global Studies All About?" In *Potentials and Challenges of Global Studies for the 21st Century*, edited by Madeleine Herren, Patrick Manning, Philip C. McCarthy, Matthias Middell, and Eric Vanhaute, 38–49. Basel: Institute for European Global Studies.

Mignolo, Walter D. 2005. *The Idea of Latin America*. Malden: Blackwell.

Mignolo, Walter D. 2008. "The Geopolitics of Knowledge and the Colonial Difference." In *Coloniality at Large: Latin America and the Postcolonial Debate*, edited by Mabel Morana, Enrique Dussel, and Carlos Jáuregui, 225–58. Durham: Duke University Press.

Morse, Richard. 1964. "The Heritage of Latin America." In *The Founding of New Societies*, edited by Luois Hartz, 123–77. Orlando: Harcourt.

Munck, Ronaldo. 2013. *Rethinking Latin America: Development, Hegemony, and Social Transformation*. New York: Palgrave Macmillan.

Naranjo, Consuelo, Miguel A. Puig-Samper, and Luis Miguel García Mora, eds. 1995. *La Nación Soñada: Cuba, Puerto Rico, y Filipinas Ante el 98*. Madrid: Doce Calles.

Perez, Michael P. 2005. "Colonialism, Americanization, and Indigenous Identity: A Research Note on Chamorro Identity in Guam." *Sociological Spectrum: Mid-South Sociological Association* 25 (5): 571–91.

Prebisch, Raúl. 1971. *Hacia una Dinámica del Desarrollo Latinoamericano: con un Apéndice Sobre el Falso Dilema Entre Desarrollo Económico y Estabilidad Monetaria*. México: Fondo de Cultura Económica.

Quijano, Aníbal. 2000. "Coloniality of Power and Eurocentrism in Latin America." *International Sociology* 15:215–32.

Radhakrishnan, Rajagopalan. 2009. "Why Compare?" *New Literary History* 40 (3): 453–71.

Rao, Nagesh. 2006. "New Imperialisms, New Imperatives: Taking Stock of Postcolonial Studies." *Postcolonial Text* 2 (1).

Reiter, Bernd, ed. 2018. *Constructing the Pluriverse: The Geopolitics of Knowledge*. Durham: Duke University Press.

Restrepo, Eduardo, and Axel Rojas. 2010. *Inflexión Decolonial: Fuentes, Conceptos y Cuestionamientos*. Popayán: Editorial Universidad del Cauca.

Roberts, Brian Russell, and Michelle Ann Stephens, eds. 2017. *Archipelagic American Studies*. Durham: Duke University Press.

Rodríguez-Silva, Ileana. 2012. *Silencing Race: Disentangling Blackness, Colonialism, and National Identities in Puerto Rico*. New York: Palgrave Macmillan.

Said, Edward. 1978. *Orientalism*. New York: Vintage Books.

San Juan, Epifanio. 1998. *Beyond Postcolonial Theory*. New York: Palgrave Macmillan.

Santos, Boaventura de Sousa. 2010. "From the Postmodern to the Postcolonial—and Beyond Both." In *Decolonizing European Sociology: Transdisciplinary Approaches*, edited by Encarnación Gutiérrez Rodríguez, Manuela Boatcă, and Sérgio Cista, 225–42. London: Routledge.

Spivak, Gayatri Chakravorty. 1988. "Can the Subaltern Speak?" In *Marxism and the Interpretation of Culture*, edited by Cary Nelson and Lawrence Grossberg, 271–313. London: Macmillan.

Spivak, Gayatri Chakravorty. 2003. *Death of a Discipline*. New York: Columbia University Press.

Stoler, Ann Laura. 2001. "Tense and Tender Ties: The Politics of Comparison in North American History and (Post) Colonial Studies." *Journal of American History* 88 (3): 829–65.

Suárez-Krabbe, Julia. 2014. "Pluriversalizing Europe: Challenging Belonging, Revisiting History, Disrupting Homogeneity." *Postcolonial Studies* 17 (2): 155–72.

Sylvester, Christine. 1999. "Development Studies and Postcolonial Studies: Disparate Tales of the 'Third World.'" *Third World Quarterly* 20 (4): 703–21.

Thompson, Lanny. 2010. *Imperial Archipelago: Representation and Rule in the Insular Territories under U.S. Dominion after 1898*. Honolulu: University of Hawai'i Press.

Véliz, Claudio. 1994. *The New World of the Gothic Fox: Culture and Economy in English and Spanish America*. Berkeley: University of California Press.

Wallaschek, Stefan. 2015. "In Dialogue: Postcolonial Theory and Intersectionality." *Momentum Quarterly* 4 (4): 218–32.

Ziai, Aram. 2012. "Postkoloniale Studien und Politikwissenschaft: Komplementäre Defizite, Stand der Forschung und Perspektiven." *Politische Vierteljahresschrift* 53 (2): 291–322.

Ziai, Aram, Bendix, Daniel, and Franziska Müller. 2020. "Decolonizing Knowledge Orders, Research Methodology and the Academia: An Introduction." In *Beyond the Master's Tools?: Decolonizing Knowledge Orders, Research Methods and Teaching*, 1–16. Lanham: Rowman & Littlefield.

CHAPTER 2

The Paradoxes of (Post-)Colonial Archipelagos—a Proposal for Postcolonizing Comparative Research

Johanna Leinius

> Incomparability compels forgetting, just as comparison prescribes some lessons and effortlessly disavows others. (Stoler 2006, 6)

Cuba, Puerto Rico, and the Philippines share not only a colonial history, having been colonized by both the Spanish Empire and the Unites States, but also a somewhat strained relation to postcolonial studies. While Puerto Ricans tend to agree that their island is a colony (Flores 2000, 35),[1] they find little resonance in postcolonial studies. Juan Flores argues that one reason is the status of Puerto Rico as a postcolonial colony:

> Puerto Rico is a colony in a different way, jibing only partially and uncomfortably with the inherited notion or stereotype of the classical colony with its earmarks of rampant socioeconomic misery, direct and total political and military control, and peripheralized public life contrasting graphically with that of the metropolis. (36)

Philippine scholars have also been critical of the relevance of postcolonial studies for the Philippines. Epifanio San Juan has famously rejected postcolonial studies as "poststructuralism regurgitated by intellectuals from the former colonies" (1995, 57) that does not take sufficiently into account contemporary US imperialism. This critique has been taken up by Alice Guillermo (1997, 16), who states with regard to the Philippines: "There is little political value in declaring oneself as a postcolonial subject while existing within a situation profoundly imbricated in neo-colonialism and imperialism." Underlining the contemporaneity of colonizing power structures, both Puerto Rican and Philippine critical intellectuals tend to reject postcolonial studies for not being sufficiently aware of the (neo-) colonial present. They echo the concerns of some postcolonial scholars who identify the tendency of postcolonial studies to locate colonial situations in the past and postcolonial ones in the present to the detriment of cases like Palestine, Morocco, the Mariana Islands, or, in fact, Puerto Rico (see Stoler 2016, 15).

Cuban scholars, in turn, usually position the colonial in the past. The Cuban government in particular has striven to act as a leader of anti-colonial and anti-imperialist movements and states; through the Cuban Revolution, the colonial past was deemed to have been overcome. Contemporary US interventions are consequently framed as neocolonialism. Tracing colonial legacies consequently has not been seen as an appropriate endeavor for Cuban scholars. Scholars located outside Cuba, in turn, have preferred to focus on evaluating the revolutionary process. Consequently, Cuban scholars as well as scholars of Cuba have not connected to postcolonial studies and its conceptual vocabulary, with the notable exceptions of literary scholars who engage with diasporic writers and their anti-colonial theorizing in prerevolutionary Cuba (see Luis-Brown 2008) or International Relations scholars who analyze revolutionary Cuba's position during the Cold War (see Laffey and Weldes 2008).

Whether Cuba, Puerto Rico, and the Philippines define their current status as postcolonial colony, target of neocolonial interventions, or decolonized revolutionary state, in all three places the impact and influence of US colonialism has been at the center of debates on colonial legacies, which has pushed reflections on the legacies of Spanish colonialism to the margins. This is the gap our volume focuses on. Unearthing colonial continuities deriving from Spanish colonialism necessitates, according to our reasoning, a comparative perspective that is conscious of both the linkages between the former colonies and the ruptures and differences that have been apparent already in times of Spanish colonialism. But how does our comparative approach based on case studies undertaken by a plurality of authors link to the debates concerning the politics of comparison in postcolonial studies? What problems, potentials, and paths does our project reveal?

In this chapter,[2] I first identify the debates concerning comparative research in the social sciences and more specifically in postcolonial, anthropological, historical, and transregional studies, showing how difference, similarity, and equality have been negotiated. I then situate the comparative approach this volume puts forward by showing how it has answered the critiques raised in these discussions. I argue that it provides a way to respect the complexity of local reality while still producing insights that point to more general patterns and processes. By employing a case study approach that assembles a plurality of voices, this strategy can, to an extent, mitigate postcolonial critiques of Eurocentrism and false universalism. By proposing the analysis of paradoxes as an entry point to the examination of the case studies assembled in this volume, I offer a path for following the traces of colonial legacies by connecting the knowledge assembled in this volume. I end by assessing the potential, but also limitations, of the proposed approach for postcolonizing comparative research.

Postcolonizing the Comparative Method

Comparisons have been a cornerstone of social science methodologies. They act as a bridging exercise between accounting for the complexity of the world and identifying general patterns by relating different cases to each other. As human sense making is to a large extent based on relationally constructing differences and similarities, and, therefore, on comparing (Saussure 1966), developing academic protocols for the exercise of comparing has been a step within the development of social science methodologies that has been seen as a natural extension of logical reasoning.

In political science and sociology, in particular, the comparative study of political systems and societies has reached a high level of sophistication. It is geared mainly toward causal explanations, hypothesis testing, and, to a lesser extent, prediction. Describing the different contexts under scrutiny and building classifications are, in most comparative methods, mere steps on the way to explaining, testing, or predicting specific outcomes (Landman 2003, 5–10; Krause 2016, 50). Quantitative paradigms are still central for comparative research. They draw on but also go beyond John Stuart Mill's methods of agreement and difference to identify the necessary and sufficient conditions that constitute the specific configurations under which certain outcomes are produced (Mahoney 2000, 388; Anckar 2008). Qualitative comparative methods, especially in the form of small-*N* comparative studies based on a case study methodology, have also become more accepted (Bennett and Elman 2006; Ragin 1987). Methods like process tracing and causal narratives have enabled thick and contextual descriptions within cases (Mahoney 2000, 412–417) and are often combined with quantitative methods in fuzzy set analyses (Ragin 2008; Rohlfing and Schneider 2018). How methods are mixed and cases are selected to improve the explanatory power of comparisons through combining inductive and deductive approaches has become the main issue of debate (Bennett and Elman 2006, 473; Ebbinghaus 2005; Hantrais 2014).

The scope of comparative approaches, however, remains restricted. In an analysis of the articles published in the three leading journals of comparative politics in the United States, Gerardo Munck and Richard Snyder show that, concerning the regional diversity of comparisons, cases are still overwhelmingly chosen from within the Organisation for Economic Co-operation and Development world (2007, 10). The issues under scrutiny are similarly limited: The state and its institutions are centered as actors, and issues of democracy and the economy are the main matters of concern (9). Comparative scholars rarely question the validity of the comparative approach as such, being more concerned with how to ensure conceptual clarity and analytical precision, or as Giovanni Sartori has already summed up the predicament of comparative studies fifty years ago: "It appears that we can cover more . . . only by saying less, and by saying less in a far less precise manner" (1970, 1035).

On the one hand, comparative methods continue to be a central methodological approach in many disciplines of the social sciences. On the other hand, critiques of comparisons are formulated from interdisciplinary and critical approaches like transregional studies and postcolonial studies, but also from within history, anthropology, and sociology. Comparisons are simultaneously ubiquitous and marginalized, fundamental for knowledge production and treated as problematic (Deville, Guggenheim, and Hrdlicková 2016, 20–21; Scheffer and Niewöhner 2010, vii; Jensen and Gad 2016, 189; Fox and Gingrich 2002).

To understand this conundrum, it is helpful to reconstruct the genealogies of comparative research. Tracing the practices of comparison, Jennifer Robinson (2011) shows that the social sciences predominantly have pursued two modes of comparison. On the one hand, societies that are seen as similar concerning their history, language, and culture are compared so that their common basis can provide a baseline against which variables can be tested. Cases that do not fit the model applied tend to be excluded from comparison. James Mahoney, for example, excludes Cuba, Panama, and the

Dominican Republic from his comparative analysis of how postcolonial legacies account for the different levels of development in former Spanish colonies, because they do not follow the trajectory of independence and sovereignty of the other Latin American colonies, as the author himself admits (2010, 33). On the other hand, comparisons juxtapose societies that are perceived as historically different in order to tease out similarities in structures or dynamics that then can provide the basis for constructing typologies or models with broader reach (Robinson 2011, 134). In both cases, "the paradox of comparison is that judgment of pertinence rests on 'the equation of unequal things'" (Stoler 2016, 15). In order to compare, things need to be similar at least concerning enough aspects to make the comparison viable, but they also need to be equal. Isabelle Stengers reminds us that, when going back to its Latin etymology, *compar* "designates those who regard each other as equals" (2011, 63).

But in the practice of comparative research, comparisons usually have rested on concepts and hypotheses developed in European and North American social sciences. Not only the material but also the conceptual center of comparisons has been Euro-America, which has served as a model for comparison with the rest of the world. Comparisons relate things to each other that are, at once, similar and different, equal and unequal. The matter of comparability is, therefore, inherently political: Comparing presupposes that things are rendered similar that might not be (entirely) similar and that the differences in the aftermath of being compared become overshadowed by their similarity. In turn, rendering something incomparable also is a move imbued with power; as Ann Laura Stoler holds in the epigraph at this chapter's opening, "incomparability compels forgetting" (2006, 6).

One has to remember that constructions of similarity, difference, and equality are not given but shaped by political events and hegemonic knowledge regimes. In many of the founding texts of the social sciences, for example, Hegel's "Lectures on the Philosophy of History" and "Lectures on the Philosophy of Religion" as well as Weber's sociology of religion in and after "The Protestant Ethic and the Spirit of Capitalism," different non-European regions are compared to Europe in order to trace specific aspects of societal development (Cheah 2003, 2). Hegel's thinking, famously, has been deeply shaped by his intellectual engagement with the Haitian Revolution, but he failed to make his comparative gaze explicit (Buck-Morss 2009, 17).

For such comparisons to become thinkable, modern structures of knowledge needed to develop, which, based on classificatory systems that allow for taxonomies to be built, could integrate the previously unknown into hierarchically ordered systems of classification. In the mid-18th century in Europe, "the emergence of natural history as a structure of knowledge" (Pratt 1992, 9) provided the background for the ordering of cultures into broader trajectories and systems of knowledge. Comparisons became a method for identifying general patterns within and between different societies and groups, allowing for the condensation of universal social laws and the building of theories with universal reach (see Tylor 1889). Based on Durkheimian sociology, among others, it was believed that

> description provided the facts, and comparative method was adopted to account for them; it was seen as a means of formulating and testing hypotheses and generalizations valid not only for one specific society or culture but cross culturally. (Holy 1987, 2)

The differentiation of the social sciences into distinct disciplines did not change this approach to comparing. While at the turn of the 20th century in Europe, social theorists like Weber and Durkheim strove to trace what made modern societies different from those defined as premodern, US sociologists took the interventions of the United States in Guam, Puerto Rico, Cuba, and the Philippines as a starting point to comparatively engage with the newly colonized territories. Moved by colonial curiosity and the perceived need to gather information about the newly subjugated territories, sociologists held courses with such titles as "The Philippine People" (Fine and Severance 1985, 118, in Go 2009, 4) or "American Race Problems" in which the West Indies, Hawaii, and the Philippines were studied comparatively (Ng 1994, 135).

Colonization stimulated the comparative imagination not only of scholars (Robinson 2011, 129) but also of those directly involved in colonial governance, as David Lambert and Alan Lester note of colonial governors:

> Since most governors dwelt in multiple colonies during their careers, so they inevitably made comparisons and connections between these colonies. Colonial governance was thus often a relative and comparative endeavour—one that was dependent on fruitfully imagining the lessons that could be learned and transferred between differently constituted colonial places. (2006, 11)

After World War II, the comparative study of colonization continued but under different auspices. In the wake of the decolonization processes of the time, the priorities changed. On the one hand, scholars like Shmuel Eisenstadt (1963, 1967) turned to the historical typologization of colonization and empire in the tradition of Weber. On the other hand, world systems theory (Wallerstein 1979) and the scholars grouped as dependency theorists (Cardoso 1977; Frank 1969) were interested in understanding the underlying patterns of the global structure of inequality and the role of colonialism in the latter. While different in ideological and analytical perspective, these approaches rest on the "capacity to examine a range of societies from the outside, and an ability to move freely from one society to another." They are based on and simultaneously provide "a synoptic view of human affairs from a great height" (Connell 2007, 12).

Additionally, the plane of equivalence—what is seen as sufficiently similar to validate comparison—assumes some sort of linearity of societal development from primitive to modern society (Robinson 2011, 133). As their trajectories are similar—either because societies are teleologically on the same path or because they are embedded in the same broader structures—different societies can be compared. Postcolonial theory has shown how such a notion of linear development is historically produced (Said 1978; Escobar 1995).

The first discipline that questioned the dominant frames of comparative research was anthropology. From the 1960s onward, it politicized the comparative practice, asked about its colonizing impetus, and strove to find other ways of generating theory (Fox and Gingrich 2002). Anthropologist questioning merged with feminist as well as science and technology studies' concern with the role and subjectivity of the researcher. Concepts were no longer seen as neutral and as unproblematically applicable in different contexts but as products of specific cultural contexts that take with them the cultural baggage of the context in which they were originally developed (Deville, Guggenheim, and Hrdlicková 2016, 21–22).

This change of perspective challenged several of the assumptions on which comparisons rest. First, methodologically, presuming the similarity and equality of the entities compared and therefore their commensurability was seen as doing violence to the complex realities on the ground (Strathern 1988). As each encounter between researcher and researched is unique and cannot be replicated, it is argued, the reduction of complexity that comparison depends on is an artificial flattening out of complexity that cannot withstand deeper scrutiny. Looking closer at the categories on which comparisons rest tends to lead to their dissolution "into dozens of other issues, pieces and fragments" (Fox and Gingrich 2002, 1). Analytical concepts, the argument goes, cannot be simply "extracted" from the context in which they were created, made transcendent, and used in other contexts as if they were clean of any contextual debris (Deville, Guggenheim, and Hrdlicková 2016, 21). Second, epistemologically, the very categories used for comparisons were charged with transporting European norms, as European developments were taken as a comparative measurement stick for all other contexts, not necessarily adequately reflecting local realities (Stoler 2001; Radhakrishnan 2009; Epple and Erhart 2015; Midell 2014, 44).

One effect of these critiques has been the rise of qualitative studies that take seriously the complexities on the ground, that either apply concepts very carefully and reflexively or forgo deduction altogether, and that argue for inductive or grounded theory (Scheffer and Niewöhner 2010, 8). A plethora of ethnographic studies have been produced that are rich in description but show little aspiration for making broader claims or for generating theory—certainly also due to anthropology's crisis of representation (Clifford and Marcus 1986). Maria de los Dolores Figueroa Romero, for example, in her impressive comparative study of the activism of Miskitu women in Nicaragua and Kichwa women in Ecuador, states that she decided to compare two cases of indigenous women's activism that share more differences than similarities to "bring to the fore the particularities of the[ir] activism" and, consequently, "to enrich the narrative of indigenous women's politics of social change more broadly" (Figueroa Romero 2011, 11). Her aim is to show the complexity of indigenous women's activism against narratives that homogenize and exoticize indigeneity. Following the outlook of many of the ethnographic studies in this tradition, she does not strive to tie her results back to more theoretical debates but chooses to formulate recommendations of how to better enter into a dialogue with indigenous women leaders instead.

When striving to contribute to the better understanding of the legacies that the colonial conquest has left on colonized as well as colonizing societies, however, tools to identify the specific patterns that can be traced back to colonial constellations of power and privilege are needed. This, inevitably, involves a certain level of generalization and, arguably, comparison. This is why Stoler insists on the continuing importance of doing comparisons or, if the method of comparisons is deemed to be unsalvageable, of finding other ways of identifying more general patterns and dynamics that point to how the colonial continues to echo in the present. She argues that postcolonial studies need "to do better comparisons, to pursue the politics and history of comparison, or to reach for connections that go beyond comparison altogether" (Stoler 2001, 864). In her recent work, she puts forward a way of examining the "strange continuity" of specific material, discursive or affective configurations, as "colonial reverberations with a difference" (Stoler 2016, 28). These configurations, she argues, are marked neither by clear breaks nor by explicit legacies but by the reanimation and rearrangement of earlier logics and practices that echo the past but appear in new figurations. She also underlines the importance of studying how comparisons have been applied and with what effects, tracing the politics of comparison in specific contexts (see also Young 2013, 688).

The historicizing of comparisons with a focus on the way comparisons have been applied has also been proposed in historical research, which has focused on interdependent dynamics to avoid a superficial reading of postcolonial processes. Neither assuming an overly dominant influence of colonial histories on contemporary structures nor denying the persistence of any colonial structures, colonialism is seen as more than a uniform force flattening out local particularities that leaves formerly colonized countries in the same state everywhere. As Anne McClintock argues:

> Yet the inscription of history around a single "continuity of preoccupations" and "a common past," runs the risk of a fetishistic disavowal of crucial international distinctions that are barely understood and inadequately theorized. (1995, 12)

Most of the historical work that responds to postcolonial concerns with overcoming Eurocentric analyses and "provincializing Europe" (Chakrabarty 2000) focuses on the British Empire and Asia (Pomeranz 2000; Parthasarathi 2011). Kenneth Pomeranz, for example, challenges the implicit normalization of Europe's historical path by turning the comparative gaze in both directions. To examine why Asia and Europe diverged in their economic path from the late 18th century onward, he compares England and the Yangzi Delta through what he calls a "reciprocal comparison," measuring the performance of England against categories developed through the analysis of the Yangzi Delta and vice versa (Pomeranz 2000, 8). His approach echoes Stengers's call for seeing the entities implicated in the comparison as active and equal parts of the comparative endeavor (Stengers 2011, 63). He expands this mode of comparison with a second mode he takes from Charles Tilly (1984): the "encompassing comparison" in which "rather than comparing two separate things (as classical social theory did) we look at two parts of a larger whole and see how the position and function of each part in the system shape their nature" (Pomeranz 2000, 10). Jan de Vries, in his history of household economies, in a similar manner, speaks of a "composite history of the common experience of a zone that is not defined primarily by political boundaries" (2008, xi). Antje Dietze and Matthias Middell, however, underline that despite changing the directionality of comparisons as well as opening spaces for questioning the units of analysis often taken for granted in comparative endeavors, these approaches are insufficient for accounting for the interactions and flows between places and peoples (2019, 60).

Other approaches that have been proposed to solve the problem of how to compare without taking for granted the entities compared, as well as to take seriously the connections that constitute these entities, are "connected histories" (Subrahmanyam 1997), "histoires croisées" (Werner and Zimmermann 2002), and "entangled histories" (Conrad and Randeria 2002). Though heterogeneous in their outlook, these approaches converge in challenging how historically diverse entities, for example, nation-states or empires, are retrospectively categorized as discrete—and similar—units of analysis to facilitate their comparison. By rendering things similar, their difference is obscured and the already existing threads between them cut. They, therefore, demand

> that we not only compare from within our boxes, but spend some time and effort to transcend them, not by comparison alone but by seeking out the at times fragile threads that connected the globe. (Subrahmanyam 1997, 762–63)

The focus on connections, networks, and entanglements has troubled historical comparisons (Potter and Saha 2015) and, according to some, has made comparisons impossible altogether (see Espagne 1994).

The archipelagic perspective that our volume takes is indebted to these debates. Seeing Cuba, Puerto Rico, and the Philippines as already entangled by networks and relations that are not always easily visible but yet there, without hastily assuming comparability, we intend to keep the tension between similarity and difference, past and present, and yet to tease out where points of connection lie. Our approach takes into account the critiques raised but does not abandon comparison altogether, nor does it presume the existence of already connected histories. It goes beyond proposals to see seas and oceans as connecting agents of different regions that, however, often tend to take entities like the Atlantic Ocean (Lachenicht 2019; Andrien 2009) or the Pacific Ocean (Wirth 2019) as objects of analysis, analyzing the flows and connections within but not beyond their borders—by relating the Philippines to Puerto Rico and Cuba, we go beyond these delineated seascapes, following the routes of colonial connections and striving to uncover the roots of the (post-)colonial present. Our approach contributes to transregional studies, which fundamentally question the concept of regions, focusing instead on the transformative connections between places and peoples in a "historically informed investigation of the reach of flows and control mechanisms that go beyond the limits and boundaries of single empires, continents, regions, or cultural spheres" (Middell 2019b, 10). In the first handbook on transregional studies, Matthias Middell (2019a) argues that rather than a discipline, transregional studies are a perspective that aims to link area studies to broader global processes, taking seriously the necessity of interdisciplinary work as well as postcolonial critiques. In the introductory chapter to the handbook, he remarks that what is needed are methodological tools to "make transregional studies more than an ambitious program" (Middell 2019b, 11).

Our volume aims to respond to this call and to offer an approach that takes into account and yet goes beyond Comparative Area Studies (CAS) (Ahram, Köllner, and Sil 2018a; Sil 2009; Berg-Schlosser 2012). CAS provides a fruitful point of reference, as it is conscious of the "political baggage of the colonial past" (Mehler 2019, 67), highlights the necessity of developing deep and interdisciplinary knowledge of the contexts under scrutiny, and sees areas as socially constituted rather than given (Hoffmann 2015). The need to work collaboratively and with the interdisciplinarity that especially cross-regional small-*N* comparisons engender, however, goes against the academic logic of developing professional expertise by focusing on single countries or areas (Sil 2009, 29; Ahram, Köllner, and Sil 2018b, 10). Immersing oneself in distinct contexts, developing the necessary language skills, and working collaboratively with native scholars takes time and resources that obstruct quick publishing—as our volume attests to. CAS, as it is put forward by, for example, the German Institute of Global and Area Studies, remains dedicated to tracing causal connections and producing generalizable conclusions, striving to balance the "deep sensitivity to context" (Ahram, Köllner, and Sil 2018b, 3) with causal inferences that transcend these contexts. In doing so, the approach is oriented toward proving the continuing relevance of area studies rather than troubling the paradigms on which comparisons rest or scrutinizing the politics of comparison critically.

In what follows, I present some possible avenues of how to undertake postcolonially informed comparative research that transcends these debates by providing a point of departure for comparative endeavors that start from the politics of comparison.

Practicing Postcolonial Comparative Research

Critically assessing and laying open for scrutiny how we have compared is, heeding the critiques not only of anthropology but also postcolonial studies, the first step in the practice of comparing. This means not only to critically reflect on the reasons for and the results of the comparative endeavor undertaken but also to reflect on the actual practices through which the comparison developed and to situate those doing the comparison socially, materially, and epistemologically.

To start with, the idea for this volume emerged from an actual encounter: the conference "Historical Legacies in Comparison: Cuba—Puerto Rico—Philippines. How Much History Can Post-Colonialism Endure?" that Hans-Jürgen Burchardt organized in March 2017 in Havana, Cuba. The conference showed that a dialogue between the social sciences and history and between the three countries can unearth previously unseen connections and linkages; it also proved that such a dialogue needed to be supported by the development of a shared analytical lens that would enable communication across the heterogeneous disciplinary and regional contexts. In the preparation of the volume, we therefore examined previous debates on colonial legacies and postcolonial histories to identify analytical dimensions that could serve as guiding posts for the case studies. We are aware that this decision already reduced the complexity of social reality and possibly obscured other relevant aspects. We hold, however, that without providing such a focus, the balance between similarity and difference would have been skewed in a way that would have made a sustained dialogue between the different times and places difficult. We identified two dimensions that, according to the literature examined, have shaped colonial rule and colonized societies in ways that provide a point of connection across contexts: first, the *political economy* and, second, the *hierarchization of difference*. Both dimensions are intersected by the *(re-)production of political power and authority*.

We derive from previous research on the (post-)colonial political economy the importance of resource extraction and of the intermeshing of economic and political power. Property relations, commerce, and the position of the colony within broader economic trade regimes shaped how political power was distributed and elites were formed (Andrien 2009). The role of the religious orders acting as economic actors (Dussel 1981; Turner Bishnell 2009, 206) and the change from mercantilism to restricted liberalization within the Spanish Empire (Mahoney 2010, 21; Schmidt-Nowara 2014, 26) are but two aspects of these dynamics. When contacting the contributors responsible for analyzing the historical and contemporary political economy of the three cases, however, we kept the task set deliberately broad, asking merely their assessment about the essential markers of the regime under scrutiny concerning the economic structures. We asked about the most dominant economic sectors, property relations, elite formation, the relative (de-)centralization of the state, and the role of geography.

Concerning the hierarchization of difference, the literature review underlined that the constitution and reproduction of unequal relations was to an important extent based on the hierarchization of especially gender, sexuality, religion, and the way "ethnoracial categories [were connected] to patterns of resource allocation" (Mahoney 2010, 19; Quijano 2000, 216; Branche 2008). Research has shown that while processes of transculturation, hybridity, and *mestizaje* took place, the ascription of difference also legitimized the unequal distribution of political authority (Klor de Alva 1995; Ibarra 1995, 87). We therefore asked the contributors of the case studies about the essential markers of the colonial regime under scrutiny concerning sociopolitical structures, especially with regard to the mechanisms of group distinction, labor regimes, slavery, migration, and access to political power. Rather than a strict questionnaire to be answered, we intended the questions we posed as guiding posts to orient the analysis and ensure the possibility of dialogue between the chapters.

The genealogy of the volume partly explains why Guam, the fourth of the last Spanish colonies, is not part of the analyses undertaken in this volume, though its history provides—even at first glance—striking similarities to the (post-)colonial experiences and dilemmas of the other three former Spanish colonies examined in this book. We discussed its inclusion in our research frame but decided against it mainly due to pragmatic reasons, such as the small size of the academic community focused on research on Guamese society and history and our complete lack of contacts to it. We are aware that this decision reproduces the marginalization of Guam in academic debates, which is connected to the silencing of Chamorro struggles.

We, therefore, decidedly encourage research on the colonial legacies of the Spanish colonization of Guam that takes into account the experiences and knowledges of the Chamorro community.

Another important aspect of the politics of comparison is the positionality and subjectivity of those undertaking the comparison. Positionality matters, and we acknowledge the extent to which the social, cultural, and geographical situatedness of the editors shaped the volume. In order to change the unidirectionality of many comparative studies in which information is extracted from the Global South by researchers from the Global North, the majority of case studies assembled in this volume are written by scholars located in Cuba, Puerto Rico, and the Philippines. We made use of previously established contacts and mapped relevant publications and their respective authors in order to identify and contact possible contributors. This strategy, of course, yielded results that were biased toward scholars visible in the research community either through their active online presence or through publications in relevant journals or edited volumes. It also revealed the difficulties in finding and contacting scholars from contexts in which reliable access to digital communication and publishing in internationally available and recognized publications are not the norm—in these cases, we relied more heavily on personal contacts and recommendations.

The contributions were written over a period of eighteen months. Apart from the challenge of going beyond our already existing scholarly networks, the material basis of academic work additionally intervened in the editing process: Hurricane María, which devastated Puerto Rico in September 2017, affected most of the Puerto Rican contributors to this volume; up to this day, infrastructural problems persist. Dialogue with the contributors from Cuba was also shaped by unreliable access to communication infrastructures.

When the case studies pointed to two topics that were of vital importance—the history and legacy of slavery as well as of the labor regime—we looked for scholars who could discuss these two topics in more depth, thus contextualizing the case studies with a more focused perspective.

Working with contributors from different contexts and disciplines also meant we had to engage with the politics of translation. Depending on the language the contributors felt most comfortable writing in, chapters were originally written in English, Spanish, or German. This meant that we had to set time—and resources—apart for translation. The work of translation was, however, not only between the three languages but also between the disciplinary and cultural codes of academic writing. We facilitated the possibility of dialogue by providing the contributors with questions to guide their analysis and by organizing an extensive review process that was not free of conflict but provided a basis for bringing the different chapters into a closer dialogue.

In what follows, I will offer an approach to the case studies assembled in this volume that engages the comparative imagination by focusing on paradoxes and ironies as analytical entry points. As an explicitly feminist and critical method, this approach complements the methodological toolbox of transregional studies, which have not yet engaged with feminist methodologies and approaches (see Middell 2019a).

Paradoxes of the (Post-)Colonial

I propose the critical analysis of paradoxes as a strategy toward the synchronic and diachronic analysis of power. It is a proposal for making tangible invisibilized connections and comparing situations that are deemed incomparable by enabling the critical analysis of the very power structures that shape how we perceive the world and can therefore reveal patterns that were previously obscured. By being open for the paradoxes that arise when distinct social realities are brought together, constructions of similarity and difference can be questioned.

The analytical strategy of scrutinizing paradoxes is ingrained in critical ethnographic and feminist work inspired by poststructuralist and postcolonial approaches (see Lather 2001; Alexander 2005; Derrida 1976). Examining paradoxes means focusing on that which goes against the *doxa*, against that which appears as normal, unquestioned, true. It denotes the simultaneous existence of "multiple yet incommensurable truths, or, truth and its negation in a single proposition, or, truths which undo even as they require each other" (Brown 2000, 238). Paradoxes are, consequently, more than analytical puzzles that need only be thought through logically to be solved—they remain irritatingly unsolvable and thus defy the academic desire to reduce complexity. The focus on paradoxes thus goes against the mainstream understanding of comparative research in the social sciences that is aimed at reducing complexity.

Translating these conceptualizations into an analytical strategy means examining that which seems irritatingly counterfactual. Probing these moments of irritation makes possible the deeper analysis of the configurations of power that urge us to draw certain conclusions more easily than others and make us feel stuck when the empirical material does not allow the drawing of these conclusions. It means enacting "a praxis of not being so sure, in excess of binary and dialectical logic that disrupts the horizon of an already prescribed intelligibility" (Lather 2001, 246). Comparative research drawing on case studies undertaken by multiple researchers anchored in different social realities is a fruitful approach in this regard because the unilateral view "from nowhere" can be troubled from the very beginning. By tracing the paradoxes identified in the case studies, an archipelagic geography of power emerges.

To start with, Fradera points out in chapter 3 the paradox that, in the Philippines, sugar production depended on the labor of free peasants, while in Puerto Rico and Cuba, the rise of sugar as the main crop led to the establishment of plantation societies dependent on slave labor. Inversely, tobacco was harvested by free peasants in Cuba and by forced peasant labor in the Philippines. What does this paradox reveal about the specific setting of the three colonies and the workings of power that link them? It underlines that there is neither a necessary correlation between plantation society and the production of certain cash crops nor one between an export-oriented colonial economy and the need for slave labor.

With natural conditions being similarly favorable for the production of sugar and tobacco in all three colonies, the distinct arrangements that developed make an analysis purely based on an economic calculus difficult. Analysis needs to look beyond the common rationale of finding ways of securing Spain's role as a colonizing power once the silver economy declined and agricultural production became more important. Contextual factors that embed the three colonies in broader networks of trade and politics as well as specific historical situations need to be taken into account. In Spanish America, the Haitian Revolution and the independence wars brought Spanish and French migrants to Puerto Rico and Cuba. They brought the necessary capital, machinery, and enslaved people to foster large-scale production and received land in turn. Cuban and Puerto Rican sugar growers subsequently increased their influence in the two colonies, but also in the Spanish Empire in general, and used it to ensure a ready supply of labor through the ongoing illegal trading of enslaved people. In the Philippines, where the galleon trade based on silver between New Spain and Asia had been at the center of economic activity, state intervention focused almost exclusively on ensuring the production and export of tobacco, because the Spanish state had a monopoly on this product. The production of other cash crops like sugar or hemp was undertaken by private individuals who sold their produce to merchants. Because these individuals lacked funds for improving and mechanizing production, their economic output remained small. Only the entrance of British capital into the Philippines motivated the Spanish to find new sources of capital to foster the Philippine economy and thus strengthen their hold on the colony.

In the absence of the necessary funds to embark on large-scale economic investments, the Spanish colonial state turned to other options to ensure the increase in capital. As Camba and Aguilar show in chapter 8, the racialized restrictions on marriage were lowered, allowing Filipino landowners to marry capital-possessing Chinese immigrants. The political economy of the Philippines was stabilized, but a new elite developed who, from this point onward, began to control political and economic power in the Philippines. In chapter 15, Cielo traces a similar pattern in contemporary times. She shows how state policies that supported the naturalization of immigrants of Chinese descent during the Marcos era intertwined with neoliberal restructuring, post-authoritarian democratization efforts, and the continuing personalization of political authority to favor "Chinese Filipinos of pure Chinese descent" to centralize economic wealth and political power. They now make up 1 percent of the population but control 60 percent of the economy (Chua 2004, 15). In chapter 9, Melgar bolsters Cielo's analysis by examining the presence of economic elites in the institutions of representative democracy as well as their influence on political decision-making. Increasing democratization in the Philippines has led, as both authors show, paradoxically, to the centralization of economic-cum-political power and authority in the Philippines.

The continuing power of hierarchies of differentiation also creates paradoxes in structuring (post-)colonial societies. Morín Nenoff, in chapter 11, comments on the paradox that in the Cuban census undertaken in 2012, 64.1 percent of the Cuban population is reported as white, 26.6 percent as mixed race, and a mere 9.3 percent as black. She holds that, taking into account the impact of slavery on the ethnic composition of the Cuban society, these numbers show the continuing influence of racism on the development of black consciousness and identity in Cuba. Denis-Rosario, in turn, in chapter 12, discusses the invisibility of Afro–Puerto Rican histories through an analysis of the central Plaza del Quinto Centenario in the capital San Juan. She writes in her chapter: "It comes across as ironic that [the sculpture on the Plaza] would celebrate the Americas' cultural heritage, since it is erected within an old Afro–Puerto Rican neighborhood—an unknown fact to most people" (214). By unearthing erased histories, she provides a distinct view on the colonial present that reveals the durability of colonial patterns not only in collective memory but also in the infrastructure of cities. The irony that she comments on reveals itself only to those conscious of how in the colonial present, the material and spatial configuration of the city reflects older colonial patterns of racialized segregation.

Another paradox that is tangible in the composition and transformation of the landscapes of Puerto Rico and the Philippines is the upsurge of shopping malls in a context in which high levels of poverty and the generally low purchasing power seem to contradict the apparent success of such economic ventures. Probing this paradox, both Cielo for the Philippines and Rivera Quiñones for Puerto Rico argue that tracing the paradox of the "malling culture" reveals the interwovenness of political and economic rule. But the authors disagree concerning the exact nature of this interwovenness: Cielo, in chapter 15, holds that private shopping malls have become constitutive of public life in the Philippines and that they show the Philippine dependence on the privatized availability of public (air-conditioned) space. According to her, the presence of shopping malls is also linked to the enormous influx of remittances by Filipino workers, which account for 9.8 percent of the gross domestic product. Dependence on remittances has shaped a "consumption-driven society not dependent on national productivity," says Cielo (262). The popularity of malls, in turn, strengthens the oligarchic hold of the economic elite who own the shopping malls and have been able to translate their economic power into political influence.

In chapter 13, Rivera Quiñones connects the contemporary omnipresence of shopping malls in Puerto Rico to the increase in retail sales during the 1990s, a time when "factories were closing down, labor rights were reduced, and US economic transfers were not increasing" (231). Nowadays, the ubiquity of American megastores and shopping malls represents the ongoing coloniality of Puerto Rico, he argues: Even though the great majority of Puerto Ricans lack purchasing power, the welfare transfers of the US government have contributed to generating a certain sense of prosperity in the poorest segments of the population as well as a consumerist orientation. Taken together, he holds, these configurations have stabilized US colonial rule and prevented anti-colonial unrest up to a certain point. Current events in Puerto Rico speak toward the unsustainability of these arrangements. Rivera Quiñones's analysis offers an entry point into understanding how the interweaving of economic and political dimensions in Puerto Rico mitigates potential grievances and stabilizes political rule.

Paradoxical Comparisons as Critical Postcolonial Method

Puerto Rico, Cuba, and the Philippines have been interlinked throughout colonial times and, as the case studies show, continue to share certain cultural, economic, and political patterns—for example, the three societies' dependence on rents, as Burchardt (chap. 18) and Kemner (chap. 17) argue—that point to the existence of colonial legacies deriving from Spanish colonialism. How we theorize these connections while also revealing their differences and how we create narratives that underline either distinctiveness or similarity are crucial for the power of these comparisons to either reproduce or trouble conventional stories of colonization and conquest. As the debates on the politics of comparative research have shown, the crucial question is: What do we compare for?

In the case of this volume, the comparison is motivated by an interest in understanding how shared histories of colonization are traceable in three contexts that, nowadays, possess very different political systems, are located in different geopolitical regions, and are objects of research in different disciplines. By linking the (post-)colonial histories of Puerto Rico, Cuba, and the Philippines, our argument goes, conventional stories of Spanish colonization might be troubled; by linking contemporary patterns of power to Spanish colonial rule, insights into the ongoing impact of colonial patterns and logics might be gained. We aim to elucidate the specificities of each context by encouraging a holistic reading of how, on the one hand, the political economy and, on the other hand, the hierarchization of differences shape the access to and the articulation of political power and authority. By providing both a synchronic and diachronic perspective, our approach refuses a superficial reading of both the past and the present by providing a detailed and multivocal account of the contexts under scrutiny.

We compare to challenge colonizing perspectives that insist on the incomparability of some contexts and the comparability of others. Our volume shows that the analysis of Spanish colonialism and its connection to contemporary patterns of rule is capable of linking three places that appear incomparable at first glance. This insight can trouble commonplace analyses of the three countries that focus on deficiencies or weaknesses derived from an analysis that separates global connections and focuses only on the particularities of the local.

Collective and interdisciplinary knowledge production organized through a case study approach is a productive entry point into this endeavor, as this volume powerfully shows. By assembling heterogeneous readings of the three contexts, we allow for a more complex reading of social realities than a single-authored text would have been able to provide. Each contribution adds a different point of view that is able to enter into a dialogue with the others because of the analytical framework provided. By allowing the richness of the different contexts to emerge, our approach goes beyond contemporary comparative approaches in the social sciences. Even in those comparative studies that apply a case study methodology, the cases studies are usually seen as providing "thick descriptions" apt for testing hypotheses that need to fit into a mixed-methods design (Munck and Snyder 2007, 7). The obstructiveness of the context is tamed through the building of variables that flatten the complexities and ambivalences contained in social realities to build paradox-free descriptions that fulfill their function without irritating the underlying paradigms of the comparison undertaken.

In this chapter, I have proposed a specific approach to analyzing case studies that engages with the irritations that paradoxical situations create. Taking into account the discussions concerning the politics of comparison reconstructed in this contribution, such an approach implements a power-conscious postcolonial sensibility. The value of this approach lies in the possibility of linking case studies in different ways, each time opening up other heuristics and singling out different dynamics and patterns. When taken together, these multiple comparisons can reveal the complexities of the (post-)colonial present.

Our analysis inevitably neglects some possibilities for comparisons that would be similarly productive. By identifying patterns of colonial rule and their refractions over time and scales, we do not focus on accounting for the presence of anti-colonial resistances up to the present day. This has been a conscious decision, as our interest is primarily in revealing how colonial patterns of rule reverberate across time and space and link situations that seem unconnected and dispersed at first glance. Linking the histories and logics of decolonizing struggles in Puerto Rico, Cuba, and the Philippines is a task left open—the methodology we propose in this volume provides a fruitful framework for this and similar projects.

Those interested in embarking on comparative endeavors from a postcolonially informed perspective can start by, first, reflecting on their motivation for comparing. Does the proposed comparison stabilize conventional histories and theories, or would it strive to read history and society against the grain and unearth new perspectives and connections? Which perspectives would be centered to the detriment of which other narratives? Second, how did the entities that are to be related comparatively come about? Are they presumed to be stable and clearly identifiable objects that function according to specific logics—like nation-states—or does the comparison strive to establish them as distinguishable but on the same plane of equivalence—think of Pomeranz's (2000) analysis of the British Empire and the Yangzi Delta—or are they seen as incomparable? What are the power effects of establishing comparative connections between these entities, which histories and linkages are erased, which ones are underlined? Which epistemic, political, and cultural communities are bolstered by how the specific constitution of these entities is imagined, and which are marginalized? Third, the research setting should be critically scrutinized. From what situated positionality do those practicing the comparison start from, and what are the specific relations of power and privilege that constitute the research situation? Is there a way to engage with multiple and differently situated voices either through directly involving differently situated researchers in the comparative process or through engaging with academic or other literature, archives, or the materiality and spatiality of the entities compared? How is the context taken into account? How do the research relationships in assembling, analyzing, and disseminating the data and results reflect power relations, and how do they shape the results of the comparative endeavor? Is there a way to use the research process to engage with previously unheard voices or unseen material and to what ends? And, fourth, the effects of the comparison should be taken into account. What impact might the comparison have and in which communities, scholarly and otherwise? Which stories are bolstered, which narratives are weakened? What can be learned from the way the comparison was undertaken both concerning the politics of knowledge production and the relationships established through the research?

For the purpose of tracing the legacies of Spanish colonialism in Spain's last colonies, multivocal and cross-regional case studies offer a fruitful starting point for rethinking comparative research as critical and postcolonial methodology that allows the colonial present to appear in its complexity and ambivalence but that yet remains dedicated to a rigorous empirical analysis. The archipelagic perspective exemplified in this volume explores the interconnections between the seemingly unconnected places of Cuba, Puerto Rico, and the Philippines, without flattening out their differences, building new "containers" for research, or subsuming local complexities under overarching categories or causal explanations. The focus on paradoxes as postcolonial comparative method, I have argued, in particular, provides a useful entry point that can strengthen the toolbox of transregional studies by engaging with feminist and postcolonial insights and methods.

NOTES

1. The term "postcolonial colony" as moniker for Puerto Rico has been used primarily by Jorge Duany, who applies it to describe Puerto Ricans as "a people with a strong national identity but little desire for a nation-state" (2002, 4, 122). He credits Juan Flores and María Milagros López (1994) with the creation of the term (Duany 2010, 49n1). Pantojas-García, in this volume, uses the term in a similar manner. Flores (2000, 36) has applied it later to compare the Puerto Rican and Martinican diaspora, finding the grounds for comparison in both islands being home to "a people wedged in an impossible situation" (39): occupied by colonial powers in a world that locates colonialism in the past.

2. I thank Regine Paul, Hannes Warnecke-Berger, Hans-Jürgen Burchardt, Tobias Kalt, and Jonas Müller for their helpful comments and feedback on earlier versions of this chapter.

REFERENCES

Ahram, Ariel I., Patrick Köllner, and Rudra Sil, eds. 2018a. *Comparative Area Studies: Methodological Rationales and Cross-Regional Applications*. Oxford: Oxford University Press.

Ahram, Ariel I., Patrick Köllner, and Rudra Sil. 2018b. "Comparative Area Studies: What It Is, What It Can Do." In *Comparative Area Studies: Methodological Rationales and Cross-regional Applications*, edited by Ariel I. Ahram, Patrick Köllner, and Rudra Sil, 3–28. Oxford: Oxford University Press.

Alexander, M. Jacqui. 2005. *Pedagogies of Crossing: Meditations on Feminism, Sexual Politics, Memory, and the Sacred*. Durham: Duke University Press.

Anckar, Carsten. 2008. "On the Applicability of the Most Similar Systems Design and the Most Different Systems Design in Comparative Research." *International Journal of Social Research Methodology* 11 (5): 389–401.

Andrien, Kennth J. 2009. "The Spanish Atlantic System." In *Atlantic History: A Critical Appraisal*, edited by Jack P. Greene and Philip D. Morgan, 55–80. Oxford: Oxford University Press.

Bennett, Andrew, and Colin Elman. 2006. "Qualitative Research: Recent Developments in Case Study Methods." *Annual Review of Political Science* 9 (1): 455–76.

Berg-Schlosser, Dirk. 2012. "Comparative Area Studies—Goldener Mittelweg zwischen Regionalstudien und Universalistischen Ansätzen?" *Zeitschrift für Vergleichende Politikwissenschaft* 6 (1): 1–16.

Branche, Jerome, ed. 2008. *Race, Colonialism, and Social Transformation in Latin America and the Caribbean*. Gainesville: University Press of Florida.

Brown, Wendy. 2000. "Suffering Rights as Paradoxes." *Constellations* 7 (2): 208–29.

Buck-Morss, Susan. 2009. *Hegel, Haiti, and Universal History*. Pittsburgh: University of Pittsburgh Press.

Cardoso, Fernando Henrique. 1977. "The Consumption of Dependency Theory in the United States." *Latin American Research Review* 12 (3): 7–24.

Chakrabarty, Dipesh. 2000. *Provincializing Europe: Postcolonial Thought and Historical Difference*. Princeton: Princeton University Press.

Cheah, Pheng. 2003. "Grounds of Comparison." In *Grounds of Comparison: Around the Work of Benedict Anderson*, edited by Pheng Cheah and Jonathan Culler, 1–20. New York: Routledge.

Chua, Amy. 2004. *World on Fire: How Exporting Free Market Democracy Breeds Ethnic Hatred and Global Instability*. New York: Anchor.

Clifford, James, and George E. Marcus, eds. 1986. *Writing Culture: The Poetics and Politics of Ethnography*. Berkeley: University of California Press.

Connell, Raewyn. 2007. *Southern Theory*. Cambridge Polity Press.

Conrad, Sebastian, and Shalini Randeria, eds. 2002. *Jenseits des Eurozentrismus. Postkoloniale Perspektiven in den Geschichts- und Kulturwissenschaften*. Frankfurt am Main: Campus.

de Vries, Jan. 2008. *The Industrious Revolution: Consumer Behavior and the Household Economy, 1650 to the Present*. Cambridge: Cambridge University Press.

Derrida, Jaques. 1976. *Of Grammatology*. Translated by Gayatri Chakravorty Spivak. Baltimore: Johns Hopkins University Press.

Deville, Joe, Michael Guggenheim, and Zuzana Hrdlicková. 2016. "Introduction: The Practices and Infrastructures of Comparison." In *Practicing Comparison: Logics, Relations, Collaborations*, edited by Joe Deville, Michael Guggenheim, and Zuzana Hrdlicková, 17–44. Manchester: Mattering Press.

Dietze, Antje, and Matthias Middell. 2019. "Methods in Transregional Studies: Intercultural Transfers." In *The Routledge Handbook of Transregional Studies*, edited by Matthias Middell, 58–73. London: Routledge.

Duany, Jorge. 2002. *The Puerto Rican Nation on the Move: Identities on the Island and in the United States*. Chapel Hill: University of North Carolina Press.

Duany, Jorge. 2010. "Anthropology in a Postcolonial Colony: Helen I. Safa's Contribution to Puerto Rican Ethnography." *Caribbean Studies* 38 (2): 33–57.

Dussel, Enrique D. 1981. *A History of the Church in Latin America: Colonialism to Liberation*. Grand Rapids, MI: William B. Eerdmans.

Ebbinghaus, Bernhard. 2005. "When Less Is More: Selection Problems in Large-N and Small-N Cross-National Comparisons." *International Sociology* 20 (2): 133–52.

Eisenstadt, Shmuel N. 1963. *The Political Systems of Empires*. Glencoe: Free Press.

Eisenstadt, Shmuel N. 1967. *The Decline of Empires*. Englewood Cliffs: Prentice-Hall.

Epple, Angelika, and Walter Erhart. 2015. "Die Welt Beobachten—Praktiken des Vergleichens." In *Die Welt Beobachten—Praktiken des Vergleichens*, edited by Angelika Epple and Walter Erhart, 7–34. Frankfurt am Main: Campus.

Escobar, A. 1995. *Encountering Development: The Making and Unmaking of the Third World*. Princeton: Princeton University Press.

Espagne, Michel. 1994. "Sur les Lomites du Comparatisme en Histoire Culturelle." *Genèses. Sciences Sociales et Histoire* 17:112–21.

Figueroa Romero, María de los Dolores. 2011. "Comparative Analysis of Indigenous Women's Participation in Ethno-politics and Community Development: The Experiences of Women Leaders of ECUARUNARI (Ecuador) and YATAMA (Atlantic Coast of Nicaragua)." PhD diss., Graduate Programme in Sociology, York University.

Flores, Juan. 2000. *From Bomba to Hip-Hop: Puerto Rican Culture and Latino Identity*. New York: Columbia University Press.

Flores, Juan, and María Milagros López. 1994. "Dossier Puerto Rico: Introduction." *Social Text Online* 38:93–95.

Fox, Richard G., and Andre Gingrich. 2002. "Introduction." In *Anthropology, by Comparison*, edited by Richard G. Fox and Andre Gingrich, 1–24. London: Routledge.

Frank, Andre Gunder. 1969. *Capitalism and Underdevelopment in Latin America: Historical Studies of Chile and Brazil*. New York: Modern Reader.

Go, Julian. 2009. "The 'New' Sociology of Empire and Colonialism." *Sociology Compass* 3:1–14.

Guillermo, Alice G. 1997. "Imperialist Globalization and Culture." *Diliman Review* 45 (1): 9–19.

Hantrais, Linda. 2014. "Methodological Pluralism in International Comparative Research." *International Journal of Social Research Methodology* 17 (2): 133–45.

Hoffmann, Bert. 2015. "Latin America and Beyond: The Case for Comparative Area Studies." *European Review of Latin American and Caribbean Studies* 100:111–20.

Holy, Ladislav. 1987. "Introduction: Description, Generalization and Comparison: Two Paradigms." In *Comparative Anthropology*, edited by Ladislav Holy, 1–21. Oxford: Blackwell.

Ibarra, Jorge. 1995. "Cultura e Identidad Nacional en el Caribe Hispánico: el Caso Puertoriceño y el Cubano." In *La Nación Soñada: Cuba, Puerto Rico, y Filipinas Ante el 98*, edited by Consuelo Naranjo, Miguel A. Puig-Samper, and Luis Miguel García Mora, 85–96. Madrid: Doce Calles.

Jensen, Casper Bruun, and Christopher Gad. 2016. "Lateral Comparisons." In *Practicing Comparison: Logics, Relations, Collaborations*, edited by Joe Deville, Michael Guggenheim, and Zuzana Hrdlicková, 189–219. Manchester: Mattering Press.

Klor de Alva, J. Jorge. 1995. "The Postcolonization of the (Latin) American Experience: A Reconsideration of 'Colonialism,' 'Postcolonialism,' and 'Mestizaje.'" In *After Colonialism: Imperial Histories and Postcolonial Displacements*, edited by Gyan Prakash, 241–77. Princeton: Princeton University Press.

Krause, Monika. 2016. "Comparative Research: Beyond Linear-Causal Explanation." In *Practicing Comparison: Logics, Relations, Collaborations*, edited by Joe Deville, Michael Guggenheim, and Zuzana Hrdlicková, 45–67. Manchester: Mattering Press.

Lachenicht, Susanne. 2019. "Multiple Atlantics." In *The Routledge Handbook of Transregional Studies*, edited by Matthias Middell, 95–101. London: Routledge.

Laffey, Mark, and Jutta Weldes. 2008. "Decolonizing the Cuban Missile Crisis." *International Studies Quarterly* 52 (3): 555–77.

Lambert, David, and Alan Lester. 2006. "Imperial Spaces, Imperial Subjects." In *Colonial Lives across the British Empire: Imperial Careering in the Long Nineteenth Century*, edited by David Lambert and Alan Lester, 1–31. Cambridge: Cambridge University Press.

Landman, Todd. 2003. *Issues and Methods in Comparative Politics: An Introduction*. London: Routledge.

Lather, Patti. 2001. "Postmodernism, Post-Structuralism and Post(Critical) Ethnography: Of Ruins, Aporias and Angels." In *Handbook of Ethnography*, edited by Paul Atkinson, Amanda Coffey, Sara Delamont, John Lofland, and Lyn Lofland. London: SAGE.

Luis-Brown, David. 2008. *Waves of Decolonization: Discourses of Race and Hemispheric Citizenship in Cuba, Mexico, and the United States*. Durham: Duke University Press.

Mahoney, James. 2000. "Strategies of Causal Inference in Small-N Analysis." *Sociological Methods & Research* 28 (4): 387–424.

Mahoney, James. 2010. *Colonialism and Postcolonial Development: Spanish America in a Comparative Perspective*. New York: Cambridge University Press.

McClintock, Anne. 1995. *Imperial Leather: Race, Gender, and Sexuality in the Colonial Contest*. New York: Routledge.

Mehler, Andreas. 2019. "Comparative Area Studies." In *The Routledge Handbook of Transregional Studies*, edited by Matthias Middell, 67–73. London: Routledge.

Middell, Matthias. 2014. "What Is Global Studies All About?" In *Potentials and Challenges of Global Studies for the 21st Century*, edited by Madeleine Herren, Patrick Manning, Philip C. McCarthy, Matthias Middell, and Eric Vanhaute, 38–49. Basel: Institute for European Global Studies.

Middell, Matthias, ed. 2019a. *The Routledge Handbook of Transregional Studies*. London: Routledge.

Middell, Matthias. 2019b. "Transregional Studies: A New Approach to Global Processes." In *The Routledge Handbook of Transregional Studies*, edited by Matthias Middell, 1–16. London: Routledge.

Munck, Gerardo L., and Richard Snyder. 2007. "Debating the Direction of Comparative Politics: An Analysis of Leading Journals." *Comparative Political Studies* 40 (1): 5–31.

Ng, Franklin. 1994. "Knowledge for Empire: Academics and Universities in the Service of Imperialism." In *On Cultural Ground: Essays in International History*, edited by Robert D. Johnson, 123–46. Chicago: Imprint.

Parthasarathi, Prasannan. 2011. *Why Europe Grew Rich and Asia Did Not: Global Economic Divergence, 1600–1850*. Cambridge: Cambridge University Press.

Pomeranz, Kenneth. 2000. *The Great Divergence: China, Europe, and the Making of the Modern World Economy*. Princeton: Princeton University Press.

Potter, Simon J., and Jonathan Saha. 2015. "Global History, Imperial History and Connected Histories of Empire." *Journal of Colonialism and Colonial History* 16 (1). https://doi.org/10.1353/cch.2015.0009

Pratt, Marie Louise. 1992. *Imperial Eyes: Travel Writing and Transculturation*. London: Routledge.

Quijano, Aníbal. 2000. "Coloniality of Power and Eurocentrism in Latin America." *International Sociology* 15:215–32.

Radhakrishnan, Rajagopalan. 2009. "Why Compare?" *New Literary History* 40 (3): 453–71.

Ragin, Charles. 1987. *The Comparative Method: Moving Beyond Qualitative and Quantitative Strategies*. Berkeley: University of California Press.
Ragin, Charles. 2008. *Redesigning Social Inquiry: Fuzzy Sets and Beyond*. Chicago: University of Chicago Press.
Robinson, Jennifer. 2011. "Comparisons: Colonial or Cosmopolitan?" *Singapore Journal of Tropical Geography* 32 (2): 125–40.
Rohlfing, Ingo, and Carsten Q. Schneider. 2018. "A Unifying Framework for Causal Analysis in Set-Theoretic Multimethod Research." *Sociological Methods & Research* 47 (1): 37–63.
Said, Edward. 1978. *Orientalism*. New York: Vintage Books.
San Juan, Epifanio. 1995. "Against Post-Colonial Theory: The Challenge of the Philippine Revolution." *Diliman Review* 43 (3): 55–67.
Sartori, Giovanni. 1970. "Concept Misformation in Comparative Politics." *American Political Science Review* 64 (4): 1033–53.
Saussure, Ferdinand de. 1966. *Course in General Linguistics*. London: Peter Owen.
Scheffer, Thomas, and Jörg Niewöhner, eds. 2010. *Thick Comparison: Reviving the Ethnographic Aspiration*. Leiden: Brill.
Schmidt-Nowara, Christopher. 2014. *The Conquest of History: Spanish Colonialism and National Histories in the Nineteenth Century*. Pittsburgh: University of Pittsburgh Press.
Sil, Rudra. 2009. "Area Studies, Comparative Politics, and the Role of Cross-Regional Small-N Comparison." *Qualitative & Multi-Method Research* 7 (2): 26–32.
Stengers, Isabelle. 2011. "Comparison as a Matter of Concern." *Common Knowledge* 17 (1): 48–63.
Stoler, Ann Laura. 2001. "Tense and Tender Ties: The Politics of Comparison in North American History and (Post) Colonial Studies." *Journal of American History* 88 (3): 829–65.
Stoler, Ann Laura. 2006. "Intimidations of Empire: Predicaments of the Tactile and Unseen." In *Haunted by Empire: Geographies of Intimacy in North American History*, edited by Ann Laura Stoler, 1–22. Durham: Duke University Press.
Stoler, Ann Laura. 2016. *Duress: Imperial Durabilities in Our Times*. Durham: Duke University Press.
Strathern, Marilyn. 1988. *Gender of the Gift*. Berkeley: University of California Press.
Subrahmanyam, Sanjay. 1997. "Connected Histories: Notes Towards a Reconfiguration of Early Modern Eurasia." *Modern Asian Studies* 31 (3): 735–62.
Tilly, Charles. 1984. *Big Structures, Large Processes, Huge Comparisons*. New York: Russell Sage Foundation.
Turner Bishnell, Amy. 2009. "Indigenous America and the Limits of the Atlantic World." In *Atlantic History: A Critical Appraisal*, edited by Jack P. Greene and Philip D. Morgan, 191–222. Oxford: Oxford University Press.
Tylor, Edwards B. 1889. "On a Method of Investigating the Development of Institutions; Applied to Laws of Marriage and Descent." *Journal of the Anthropological Institute of Great Britain and Ireland* 18:245–72.

Wallerstein, Immanuel. 1979. *The Capitalist World-Economy*. Cambridge: Cambridge University Press.

Werner, Michael, and Bénédicte Zimmermann. 2002. "Vergleich, Transfer, Verflechtung. Der Ansatz der Histoire Croisée und die Herausforderung des Transnationalen." *Geschichte und Gesellschaft* 28 (4): 607–36.

Wirth, Christa. 2019. "Movements, Sites, and Encounters of (Post-)Colonial Knowledge." In *The Routledge Companion to Transregional Studies*, edited by Matthias Middell, 110–16. London: Routledge.

Young, Robert C. 2013. "The Postcolonial Comparative." *PMLA* 128 (3): 683–89.

CHAPTER 3

Cuba, Puerto Rico, the Philippines, and the Crisis of the Great Empire

Global Dynamics and Local Developments

Josep M. Fradera

The Spanish Empire, established in the last decade of the 15th century, expanded relentlessly until the end of the 18th century, a remarkable case of longevity, though by the very end of the eighteenth and into the following century it began falling apart. The Napoleonic invasion of May 1808 furthermore led to the military and financial collapse of the metropolis. Under these dramatic circumstances, the only possibility for survival lay in resisting the French on the peninsula and trying to reach some sort of consensus with the Creole elites who remained loyal to the monarchy. With that objective in mind and in the absence of a monarch, the Cortes were summoned to the city of Cadiz, the center of transoceanic navigation, which was under Spanish sovereignty and British protection. Even so, the empire collapsed like a house of cards between 1808 and 1824. By the end of that period, with the emancipation of the entire South American continent after the defeat of the Spanish army in Ayacucho, the only remaining Spanish possessions were island colonies, two in the Antilles and the other in the China Sea. On the periphery of the great silver empire, Cuba, Puerto Rico, and the Philippines became the raison d'être of Spain's continued colonial existence throughout the 19th century. From being possessions on the margins of an empire centered in New Spain and Peru, the suppliers of the silver that was minted and used universally, the three insular possessions allowed Spain to remain a colonial power until 1898. To understand how this happened, we must look back to the time when the monarchy's military needs were such that the approach toward those enclaves underwent a shift and new relations were forged with their modest but active landowners and merchants.

The origin of that shift in the mid-18th century lay in the outcome of the intercolonial wars among the old transatlantic and Asian worlds of the Iberian nations and the emerging powers of Great Britain and France, whose expansion was going to dominate the world throughout the 19th century and much of the 20th. War preparations by the emerging nations were characterized by new military organization, and the Iberian empires tried to respond. From pursuing the old strategy of fortifications in the nerve centers of the empire—places such as the Spanish cities of Veracruz, Callao, Cartagena de Indias, and Manila, which ensured maritime traffic between Europe and the overseas possessions—the imperial powers began using occupation instead, along with the more extensive, flexible, and costly deployment of armed forces. To protect Spain's enormous holdings throughout America, the Crown launched an ambitious policy of territorial expansion and border control. This required controlling peoples who earlier had not been subject to control and who were unwilling to accept new lords, as can be seen with the wars in Patagonia, Yucatan, Central America, northern Mexico, Mindanao, and the Visayas Islands in the Philippines. Territorial control was a matter of urgent military necessity, and it entailed conflicts with neighboring powers, be they the Portuguese in Guaraní Brazil; British colonists in the Carolinas, on the Florida border, and in the Gulf of Mexico; or Muslim sultanates in Mindanao, where the population was neither assimilated nor Christian.

Occupying a territory—imposing first administration, then dominion, and then laws, in that order—and establishing a permanent colonial presence was a costly logistical and financial exercise. The result of this incremental growth of state military and financial capacity, especially in the so-called amphibious states that waged war on land and on sea, has been referred to as the "fiscal-military state" (Brewer 1988; Stone 1994). Until the Bourbon Reforms of the 1770s and 1780s, the effort was almost entirely centered in the great mining areas of Peru and New Spain, especially the latter. Technological changes in Zacatecas, especially deeper mining to reach better veins and the supply of mercury for amalgamation, ensured the viability of this new colonial cycle (Langue 1991). As a result, New Spain continued functioning as the imperial bank until the final collapse of the viceroyalty (Marichal Salinas 1999). The effort to ensure resources for an unprecedented military campaign forced the Crown to face the fact that it had to reform the old ways of controlling transatlantic commerce, held in place by the port monopolies of Cadiz in Spain; Veracruz, Acapulco, and Portobelo in America; and Manila in the Pacific. From the first reforms in the 1750s up to those of the 1790s, the addition of new contact ports in America, tariff reforms, and "forced distribution" of merchandise in America, a way of guaranteeing the placement of European products (whether peninsular or re-exported) in colonial markets, led to increased earnings from commerce and mining and the flow of American precious metals from America to Cadiz, which was key to the entire system (Delgado Ribas 2007). This new arrangement was, to some degree, the outcome of changes in American and peninsular societies, especially the former, which saw numeric growth, urbanization, and broader commercial circulation.

From the Imperial Periphery to the Colonial Center

The integration of the periphery of Spain's vast dominions, both for economic reasons and for questions of security, was critical to this organization. The three insular enclaves were particularly challenging. The most promising crops for developing Cuba and Puerto Rico were coffee, sugar, and tobacco, the latter a native crop that had drawn the attention already of the first Europeans on the islands. There was also a ranching economy that served cities, supplied salted meat for the fleet, and sold it to neighboring islands thanks to an extensive contraband network that the authorities neither could nor tried to control. In the Philippines, agricultural products throughout the archipelago also were native or introduced, the latter including coffee, sugar, indigo, and tobacco (McCoy and de Jesús 1982). Rice fields ensured the subsistence of the population and the prosperity of estates surrounding the capital, many of them owned by religious orders. The combination of increased maritime commerce and rising demand in Europe for dyes and tropical consumer products led to some tolerance for organizational modifications in the production of certain products; these included cacao and sugar in the continental and insular Caribbean, yerba mate in the Guaraní region, indigo in Tucumán, and extensive ranching in the Río de la Plata area, sometimes with spectacular results and always in detriment to the native inhabitants whose living spaces were being radically curtailed.

Two of these changes turned out to be enormously important, both productively and socially. The first was the long-term development of sugar plantations in the Antilles. Historically, Cuba had been the main producer of tobacco and wood for repairing the ships traveling from Cadiz, Veracruz, or Panama via Havana (de la Fuente 2008). In the mid-18th century, as a consequence of the productive revolution in the British and French Antilles, sugar became the most dynamic force for change in western Cuba and around Ponce, in Puerto Rico, though the latter case was incipient (Scarano 1984). This was still an agrarian sector that relied upon small-scale producers, but it was dynamic, using slave labor on a reduced scale. Coffee and tobacco, meanwhile, attracted small independent growers who sold to wholesalers in contact with Havana merchants (Bergad 1983). The slave uprising and revolution in French Sante-Domingue (Haiti), leading both to emigration to Cuba by wealthy sugar growers and to a sharp increase in the price of sugar on international markets, were the decisive steps for transforming the sector into one of larger holdings (Ferrer 2014). The liberalization of the slave trade for the Spanish navy in 1789 (earlier it had been in the hands of foreign contractors) was essential. Freedom to import labor to America would remain in place until the first abolition treaty between Spain and Britain was signed in 1817; that treaty went into effect three years later, the high point of the importation of Africans, forcing traders to make clandestine trips from the African coast to the Spanish Antilles. Fifty years later, the last of the slave ships were still arriving on Cuban shores.

The Philippines had been in Spanish hands for more than 200 years, thanks to linkages between American silver and Asian markets, including China. But colonization there had never been successful, and that would remain the case until after the US arrival in 1898. Even so, the archipelago's economy began diversifying already in the second half of the 18th century. Market crops (including for supplying military installations and the Manila transpacific nexus) often were controlled by the religious orders, especially Dominicans and Jesuits, though Asian commercial diasporas were also there. Mexicans, Chinese, Gujaratis, and Armenians all had established societies inside the city walls and in the Tondo neighborhood, largely inhabited by Chinese (Yuste López 2007). But this economy relied upon the arrival of galleons carrying silver from New Spain. That was what drew foreign merchants and fed the circuits of exchange with the Visayas and the interior of Luzon Island.

The colonial government was not content with the negligible tariffs or with head taxes on natives and mestizos (Sangley-Chinese), and in the

1820s it encouraged a new sort of agricultural labor in the archipelago. The sector chosen was tobacco, to be produced under the direction of the state in the framework of social units known as *colecciones* (de Jesús 1999). The largest among them was Cagayán, an example of Asian adaptation of productive and labor resources, that is, not by using slaves but rather by imposing strict obligations on the peasantry. Northeast Luzon was the center of large-scale tobacco production under state monopoly. There, in the decades following the great imperial crisis, an important labor experiment took place under the supervision of, and of great benefit to, Spanish financial authorities. The result was the absolute financial protection of the possessions. This took place at a time when all indications were that Spain would not be able to hold on to the Philippines because of the interruption of the ocean travel that had ensured its connections with the rest of the empire since the 16th century. The organization of regulated labor aimed at producing just one product, whose commercialization favored colonial interests, was obviously a form of taxation in kind (Fradera 1999). It is reminiscent of what the Dutch did in Java when Van den Bosch took control of that island after Napoleon's armies withdrew from the Netherlands and the Dutch recovered the islands from Britain, setting up highly detailed and large-scale production of coffee, sugar, and indigo by peasant communities (Boogmaard 1989).

Slavery and the Global Market

Changes in colonial policy would have been neither sufficient nor viable if not for the fact that they took place alongside the appearance of societies that were entirely different from those of the first half of the 18th century. In the Antilles, the key factor was, as mentioned earlier, the adoption of slave labor in the sugar sector typical also of rival countries' large and small insular possessions. Slavery was present throughout the plantations of the central product connecting the islands with international commercial circuits, while free peasants who sold products to wholesalers on the unregulated market were the dominant feature in tobacco, coffee, and food, a continuation of the old way of doing things. But in sugar, semi-mechanized production and mass slave labor proved to be extraordinarily successful (Moreno Fraginals 1978). The paradox was obvious: sugar depended on free peasants in the Philippines, while tobacco was being harvested by free peasants in Cuba; inversely, forced non-slave labor by some 10,000 Filipino peasants assured production in the Cagayán *colección*, and sugar was grown in the Visayas Islands, especially Iloilo, using free peasant labor. Cuban sugar production would eventually count on some 400,000 African slaves at the height of mechanization in the 1840s and 1850s (Knight 1970; Bergad, Iglesias García, and Barcia 1995).

These various methods of agricultural production aimed at reaching expanding world markets during the first half of the 19th century were critical for ensuring colonial continuity in the three insular possessions. It was no simple matter, particularly in the Caribbean and especially with Cuba. The principal difficulty was obvious: importing African slaves entailed confronting the world's first great humanitarian cause, the British campaign to abolish the slave trade. The campaign began in the 1790s, propelled largely by religious activists and followers of Wilberforce (Brown 2006). The first tangible result was British and US abolition of trafficking, in 1807 and 1808, respectively. Later, after the Congress of Vienna, there would be a shift toward bilateral treaties including Spain, Portugal and Brazil, and the Netherlands; the establishment of mixed courts in Sierra Leone and Liberia; and the right to inspect ships, all of which made slave trafficking absolutely illegal (Murray 1980). Nevertheless, high demand for labor spurred the arrival of *bozales*, or slaves born in Africa, in the Spanish Caribbean colonies, on a massive level in Cuba. When clandestine trafficking proved insufficient, the importation of Chinese contract laborers during two more decades satisfied sugar's insatiable needs.

The great imperial crisis, the Napoleonic wars, and difficulties during the absolutist monarchies of Charles IV and Ferdinand VII of Spain all had varied economic repercussions, which cannot be explained here. But some considerations can be stated succinctly. First, there was a new and complex symbiosis between colonial power and local forces participating in the formation of new societies at the turn of the century, which were well established by the 1830s. At that point, as liberalism in Spain was being consolidated, the three insular possessions were excluded from political representation, elections, and citizenship via a maneuver that Napoleon had introduced in 1799 in France consisting of promising 'special laws' that were never implemented, distinguishing political measures in the metropolis from those in the colonies (Bénot and Dorigny 2003). Colonial subjects were relieved of the burden of corruption and influence peddling by civil servants but by the same token were placed under the authority of military powers that governed Havana, San Juan, and Manila with few restrictions (Fradera 2005). If the aforementioned Bourbon Reforms were the last large-scale attempt to impose fiscal and commercial structures to maximize the Crown's extractive capacity, the 19th-century reforms were on a different scale. The emergence of the Cuban sugar plantations amid the upheavals of war in 1815 maintained the imperial nexus with the Antilles and Spain's presence in America. The development of large-scale production in the hands of local Creole landowners was the product of the disappearance of the largest producer at the time, the migration of sugar technology and capital to the neighboring island, plenty of available fertile land, and the absence of any significant abolition movement in Spanish Catholic and liberal circles. Growers' wish for reforms and tax deregulation quickly bumped up against their need for Spanish colonial authorities to protect them against denunciations from abolitionists, along with the fact that abolition in the Caribbean islands belonged to Britain and other European countries from 1833 to 1848 (Drescher 2002).

Meanwhile, Havana and Matanzas became large commercial ports, indirectly spurring the export of other products, some of which, including tobacco, quickly reached the accessible and constantly growing market in the United States. The case of the Philippines was not much different. Since the late 18th century, Filipino Creoles and Chinese Filipino elites had taken advantage of markets in China and Southeast Asia. They saw the British presence in India, Southeast Asia, and southern China, the Dutch in Java, the French in the Mascarenes and India, and the Portuguese presence throughout southern Asia, and they imagined a new mercantile order between the Indian Ocean and the China Seas. Expansion of the opium trade allowed them to envision the growth of that new market (Trocki 1999). That project would collide both with state priorities and with those of the state's proverbial and interested allies in the religious orders, but nevertheless the Asianization of the Philippines was inexorable, especially after the final collapse of the transpacific route between Manila and Acapulco in 1824 (Legarda 1999).

The second consideration is that the Cadiz Cortes and their aftermath in 1820–23 were the last attempt at imperial reform based on a liberal consensus with leaders in Santiago de Chile, Guanajuato, Havana, San Juan, and Manila. The voices of "American Spaniards" are perfectly reflected in the minutes. The failure of the desired colonial pact and the return of absolutism put matters in an entirely different light. With the loosening of the colonial nexus thanks to wars in the metropolis and in America, the affirmation of native capitalism, with its ties to international commerce, was such that once liberals were in power in Spain, the exclusion of the colonies from decision-making led to their elimination from political representation and the subsequent spectacular expansion of military authority in all three possessions. That model allowed Spain to prolong the colonial cycle for decades, ensuring accumulation thanks to exports, especially from the Antilles. The crisis at the end of the 19th century signaled the reverse of that dynamic: it became impossible to avoid the tensions resulting from the last gasps of slavery, which had definitively been abolished in 1886 (republican Brazil would do so in 1888), and from the new competition arising from the Conference of Berlin in 1885, with the United States emerging as a new power, signaling the inevitable demise of imperial Spain. The offer of political reforms along the lines of the Canadian model that the Antilles upper class aspired to, along with growing emigration from the peninsula to the American enclaves, was not enough to compensate for the shattered historical links with the three possessions.

Political Economy and the Colonial Model

The Spanish silver empire turned into a tropical agricultural empire at the turn of the 18th century. When the old empire vanished with the wars of independence, indigenous uprisings, and the subsequent disintegration of the mining industry, new networks of interests appeared on the periphery of the continental empire. New economic forces in the Antilles and the Philippines were the only viable alternatives. All efforts by the old metropolis were aimed at protecting and consolidating the imperial nexus.

This new colonial reality was the outcome of three interrelated planes: (1) massive supply of slave and contract labor, which would endure until the 1860s; (2) elastic and expanding demand for raw materials, tobacco, and tropical agricultural consumer products; and (3) colonial policies that benefited the interests of privileged groups in the Antilles and the Philippines, along with political measures by the late imperial and liberal state after the 1820s and after the Liberal Revolution of 1836–37. The combination of these factors provided a window of opportunity for Spain's colonial tradition to adapt to the new 19th-century capitalism, which was based on manufacturing in Europe and the United States and which required growing amounts of raw materials, tobacco, and sugar. So, the colonialism that would last until the Spanish-American War was simply a new episode in the old story of Spain's overseas efforts across the Atlantic and the China Seas.

Let me now turn to the significance of the new economic model and its limits in order to examine the functions of the colonial political system that would govern for an entire century. The emergence of the three colonies amid wider imperial collapse, as we saw, was clearly based on incremental production of tropical products in the three insular possessions. The three most important of these products were sugar, coffee, and tobacco, along with those of lesser importance such as indigo in the Philippines and copper in Cuba. But there were regional differences; Cuban sugar was at the center of it all, and already in the 1820s it was the most important crop. At the same time, coffee production was advancing in the zone of Utuado, in Puerto Rico. As the great Cuban historian Manuel Moreno Fraginals showed in his work *El Ingenio: Complejo social cubano del azúcar*, sugar required three conditions in order for the sector to grow: easily accessible and fertile land, the conversion of forests into wood that could be used as fuel; and a supply of slaves proportionate to the land under cultivation. Western Cuba easily fulfilled the first two conditions and, furthermore, had an excellent port, Havana, where the fleets from Cadiz stopped off before going to Veracruz or Portobelo. Havana also provisioned ships on their way to a variety of destinations in New Spain, New Granada, Venezuela, Louisiana, and Florida during the years of Spanish sovereignty. The most serious danger for the sugar sector was insufficient labor, given that from the start independent peasant labor—used with tobacco and also in the Gulf of Mexico, as reported by Alexander von Humboldt on his visit to America subsidized by Charles IV (Covarrubias and Souto Mantecón 2012)—had been excluded in favor of slave labor. The problem was that the period when the sugar industry took off (1811–15) coincided with Britain's switch regarding slave trafficking. Furthermore, in 1817 the Spanish Crown gave in to British pressure and, in extreme financial difficulty, signed a treaty prohibiting trafficking with its American possessions. From then on, British authorities could inspect Spanish and other ships going back and forth between Africa and the Antilles. But that did not impede the shipment of 400,000 Africans to the islands to work on the plantations. As the United States and the British West Indies could no longer receive slave ships, part of the US and British fleets that had participated in that traffic shifted to Spanish and Brazilian markets. The subsequent Royal Navy embargo was unable to prevent them from arriving in Cuba (Edwards 2007). And starting in the 1850s, slaves were joined by smaller but not irrelevant numbers of Asian contract laborers, especially from China, who were known as the Manila Chinese. The Spanish Antilles (along with Brazil) became an extraordinary case of resistance to salaried agricultural labor; reasons for this include both government policies and the weakness of Spanish abolitionists. The perseverance of slavery in Cuba and the growth of exports from there point to the truth uttered by planters everywhere, that slave labor was essential for industrial crops like sugar and cotton (Beckert 2014).

Tobacco, on the other hand, was cultivated year-round by peasants who had to pay close attention to how the leaves matured. This was a sector with a variety of labor formulas: individual growers, manufacturing and marketing centers, and, in the case of the Philippines, state intervention through the establishment of *colecciones*, where heads of peasant families were forced to work. In that case, the state purchased leaves that would then be shipped to state monopoly factories in Spain or to other buyers, especially in the Netherlands.

Nineteenth-century capitalism was built as a global market in which private parties and the state could profit from elastic global demand beyond national markets. In the Philippines, state intervention was centered on tobacco, which became crucial once the silver routes between New Spain and Asia ended, but the state did not get involved in other areas. In the Caribbean, in contrast, the state's principal function was to favor the slave plantations, ensure order, and protect Cuban and Puerto Rican sugar growers and the ongoing illegal importation of slaves. In both the Philippines and the Antilles, the state pocketed hefty customs payments. This model lasted until at least the 1870s, slowly undone by the political changes in 1868, the first Cuban war of independence, the abolition of slavery in Puerto Rico, and, later, the complete privatization of the tobacco industry and its fleets in 1882, when they became part of a business consortium funded by Antonio López y López in Barcelona (Rodrigo Alharilla 2009).

This economic model ensured the survival of colonialism and a particular form of capitalism, which may have been inferior but remained effective until the Spanish-American War. The model had been built step-by-step after the great imperial crisis and the wars of independence (Rodríguez 1998). In the early 19th century, the Cortes of Cadiz included representatives from throughout the Spanish Empire, Spaniards from "both hemispheres," as they were called (Portillo 2000, 2006). This form of representation was echoed a few years later, after the first absolutist period and the reaction by Ferdinand VII. This second constitutional period, the so-called Liberal Triennium of 1820–23, replicated the transatlantic representational scheme in the context of reformist radicalization. At that time, however, much of continental America was not sending representatives to take their seats in Madrid. Ferdinand's second neo-absolutist period put an end to any possibility of constitutional protection for the negotiations between metropolitan Spaniards and those parts of the empire under Spanish sovereignty.

The reestablishment of liberal political representation during the revolutionary years of 1835–36 is rarely taken into account by historians, but it led directly to a new constitution that replaced the one approved in Cadiz in 1812. The Constitution of 1837 definitively provided a political framework for all the economic and social contexts I have described. Indeed, the new constitution expelled colonial representatives, in line with Napoleon's 1799 "special laws" that were never implemented. In practice, colonists were ostracized, and any discussion concerning military power in the three insular possessions was silenced. Thus, the metropolitan government was from then on able to address the question of Spain's position in the context of imperial rivalries and to avoid public debates regarding British pressure or efforts by slave owners in Louisiana in the 1850s, with the support of Cuban slave owners, to militarily occupy Cuba. Spain's involvement in subsequent neocolonial adventures in Morocco (1859), Mexico (1861–62), the Peruvian Chincha Islands (the site of enormous guano deposits), and Chile and Peru (where imaginary debts were claimed in 1864–66) was generally marked by failure. The goal, finally, was to eliminate any political trouble that might result from elections in the colonies or from colonial participation in parliament. In short, by excluding the colonies from formal political life, Spain avoided unrest, empowered the military captains general in the colonies, and forced Creole leaders, no matter how powerful, to channel their interests through lobbies or, at the end, open insurgency.

Though brief, this summary explains how Spain managed to transform peripheral territories into dynamic and important enclaves of agrarian capitalism. It is the tale of how one of the oldest European colonial powers managed to remain for an additional century among the imperial family that governed much of the world.

REFERENCES

Beckert, Sven. 2014. *Empire of Cotton: A Global History*. New York: Vintage Books.

Bénot, Yves, and Marcel Dorigny, eds. 2003. *Rétablissement de l'Esclavage Dans les Colonies Françaises. Aux Origines d'Haïti*. Paris: Maisonneuve et Larosse.

Bergad, Laird W. 1983. *Coffee and the Growth of Agrarian Capitalism in Nineteenth-Century Puerto Rico*. Princeton: Princeton University Press.

Bergad, Laird W., Fe Iglesias García, and María del Carmen Barcia. 1995. *The Cuban Slave Market, 1790–1880*. Cambridge: Cambridge University Press.

Boogmaard, Peter. 1989. *Children of the Colonial State: Population Growth and Economic Development in Java, 1795–1880*. Amsterdam: Free University Press.

Brewer, John. 1988. *The Sinews of Power: War, Money, and the English State, 1688–1783*. Cambridge, MA: Harvard University Press.

Brown, Cristopher L. 2006. *Moral Capital: Foundations of British Abolitionism*. Chapel Hill: University of North Carolina Press.

Covarrubias, José Enrique, and Matilde Souto Mantecón, eds. 2012. *Economía, Ciencia y Política. Estudio Sobre Alexander von Humboldt a 200 Años del Ensayo Político Sobre el Reino de Nueva España*. México: Instituto Mora/UNAM.

de Jesús, Ed. C. 1999. *The Tobacco Monopoly: Bureaucratic Enterprise and Social Change, 1766–1880*. Manila: CSIC.

de la Fuente, Alejandro. 2008. *Havana in the Atlantic in the Sixteenth Century*. Chapel Hill: University of North Carolina Press.

Delgado Ribas, Josep M. 2007. *Dinámicas Imperiales (1650–1796). España, América y Europa en el Cambio Institucional del Sistema Colonial Español*. Barcelona: Ediciones Bellaterra.

Drescher, Seymour. 2002. *The Mighty Experiment: Free Labor versus Slavery in British Emancipation*. Oxford: Oxford University Press.

Edwards, Bernard. 2007. *Royal Navy versus the Slave Traders: Enforcing Abolition at Seas, 1808–1898*. Barnsley, UK: Pen and Sword Books.

Ferrer, Ada. 2014. *Freedom's Mirror: Cuba and Haiti in the Age of Revolution*. Cambridge: Cambridge University Press.

Fradera, Josep M. 1999. *Filipinas, la Colonia más Peculiar: La Hacienda Pública en la Definición de la Política Colonial (1762–1868)*. Madrid: CSIC.

Fradera, Josep M. 2005. *Colonias para Después de un Imperio*. Barcelona: Edicions Bellaterra.

Knight, Franklin W. 1970. *Slave Society in Cuba during the Nineteenth Century*. Madison: University of Wisconsin Press.

Langue, Fréderique. 1991. "Mineros y Poder en Nueva España. El Caso de Zacatecas en Vísperas de la Independencia." *Revista de Indias* 51 (192): 327–42.

Legarda, Benito J., Jr. 1999. *After the Galleons. Foreign Trade and Entrepreneurship in the Nineteenth-Century Philippines*. Manila: Ateneo de Manila Press.

Marichal Salinas, Carlos. 1999. *La Bancarrota del Virreinato, 1780–1810: La Nueva España y las Finanzas del Imperio Español*. México: El Colegio de México.

McCoy, Alfred W., and Ed. C. de Jesús. 1982. *Philippine Social History: Global Trade and Local Transformations*. Quezon City: Ateneo de Manila University Press.

Moreno Fraginals, Manuel. 1978. *El Ingenio. Complejo Económico Social Cubano del Azúcar*. Havana: Editorial de Ciencias Sociales.

Murray, David. 1980. *Odious Commerce. Britain, Spain and the Abolition of the Cuban Slave Trade*. Cambridge: Cambridge University Press.

Portillo, José María. 2000. *Revolución de Nación. Orígenes de la Cultura Constitucional en España, 1780–1812*. Madrid: Centro de Estudios Políticos y Constitucionales.

Portillo, José María. 2006. *Crisis Atlántica. Autonomía e Independencia en la Crisis de la Monarquía Hispana*. Madrid: Marcial Pons.

Rodrigo Alharilla, Martín. 2009. "Del Desestanco del Tabaco a la Puesta en Marcha de la Compañía General de Tabacos de Filipinas (1879–1890)." *Boletín Americanista* 59:199–221.

Rodríguez, Jaime E. 1998. *La Independencia de la América Española*. México: Fondo de Cultura Económica.

Scarano, Francisco A. 1984. *Sugar and Slavery in Puerto Rico: The Plantation Economy of Ponce, 1800–1850*. Madison: University of Wisconsin Press.

Stone, Lawrence, ed. 1994. *An Imperial State at War: Britain from 1689 to 1815*. London: Routledge.

Trocki, Carl. 1999. *Opium, Empire and the Global Political Economy: A Study of the Asian Opium Trade*. New York: Routledge.

Yuste López, Carmen. 2007. *Emporios transpacíficos. Comerciantes mexicanos en Manila*. México: Universidad Nacional Autónoma de México.

PART 2

The Past and Present of the Political Economy and Authority in Cuba, Puerto Rico, and the Philippines

CHAPTER 4

Spain in Cuba

Policies, Structures, Economic Practices, and Colonial Relations

Antonio Santamaría García

The Spanish colonial regime in Cuba was altered at the end of the 18th century and augured great economic growth based on export agriculture and the slave trade, which worked in line with the interests of the elite island producers. However, Spain lacked a market for the Cuban supply, thus leading the regime to support itself through business relations between the island's and metropole's elites and through the extraction of the territory's revenue. This system (considered anachronistic due to its divergence from the British model, though its conditions were different as well) lasted 140 years and obtained a level of economic expansion unequaled in the English dominions. The following pages will present an analysis of the elements that constituted this system and an explanation of how, with time, the aforementioned harmony of Spanish-Cuban interests weakened due to the crisis of slavery and the concentration of colonial trade in the United States, factors that contributed to the end of Spanish rule.

Colonial Relations, Slavery, and Sugar Production in Cuba

Traditionally, Cuba's tobacco trade and supply, its principal export, were under metropolitan monopoly control. The island was considered strategic for the defense of the Spanish American Empire. The West Indies Fleet convened in Havana before returning to Europe, for which it was accorded a *situado* (remittance issued to sustain the colony) from the capital of the viceroyalty of New Spain, on which it depended (Fuente 2009).

In other Caribbean islands, commercial sugar production had progressed since 1640 through the use of slave labor, and Cuba planned to follow this example, considering that sugar was already produced in the Havana region thanks to reforms dating from the end of the 18th century that commercialized the land, but this region's growth required the deregulation of trade and slavery given the population shortage at that time (171,600 people in 1770–74, with 1,805,000 in 1890–94 following the introduction of at least 600,000 slaves; see fig. 4.1).

The modification of the colonial system in Cuba was the result of a series of events. In 1762, the British invaded Havana, and, upon recapturing it, the Spanish Crown created policies that would ensure that the island would be self-financed and would improve its defenses. The cornerstones of these policies were to outfit Havana with its own treasury and deregulate commerce and the African slave trade, including trade with friendly countries, authorized during the United States' independence (1775–83) and prolonged de jure or de facto due to the need to provide the territory with provisions, which the West Indies Fleet no longer guaranteed, and to export its products (Amores 2005).

Once independent from Great Britain, the United States stopped importing goods from British territories. Cuba's supply profited from this as well as from a market that Haiti ceased to supply and the slave trade that was no longer directed to the former French colony after its revolution (1791). The producing elite of the island thus formulated a project to take advantage of these opportunities, to expand the policies initiated in 1762 and enhance its participation in decision-making, which resulted in the creation of institutions like the Sociedad Económica (1784) and the Consulado de Comercio y Junta de Agricultura (1792), advisory organizations that also exercised authority over trade and the boosting of production and infrastructure development (Vázquez and Santamaría 2012).

The colonial reforms were a necessary condition for Cuba's economic growth. Its real gross domestic product (GDP) per capita increased 6.5% annually between 1775 and 1850, while Mexico's increased only 0.5% (Santamaría 2011). The sufficient condition, however, was the business abilities of the elites, especially those in Havana, who focused on agriculture (due to the island's lack of minerals, as in other parts of the Americas) and on founding a metropolitan trade monopoly. These elites benefited from the

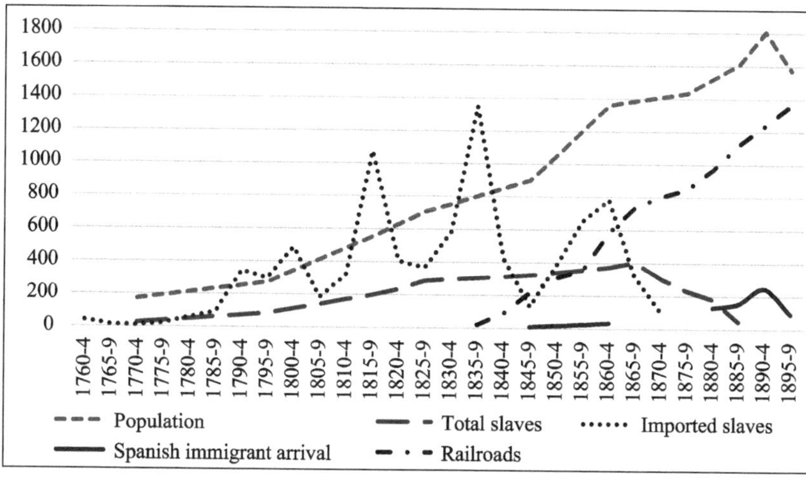

Fig. 4.1. Population and total slaves in Cuba (in thousands), imported slaves, immigrant arrivals (in hundreds) and railroads (in thousands of miles) (five-year averages)
Source: Adapted from Pérez de la Riva (1987); Zanetti and García-Álvarez (1987); Maluquer (1992); Santamaría and García-Álvarez (2004).

privilege accorded to the city's cabildo to rent out land until 1729, at the demand of the army and fleet, which enabled them to accumulate land and capital from the remittances they received and from official permissiveness regarding exportations that weren't approved by the Spanish treasury and to control the tobacco supply (also acquired with the remittance money) (Santamaría and García Álvarez 2004).

The series of events and policies that favored Cuba's growth continued into the 19th century. Napoleon invaded Spain in 1808, and independence began in its American empire. Although the island's agricultural and commercial elites debated over how to proceed, they remained loyal to the metropole. The island's economic progress and the possibility that political changes would halt it or lead to unrest within its growing African population (like that which took place in Haiti) help to explain this decision. Furthermore, Great Britain abolished the slave trade in 1808 and slavery in 1838, which damaged their sugar supply and benefited Cuba's (see fig. 4.2), which surpassed that of the English Caribbean around 1845.

The Latin American independence movements resulted in the strengthening of Cuba's previously implemented reforms in 1818. Cuba decisively deregulated its foreign trade and perpetuated its slave trade, despite the

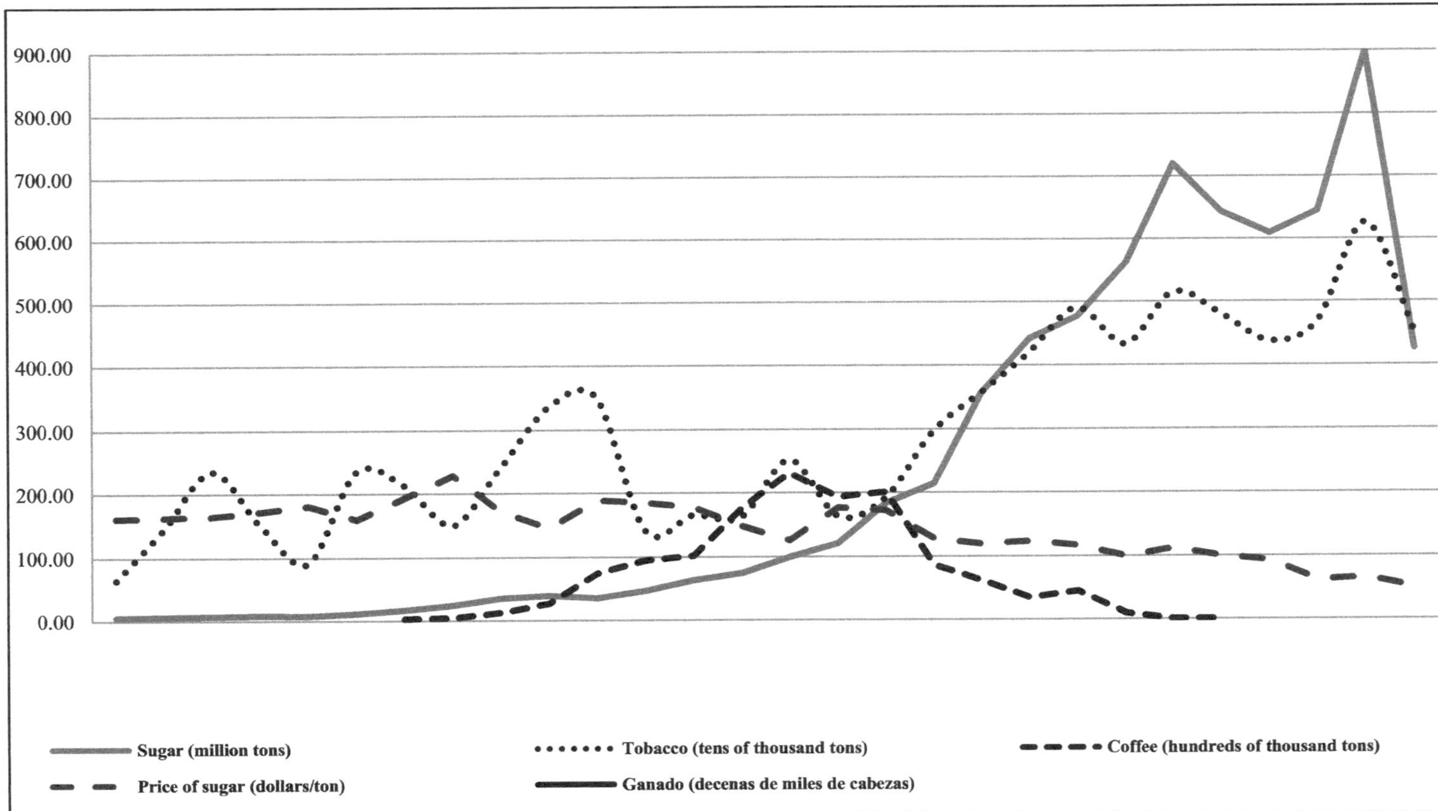

Fig. 4.2. Supply of sugar, coffee, tobacco, and livestock in Cuba and the price of sugar (five-year averages)
Source: Adapted from Moreno-Fraginals (1978); Stubbs (1989); Santamaría and García-Álvarez (2004); García-Álvarez (2015)

fact that the Spain and British governments signed a treaty prohibiting the slave trade in 1815. And, as these policies aimed to incentivize the growth of the island's economy, which was based on its exportations (given that the metropole lacked the market for them and that the reason for having colonies is to exploit them), a tax system was established on the island that protected importations from the mother country through tariffs, levied tariffs on all commercial trade, and favored the transportation of goods on national ships (Roldán 1997).

The extraction of Cuba's fiscal revenue was established by tariff laws in 1822, which would remain essentially unaltered until the end of Spanish rule on the island. However, belying the enduring nature of this fiscal system, a number of factors would ultimately lead to the demise of Spain's dominion. First was the need for slaves to maintain its economic growth, given the limited population on the island. Second was the cover offered through Cuba's colonial status that enabled it to continue the slave trade, which lasted until 1872 thanks to British-American conflict in the Caribbean, a balance of powers that allowed Cuba to remain in Spanish hands. The protraction of a slave-based social order was further guaranteed by the stationing of the metropolitan army on the island. These features, which determined the island's economic and social structure, also explain how the political position attained by the elites around 1790 would ultimately be undermined.

The Beginning of the Slavery Crisis, the Extraction of Colonial Revenue, and Cuba-Spain Ties

In the absence of market ties and given that the elite producers were Creoles, colonial relations in Cuba were based on the previously cited factors: free trade, the extraction of fiscal revenue, the maintenance of the slave trade, and shared trade between the island and metropolitan elite (Cayuela 1993). The alignment of interests that modified this relationship, however, progressively deteriorated at the same time as processes were modifying sugar production and markets. The end of the slave trade in Great Britain increased pressure to put an end to the practice, and the prohibition against it in Spain was toughened, albeit briefly, in 1845. In the end, the economic-strategic criteria that had previously permitted the perpetuation of slavery prevailed, though at the cost of a steep rise in the price of Africans.

The escalating cost of slaves led to their concentration in Cuba in the business that was most profitable: sugar cane plantations. Additionally, to counteract this cost and the rising competition resulting from Europe's progress in the manufacturing of beet sugar following the Napoleonic Wars, sugar mills were mechanized and, in the west of the island, where the greatest concentration of factories was found (Cantero [1856–57] 2005), railways were constructed beginning in 1837, which would come to span 2,225 kilometers by 1898 (see fig. 4.1).

The difficulties involved in the slave trade—the high cost of slaves, the railway's reach, and the modernization of the factories—led to increasingly pooled resources in these endeavors and in the west of Cuba. This ended up damaging the supply of goods that were formerly favored by the very policies that backed their expansion. Coffee, which was grown in the island's east and west and whose production had increased since the 1790s, was particularly affected. It would end up attaining the same value as sugar, but, due to the aforementioned conditions and the increase in international competition, it crashed in the 1840s and was unable to recover (García Álvarez 2015). On the other hand, the cultivation and trade of tobacco survived, thanks to internal consumption, an external demand for Havanas, and the fact that it required less capital and fewer slaves and occupied space unsuitable for sugarcane (Stubbs 1989).

Other supply sectors that subsisted included stockbreeding, since it was needed as a food source; farming and the transportation of agricultural products (see fig. 4.2); copper mining and the banana plantations, which were limited to small regions; and foodstuffs for the population and the plantations, although these necessities were covered by the growing importation of food products (Le Riverend 1985; Santamaría and García Álvarez 2004).

Since the 1840s, Cuba's economy specialized in supplying sugar, and its territorial imbalances worsened. In the 1800s, the eastern half of the island was home to only 25% of the population, and production, trade, and the railways were concentrated in the west, which reduced relative agricultural diversification in the period 1790–1840. Additionally, the protection of the sugar beet industry in Europe led to the concentration of the island's confectionery sugar exports in the United States (30% in 1850, 70% in 1870, and 80% in 1880), which would effectively confer decisive power over the exports to a foreign country, something that was impossible to predict at the time of the reformation of colonial relations, and which, in 1854, gave rise to an increase in sugar tariffs in retaliation to tariffs applied to US flour sent to the Great Antilla (Moreno-Fraginals 1978).

The processes mentioned above occurred when the old regime gave way

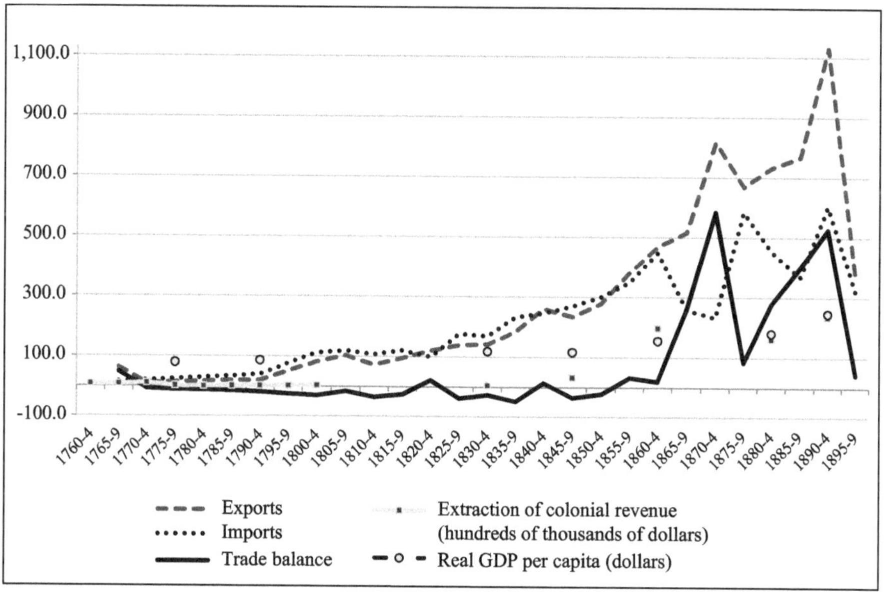

Fig. 4.3. Exports, imports, trade balance, the extraction of colonial revenue, and the real GDP per capita in Cuba (five-year averages)
Source: Data from Santamaría (2011); Maluquer (1974); Roldán (1997).

to liberal governments in Spain, whose plan was to increase Cuba's contribution to its development through a higher tax burden (see fig. 4.3) and to recuperate power that had been ceded to its elites during the time of the colonial reforms. These elites had grown old or died and had not passed on their investment habits to their descendants, whereas the metropolitan immigrants working in commercial and slave trade, though they continued their association with the Creole trade oligarchy, inherited economic hegemony over it (Bahamonde and Cayuela 1992). This was made evident by their acceptance that the constitution approved by the Courts of Madrid in 1837 would not apply to the Great Antilla and that the territory would remain under the rule of a general with plenipotentiary capacities (Gonçalvès 2008). The reason for this decision was based on slavery and meant that the Cuban population was not given the same rights as the Spanish.

This greater fiscal pressure led to a rise in the revenue that Spain extracted from Cuba—from 2.7% to 3.3% of its GDP between 1840 and 1870—but since GDP increased 33% during the same period, the drain of wealth did not lead to any conflicts as long as the economy maintained its upward trend and slavery did not reach a point of crisis. However, these same reasons paved the way for the political inaction that played out in response to progressive demands for reform on the island, despite the fact that recessions in 1857 and 1866 diminished its growth. This, along with the outflow of resources by way of taxes and the commercial imbalance with the metropole (Maluquer 1974; Roldán 1997), led to problems in raising the necessary investment to modernize its factories. Additionally, the colonial tariff negatively affected trade with the United States, and the country's abolition of slavery following its Civil War (1861–65) foretold the demise of slavery in the Great Antilla.

The Beginning of Colonial Crisis: Cuba without Slaves, Spain, and the United States

Following the abolition of slavery in the United States, a committee was convened in Madrid to address its economic problems of Cuba and the equalization of rights to those of Spain. In the end, it yielded no results besides the implementation of a new tax on the island. This, along with the reformist colonial movement's participation in the revolution that abolished the Spanish monarchy in 1868, helps to explain the outbreak of a war of independence in the Great Antilla in 1868 (Santamaría and García Álvarez 2004). Territorial imbalances were an additional factor contributing to the outbreak, since the conflict started in the east and was restricted at the western half of its territory.

With the war began the abolition of slavery in Cuba. The rebels proclaimed abolition in the territories they controlled, and the government responded with free womb laws, emancipation of the elderly, and emancipation of those who served in the army; the slave trade came to an end in 1872. The conflict lasted until 1878, and, although the majority of Creole elites supported and funded the metropole, this reinforced Spanish power on the island through the transfer of seized goods to the rebels, leading to immigration from the motherland that Hispanicized colonial society (Naranjo and García González 1996), since Cuba remained underpopulated and the end of slavery led to the need to import other workers (see fig. 4.1).

The Ten Years' War (1868–78) caused inflation, since money was minted to finance it, and an enormous public debt emitted by a bank set up in Spain was dumped on Cuba's treasury. Inflation ended only after the Bourbons were restored to power in the monarchy (1874) and the promised reforms were thwarted in 1866. In exchange for these reforms, abolition was declared (without reparations), and, in 1866, slavery ended in the Great Antilla, which promoted the equalization of rights in the island to those of the metropole. Liberty of association, freedom of the press, and the creation of political parties were declared; elections were held; and colonial representatives were sent to the Courts of Madrid. But these advances created an imbalance in progress achieved in the social, political (authority was still held in the island by the captain general), and economic realms (Piqueras 2003).

Spain's export interests obstructed economic reforms in Cuba. In 1882, Spain managed to increase protection for products sent to the island and ensured that the promised elimination of Spanish island trade tariffs would be gradual. The extraction of colonial revenue grew due to the increasing commercial imbalance between Spain and the Great Antilla as well as the debt—which in 1881 accounted for 6.3% of the GDP and had increased 91% since 1860 while the GDP had increased a mere 17%. However, the island compensated for this loss with its credit balance from trade with the United States and its current account balance, which went from –3% to –0.9% of its GDP during the same time period thanks to the stoppage of the drain on resources in the purchasing of slaves, the inflow of British capital for the purchase of railways, and North American capital put into factories and mines (Santamaría 2011; see fig. 4.3).

The problem of the lack of economic reforms in Cuba was further aggravated by the crisis of 1883–84, which plunged the price of sugar below that of US tariffs (see fig. 4.2). The Creole elite assembled to demand these reforms, but the 1884 signing of a Spanish–North American modus vivendi, which reduced the abovementioned tariff by 15%, succeeded in placating them. The island's budget returned to prewar levels, albeit with less income, and it began to incur deficits (Roldán 1997). Additionally, US sugar refiners formed a trust in 1887, and, in 1891, they succeeded in getting the US government to modify its customs duties on sugar confectionery, raising their cost and favoring the importation of raw sugar, which compelled Cuban sugar plantation owners to manufacture it as such, thus increasing their dependence on the North American market to export their products (Santamaría and García Álvarez 2004).

Securing the US market was of fundamental importance in optimizing the large investments made to modernize Cuban sugar plantations, since making a profit from economies of scale from the technology that had been installed required increasing their production (Iglesias 1998).

It was likewise essential for the metropole that the island's economic growth enable the continued extraction of revenue for the importation of provisions (on which its population's diet depended), and to alleviate territorial imbalances caused by resource concentration in its sugar supply. These imbalances were exacerbated by the War of '68 and its effect on the eastern half of the island, as well as by failed projects to construct a railway that would have enabled communication with the west (Zanetti and García Álvarez 1987).

The effect of the change in US tariffs led the Cuban elite to assemble again as the "Movimiento Económico" to call for the endlessly deferred reforms, due to the fact that Spain was undermining the foundation of the island's exports. This time they were joined by the metropolitans who operated in the Great Antilla, joining interests that affected the colonial agreement. Nevertheless, a Spanish–North American treaty again succeeded in deferring any resolution.

The Foster-Cánovas Treaty of 1891 reduced the US tariff on Cuban sugar, but, in exchange, it divided the island market between North American and Spanish exportations, reducing customs tariffs for both (Zanetti 1998). As a result, the Cuban sugar output grew to 1,100,000 tons (see fig. 4.2), but at the cost of ceding even greater control of its economy to a foreign country.

The Spanish–North American treaty of 1891 enabled Spain to increase its positive trade balance with Cuba during the periods 1885–89 and 1890–95 from $7.5 million to $14 million per year and enabled the taxed revenue extracted from the island to rise from $16 million to $24 million, thanks to the 3.3% annual increase of the real GDP per capita (see fig. 4.3), a similar increase to that of Germany or the United States, both leaders of the Second Industrial Revolution. However, without the slavery on which the colonial system in the Great Antilla had been based, the constant worsening of problems caused by the insufficient and postponed reforms, and the social polarization stemming from the increased number of migrants coming from the mother country and the Spanish business owners operating on the island, the decisive capacity that the United States achieved over the island's economy could lead to devastating outcomes.

In effect, in 1895, the United Stated declined to renew its treaty with Spain, and that same year marked the beginning of Cuba's second war of independence. This time, the conflict was to extend throughout the island's territory, and the Creole elite did not demonstrate the same level of attachment to the metropole as they did in 1868–78 (Zanetti 1998).

Cuba's postponed colonial reforms began after the outbreak of war in 1895. The territory was granted political autonomy, but it was not sufficient enough to tilt the balance of the conflict in favor of the Spanish. The devastating conflagration lasted from 1895 to 1898, until the US intervened, putting an end to Spanish dominion on the island.

Conclusion: Epilogue on Spain in Cuba

The colonial relationship between Spain and Cuba, reformed at the end of the 18th century, satisfied interests on both sides. It favored economic growth for the former and a share in its earnings for the latter, because it was in line with the conditions of both parties: for the island, it facilitated the supply of resources they lacked internally and the necessary means for its growth—slaves and free trade; for the motherland, it established the instruments enabling its fiscal exploitation, given Spain's lack of internal demand and the industrial capacity that would have allowed it to have a level of control and exploitation over its territories like that of the British Empire.

The conditions that the reforms of the ruling relationship of Spain over Cuba were based on also guaranteed its success and perpetuation, but only until it led to substantial changes in those same conditions, since it established a strict adherence to the foundations of the colonial pact and an inability to adapt or modify them.

For the aforementioned reasons, the tools of control used by the Spanish government in Cuba were strengthened, rather than relaxed, in response to changes in the island's economy and society, which hampered the prolongation of colonial relations after the abolition of slavery. This inability to adapt explains why the dissociative elements behind this relationship ultimately prevailed. The slave trade and forced work of Africans enabled great growth on the island, but it also led to a specialization in products that created serious territorial imbalances and an export concentration in the US market, which in turn led to the United States' holding decisive power over the Great Antillean economy, a prospect that was not contemplated when ties were reestablished with the metropole at the end of the 18th century.

The colonial relationship with Spain would end up seriously stunting the economic growth in Cuba that the relationship had been based on and that had made the territory valuable to the metropole. Furthermore, the endurance of this relationship also depended on the volition of a foreign country, which was the island's market and, as long as it existed, enabled the changes needed in the relationship to be further postponed.

Along with the social problems that were passed down from slavery and inequalities, which after the disappearance of the institution of slavery were perpetuated in the labor market and in practices and customs, the hyper-specialization of production in Cuba, which ultimately was one of the motives leading to its independence and which endured even after it was achieved, as well as the asymmetrical relationship with the United States, constituted the legacy inherited from the colonial period that marked the history of the island to come.

NOTE

Work for this chapter was financed by the European project Research and Innovation Staff Exchange, H2020-MSCA-RICE-2018, Connected Worlds: the Caribbean, Origin of the Modern World, ConnectCaribbean-823846, and the Spanish projects Las Crisis Económicas en el Caribe Hispano en Perspectiva Comparada (Ministerio de Ciencia e Innovacion, PID-2020-119888GB-Ioo), y Los Desafíos del Orden en el Circuncaribe Hispano (Ministerio de Ciencia e Innovación, MICU, 1789-1960, RTI2018-094305-B-100).

REFERENCES

Amores, Juan B. 2005. "Las Elites Cubanas y la Estrategia Imperial Borbónica en la Segunda Mitad del Siglo XVIII." In *Elites Urbanas en Hispanoamérica*, edited by Luis Navarro, 187–97. Sevilla: Universidad de Sevilla.

Bahamonde, Ángel, and José Cayuela. 1992. *Hacer las Américas. Elites Coloniales Españolas en el Siglo XIX.* Madrid: Alianza.

Cantero, Justo. (1856–57) 2005. *Los Ingenios. Colección de Vistas a los Principales Ingenios de Azúcar de la Isla de Cuba.* Edited by Luis Miguel García Mora and Antonio Santamaría. Aranjuez: Doce Calles.

Cayuela, José. 1993. *Bahía de Ultramar. España y Cuba en el Siglo XIX.* Madrid: Siglo XXI.

Fuente, Alejandro de la. 2009. "Economía." In *Historia de Cuba*, edited by Consuelo Naranjo, 59–68. Aranjuez: Doce Calles.

García Álvarez, Alejandro. 2015. "Los Primeros Tiempos en la Ruta Antillana del Café." *Revista de Indias* 263:117–48.

Gonçalvès, Dominique. 2008. *Le Planteur et le Roi. L'Aristocratie Havanaise et la Couronne d'Espagne.* Madrid: Casa de Velázquez.

Iglesias, Fe. 1998. *Del Ingenio al Central.* San Juan: UPR.

Le Riverend, Julio. 1985. *Historia Económica de Cuba.* Havana: Pueblo y Educación.

Maluquer, Jordi. 1974. "El Mercado Colonial Antillano en el Siglo XIX." In *Agricultura, Comercio Colonial y Crecimiento Económico en la España Contemporánea*, edited by Jordi Nadal and Gabriel Tortella, 322–57. Barcelona: Ariel.

Maluquer, Jordi. 1992. *Nación e Inmigración: los Españoles en Cuba*. Oviedo: Júcar.

Moreno-Fraginals, Manuel. 1978. *El ingenio. Complejo Económico Social Cubano del Azúcar*. Havana: Ciencias Sociales.

Naranjo, Consuelo, and Armando García González. 1996. *Racismo e Inmigración en Cuba en el Siglo XIX*. Aranjuez: Doce Calles.

Pérez de la Riva, Juan. 1987. *El Barracón. Esclavitud y Capitalismo en Cuba*. Barcelona: Grijalbo.

Piqueras, José A. 2003. *Cuba, Emporio y Colonia*. Madrid: FCE.

Roldán, Inés. 1997. "España y Cuba. Cien años de relaciones financieras." *Stvdia Historica* 20:35–69.

Santamaría, Antonio. 2011. "Dos Siglos de Especialización y dos Décadas de Incertidumbre. La historia Económica de Cuba, 1800–2010." In *Institucionalidad y Desarrollo Económico en América Latina*, edited by Luis Bertolá and Pablo Gerchunoff, 135–90. Santiago: CEPAL.

Santamaría, Antonio, and Alejandro García Álvarez. 2004. *Economía y Colonia: la Economía Cubana y la Relación con España, 1765–1902*. Madrid: CSIC.

Stubbs, Jean. 1989. *El Tabaco en la Periferia*. Havana: Ciencias Sociales.

Vázquez, Sigfrido, and Antonio Santamaría. 2012. "Cuba Económica en Tiempos de las Independencias Americanas: la Hacienda y la Consolidación de los Vales Reales en Comparación con el Caso de México." *Revista de Historia Económica* 30 (1): 91–124.

Zanetti, Oscar. 1998. *Comercio y Poder. Relaciones Comerciales Hispano-Cubanas-Norteamericanas en Torno a 1898*. Havana: Casa.

Zanetti, Oscar y Alejandro García Álvarez. 1987. *Caminos Para el Azúcar*. Havana: Ciencias Sociales.

CHAPTER 5

The Political Economy of Contemporary Cuba

Jacqueline Laguardia Martinez

To evaluate contemporary Cuba from any dimension, be it economic, political, or sociocultural, is a challenging exercise. This is particularly true at the current moment, when significant changes have occurred in the political scenario of an island that has been striving for an ambitious socioeconomic reform in recent years. The main objective of this chapter, therefore, is to identify key characteristics of Cuba's economic systems in the midst of the many transformations registered throughout the country's history. In that regard, the chapter briefly covers the first 50 years of the revolution as the necessary preamble in understanding Cuba's economy and society. It evaluates the political economy of contemporary Cuba in order to allow a comparison of Cuba's socioeconomic structures from the colonial era until present day.

Breaking with the Colonial Legacies of the Socioeconomic System: The Impact of the Cuban Revolution

On January 1, 1959, a new period started in Cuban history. Two years later, after continuous and monumental changes that included the nationalization of foreign enterprises—most of them US companies—the approval of the First and Second Agrarian Reform laws, and the creation of several institutions and organizations—for instance, the Federation of Cuban Women and the Cuban Institute of Cinematographic Art and Industry—Cuban society turned around social relations and, consequently, the economic system. In 1961, when Cuba declared itself a Socialist country, the determination of building a different type of society required the island to look for new ways of organizing its economic activity and socioeconomic relations. A key pillar in this direction was to give a central role to the state as the main economic actor as well as to increase the use of central planning and the control of market forces.

The overarching economic goal was to eradicate underdevelopment. For Cuba to rapidly advance toward a diversified economy encompassing agricultural and industrial activities, the country had to overcome its colonial history of monocrop and dependency. The Cuban government promoted boosts in productions and exports, the abandonment of sugar dependency, full employment, and the use of science and technology as integral components of the economy. Since the revolutionary government became conscious of the economic fragility of the existing model,[1] it decided to radically modify it together with the rationale that shaped it.

By 1959, the Cuban economy faced serious problems: low economic growth rates, a stagnant sugar sector and a limited non-sugar sector, high unemployment that worsened once the sugar harvest ended, substantial gaps between urban and rural areas, and high dependency on sugar exports and on the economic links with the United States (Mesa-Lago 2009, 368).

Most of these problems can be traced to the political and economic organization imposed by Spain on its island colonies: the plantation economy. The Cuban colony flourished on the production of sugarcane and had the task of satisfying the increasing demands of the European and North American markets. The Spanish Crown, together with the Creole elite, enforced production and trade mechanisms that had revolved around sugar since the 17th century. By inserting Cuba into the role of monocrop producer and exporter in the global market, the underdevelopment of the Cuban economy was decided.

During the first half of the 20th century, the sugar dependence deepened. The onset of the world wars led to an increase in sugar prices, allowing Cuba to enjoy periods of economic prosperity, which soon after gave rise to cyclical crises with the adjustment of global markets once military campaigns ended. The overwhelming dependence on the export of a single product persisted in spite of diversification attempts during the 1930s and 1940s. This placed the economy in an unresolved situation of vulnerability determined by the evolution of sugar prices, which were decided by exogenous actors and events, most of them linked to US political will and domestic political affairs. Since the end of the 19th century, the United

States had increased its presence in the Cuban economy to become the primary market for exports and the primary source of imports, which lasted until the 1960s.[2]

After 1959, transformations were conducted briskly, fiercely, boldly, and someway chaotically, and they altered the property relations on the island. Changes were also made to the overall social structure since property is not merely an economic concept but a social category (Valdés Paz 2016). The bourgeoisie and previous economic elites were undermined by Socialist ideology and the new socioeconomic organization.

The Agrarian Reform of 1959 resulted in the creation of cooperatives, which amounted to 3.6 million hectares, representing about 44% of all expropriated land. These cooperatives were later transformed into state farms. After the Second Agrarian Reform in 1961, more than 30% of the country's agricultural lands returned to the state (Molina Molina 2007, 191). The state became the dominant actor in the agricultural sector, holding most of the arable lands, technology, and resources to conduct the agricultural activity on the island. Until 1993, the state was in charge of 83% of the agricultural activity (Nova González 2012, 130).

By the end of the 1960s, the state had become the central economic actor by controlling all banking, foreign trade, and wholesale trade activities, as well as 50% of retail trade, 92% of transport, 80% of construction, 85% of industry, and 37% of agriculture. To a lesser degree, cooperative and small private property continued to exist, mostly in the agriculture sector. Self-owned employment (*trabajo por cuenta propia*) was first authorized in 1978 and lasted until 1986, when the debate concerning the high prices on the agricultural market provoked its temporary suspension (Rodríguez 2016a).

Foreign economic partners changed during the revolutionary period for ideological and political reasons. In October 1960, President Eisenhower imposed the trade embargo on Cuba, which covered US exports to the island except for medicine and some foods. President Kennedy expanded it later, turning it into an economic blockade (Fabry 2015).[3]

In 1972, Cuba entered into the COMECOM (Council for Mutual Economic Assistance). For the next 20 years, around 80% of Cuban imports came from COMECOM countries, gaining preferential prices, commercial credits, and developmental aid (Bell Lara et al. 2017, 17).

In 1975, the First Congress of the Communist Party of Cuba (PCC) approved the economic plan for the 1976–80 period. Its main goal was to accelerate industrialization by increasing sugar production and other agricultural activities. In 1982, foreign investment in joint ventures was legalized.

Between 1988, when Cubanacan was installed as the first joint venture, and 1991, 20 joint ventures were agreed upon. During the Fourth Congress of the PCC in 1991, the further expansion of foreign direct investment (FDI) was approved. The following year, the increased opening to FDI was codified in the constitutional reform (Morris 2008, 777), which allowed the coexistence of various forms of property within the framework of the Socialist economy.

By the end of the 1980s, Cuba's economic strategies since the triumph of the revolution had intended to deal with and effectively solve key questions for accomplishing economic development, for example, how to achieve economic independence, how to socialize agricultural and industrial property and boost productivity and economic efficiency, how to distribute economic wealth, how to successfully design and implement economic plans and management systems, and how to insert Cuba in the international economy (Molina Molina 2007, 187).

The results, however, were mixed. Industrial production grew at an annual average rate of 2.9% between 1959 and 1989. Construction increased around 6%, while agricultural production only grew 0.9%. By 1989, Cuba had multiplied its steel production 14 times, cement production 6 times, nickel production and oil refinement 4 times, fertilizers production 10 times, and textiles production 7 times. Between 1959 and 1983, 1,100 new industries were created (Bell Lara et al. 2017, 17). As such, even if industrialization was possible, the Cuban industry still relied heavily on imported inputs, imported technologies, and oil-intensive machinery.

In spite of the profound changes in the political, economic, and social dynamics registered in the first 30 years of the Cuban Revolution, the country was unable to break its pattern of exporting items such as sugar, citrus fruits, and nickel and also failed to overcome its economic linkages with a limited number of foreign partners, mostly the USSR. Cuba remained an exporter of raw materials and an importer of technology and high-value goods. Due to ideological alignments and to the US hostility during the Cold War, the pattern of condensing trade and economic relations with a few partners persisted. The promotion of the service sector slowed down due to the economic model adopted and the disconnection with key foreign markets. In 1987, trade with the COMECOM was at 86.4%. Cuba sold 63% of its sugar exports, 73% of nickel, 95% of citrus fruits, and 100% of electronic spare pieces and components to the Socialist countries in Europe; in turn, it imported 63% of food, 86% of raw materials, 98% of oil, 80% of machineries and equipment, and 74% of manufactured goods from the COMECOM (Bell Lara et al. 2017, 19).

The Special Period: A Breaking Point in the Political Economy of Cuba

Starting in the late 1980s, there were signs indicating the exhaustion of the economic model (Pérez Villanueva 2012; Sánchez Egozcué 2015), which, together with the breakdown of the USSR and its European Socialist allies, forced Cuba to embark, yet again, on a brisk, fierce, bold, and someway chaotic adjustment process. Between 1989 and 1993, the gross domestic product (GDP) decreased by 34.7%, imports decreased by 78%, and the fiscal deficit reached 33.5% of the GDP (Banco Central de Cuba n.d., 7).

The disruption of the socioeconomic organization delinked many economic actors from the state-controlled mechanisms and opened the gate for more diverse property relations, causing a reduction in the state's economic activities. State-owned lands were transferred to the cooperatives and small farmers. Ministries and other governmental institutions were reduced from 50 to 31. The possession and circulation of foreign currency was permitted, and new norms to legally frame the novel political economy system were approved as the Foreign Investment Law of 1995 and the Tax System Law of 1994 (Banco Central de Cuba n.d., 8). In Havana, Moa, and other tourist destinations, the FDI increased. Alliances changed once again, and European and Latin American companies, together with companies from Canada and China, added Cuba to their business portfolios and created joint ventures in the island.

The economic crisis forced many Cubans to migrate. The main destination was the United States, particularly Florida, because of its closeness to Cuba, the existence of a large Cuban diaspora, its economic development, and the special provisions put in place to accommodate Cuban migrants. Between 1989 and 1994, the US Coast Guard intercepted 45,930 Cubans on the high sea. Between 1989 and 2004, almost 302,000 Cubans migrated to the United States, of which 18% arrived by sea. In 2005, around 180,000 Cubans lived in other countries apart from the United States, mainly Venezuela, Mexico, and Spain, as well as in Puerto Rico, which is not usually included in official US migration statistics (Duany 2005, 165–69). The figures have continued to increase, mostly after January 2013, when Cuba implemented a migratory reform (Gaceta Oficial de la República de Cuba 2012). Between 2013 and 2018, Cuban citizens made more than 3 million trips abroad (Figueredo et al. 2019).

In January 2017, a few days before the end of his second term, President

Barack Obama decided to end the "dry feet, wet feet" policy. This change modified Cuban migratory flows in view of the novel difficulty of settling in the United States—a difficulty that was significantly increased by the Trump administration's policy toward Latin American and Caribbean migration. In recent years, a growing number of Cubans have preferred to migrate to South America and Central America instead of heading immediately to the United States.

Migration has resulted in mounting remittance flows. Remittances have become a central income source for Cuban households: Around 25% of Cubans receive remittances (Rodríguez 2016a), and they have been estimated between USD 3,000 million and 3,500 million annually for the last decade (Triana Cordoví 2017, 38). Even when there were no accurate figures for remittances, in 2008 they were estimated to be USD 1,447.06 million, and, by 2018, they had increased to USD 3,691.68 million, a growth of 3.6% over the previous year. Around 90% of these money transfers came from the United States (Morales 2019). This trend indicates that there is a sector within Cuba society that has been able to sustain and reproduce itself without relying on the state as the main provider of employment, subsidized products, and services.

It is estimated that the amount of remittances sent to Cuba has dropped since 2019 as a result of various factors, notoriously the increasing restrictions that the Trump administration imposed on the Cuban economy in its aim to pressure the government toward a change of regime and to cut cooperation with Venezuela. In September 2020, the US government limited the amount of money that Cubans living in the United States can send to their relatives in Cuba to USD 1,000 every three months (EFE 2019). Starting in February 2020, Western Union suspended sending remittances to Cuba except from its offices in the United States (Pentón 2020). In November 2020, Western Union ceased all its operations in Cuba.

Some of the changes of the 1990s led to ruptures with the major aspects of the Cuban economy rooted in colonial and neocolonial history, for example, sugar dependence. By the end of the first decade of the 21st century, sugar production and exports had diminished considerably, with most of its decline occurring after the 2002 restructuring of the industry, which led to the reduction of the allotted land to sugarcane plantations and the number of sugar mills by half. After 2008, Cuba no longer depended primarily on sugar exports (see table 5.1).

The distribution of exports shows a larger diversification, with the great-

TABLE 5.1. Cuban Production Indicators, 1957–58, 1989, and 2007–8

Production (tons per 1,000 inhabitants)	1957–58	1989	2007–8	Change % 2008/1958	Change % 2008/1989
Mining					
Nickel	3	4	7	133	75
Oil	7	68	258	3,585	279
Natural gas	9	3	108	1,100	3,500
Industry					
Sugar	859	768	106	–88	-86
Electricity (1,000 Kw/h)	379	1,440	1,574	315	9
Steel	9	30	23	156	-23
Cement	108	355	158	46	-55
Textiles (m^2)	17	21	2	-88	-90
Agriculture					
Tobacco leaf	8	4	2	–75	-50
Citrus	16	96	31	94	-67
Coffee	6	3	0.4	-93	-87
Eggs (1,000 units)	46	254	202	339	-20
Rice	37	50	39	5	-22
Milk	113	107	48	-57	-55
Chicken meat	7	14	4	–43	-67
Fish and seafood	3	18	6	100	-67

Source: Adapted from Mesa-Lago (2009, 372).

est change being the notable increase in the share of minerals. According to Mesa-Lago, this resulted from the substantial increase in nickel output stimulated by the jump in world prices for nickel in 2006–7 (2009, 374).

Cuba has not been able to boost exports to cover for import demands of a population that has doubled since 1959 (see table 5.2). The import share of food and fats rose to 23% after the 1990s. By 2008, Cuba was importing 84% of its basic food basket at a cost of USD 2.5 billion (Mesa-Lago 2009, 374). Cuba's political economy remains hampered by its large dependence on the imports of basic goods and, most specifically, its inability to foster an agricultural sector capable of meeting the needs of domestic consumption and also to export.

The Special Period[4] forced Cubans to engage with small farming practices due to the lack of fertilizers and machineries and the abrupt shrinking of food imports. During the 1990s, Cuba registered an increase in the organic production of coffee, cocoa, sugar, oranges, grapefruits, honeybees, and medical herbs (Rodríguez Castellón 2004). Unfortunately, the wide national movement toward small urban farming and organic agriculture has been gradually neglected. What could have been an innovative solution

TABLE 5.2. Cuban External Economic Indicators, 1957–58, 1989, and 2007–8

Indicators	1957–58	1989	2007–8	Change % 2008/1958	Change % 2008/1989
External trade of goods					
(Cuban pesos per capita)					
Exports	108	514	336	211	-35
Imports	114	774	1,290	1,032	67
Trade balance (deficit)	-6	-260	-953	15,783	266
Deficit (% of GDP)	2	9	19	850	111
Export distribution (%)					
Sugar	81	73	5	-94	-93
Tobacco	7	2	6	-14	200
Minerals (mainly nickel)	6	9	57	850	533
Others	6	16	32	433	100
Import distribution (%)					
Food and fats	21	13	16	-23	23
Manufactures	24	14	20	-16	43
Machinery and transport equipment	31	31	30	-3	-3
Fuels and minerals	11	32	24	118	-25
Trade partner concentration	62	65	20	-68	-69
(% of total trade)					
Tourism					
Visitors (per 1,000 inhabitants)	40	26	209	490	704
Gross income (pesos per capita)	9	16	226	2,411	1,067

Source: Adapted from Mesa-Lago (2009, 373).

for promoting food security, ensuring ample and diverse agricultural production, and diversifying exports has been reduced to limited productions in specific zones, with only a few organic farms remaining.

Cuban agriculture exhibits one of the lowest yields in Latin America, with losses of around 57% of agricultural production—30% during harvest and post-harvest phases and 27% during distribution. The cooperative sector owns 80% of the land and produces 90% of the national food but only satisfies 20% of the demand. Cuba's food imports are around USD 2,000 million every year (UEPESC 2017b). In 2018, the imported food bill amounted to around USD 1,700 million, of which an estimated 35%–47% could be replaced by domestic production (Rodríguez 2019).

The tourism renaissance after 1989 appeared as a curious trend connected to the service vocation of the Cuban economy and to the colonial pre-sugar past when Havana was an open economy specialized in services,

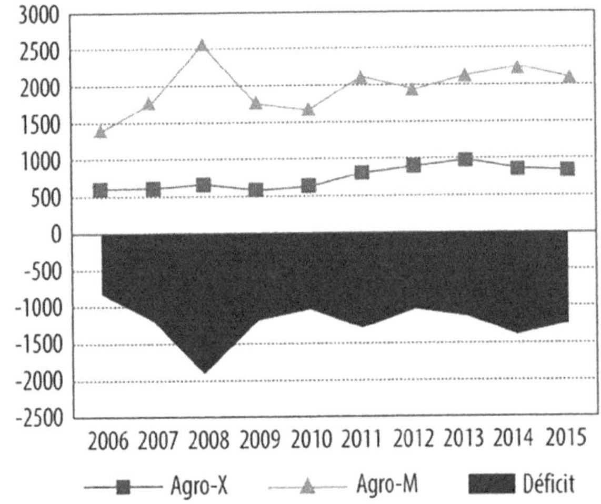

Fig. 5.1. Trade in Cuban agricultural products (in million Cuban pesos)
Source: Data from Anaya Cruz and García Álvarez (2017, 64).

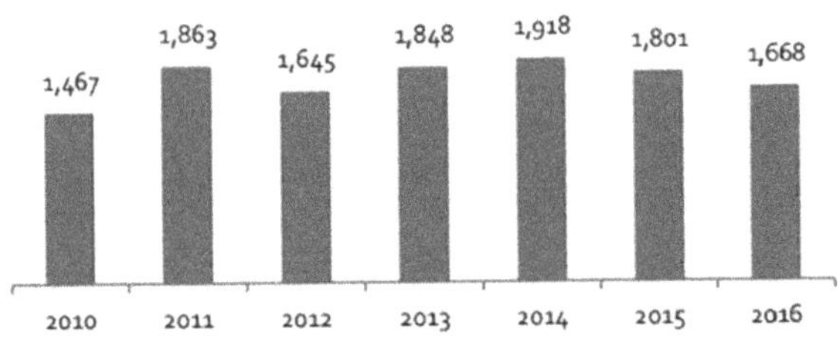

Fig. 5.2. Food imports (in million Cuban pesos)
Source: Data from UEPESC (2017a).

thanks to its favorable geographic position that had made it the American hub of the fleet system of the Spanish Empire since the 1560s. Tourism was one of the main avenues for lifting up the economy during the Special Period, and, since then, it has remained one of the country's key economic activities. In the tourism sector, investors come from, among others, Spain, France, Canada, Germany, Switzerland, Canada, and China (Feinberg 2017). Since 1995, exports of the tertiary sector have surpassed goods exports, with tourism and the exports of professional services being leading items (Torres Pérez 2012, 71).

After December 17, 2014, when Presidents Raúl Castro and Barack Obama announced the normalization of bilateral relations, tourism blossomed.[5] US citizens were allowed to travel to Cuba under 12 categories of authorized travel; therefore, the statutory prohibition of tourism could be eluded. The growing interest in Cuba and the rush to visit "before Americans arrive" triggered a notable increase in tourism starting in 2015. In 2016, Cuba received 4,029,000 foreign visitors (Perelló Cabrera 2017, 68–71). According to the World Travel & Tourism Council (WTTC), the direct contribution of travel and tourism in 2016 to Cuba's GDP was USD 2,074.9 million, representing 2.2% of its GDP. In 2016, the total contribution of travel and tourism to employment, including jobs indirectly supported by the industry, was 8.9% of total employment, which represented 462,000 jobs (WTTC 2017).

By 2020, a more pronounced blow to tourism activity in Cuba was expected, not only as a result of the pandemic associated with COVID-19 but also as result of the increased restrictions imposed by the Trump administration. Between January and June 2020, Cuba merely received 1,236,461 visitors, including 106,940 Cubans living abroad (ONEI 2021). After the first wave of the pandemic, the country reopened the borders in October 2020, but limited tourism activity has been reactivated since. The Trump administration activated Title III of the Helms-Burton Act, the restriction of travel categories for Americans wishing to travel to Cuba, and the prohibition of cruises to Cuba, among other measures, as of December 10, 2019, US commercial airlines are prohibited from traveling to Cuba, with the exception of flights to Havana (BBC 2019).

The Trump administration's policy toward Cuba, which took a step back from the progress made by President Obama when reestablishing bilateral diplomatic relations, turned back to the usual confrontation and hostility. The Trump strategy toward Cuba negatively affected the arrival of international visitors to the island. While in 2018 Cuba received 4,711,910 visitors, in 2019 the figure fell to 4,275,558. While decreases in European tourist arrivals were reported, the most drastic drop was led by the United States. In 2018, 637,907 Americans traveled to the island, while only 498,067 did so in 2019 (ONEI 2020, 6).

Since the strategies that were embraced to navigate the crisis of the 1990s—even when bringing considerable changes to the economy and society—were unable to achieve larger ruptures with the colonial past and—while the sugar dependency was broken years after—Cuba increased its dependence on remittances and tourism, new changes were demanded.

The more recent attempt to boost the Cuban economy and break with the colonial heritage and the patterns of economic underdevelopment is the reform that was undertaken in 2011 and continues today. Without discussing its specific pillars and objectives, the next section delves into some of its impacts on Cuba's economy and society.

"Updating the Cuban Socioeconomic Policy": Initial Results

In 2006, President Raúl Castro spearheaded a debate on economic and social changes in which Cuban economists proposed reforms ranging from the transformation of property relations to a greater opening to FDI. In 2008, hurricanes caused substantial damage equivalent to 20% of Cuba's GDP (Mesa-Lago 2009, 369) and, together with the global economic crisis and its regional impacts, slowed the pace of the reforms. In 2011, at the Sixth Congress of the PCC, the program "Updating the Cuban Socioeconomic Policy" (Lineamientos de la Política Económica y Social del Partido y la Revolución) was officially launched as the continuum of a wave of changes initiated in 2007.

The program, besides keeping the overarching ambition of building a resilient and solid economy devoid of the remnants of the colonial past, strives to adapt the Cuban model to a world in which the predominant economic logic is not aligned with Cuba's ideological and social orientation. Even in Latin America, major changes have tipped the favorable balance of progressive political forces and undermined leaderships openly sympathetic to Cuba—such as Nicolás Maduro in Venezuela, Lula and Dilma Rousseff in Brazil, Rafael Correa in Ecuador, and Evo Morales in Bolivia. The circumstances that made the advancement of economic partnerships, such as the ALBA–TCP and Petrocaribe, are no longer there.

A quick evaluation of the Cuban reform up to the beginning of 2020 shows that results have been mixed. On the positive side, Cuba has been able to partially diversify its economic ties, although trade concentration remains with China, Spain, Canada, and Venezuela, which are also the main destinations for exports. In 2018, these four countries accounted for 68.6% of the value of Cuban exports. The concentration remains when examining Cuba's export items, where the main products still correspond to raw materials associated with mining activity, agriculture (sugar and tobacco), beverages (rum), and chemicals (ONEI 2019, 9–28).

The economic performance has not met the expectations, and economic growth has remained under the 5–7% rate (Monreal González 2017c). The Cuban economy reached a peak of 12% GDP growth in 2006 but averaged around 2% annual growth between 2009 and 2017 (Mesa-Lago 2019). Vulnerabilities associated with geographic conditions, size, insularity, demographic trends, high exposure to extreme meteorological events, and high susceptibility to climate change remain, and they continue to weaken the

Cuban economy within the current unstable global economic environment, especially with regards to Latin America and the Caribbean.

The reform has not been able to break the vicious circle that entraps the Cuban economy: weak economic growth, growing fiscal deficits, macroeconomic imbalances as well as distortions in the monetary regime, market segmentation, and insufficient FDI to modernize and recapitalize obsolete infrastructure. High import demand coexists with limited import substitution capacity and with the inability to convert domestic production into exports (Triana Cordoví 2017; Mesa-Lago 2019).

Despite the cautiousness of the reform, property relations have become more diverse and complex by incorporating new social actors (Valdés Paz 2016). For example, reforms in the structure of land ownership have deepened since 2007, the facilitation of self-employment followed in September 2010, the authorization for the creation of nonagricultural cooperatives was approved, and, as a result, the non-state sector has grown to a size not seen since the mid-1960s (Torres Pérez 2016, 6). Since 2010, private employment has been the only form of employment that has increased continuously, as opposed to the public sector, which lost almost 153,000 employment positions, while the cooperative sector did not generate net employment (Monreal González 2017c).[6]

Incomes in Cuban households are compounded by salaries associated with formal employment together with private transferences such as remittances and public transferences such as pensions, social assistance, and subventions to products and services like the ration card (*libreta de abastecimientos*) (Galtés Galeano 2017, 68). In 2015, between 43% and 46% of the average household income was obtained via formal salary (Torres Pérez 2017; Galtés Galeano 2017). Incentives to work come mostly from the non-state sector, and young Cubans prefer to work in the private sector, where they make up 24% of the workforce (Cubadebate 2015). The income generated by the private sector is superior to the average income received by the employees of the public sector. Even unemployed people with access to remittances can obtain a higher income than the formally employed workforce, a fact that evidences the instability, inequity, and social polarization in a society where formal salaries play a minor role (Galtés Galeano 2017, 69–73).

The ongoing reform should also be evaluated from a social perspective. Without exhausting the analysis of the social dimension of the reform, which deserves a chapter by itself, it is important to mention a few key features. The scope of the recent changes has had a profound social impact and has enlarged the social gaps within a diverse society that tends to become more heterogeneous (Valdés Paz 2016; Torres Pérez 2017, 29). After the 1990s, differences between rural and urban areas and between provinces and municipalities became more accentuated (Serbin 2017; Grabendorff 2017; Monreal González 2017a; Íñiguez Rojas 2013; Espina Prieto 2004, 2008, 2010). Inequality has resurfaced, to the surprise and worry of many who thought poverty and social stratification were unhappy memories of the past. Significant differences between households exist and have become more pronounced (Barbería 2008; Zabala Arguelles 2013; Espina Prieto and Echevarría 2015; Feinberg 2017; Íñiguez Rojas and Pérez Villanueva 2004). Gender inequality and racial prejudice persist.

From the 1990s until the beginning of the 21st century, the Gini coefficient deteriorated from 0.38 to 0.407 (Monreal González 2017a; Barbería 2008). In 2000, 20% of Cubans suffered from insufficient incomes and unfulfilled basic needs (Espina Prieto 2008). Nowadays, it is estimated that one in four Cubans is affected by some type of income poverty. It is expected that the Gini coefficient for Cuba in 2017 could be worse than the 0.407 calculated almost 20 years ago (Monreal González 2017b; Rodríguez 2016b). Differences are obvious when compared to the Gini coefficient during the 1970s and the 1980s: in 1978 it was 0.25, while in 1986 it was 0.22 (Zabala Arguelles 2013, 340). In the mid-1980s, the Gini coefficient was an estimated 0.24 (Espina Prieto 2008).

In 2017, at the Seventh Congress of the PCC, it was recognized that the planning of the reform program exceeded its execution since merely a little more than 20% of the guidelines had been implemented, while almost 80% were still in the process of implementation (PCC 2017). Almost a decade after its launch, it can be concluded that the reform has not been able to fundamentally transform Cuba's economy or to reduce, or even contain, economic distortions and social differentiation.

Final Comments

Cuba's economy and society underwent dramatic changes after the 1960s when the government declared the Socialist character of the revolution and assumed the task of breaking with the colonial past. More than half a century later, after having embraced a conscious transformation attempt anchored in Socialist political economy under the US embargo that is still operative, surviving a colossal crisis in the 1990s, and having been forced to adapt to a profoundly different world characterized by the hegemony of neoliberal capitalism, the country exhibits a mixed scenario of rupture and continuity with the colonial past.

Cuba is no longer a sugar island depending on a single export market. The country has become a service economy, where tourism and the export of professional services partially compensate for the deficit of the balance of trade for goods. However, traces of colonial legacies remain in Cuba's patterns of insertion into the global economy. The main exports are still raw materials associated with agriculture and mining, and the beaches. Jumping into producing high value-added products and services for domestic and foreign consumption has not been achieved despite several attempts at social and economic restructuring. The structural weakness of the economy persists since it is highly vulnerable to exogenous events and dependent on imports and remittances, with limited economic diversification, technological lags, and low productivity.

The permanence of colonial footprints is visible in territorial disparities. Urban settlements near bay areas—such as Havana and Santiago de Cuba—continue to be at the core of economic dynamism, together with coastal zones turned into tourism attractions. Social gaps born in the colonial period still remain, in spite of the significant social transformation achieved after 1959 in terms of diminishing racial and gender inequalities. Poverty has not been eradicated, and, since the crisis of 1990, it has deepened.

Although the ambitious goal of transforming Cuba's economic structure seems to have stalled in recent years as a result of a volatile global economy, the rightward shift of important regional allies such as Brazil and Ecuador, the Venezuelan crisis, and the aggressiveness of the Trump administration, all of it in a scenario of increasing extreme weather events and transnational health threats, the country has made progress in the process of renewing its political institutions.

In February 2019, the new constitution was approved, with 73.3% of the vote in favor of the "yes" option of the registered Cuban citizens (Granma Redacción Digital 2019). In October 2019, the Cuban Parliament elected Miguel Mario Díaz-Canel Bermúdez as president of the Republic of Cuba during the Fourth Extraordinary Session of the National Assembly of People's Power (Telesur 2019). The new constitution recognizes private property and foreign investment, an act that constitutes decisive support to the private sector of the Cuban economy (Malkin 2019).

Cuba is considered a Small Island Developing State (SIDS). To break from the specific constraints of social and economic development has proven difficult for the ensemble of Caribbean SIDS, who all share a similar history of colonial exploitation regardless of their colonial masters. Cuba, contrary to its neighbors, has chosen the Socialist option as an alternative approach of moving away from the colonial legacy. In spite of the changes previously discussed, there is still much work to do.

Key lessons for pursuing transformations in order not only to transform the colonial legacy but also to make the socioeconomic model more resilient, stable, diverse, inclusive, and participatory could be found, ironically, when revisiting the past: History teaches us that Cuba's geographic location places it in a privileged position for becoming a Latin American and Caribbean hub, even under a scenario of US blockade. Cuba has extensive expertise as a service economy that cumulates savoir faire on how an open small economy[7] is capable of building resilience as it has been forced to deal with foreign actors and events to rapidly adjust in order to survive. Having a healthy and educated population should reinforce the conviction that the most valuable resource is its population, capable of creating and innovating in the toughest circumstances.

How to shape and implement the future path of the social and economic changes is fundamental for the novel architecture of the political economy of Cuba. The challenge is not only to overcome the colonial legacy but to achieve economic success and improve people's welfare in a context of political rights, social justice and equity. More than four centuries of colonial rule have proven difficult but not impossible to overcome. Lessons have been learned. The real challenge is to accept the need to drop what does not work and to create new paths and take risks. By doing so, maybe history can be different.

NOTES

1. Focusing on sugarcane resulted in the dependence on a single product to be exported—most of it to a single market, the United Sates—which, due to the seasonality of the harvest and the occurrence of climatological events, was incapable of guaranteeing full employment. It also remained vulnerable to the impact of exogenous events that forced a shorter harvest as an attempt—usually useless—to sustain higher prices or to secure the US export quota.

2. Merchants in Cuba and the American colonies established illicit contacts to trade on commodities as well as to avoid colonial taxes on imports, evading the trade monopoly system in force since the 17th century. By 1818, trade agreements between companies in Cuba and in the United States began to replace the trade agreements with Spain (Pérez 2015). In 1860, 20% of Cuba's imports came from

the United States, 20% from Great Britain, and 30% from Spain. However, 62% of its exports went to the United States (Le Riverand 1965).

3. From April 2018 to March 2019, the US blockade caused losses to Cuba of around USD 4,343.6 million. At current prices, accumulated damage is estimated at USD 138,843.4 million (MINREX 2019).

4. The Special Period refers to the extended period of deep economic crisis during the 1990´s that resulted primarly from the disappearance of the USSR and socialist countries in Eastern Europe.

5. The optimism born from the normalization process of bilateral relations between Cuba and the United States diminished with the Trump administration. The Trump administration tightened the restrictions on travel, banned any transactions that could benefit Cuban armed forces, froze consular operations by retiring and expelling diplomatic personnel, and retained the embargo.

6. Cuba's workforce has around 4,500,000 workers. Almost 30% of them are not employed in the public sector. In 1989, however, almost 90% were (Torres Pérez 2017, 58). The 30% consists of the self-employed (*cuentapropistas*), members of cooperatives, and employees in foreign firms or joint-venture enterprises (Rodríguez 2016b; Torres Pérez 2017; Triana Cordoví 2017). Among them, the self-employed account for 42% (Galtés Galeano 2017, 70).

7. The coefficient of openness of the economy (*coeficiente de apertura externa*)—understood as the ratio of total exports and imports divided by the GDP—grew from 38.2% in 2007 to 47.5% in 2015 (Romero Gómez 2017, 13).

REFERENCES

Banco Central de Cuba. N.d. *La Economía Cubana en el Periodo Especial 1990–2000.* http://www.bc.gob.cu/Anteriores/Otros/economia%20cubana.pdf

Barbería, Lorena. 2008. "Remesas, Pobreza y Desigualdad en Cuba." *Espacio Laical* 2:18–21.

BBC. 2019. "Vuelos a Cuba: Trump Prohíbe a las Aerolíneas Comerciales Estadounidenses Volar a la Isla, con Excepción de La Habana." BBC News Mundo, October 25. https://www.bbc.com/mundo/noticias-internacional-50147618

Bell Lara, José, Tania Caram León, Dirk Kruijt, and Delia Luisa López García. 2017. *Cuba: Período Especial.* Havana: Editorial UH.

Cubadebate. 2015. "El 24 % de los Jóvenes en Cuba Trabajan en el Sector no Estatal." *Cubadebate*, September 7. http://www.cubadebate.cu/noticias/2015/09/07/el-31-de-los-jovenes-en-cuba-trabaja-en-el-sector-no-estatal/

Duany, Jorge. 2005. "La Migración Cubana: Tendencias Actuales y Proyecciones." *Encuentro de la Cultura Cubana* 36 (spring): 164–79.

EFE. 2019. "EE.UU. Limita el Envío de Remesas Hacia Cuba." *EFE Washington*, September 6. https://www.efe.com/efe/america/economia/ee-uu-limita-el-envio-de-remesas-hacia-cuba/20000011-4058483

Espina Prieto, Mayra P. 2004. "Efectos Sociales del Reajuste Económico: Igualdad, Desigualdad y Procesos de Complejizarían en la Sociedad Cubana." In *Reflexiones sobre Economía Cubana*, edited by Omar E. Pérez Villanueva, 385–419. Havana: Editorial de Ciencias Sociales.

Espina Prieto, Mayra P. 2008. "Desigualdad y Política Social en Cuba Hoy." Paper presented at the Future of Social Justice in Cuba conference, Bellagio Conference Centre, Italy, May 27–29.

Espina Prieto, Mayra P. 2010. *Desarrollo, Desigualdad y Políticas Sociales. Acercamientos Desde una Perspectiva Compleja*. Havana: Acuario.

Espina Prieto, Mayra P., and Dayma Echevarría. 2015. *Los Correlatos Socioculturales del Cambio Económico*. Havana: Ruth Casa Editorial.

Fabry, Merrill. 2015. "The U.S. Trade Embargo on Cuba Just Hit 55 Years." *Time*, October 19. http://time.com/4076438/us-cuba-embargo-1960/

Feinberg, Richard E. 2017. "Order from Chaos: What Will Be Raúl Castro's Legacy?" *Brookings Institution*, December 4. https://www.brookings.edu/blog/order-from-chaos/2017/12/04/what-will-be-raul-castros-legacy/

Figueredo Reinaldo, Oscar, Lissett Izquierdo Ferrer, and Edilberto Carmona Tamayo. 2019. "Cuba en Datos: Migraciones, ¿Hacia Dónde Nos Movemos?" *Cubadebate*, April 2. http://www.cubadebate.cu/especiales/2019/04/02/cuba-en-datos-migraciones-hacia-donde-nos-movemos/#.XoED0OpKjIU

Gaceta Oficial de la República de Cuba. 2012. "Decreto-Ley No. 302 Modificativo de la Ley No. 1312, 'Ley De Migración' de 20 de septiembre de 1976." *Cubadebate*.

Galtés Galeano, Indira. 2017. "Desigualdad de Ingresos en Cuba: ¿Qué Papel Juegan los Salarios?" In *Miradas a la Economía Cubana. Un Acercamiento a la 'Actualización' Seis Años Después*, edited by Ricardo Torres Pérez and Dayma Echevarría León, 68–80. Havana: Ruth Casa Editorial.

Grabendorff, Wolf. 2017. "Cuba: The Challenges of Change." In *Pensamiento Propio: Cuba y el Proceso de Actualización en la Era de Trump*, edited by Andrés Serbin, 33–56. Buenos Aires: Centro de Estudios Globales y Regionales.

Granma Redacción Digital. 2019. "Cuba Dijo Sí a la Nueva Constitución." *Granma*, February 25. http://www.granma.cu/reforma-constitucional/2019-02-25/cuba-dijo-si-por-la-nueva-constitucion-25-02-2019-16-02-47

Íñiguez Rojas, Luisa. 2013. "Desigualdades Territoriales y Ajustes Económicos en Cuba." In *Miradas a la Economía Cubana. Entre la Eficiencia Económica y la Equidad Social*, edited by Omar E. Pérez Villanueva and Ricardo Torres Pérez, 101–16. Havana: Editorial Caminos.

Íñiguez Rojas, Luisa, and Omar E. Pérez Villanueva. 2004. "Espacio, Territorio y Desigualdades Sociales en Cuba. Precedencias y Sobreimposiciones." In *Reflexiones Sobre Economía Cubana*, edited by Omar E. Pérez Villanueva, 420–70. Havana: Editorial de Ciencias Sociales.

Le Riverand, Julio. 1965. *Historia Económica de Cuba*. Havana: Editora Universitaria.

Malkin, Elisabeth. 2019. "Los Cubanos Respaldan la Nueva Constitución, Pero los Disidentes se Hacen Oír." *New York Times*, February 25. https://www.nytimes.com/es/2019/02/25/espanol/america-latina/constitucion-cuba.html

Mesa-Lago, Carmelo. 2009. "Economic and Social Balance of 50 Years of Cuban Revolution." In *Cuba in Transition*, edited by the Association for the Study of the Cuban Economy (ASCE), 368–82. http://citeseerx.ist.psu.edu/viewdoc/summary?doi=10.1.1.403.8964

Mesa-Lago, Carmelo. 2019. "El 'Enfriamiento' de la Economía Cubana." *Nueva Sociedad (NUSO)* 279 (Jan.–Feb). https://nuso.org/articulo/el-enfriamiento-de-la-economia-cubana/

Ministerio de Relaciones Exteriores de Cuba (MINREX). 2019. *Informe de Cuba sobre la Resolución 73/8 de la Asamblea General de las Naciones Unidas. "Necesidad de Poner Fin al Bloqueo Económico, Comercial y Financiero Impuesto Por los Estados Unidos de América Contra Cuba."* Havana: Ediciones MINREX.

Molina Molina, Ernesto. 2007. *El Pensamiento Económico de la Nación Cubana.* Havana: Editorial de Ciencias Sociales.

Monreal González, Pedro. 2017a. "Desigualdad en Cuba: ¿Combatiendo la Riqueza o la Pobreza?" *Cubaposible*, April 25. https://cubaposible.com/desigualdad-cuba-combatiendo-la-riqueza-la-pobreza/

Monreal González, Pedro. 2017b. "Irma en el Tejado: Desastres, Pobreza y Desarrollo en Cuba." *Cubaposible*, September 21. https://cubaposible.com/irma-en-el-tejado-desastres-pobreza-y-desarrollo-encuba/

Monreal González, Pedro. 2017c. "Un Programa de Estabilidad Económica para Cuba." *Cubaposible*, November 14. https://cubaposible.com/programa-estabilidad-economica-cuba/

Morales, Emilio. 2019 "Remesas, ¿Una Ruta de Inversión Para los Cubanos?" *Havana Consulting Group and Tech*, September 27. http://www.thehavanaconsultinggroup.com/es-es/Articles/Article/69?AspxAutoDetectCookieSupport=1

Morris, Emily. 2008. "Cuba's New Relationship with Foreign Capital: Economic Policy-Making since 1990." *Journal of Latin American Studies* 40 (4): 769–92.

Nova González, Armando. 2012. "La Propiedad en la Economía Cubana. Recientes Cambios en las Formas de Propiedad y su Impacto en el Sector Agrícola Cubano." In *Cuba. Hacia una Estrategia de Desarrollo Para los Inicios del Siglo XXI*, edited by Mauricio de Miranda Parrondo and Omar E. Pérez Villanueva, 127–57. Cali: Sello Editorial Javeriano.

Oficina Nacional de Estadística e Información (ONEI). 2019. *Anuario Estadístico de Cuba 2018. Sector Externo. Edición 2019.* http://www.onei.gob.cu/node/14211

Oficina Nacional de Estadística e Información (ONEI). 2020. *Turismo Internacional. Indicadores Seleccionados: Enero—Diciembre de 2019. Edición Marzo 2020.* http://www.onei.gob.cu/sites/default/files/06_completa.pdf

Oficina Nacional de Estadística e Información (ONEI). 2021. *Arribo de viajeros. Visitantes internacionales. Información preliminar. Enero-junio.* http://www.onei.gob.cu/node/14661

Partico Comunista de Cuba (PCC). 2017. "Actualización de los Lineamientos de la Política Económica y Social del Partido y la Revolución para el periodo 2016–2021." Document presented at the Seventh Congress of the PCC, Havana, Cuba. http://www.cubadebate.cu/especiales/2017/07/13/lea-los-textos-definitivos-de-la-conceptualizacion-del-modelo-cubano-y-la-actualizacion-de-los-lineamientos/

Pentón, Mario J. 2020. "Western Union Corta el Envío de Remesas a Cuba Excepto Desde EEUU." *El Nuevo Herald*, February 27. https://www.elnuevoherald.com/noticias/mundo/america-latina/cuba-es/article240709471.html

Perelló Cabrera, José Luis. 2017. "El Turismo Internacional en Cuba y sus Implicaciones en el Caribe Ante un Escenario de Relaciones Diplomáticas con los Estados Unidos." In *Cuba en sus Relaciones con el Resto del Caribe. Continuidades y Tupturas tras el Restablecimiento de las Relaciones Diplomáticas entre Cuba y los Estados Unidos*, edited by Jacqueline Laguardia Martínez, 63–76. Buenos Aires: CLACSO. http://biblioteca.clacso.edu.ar/clacso/gt/20171123054316/Cuba_en_sus_relaciones_con_el_resto_de_Caribe.pdf

Pérez, Louis A. 2015. *Cuba: Between Reform and Revolution*. 5th ed. New York: Oxford University Press.

Pérez Villanueva, Omar Everleny. 2012. "Problemas Estructurales de la Economía Cubana." In *Cuba. Hacia una Estrategia de Desarrollo Para los Inicios del Siglo XXI*, edited by Mauricio de Miranda Parrondo and Omar E. Pérez Villanueva, 1–50. Cali: Sello Editorial Javeriano.

Rodríguez, José Luis. 2016a. "El Socialismo, si no se Asimila Conscientemente, se Queda en la Superficie." Interview by Fernando Luis Rojas and Carolina García Salas. *Catalejo*. http://www.temas.cult.cu/catalejo/jos-luis-rodr-guez-el-socialismo-si-no-se-asimila-conscientemente-se-queda-en-la-superficie

Rodríguez, José Luis. 2016b. "Los Lineamientos para la Política Económica y Social y su Evolución 2011–2016." *Cubadebate*, April 14. http://www.cubadebate.cu/opinion/2016/04/14/los-lineamientos-para-la-politica-economica-y-social-y-su-evolucion-2011-2016/

Rodríguez, José Luis. 2019. "Balance Económico Preliminar del 2018 en Cuba y Plgunas perspectivas Para el 2019 (Parte I)." *Cubadebate*, March 2. http://www.cubadebate.cu/opinion/2019/03/02/balance-economico-preliminar-del-2018-en-cuba-y-algunas-perspectivas-para-el-2019-parte-i/#.XoERJ-pKjIU

Rodríguez Castellón, Santiago. 2004. "La Agricultura Orgánica en Cuba. Avances y Retos." In *Reflexiones sobre Economía Cubana*, edited by Omar E. Pérez Villanueva, 367–84. Havana: Editorial de Ciencias Sociales.

Romero Gómez, Antonio F. 2017. "Los Desafíos del Escenario Externo para la Economía Cubana." In *Miradas a la Economía Cubana. Un Acercamiento a la 'Actualización' Seis Años Después*, edited by Ricardo Torres Pérez and Dayma Echevarría León, 13–22. Havana: Ruth Casa Editorial.

Sánchez Egozcué, Jorge Mario. 2015. "Challenges of Economic Restructuring in Cuba." In *A Contemporary Cuba Reader: The Revolution under Raul Castro*, edited by Philip Brenner, Marguerite Rose Jiménez, John M. Kirk, and William M. LeoGrande, 125–39. Lanham: Rowman & Littlefield.

Serbin, Andrés. 2017. "Cuba: Legados del Pasado y Retos del Presente." In *Pensamiento Propio: Cuba y el Proceso de Actualización en la Era de Trump*, edited by Andrés Serbin, 7–32. Buenos Aires: Centro de Estudios Globales y Regionales.

Telesur Noticias. 2019. "Diputados Cubanos Eligen a Díaz-Canel Como Presidente del País." *Telesur*, 10 October. https://www.telesurtv.net/news/cuba-diputados-eleccion-presidentes-altos-cargos-estado--20191010-0008.html

Torres Pérez, Ricardo. 2012. "Estructura Económica y Crecimiento. Apuntes Sobre Políticas de Desarrollo Productivo en el Nuevo Contexto de la Economía Cubana." In *Cuba. Hacia una Estrategia de Desarrollo Para los Inicios del Siglo XXI*, edited by Mauricio de Miranda Parrondo and Omar E. Pérez Villanueva, 51–89. Cali: Sello Editorial Javeriano.

Torres Pérez, Ricardo. 2016. "Economic Transformations in Cuba: A Review." *Third World Quarterly* 37 (9): 1–15.

Torres Pérez, Ricardo. 2017. "El Proceso de Actualización del Modelo Económico y Social de Cuba." In *Pensamiento Propio: Cuba y el Proceso de Actualización en la Era de Trump*, edited by Andrés Serbin, 57–80. Buenos Aires: Centro de Estudios Globales y Regionales.

Triana Cordoví, Juan. 2017. "Economía Cubana 2016 y 2017: La Coyuntura y los Retos del Crecimiento." In *Miradas a la Economía Cubana. Un Acercamiento a la 'Actualización' Seis Años Después*, edited by Ricardo Torres Pérez and Dayma Echevarría León, 37–48. Havana: Ruth Casa Editorial.

Unidad de Estudios de Políticas Económicas y Sociales del Caribe (UEPESC). 2017a. "Monitor Caribe—Haití Año 2, Numero 20, 16–31 Octubre 2017." *UEPESC.* http://economia.gob.do/wp-content/uploads/drive/UEPESC/Monitor%20Caribe%20Haiti/Monitor_Caribe_Haiti_10_2017_Q2_No._20.pdf

Unidad de Estudios de Políticas Económicas y Sociales del Caribe (UEPESC). 2017b. "Monitor Caribe—Haití Año 2, Numero 10, 16–31 Mayo 2017." *UEPESC.* https://drive.google.com/file/d/0B1lebicmb1OkaDh0XzVBNXB3eGM/view

Valdés Paz, Juan. 2016. "El Socialismo no Puede Posponer la Democracia que ha Prometido." Interview by Fernando Luis Rojas and Carolina García Salas. *Catalejo.* http://www.temas.cult.cu/catalejo/juan-vald-s-paz-el-socialismo-no-puede-posponer-la-democracia-que-ha-prometido

World Travel & Tourism Council (WTTC). 2017. "Travel & Tourism. Economic Impact 2017 Cuba." WTTC. https://www.wttc.org/-/media/files/reports/economic-impact-research/countries-2017/cuba2017.pdf

Zabala Arguelles, María del Carmen. 2013. "Los Retos de la Equidad Social en el Actual Proceso de Cambios Económicos." In *Cuba: la Ruta Necesaria del Cambio Económico*, edited by Omar E. Pérez Villanueva and Ricardo Torres Pérez, 338–59. Havana: Editorial de Ciencias Sociales.

CHAPTER 6

Puerto Rico's Colonial Legacies and Postcolonial Constellations

Economy, Society, and Polity

Emilio Pantojas-García

Since its "discovery" in 1493, Puerto Rico has never been anything but a colony. Settled in 1508, it remained a colony of Spain until it was invaded by the United States in 1898 and ceded to that empire as part of the Treaty of Paris, which brought the Spanish-American War to an end.[1] Puerto Rico's colonial legacies come, therefore, from these two empires. Contemporary Puerto Rico is a true hybrid. After 1898, for example, the island's legal system was forced to transition between the "civil law judicial tradition" of Spain and the North American common-law court framework (Rivera Ramos 2001, 70). An intense process of "Americanization" was implemented as the central educational and cultural policies of the American colonial state (Pantojas-García 1974; Negrón de Montilla 1975).

In the 21st century, Puerto Rico is a Latin American nation inhabiting a postcolonial colony "enjoying" the "advantages" of post–World War II colonialism: metropolitan citizenship, social welfare programs, constitutional guarantees, and, until recently, economic protectionism and subsidies. In this chapter, I show how the colonial configurations of economy and society have resulted in the formation of a postcolonial colony characterized by an absentee ruling class, a weak local entrepreneurial elite, and a rentier political class dependent on metropolitan transfers and subsidies to secure local dominance.

Economy and Society

Until the 19th century, Puerto Rico was mainly a colony of settlers with a defensive military bastion in the port of San Juan Bautista. As the easternmost of the Greater Antilles, Puerto Rico was the first major harbor that the Spanish fleet would encounter on the trip to America from Spain and the last on the trip to Spain.[2] Puerto Rico was a defensive military outpost supported from 1587 to 1810 by an allowance from New Spain called the *Situado Mexicano*, which provided for the military expenses of the *Capitanía General* that guarded the port of San Juan with an elaborate fortress system. After brief periods in the 16th century when gold mining and sugar milling flourished, the island's economy became mainly a subsistence economy that produced some agricultural exports (ginger and hides) traded through a steady smuggling system (see Scarano 1994, chaps. 9–12; Morales-Carrión 1971, chap. 3).

After the Bourbon Reforms were initiated in 1765, the island was set on a course of integration into the international economy, first exporting sugar and later coffee becoming the most important export product. The Real Cédula de Gracias of 1815 opened the island to Catholic migrants fleeing the independence revolutions in Spanish America and the Haitian Revolution. The Spanish and French exiles brought with them capital, machinery, and slaves and were provided lands by the Crown to produce sugar and other export products.

The abrupt decline in sugar exports from Haiti also stimulated the growth of sugar production and export in Puerto Rico as well as the importation of slaves. In 1812, the land dedicated to sugar cultivation was 5,765 *cuerdas* (5,598 acres), with a production of 838 tons of sugar. Likewise, 3,905 tons of coffee were produced on 9,493 *cuerdas* (9,218 acres). Driven by the immigrant entrepreneurs who brought machinery and slaves with them, by 1830 the land cultivated in sugar nearly doubled to 11,103 *cuerdas* (10,781 acres) with a production of 14,126 tons, an increase of 1,585 percent. Coffee production grew to 6,569 tons, an increase of 112 percent (Dietz 1986, 17–18).

The labor needed to support this rapid growth came from two sources. First, an estimated 60,000–80,000 slaves, an unprecedented number, were brought to Puerto Rico between 1815 and 1845. Second, the colonial government proclaimed vagrancy laws compelling anyone not engaged in a craft or not owning land to carry a workbook as proof of gainful employment. Thus, the subsistence peasants displaced from Crown lands, now given to immigrants and larger landowners who could pay taxes, were compelled to become wage laborers (*jornaleros*) (Scarano 1994, 405, 416–19).

Sugar exports led economic growth during the first half of the 19th century. Between 1814 and 1854, foreign trade increased by nearly 2,100 percent. But the decline in the prices of sugar, technological advances by competitors, increases in the prices of land and slaves, and sugarcane disease slowed the growth of the sugar industry (Dietz 1986, 20–21, 26–27; de Jesús Toro 1982, 20).

In the second half of the century, therefore, coffee became the engine of economic growth, and the coffee hacienda of the highlands was the axis of economic and sociocultural production. The growth of coffee as the leading export commodity was driven by the growth in demand and prices in Europe (Scarano 1994, 466–67). By 1881, coffee became the leading export product, representing 54.5 percent of the value of exports, while the share of sugar declined to 28.9 percent. In 1896, two years before the US invasion, coffee exports represented 76.9 percent of the value of exports, while sugar represented only 20.7 percent (Dietz 1986, 27).

The markets and geographical spaces of coffee and sugar production were different. Coffee was grown in the highlands, while sugar was cultivated and processed mainly in the coastal valleys. The main markets for Puerto Rican coffee exports were Spain, France, Germany, Italy, and Cuba, while the main market for sugar was the United States. In the 1880s, Puerto Rico became the fourth largest coffee producer behind Brazil, Venezuela, and the Dominican Republic (Scarano 1994, 466).

The hacienda became the dominant economic unit, and coffee hacendados became the socially hegemonic class. The main sources of labor for the coffee haciendas were sharecroppers (called *agregados* and *medianeros*). Other rural laborers (*jornaleros*) were those who had been displaced from common lands distributed by the Crown to exiles from the Spanish American independence wars and other Catholic migrants under the Real Cédula de Gracias (Quintero 1980a, 102–8).

Seignorial relations of production created a patriarchal outlook of culture and society begetting the notion of the "great Puerto Rican family" (*la gran familia puertorriqueña*) as the foundational component of social and political identity. As Quintero Rivera argues, the southern city of Ponce became the principal port for exports of coffee and sugar and the social epicenter of the emerging Creole class of hacendados. The capital of San Juan was the center of colonial government, but Ponce became the alternate capital, where the Creole elite would affirm its social and cultural supremacy without necessarily advocating for independence (Quintero Rivera 1988, 42–53).

Social stratification in the 19th century differentiates a ruling colonial elite and a Creole elite. The ruling elite was led by the Spanish military and government officials and a class of merchants led by Catalonian immigrants. The socially and culturally hegemonic Creole elite was led by the hacendados and Puerto Rican–born liberal professionals (lawyers, doctors, writers). There was a class of small landowners who were not only Creole but also immigrants from Spanish America, Haiti, and even Corsica. Creole sharecroppers and landless peasants provided labor for haciendas and small farms, while artisans and wage laborers worked in the cities. Because of the relatively late development of sugar as a major export commodity, African slaves never became a major proportion of the population, except in the sugar-growing regions of the coastal valleys, which greatly influenced the popular culture of the island (see Quintero Rivera 1980a, 1988; Bergad 1980). The working classes lived in poverty and squalor in the countryside and the urban centers, subject to the whims and needs of the paternalistic hacendados in the countryside and the Spanish and Creole elites in the cities.[3]

Political autonomy became the political alternative of the Creole elite to Spanish military rule. It is argued that, with the island having become a political haven for exiles from Latin America and Haiti, the local elites were more fearful of popular uprisings than of the Spanish "iron fist" policies (see Scarano 1994; Quintero Rivera 1988).

The New Metropolis: Conflict and Accommodation

When the United States invaded Puerto Rico, there was a clear and distinct Puerto Rican national character, with literary, musical, and sociocultural traditions. The coffee hacendados led a Creole social coalition that favored provincial autonomy within the Spanish political system. Although socially hegemonic and economically dominant, the hacendados did not aspire to become a "ruling" class (Quintero Rivera 1980b, 217). There was never a strong independence movement led by the Puerto Rican hacendados; autonomy was the political aspiration of this class.

Under American rule, the economy was transformed from a mercantile economy based on the export of coffee produced in haciendas to a capitalist plantation economy exporting sugar. In turn, the axis of social relations in Puerto Rican society shifted from seignorial relations between hacendados and peasants to capitalist relations between absentee owners, plantation managers, and rural proletarians (Quintero Rivera 1980a, 113–20).

American sugar, tobacco, and fruit companies came to dominate agricultural production. By 1925, sugar exports accounted for 56.2 percent of the value of exports, up from 20.7 percent in 1896, while coffee only amounted to 7 percent. Fruit exports amounted to 5.2 percent of total exports, tobacco to 10.4 percent, and cigars to 7.5 percent. Put another way, the sectors dominated by American corporations produced 79.2 percent of total exports by 1925 (calculated from Dietz 1986, 117–20).

In the pioneer study of the island's political economy, *Porto Rico: A Broken Pledge* (1931), Bailey Diffie and Justine Diffie meticulously describe the economic penetration of American corporations. In the 1930s, four American sugar corporations owned or rented 68 percent of the 251,000 acres of land dedicated to sugarcane cultivation, owned 11 of 42 sugar mills, and produced over 50 percent of the sugar on the island. Puerto Rico became the third major supplier of cane sugar for the US market behind Cuba and Hawaii. Alongside these four sugar giants, American companies came to dominate cigar production and tobacco exports and controlled 64 percent of the land dedicated to fruit production for exports. Two American and two Canadian banks were established alongside, and in competition with, the two existing local banks, just founded in the 1890s. Another four American shipping companies came to control all freight movements between the island and the ports of the United States. American companies also controlled railway transportation and utilities (Diffie and Diffie 1931, 52–65, 100–117; Quintero Rivera 1980a, 114).

By the 1930s, however, the sugar economy of Puerto Rico had turned the island into the "poorhouse of the Caribbean." The wages of sugarcane workers in Puerto Rico were lower than in Cuba, Hawaii, Honduras, and the Bahamas (Diffie and Diffie 1931, 86). The mass of landless peasants and rural proletarians remained poor and illiterate, while the hacendados were displaced from political power and came to occupy a new position in the middle classes in business and liberal professions. The Puerto Rican sugar growers, mostly pro-American, emerged as a new "dominant" sociopolitical elite (Quintero Rivera 1988, 133).

The first three decades of American colonialism were dominated by a "triangular conflict" between three local political forces: (1) the hacendados, facing the displacement of coffee production and the haciendas as the most dynamic sector of the economy and polity; (2) the sugar growers and exporters, linked since the 19th century to the sugar interests of the United States; and (3) the trade union movement, made up of urban workers and artisans, which had been persecuted by the Spanish colonial government and now "enjoyed" the extension to Puerto Rico of workers' rights achieved by the American Federation of Labor. The new colonial metropolis redefined the limited political space conceded to the local political forces. While the executive branch of government was directly controlled by the metropolis through the appointment of a governor and all the heads of the colonial cabinet by the US president, an elected House of Representatives and municipal governments became the center of local political conflicts. A highly centralized colonial government severely limited the realm of action of local political forces that vied for the favor of the colonial administrators (see Quintero Rivera 1980b).

Along with integrating Puerto Rico into the American economy, the United States promoted a process of cultural assimilation and eventual political annexation of the island as a state of the Union. During the first four decades of the 20th century, English was the medium of education in Puerto Rican public schools. Protestant missionaries established churches, schools, and other educational and charitable institutions with the objective of "lifting" Puerto Ricans to the standards of American citizenship. The politically emergent sugar elite as well as organized labor, which was accorded freedom to organize under the new regime, became supporters of assimilationist policies and promoted the annexation of the island as a state of the Union (see Pantojas-García 1974; Negrón de Montilla 1975; Quintero Rivera 1980b).

The Great Depression and World War II drove social and economic change in Puerto Rico. The decline of sugar exports, after the import quotas imposed by the Smoot-Hawley Act of 1934,[4] and the need to substitute imports during the war imposed the need for short-term changes and a strategic long-term economic shift. During the 1930s, the Roosevelt administration extended to Puerto Rico welfare benefits administered by the Puerto Rico Emergency Relief Administration and the Puerto Rico Reconstruction Administration. Transfer payments to individuals, public works, and land distribution to peasants (akin to the American Homestead Act) became major sources of support for the working population. American sugar companies retrenched production, as they were the main recipients of the government-issued import quotas. Local sugar growers who sold their sugarcane to the companies' mills suffered the brunt of the cuts in production. Discontent and political unrest intensified as sugar workers' salaries shrunk and unemployment grew. Repression against both the

Nationalist Party and the labor unions and welfare relief were the answer of the American colonial government (Dietz 1986, 171–73; Pantojas-García 1990, 39–57).

The war changed everything and paved the wave for the transformation of Puerto Rico from an agricultural export-oriented economy to the first export-manufacturing platform in the world. The post–World War II demand to decolonize the world led to a policy of colonial reforms whose outcome was that the island would be better off than its Latin American and Caribbean neighbors but not equal to the states of the Union (Pantojas-García 2005, 172, 175). What is today known as the *maquiladora* model, which imports manufacturing components for processing and assembly for export to the metropolitan economy, was first implemented in Puerto Rico. After World War II, the United States emerged as the hegemonic industrial power in the world. Manufacturing shifted from consumer goods to durable consumer and capital goods. This change converged with the search for economic investment in Puerto Rico (Pantojas-García 1990, 4).

The Puerto Rico Industrial Development Company was established in 1942 to promote economic development and investment. After a brief experiment on state-based import substitution industrialization, when the government owned and operated five manufacturing companies (cement, paper, cardboard, glass, and clay products), a new industrial incentives law was passed. The law offered tax holidays, subsidized rent, and wages to attract investment from American entrepreneurs in assembly manufacturing (Pantojas-García 1990, 43–45).

The government of Puerto Rico hired American consultants to advise them on potential industrial investment opportunities. A series of viability studies and later promotion materials were produced by these consultants on the advantages of investing in Puerto Rico on light industries, especially apparel (Little 1942; O'Connor 1948). The local incentives, combined with low wages, relative to other areas in the United States, and no federal taxes, resulted in the transformation of Puerto Rio into the first export-led industrialization experience in the world. This "model" would later be adopted by other small economies, such as Ireland, Taiwan, Singapore, South Korea, and Hong Kong (Pantojas-García 1990, 1–5).

Export-led industrialization transformed Puerto Rico from a predominantly rural-agrarian society to a predominantly urban-industrial society. It succeeded in terms of economic growth and improvement in standards of living. The Puerto Rican model of export-led industrialization, however, was different from that of the Asian Tigers or Ireland. The key competitive advantages of the island were based on the colonial relationship it had with the United States: (1) free access to the US market; (2) exemption from US federal and local taxes; (3) preferential treatment for certain imports; and (4) common currency (the US dollar).

During the 1950s and 1960s, assembly manufacturing was dominated by American subcontractors that established assembly plants processing components into final consumer goods for export to the United States. With the Kennedy rounds of the General Agreement on Tariffs and Trade and the reduction of import tariffs from Asia and Europe, labor-intensive assembly plants located on the island faced stiff competition and started moving to other locations in the Caribbean and Asia. A second stage of export-led industrialization was promoted with the extension to Puerto Rico of special oil import quotas in 1965. The island became a major center for refined oil products and petrochemical components (Pantojas-García 1990, 73–80, 107–9).[5]

As the oil refining industry sank into crisis with the abolition of oil import quotas and the 1973 oil embargo, yet another exceptional advantage made economic restructuring viable. The inclusion of Section 936 of the US Internal Revenue Code in the 1976 federal tax reform provided new exemptions for repatriation of profits to the parent companies of American corporations operating on the island. This measure stimulated the establishment of pharmaceutical companies making billions of dollars in the production of "miracle drugs" and other medicines for the US market (Pantojas-García 1990, 153–55).

The process of export-led industrialization radically changed the social structure of Puerto Rico. Agriculture declined dramatically, becoming the less dynamic sector of the economy and expelling thousands of workers from the countryside to the cities and eventually to the United States. Agriculture's share of net income declined from just over 20 percent to less than 8 percent in the 1950s. Migration to the United States in the 1950s averaged 446,693 per year (Duany and Pantojas-García 2005, 26). Manufacturing and services became the most important sources of income and employment, along with the expansion of trade, as domestic consumption increased. A mass of marginalized agricultural workers and urban poor migrated or found jobs in the informal sector of the economy. The middle sectors grew, fostered by the increase in industrial workers, a new petty bourgeoisie (retail shop owners, contractors, etc.), and an emerging managerial class. Among the working classes, a virtually new phenomenon emerged, the two-income family, as women joined the industrial labor force in significant numbers, adding a new dimension to the middle classes (Acevedo 1990, 250; Pantojas-García 1990, 80–88).

Puerto Rico became a link in a vertically integrated production chain that began and ended in the headquarters and financial centers of the American transnational corporations that operated on the island. Contrary to the Asian Tigers or Ireland, a local class of modern and export-oriented industrialists never developed. Studies on Puerto Rican entrepreneurs in the 1950s describe them as traditional, conservative, family-centered, and aristocratic in attitude (Cochran 1959: 149; see also Scheele 1956). A study of the Puerto Rican entrepreneurial class in the late 1980s concluded that it adapted to the dominance of American capital and occupied a space in the entrepreneurial life of the island but did not emerge as an autonomous Creole bourgeoisie (*burguesía criolla*) (González Díaz 1991, 124). Even in the 21st century there are a few Puerto Rican businesses organized as public companies traded on the stock market. The dominant sectors of the local entrepreneurs remain in wholesale and retail trade, finance, health and health insurance, and services.[6]

Puerto Rico thus became integrated into the American economy, while at the same time the culture and the traditions of its population remained in many respects Latin American. The island could be described as a Latin American nation subsumed within the US economy and its colonial policies. Claims to a distinct Puerto Rican national identity are ultimately constructions of a common foundational myth that sets the Puerto Rican people vis-à-vis "the other," whether Spanish or North American. This foundational myth is grounded in the notion of "the great Puerto Rican family" (*la gran familia puertorriqueña*) advanced by the Creole elites in the 19th century. This myth may be told from different perspectives of class, gender, race, and so forth, and claimed in contested terms, but taken together, the different versions represent an imagined common ground: "Puerto Ricaness" (*la puertorriqueñidad*).

For Puerto Ricans, the island provides the fulcrum that affirms Puerto Rican national identity. On the island, unlike in the United States, Puerto Ricans are not a minority, and Puerto Rican culture flourishes as an autonomous force on equal terms with other world cultures. Spanish continues to be the Puerto Rican vernacular, and Puerto Rican literature is considered part of Spanish American literature in global literary, cultural, and academic circles. For the Puerto Rican diaspora in the United States, Spanish is the language of resistance. Switching to Spanish in the middle of a conversation or interjecting a word or phrase in Spanish provides a way of identifying with the Puerto Rican ethos for English-speaking second- or third-generation Puerto Ricans living in the United States. Spanish thus functions as the language of the "initiated," the "citizens" of the Puerto Rican nation. To be a "real" *boricua* (Spanish colloquial for "Puerto Rican" derived from the Taino name for the island, Borikén), one needs to be able at least to sing along with a salsa song, make a witty comment in Spanish, and know the "language" of the Puerto Rican household, where Spanglish may be spoken (Pantojas-García 2005, 168, 174).

Polity and Ruling Elites

As the oldest colony in the world, Puerto Rico was ruled directly by colonial bureaucrats from Spain and the United States until the end of World War II. The Creole colonial elite established a subordinate political partnership, in this process benefiting from the "privileges" of government employment and patronage under both empires, Spain and the United States. As a postcolonial world order was to emerge in the postwar era, the US government was compelled to design a political alternative that would ensure its control over Puerto Rico, while providing a measure of self-rule.

In 1946, President Harry S. Truman appointed the first Puerto Rican governor in the history of the island. In 1948, the US Congress passed a law allowing the governor's election by direct vote of the people of Puerto Rico. In 1950, Congress passed Law 600, authorizing a convention to draft the constitution of the Estado Libre Asociado (Free Associated State) of Puerto Rico, named in English the Commonwealth of Puerto Rico.[7] The new constitution was subordinate to that of the United States. After the members of the convention drafted the constitution, it was modified and approved by Congress and then approved by the people of Puerto Rico in a referendum held on March 3, 1952 (Pantojas-García 1990, 66–68).

The new political status did not substantially alter the legal-political and economic relations between Puerto Rico and the United States. Because the Commonwealth formula is not part of US federal doctrine, the prevailing judicial interpretation continues to be an unincorporated territory that belongs to but it is not a part of the United States. In an article published a year after the creation of the Commonwealth, Harvard law professor Rupert Emerson emphasized the essentially symbolic character of the change in political status (1953, 10).

Nonetheless, Commonwealth status provided a measure of self-rule. The elected governor would appoint all cabinet officials and other members of the executive branch. The local legislature could pass legislation on local affairs, as long as these laws did not conflict with the US Constitution, laws, and federal regulations. The Commonwealth judicial system operated autonomously from the federal system, although decisions of the Puerto Rico Supreme Court could be appealed in the Federal Court of Appeals and the US Supreme Court. Under Law 600, the US Congress retained sovereignty over Puerto Rico and can unilaterally dictate policy relating to defense, international relations, foreign trade, and investment. Congress also has the right to revoke any insular law inconsistent with the US Constitution. Federal regulations may be applied selectively at the discretion of the US Congress or the president. In 2016, responding to the Puerto Rican government's default on its debt, Congress unilaterally appointed a Fiscal Oversight and Management Board, which took control of government finances.

The transition from direct metropolitan rule to local self-rule was presided over by a colonial elite under the leadership of Luis Muñoz Marín. A populist leader, Muñoz in the late 1930s and 1940s led a group of "modern" professionals who worked with the Roosevelt administration in Washington to extend to Puerto Rico a version of the New Deal policies to address the effects of the Great Depression on the rural population and the urban poor. Muñoz and the "techno-bureaucracy" linked to the New Deal programs known as the Puerto Rico Emergency Relief Administration and the Puerto Rico Reconstruction Administration led a process of politico-economic restructuring of the colonial relation. In exchange for federal assistance and local self-rule, the Popular Democratic Party led by Muñoz legitimated the new shape of the colonial relation in the international community. Following the 1952 plebiscite, the US government informed the United Nations that Puerto Rico had exercised its right to self-determination. In 1953, the United Nations passed resolution 748 (VIII) recognizing Puerto Rico as a self-governing territory, thus removing the island from the list of nonindependent territories, which exempted the United States from reporting on its status and affairs (Pantojas-García 2013, 42–44).

The new colonial techno-bureaucracy led the process of the "modernization" of Puerto Rico, transforming the island into the first small economy to embark on export-led industrialization as its axis of development (Pantojas-García 1990). Henry Wells (1969) and Kenneth Farr (1973) characterize this as a process of change from traditional to modern values presided over by the personal politics and vision of a populist leader.

As was the case of the hacendados in the 19th century, the techno-bureaucracy became a hegemonic social actor that was not the dominant class. As in the sugar economy, the dominant economic sector was American capital, linked initially to light manufacturing as contractors or subsidiaries of American international corporations and later to transnational companies (TNCs) in petrochemicals and pharmaceuticals, integrating the island's economy into a global chain of production and trade.

The Emergence of a Puerto Rican Rentier Elite

After 1976, the main economic competitive advantage of Puerto Rico was Section 936 of the US Internal Revenue Code. This section allowed TNCs to repatriate profits from their Puerto Rican subsidiaries after five years of being deposited in local banks without paying federal taxes, though they did have to pay a "tollgate tax" to the local government of between 2 and 5 percent on repatriated profits. The island became a unique tax haven, where American TNCs needed to establish a "possession corporation" that had manufacturing operations to legally avoid paying federal taxes in the repatriation of globally earned profits (US Department of the Treasury 1989, 19).

Under Section 936, billions of dollars in profits exempt from federal taxes were deposited in the subsidiaries of American and Puerto Rican banks operating in Puerto Rico. This created a bonanza for the government and for the banking and financial industries operating on the island.[8] The tollgate tax amounted to hundreds of millions of dollars in "new" revenues and bank deposits (Miller 1999). American TNCs in pharmaceutics, medical equipment, and electronics began to use transfer pricing mechanisms to funnel profits to the island from all over the world. Section 936 of the federal tax code made Puerto Rico the most profitable tax haven in the world (Pantojas-García 1990, 166–67).

To illustrate the magnitude of the importance of Puerto Rico as a manufacturing tax haven, we can compare the profits from the island to those of the United Kingdom and Canada in 1996, the year Section 936 was repealed by Congress. In 1996, Puerto Rico generated the largest amount of income on US direct investment abroad, $15,423 million, or 13.8 percent of global income. By comparison, the United Kingdom generated $13,862 million and Canada $8,642 million, or 12.4 percent and 7.7 percent, respectively, of income generated by US direct investment abroad. In 1996, Puerto Rico's gross domestic product was $45.3 billion, the United

Kingdom's was $1,180 billion, and Canada's was $601.6 billion. By this measure, the economy of the United Kingdom was 26 times bigger than Puerto Rico's, and Canada's was 13 times bigger, yet Puerto Rico produced nearly twice as much income for US direct investment as Canada and more than 11 percent of that of the United Kingdom (Pantojas-García 2007, 217–18).

This unique tax haven's economy, anchored in colonial exceptionality, led to the transformation of the developmentalist techno-bureaucracy into what can be termed a "state-based rentier elite." Like the Spanish colonial elite lived off the *Situado Mexicano* from the 16th to the early 19th centuries, the Puerto Rican colonial elite has come to rely on US federal government transfers and the direct and indirect tax revenues of "936 corporations" as the economic basis of its existence and economic position at the top of the social hierarchy.[9] This state-based kakistocracy has "patrimonialized" public revenues and government positions, using its relative political power to enrich themselves and the members of the two dominant political parties, the Popular Democratic Party (Partido Popular Democrático, or PPD) and the New Progressive Party (Partido Nuevo Progresista, or PNP) (Pantojas-García 2016).[10]

Two examples will illustrate this process of personal arrogation of public revenues and positions referred to as "patrimonialization." In 1998, the mayor of the small town of Orocovis died, and his son, who lived in a different town, was elected by a party assembly as his successor in violation of the legal requirements of residence. Since then, this has become a common practice shared by both governing parties, the PNP and the PPD. In the towns of Carolina (2007) and Caguas (2010), the PPD mayors died, and their sons "inherited" the position. Another three PNP mayors have "inherited" their position: In Bayamón in 2001 and in Las Piedras in 2005, this happened through an election with the father's blessing; in Canóvanas in 2014, this happened in a midterm primary where the contestants were both a son and a daughter of the retiring mayor.

In 2013, the governor signed a special tax called the *patente nacional* (national patent). Law 40 was to be imposed on those corporations and financial entities with a gross income of over 1 million dollars. As the name suggests, this was a tax for doing business on the island, a sort of "rent" or "tribute" in the most classic sense. The law was repealed but was one of many new taxes imposed to provide revenue to the government at the height of the current economic depression.

Conclusion

Puerto Rico is a postcolonial colony. Its legacies come from both Spain and the United States. The dominant classes have been and are metropolitan, and the Creole colonial elites have never expressed a majority desire for independence. Socioculturally, Puerto Rico survives as a Caribbean Latin American nation with a distinct national identity expressed in literature, music, sports, and even international beauty pageants.

The Puerto Rican "political class" has typically been integrated by liberal professionals (lawyers, physicians, writers, etc.) and technocrats (engineers, accountants, planners, bankers, and entrepreneurs). The Puerto Rican businessmen and the wealthy have never achieved the status of a "national bourgeoisie" or a dominant class with a political project of independence. Historically, they have managed to accommodate their interests with those of the metropolitan ruling classes, accepting its subordinate position and role in the economy and polity of the colony. Presently, this accommodation as a lucrative backyard of the American economy is in crisis. Colonial rentiers of various kinds now struggle to accommodate and survive.

NOTES

1. On November 25, 1897, the Puerto Rican colonial elite had achieved self-rule as Spain granted provincial autonomy to Cuba and Puerto Rico. An autonomous government was appointed on February 10, 1898, and the provincial parliament was inaugurated on July 17, but the American invasion on July 25, 1898, ended this process (Scarano 1994, 540–41, 548–49).

2. The ports of Cartagena de Indias in New Granada and Veracruz in New Spain were the main destinations for collecting the gold and silver of the New World. The port of Havana was the point of encounter of the fleet before the return to Seville.

3. The dire living conditions of the rural workers are depicted in the classic Puerto Rican novel *La Charca* (*The Pond*). Written by Manuel Zeno Gandía, a Puerto Rican Creole who studied medicine in Madrid, this novel was published in 1894, and it portrays the lives of a poor family driven by "base passions" that lead to problems such as abuse and incest. The title symbolizes the stagnant and murky living conditions of the poor in late 19th-century Puerto Rico (Zeno Gandia [1894] 2003).

4. Sugar prices fell during the 1920s due to overproduction. Sugar-producing countries consequently agreed to limit exports to remedy price decline through self-imposed quotas by signing what became known as the "Chadbourne Plan." The United States did not abide by this plan and imposed quotas and a tariff on sugar imports established by the Smoot-Hawley Act. This provided an advantage to American sugar companies, within the constraints of the quota system.

5. By 1972, US petrochemical transnationals produced in Puerto Rico 40 percent of all the paraxelene, 30 percent of all the cyclohexane, 26 percent of all the benzene, 24 percent of all the propylene, and 12 percent of all the vinyl chloride consumed in the United States (Pantojas-García 1990, 118).

6. Of the top 100 locally owned businesses in 2017, 29 are wholesale trade, 27 are retail trade, 11 are hospitals, 6 are insurance companies, 4 are hospital management companies, and only 6 are manufacturing companies, of which 5 are in food and beverages. There are only 5 Puerto Rican public companies, 3 of which are banks (Caribbean Business 2017).

7. The colonial constitution created the Free Associated State of Puerto Rico, or Estado Libre Asociado de Puerto Rico. The adopted translation, however, was the Commonwealth of Puerto Rico. Nonetheless, a recent decision of the US Supreme Court upheld the view that the sovereignty of Puerto Rico resides with the US Congress. Syllabus, Supreme Court of the United States, *Commonwealth of Puerto Rico v. Sanchez Valle et al.* (October 2015). https://www.supremecourt.gov/opinions/15pdf/15-108_k4mp.pdf

8. Even two Spanish banks established operations on the island in the late 1970s, lured by 936 deposits: Banco de Santander bought the First National Bank of Puerto Rico in 1976, and Banco Bilbao Vizcaya bought the Banco de Mayagüez in 1979.

9. After the expiration of Section 936 in 2006, most of this companies shifted to the status of Controlled Foreign Corporations (CFCs), under Subsection F of Section 952 of the U.S. Internal Revenue Code.

10. "Kakistocracy" literally means the government of the worse. The concept was developed by Italian political philosopher Michel Angelo Bovero to describe the Berlusconi government. The PPD is the party that created the Commonwealth and ruled from 1948 to 1968. The PNP is the party that favors statehood (annexation as the 51st state of the Union) and has alternated governing from 1969 to the present.

REFERENCES

Acevedo, Luz del Alba. 1990. "Industrialization and Employment: Changes in the Patterns of Women's Work in Puerto Rico." *World Development* 18 (2): 215–29. https://doi.org/10.1016/0305-750X(90)90049-4

Bergad, Laird W. 1980. "Toward Puerto Rico's Grito de Lares: Coffee, Social Stratification, and Class Conflicts, 1828–1868." *Hispanic American Historical Review* 60 (4): 617–42.

Caribbean Business. 2017. *Book of Lists.* http://caribbeanbusiness.com/cbepaper/bol2017.html

Cochran, Thomas. 1959. *The Puerto Rican Businessman: A Study in Cultural Change.* Philadelphia: University of Pennsylvania Press.

de Jesús Toro, Rafael. 1982. *Historia Económica de Puerto Rico.* Cincinnati: South-Western.

Dietz, James L. 1986. *Economic History of Puerto Rico: Institutional Changes and Capitalist Development.* Princeton: Princeton University Press.

Diffie, Bailey W., and Justine W. Diffie. 1931. *Porto Rico: A Broken Pledge*. New York: Vanguard Press.

Duany, Jorge, and Emilio Pantojas-García. 2005. "Fifty Years of Commonwealth: The Contradictions of Free Associated Statehood in Puerto Rico." In *Extended Statehood in the Caribbean: Paradoxes of Quasi Colonialism, Local Autonomy and Extended Statehood in the USA, French, Dutch and British Caribbean*, edited by Lammert de Jong and Dirk Kuijt, 21–57. Amsterdam: Rozenberg.

Emerson, Rupert. 1953. "Puerto Rico and American Policy Toward Dependent Areas." *Annals of the American Academy of Political Science* 285:9–15.

Farr, Kenneth R. 1973. *Personalism and Party Politics: The Institutionalization of the Popular Democratic Party*. Hato Rey, PR: Inter American University Press.

González Díaz, Emilio. 1991. *La Política de los Empresarios Puertorriqueños*. Río Piedras: Ediciones Huracán / Centro de Investigaciones Sociales.

Little, Arthur J. 1942. *Report on New Industries for Puerto Rico*. Cambridge, MA: Arthur D. Little.

Miller, Randy. 1999. "U.S. Possessions Corporations, 1995." *SOI Bulletin* 17:168–84.

Morales-Carrión, Arturo. 1971. *Puerto Rico and the Non-Hispanic Caribbean: A Study in the Decline of Spanish Exclusivism*. San Juan: University of Puerto Rico Press.

Negrón de Montilla, Aida. 1975. *Americanization in Puerto Rico and the Public-School System, 1900–1930*. Río Piedras: Editorial Universitaria.

O'Connor, Donald J. 1948. *Puerto Rico's Potential as a Site for Textile, Apparel and Other Industries*. Washington, DC: Office of Puerto Rico.

Pantojas-García, Emilio. 1974. "La Iglesia Protestante y la Americanización de Puerto Rico: 1898–1917." *Revista de Ciencias Sociales* 17 (1–2): 98–122.

Pantojas-García, Emilio. 1990. *Development Strategies as Ideology: Puerto Rico's Export-Led Industrialization Experience*. Boulder: Lynne Rienner / University of Puerto Rico Press.

Pantojas-García, Emilio. 2005. "The Puerto Rican Paradox: Colonialism Revisited." *Latin American Research Review* 40 (3): 163–76.

Pantojas-García, Emilio. 2007. "Federal Funds and the Puerto Rican Economy: Myths and Realities." *CENTRO Journal* 19 (2): 207–23.

Pantojas-García, Emilio. 2013. "The Puerto Rican Status Question: Can the Stalemate be Broken?." *Caribbean Journal of International Relations* 1 (2): 41–52.

Pantojas-García, Emilio. 2016. "Is Puerto Rico Greece in the Caribbean?" *Fletcher Forum of World Affairs* 40 (1): 63–71.

Quintero Rivera, Angel G. 1980a. "Background to the Emergence of Imperialist Capitalism in Puerto Rico." In *The Puerto Ricans: Their History, Culture, and Society*, edited by Adalberto López, 97–127. Cambridge: Schenkman.

Quintero Rivera, Angel G. 1980b. "The Development of Social Classes and Political Conflict in Puerto Rico." In *The Puerto Ricans: Their History, Culture, and Society*, edited by Adalberto López, 213–231. Cambridge: Schenkman.

Quintero Rivera, Angel G. 1988. *Patricios y Plebeyos: Burgueses, Hacendados, Artesanos y Obreros; Las Relaciones de Clase en el Puerto Rico de Cambio de Siglo*. Río Piedras: Ediciones Huracán.

Rivera Ramos, Efrén. 2001. *The Legal Construction of Identity: The Judicial and Social*

Legacy of American Colonialism in Puerto Rico. Washington, DC: American Psychological Association.

Scarano, Francisco A. 1994. *Puerto Rico, Cinco Siglos de Historia*. México: McGraw-Hill.

Scheele, Raymond L. 1956. "The Prominent Families of Puerto Rico." In *The People of Puerto Rico: Study in Social Anthropology*, edited by Julian H. Steward et al., 418–62. Urbana: University of Illinois Press.

US Department of the Treasury. 1989. *The Operation and Effect of the Possessions Corporation System of Taxation, Sixth Annual Report*. Washington, DC: Department of the Treasury.

Wells, Henry. 1969. *The Modernization of Puerto Rico: A Political Study of Changing Values and Institutions*. Cambridge, MA: Harvard University Press.

Zeno Gandía, Manuel. (1894) 2003. *La Charca*. Biblioteca Virtual Universal. http://www.biblioteca.org.ar/libros/71048.pdf

CHAPTER 7

The Political Economy of Contemporary Puerto Rico

Argeo T. Quiñones Pérez and Ian J. Seda-Irizarry

Any approach toward comprehending the evolution and current state of the socioeconomic situation of Puerto Rico has to recognize both continuity and rupture in the economic history of this colonial possession of the United States.[1] The type of characterization provided to unravel this process will be inextricably tied to the types of solutions proposed, discussed, and maybe even implemented. In the particular case of Puerto Rico, for reasons that go beyond the immediate focus of this chapter, most of the problems encountered on the island are explained on the basis of Puerto Rico's colonial condition as a territorial possession of the United States. The lack of sovereignty in such areas as monetary policy, food production and consumption, and power in international affairs highlights how the country has its hands tied behind its back in, for example, tackling the current economic depression. The logic of this explanation usually dictates that if Puerto Rico were not a colony of the United States, then the residents of the island would not be the victims of the plethora of problems currently suffered.

We find that these explanations, whose coordinates of discussion are defined by power relations between nation-states (Puerto Rico subjugated as a colony to the United States), need to be further fleshed out by bringing into the picture the socioeconomic system in which this particular colonial relationship plays out. By highlighting *capitalism* alongside colonialism in our understanding of the current situation of Puerto Rico, other protagonists are brought forward into the picture and an inescapable and provocative conclusion is reached: ending the colonial relationship might be a necessary but not sufficient condition for solving the problems of the vast majority on the island. In other words, the analysis of colonialism in Puerto Rico has usually been silent regarding *internal power and economic relations in a capitalist class structure*. This silence could potentially entail the reproduction of the same type of relations and economic model even in a postcolonial moment.

The purpose of this chapter is to add to the present discussions pertaining to the future of Puerto Rico within the context of the economic depression of the past decade and a half so that new conversations can take place to produce richer characterizations that hopefully feed political reactions against the social decomposition happening on the island.

A Dependent Economy

While the economy of the island of Puerto Rico is one that has passed through different stages since the period of industrialization began in the late 1940s, the understanding of how to achieve and sustain industrialization, and by extension economic development, has basically remained the same: phases pertaining to light industry, that is, apparel (1947–67); heavy industry, that is, petrochemicals (1968–75); and high technology, that is, pharmaceuticals and electronics (1976–2006) all have had the common denominator of using substantial tax incentives (exemptions, preferential treatment, credits, subsidies, etc.) for foreign capital as the spearhead of a strategy to achieve capital accumulation and economic development.[2]

The general practical and ideological contours behind this project of *industrialization by invitation*, known as Operation Bootstrap, are ones that during the last decades have still permeated the policy approaches of the different governmental administrations of the colony.[3] Important among these is the idea that benefits generated at the top, that is, in the private business sector, will somehow "trickle down" to the rest of society. While it is true that some limited success in terms of economic growth was achieved during the initial decades of Operation Bootstrap (6% average growth between the years 1947 and 1973), what is undeniable is that the perpetuation of the model has not contributed to the creation of a dynamic and sustainable economy; on the contrary, it has created both *economic dependence* on foreign capital, an unproductive local capitalist class that has focused on financial and merchant activities, and a highly skilled working class with limited access to employment and substantial incentives for emigration.

Currently, the size of the economy of Puerto Rico, measured in terms of its gross domestic product (GDP), totals $105 billion, while measured in terms of its gross national product (GNP), it totals $70 billion. This gap between GDP and GNP represents an approximation of the total amount of money that is extracted from the island and sent to the US mainland by US multinational firms.

The level of internal investment by the private sector equals 12% of GNP and is seven times smaller than the level of aggregate internal consumption, while imports outpace exports by 10%.[4] More than 80% of what is consumed within the island is imported, while less than 15% of the purchases by multinationals are from local suppliers. Manufacturing accounts for 47% of GDP, followed by real estate with 15% and finance and insurance with 5%.[5] Employment in the tourism sector (80,000 jobs) has recently outstripped that of manufacturing (76,000 jobs), even though it only provides a small fraction of what manufacturing adds to the economy.[6] Finally, the unemployment rate, as of February 2020, is 8.8%.

The statistical description provided above points to an economy that does not produce any substantial domestic capital accumulation, and therefore employment, and is one that consumes what it does not produce and produces what it does not consume. Not surprisingly, its dependence on foreign capital, its anemic performance in the local capitalist sector, the changes in the global economy, and a relationship with the United States that imposes political and economic constraints have all combined to transform Puerto Rico from a supposed "success" story in the economics literature into an evident catastrophe.

A Decade of Economic Depression

It is not an exaggeration to claim that the performance of the economy of Puerto Rico during the last decade and a half evokes images of a disaster whose magnitude—in all its qualitative, quantitative, and temporal determinations—is difficult to grasp. A couple of years ago, the Economic and Intelligence Unit, a research division of the London-based *The Economist*, declared that Puerto Rico would be among the list of "slowest growing economies" (just behind Venezuela) with no foreseeable recovery in the near future (The Economist 2018). While the catastrophic nature of the socioeconomic reality on the island has been significantly augmented by recent natural disasters, there is no denying that the outcome of devastation was already visible on the horizon.[7]

Years of relative economic stagnation since the 1970s (less than 1.5% growth per year), followed by more than a decade of economic depression and a severe fiscal crisis (current public debt equals 100% of GNP), have been caused and shaped by both endogenous and exogenous factors. The results are staggering: Since 2006, the total economic contraction of the economy, measured in terms of the GNP, has reached 14%,[8] while nonagricultural wage labor has fallen 16% (168,000 jobs).[9] There has also been a general collapse in the real estate market in terms of loss of value, mortgage foreclosures, and abandoned housing properties.[10] Not surprisingly, inequality and poverty have increased, placing Puerto Rico among the most unequal countries in the world.[11] Finally, increasing waves of emigration and a lowering of the natural growth rate of the population have translated into a demographic imbalance.[12] The long-term impact of these and other results is practically impossible to foresee, but one thing is sure: they are affecting different social sites in very grave ways.[13]

In response to this scenario, government administrations with different views on the colonial situation of the island in relation to the United States have converged in their responses by putting forward various regressive policies that have included an increase in the tax burden of consumption, the firing of thousands of public employees with a reduction in the fringe benefits of those remaining, big privatization projects, and market liberalization policies.[14] While the difference between administrations is one of degrees, a constant among them has been their attack on labor based on an *internal devaluation* strategy that seeks to make Puerto Rico more "competitive" and "attractive" for foreign investment by reducing labor costs. This approach has echoed the general global offensive by capital against labor in a moment when, contrary to the offensive of the 1970s and early 1980s, labor's institutions are weak and on the retreat.[15]

Another important dimension of the offensive on labor has been the standard neoliberal attack based on the size of the government, which in this case has gone beyond the mere rhetoric and has been put into practice.[16] Between 2009 and 2016, over 73,000 public employees were fired, a drop of around 24% in public employment. This and other measures concerning cuts in public spending are aligned with the discredited ideology of "expansive austerity," an ideology embraced by the different governmental administrations to supposedly revitalize the economy and be able to pay off the public debt.[17] This approach to confronting the double whip of the economic depression and the massive fiscal crisis, instead of laying the foundations for a future recovery, has facilitated a process of "accumulation by dispossession" (Harvey 2003) where public assets have been sold, pensions and retirement systems have been unfunded, and other public budgets have been reallocated with the aim of paying a stratospheric public debt in a country with a real budgetary fiscal constraint given the absence of monetary sovereignty.[18] The combined efforts of the government, banks, insurance firms, credit rating agencies, hedge funds, local intermediaries, and the recently imposed Fiscal Control Board (FCB) have supposedly been oriented toward making Puerto Rico regain access to credit markets to fund the reconstruction of the island's economy. Instead, the socialization of costs within a regime of austerity to try and pay off the debt has further undermined the capacity of the economy to grow, an outcome that is leading the island to a guaranteed future of *debt peonage*.

At the same time, the status of the island and the politico-economic constraints that it enforces have limited some of the maneuvering space for the local economy. Century-old merchant laws that to a certain extent put a constraint on commerce, the double standards in terms of the lack of applicability of bankruptcy laws (e.g., Chapter 9),[19] and the lack of monetary policy are but some of these dimensions.

Contending Explanations of the Crisis

When it comes to understanding what brought the island's economy to this debacle, explanations range from (1) finger pointing to the history of colonial Puerto Rico to (2) the inept and corrupt management of local government administrations to (3) the transformations in the global economic system during the last four decades that have, for example, provided capital with greater flexibility to move around its profits.

A good example that to some extent combines all three perspectives focuses on the effects of the elimination of Section 936 of the US tax code, which provided the axis for manufacturing on the island. Since 1976, this tax regime gave red-carpet treatment to multinational subsidiaries operating in Puerto Rico to remit profits earned on the island back to their parent company in the United States without paying taxes. Because of political pressure pertaining to tax revenue lost to the mainland, the mechanism was eliminated by the US Congress in 1996 with a 10-year transitional phase-out period. Three main empirical observations highlight the relationship between the economic depression and the elimination of Section 936:

(1) Since the mid-1990s, industrial employment has decreased and firms have left in what is usually described as a process of *deindustrialization*.
(2) The public debt of the government and its corporations experienced an increase starting in the 1990s. Deindustrialization implied fewer jobs, and fewer jobs implied less revenues for the government via tax collections. A choice was then made to close the gap between revenues and government spending via the emission of debt.
(3) The year 2006 marks the end of the phase-out transition period for Section 936, and that same year, according to official statistics, also marks the beginning of the economic depression of the island.

The colonial legacy of Section 936 could be interpreted in terms of the huge sums of money *extracted* from Puerto Rico, mainly by American firms, and not reinvested in the island's economy. The transformations of global capitalism associated with financial flexibility can be seen in terms of the quantum of profits reported on the island (though not necessarily produced there) by firms to escape taxation.[20] Finally, the role of inept administrations is usually highlighted, given the lack of a comprehensive strategy for economic growth and development that should have been worked out and implemented once the elimination of Section 936 was finalized.

A critical political economy approach recognizes all of the above specifications to comprehend the complexities that shape the socioeconomic fabric of Puerto Rico. Still, what we would like to do with our contribution in this book is to reposition the above characterizations within a slightly different set of coordinates to try and highlight the perpetuation of a failed model of economic development mentioned in the introduction, while recognizing the local determination of policies aligned with it. This perspective is usually not emphasized in the analysis provided by economists within and outside the island and has important implications for any political strategy seeking to alter the current status quo on the island.

An Alternative Outlook

The first step in our endeavor to explore the contemporary political economy of Puerto Rico is to emphasize that the crisis of Puerto Rico's Commonwealth, that is, the Estado Libre Asociado, and the crisis of its economic model, although intertwined, have to be kept conceptually distinct from one another. It is our position that collapsing one into another has obscured the *internal relations of power* at play on the island, relations that have shaped the responses to the economic crisis and are useful for explaining the fiscal crisis and the neoliberal structural adjustment that has been imposed to pay off the debt.

As in any other society, relations of power run at different levels throughout the economic fabric of Puerto Rican society. Unfortunately, and for reasons that go beyond the space and purpose of this chapter, politics and power in Puerto Rico have historically been reduced and understood in relation to the colonial condition of the island as a territory of the United States. In that understanding, to say that the problem of the crisis is political is usually translated into a belief that if the colonial condition is abolished, the crisis will be solved. Common in these approaches is the *unilateral* emphasis on the politico-legal relationships with the United States. Also, the fact that the economic downturn of the island predated the global recession by two years is taken by many as evidence that this is a crisis of the colonial model and that, therefore, the solution has to be sought in changing the present colonial relationship to a non-colonial status, be it statehood, independence, or variants of so-called sovereignty.[21] As we hope to make clear by the end of this chapter, the ending of the colonial relationship with the United States is a necessary but not sufficient condition to address the deep roots of the crisis. Important dimensions of the current socioeconomic arrangement can still be compatible with non-colonial status options.

Another important dimension for understanding the current political economy of Puerto Rico is the recognition that certain individuals and groups within the island have benefited during the economic depression. As in many other parts of the world, income inequality has been one of the major plot stories in Puerto Rico. Not only is the distribution of income on the island more unequal than in any state in the United States, but the island is also one of the most unequal countries in the world. From a critical political economy perspective, this fact has to be further deconstructed by looking at the distribution of income in relation to its sources. For example, during the first 10 years of economic depression (2006 to 2016), data on the functional distribution of income pointed to a decrease in income of 3.9% for those whose income was based on employee compensation, while income based on property (profits, interests, etc.) increased by 59%. Another way to visualize the impact of this massive redistributive outcome is to directly compare the relative sizes of income going to property vis-à-vis that going to labor. For the year 2006, the total income based on property amounted to 56% of the total income based on employee compensation. By 2016, that proportion had increased to 92%.[22] These and other statistics show the class bias of the redistributive effects of the crisis, where not everybody on the island is experiencing the economic depression in the same way. These results are in part explained by the regressive tax policies that have characterized the different administrations in power. These policies have been the outcome of the common ideological beliefs of the different governmental administrations as well as of the intense pressure from socioeconomic interests that represent the organized strata of the local business and political elites.[23] A case in point is the Coalition of the Private Sector, an umbrella organization constituted by more than two dozen associations of the private sector on the island that have historically pushed for conservative/pro-market policies regarding the labor market while seeking to push for more corporate welfare for themselves.

Another important methodological step in understanding the crisis of Puerto Rico is to place it in a historical context. The current socioeconomic catastrophe of Puerto Rico has to be understood in relation to the crisis conjuncture of the mid-1970s and the "development" project begun in the mid- to late 1940s. Critical in this is the recognition of the *relative autonomy* that different governmental administration have had in fiscal matters, be it in terms of, for example, levels of public spending, types of public spending, and incentives provided to the private sector (both foreign and local). Specifically, we want to highlight the perpetuation of a failed model of economic development that privatizes the gains and socializes the costs via the continued reliance on all types of tax incentives (credits, preferential rates, subsidies, etc.) with no connection to a well-developed and long-term industrial policy.

Perpetuation of a Failed Economic Strategy

Puerto Rico faced its first postwar fiscal and economic crisis during the mid-1970s. This conjuncture demonstrated that the economic model in place had run its course and that fundamental changes were required so that its inherent structural deficiencies would not be triggered by new historical circumstances.

As mentioned at the beginning of this chapter, the strategy of "industrialization by invitation" provided substantial incentives to attract foreign direct investment. These included subsidized public utilities, infrastructure, and land; the provision of environmental subsidies; and tax credits and exemptions. This arrangement had originally been seen as an initial stage in the industrialization process to plant the seeds for the development of a robust local industry that would then "take off" and compete in world markets.[24]

Since the 1940s, various warnings had been made, especially about the excessive use of tax exemptions as the spearhead for an attempt at equitable and sustainable growth and development. The crisis of the mid-1970s, which disrupted the fragile relative balance that had been attained between economic growth and distribution that had sought to legitimize the capitalist colony since 1947, showed the limits of dependent growth, limits that were not addressed. Instead, the dependency on foreign capital was further strengthened with the implementation of Section 936 in 1976.[25] The new tax exemption incentives for firms reflected the new global landscape in terms of flexibility for financial flows, as well as a continuation of the failed strategy of industrialization by invitation. As Dietz (1986, 251) states, "The tax-exemption program shifted from being a temporary measure, as originally conceived, to being a permanent feature of the development strategy."

When examining the reactions to the current economic depression by the various administrations, one cannot fail to notice the continuation of the failed strategy of development based on tax incentives to both local and foreign capital. In 2004, two years before the economic crisis began, there were around 40 tax exemption laws. In 2008, two years after the start of the crisis, there were around 60 laws. Now there are more than 90 tax exemption laws, and the current government administration does not show any signs of diverting from this path.

Apart from the number of laws, what jumps out is the fact that none of these laws have been ever submitted to a thorough analysis to see if their purported aims actually materialized.[26] Given the double-digit unemployment rate, the severe economic contraction with no end in sight, the increase in inequality, and the increase in the money being extracted from the island, one would think that there would be an urgent need to revisit this approach.[27]

What has indeed come out of this arrangement is a parasitic local private sector that cannot create jobs and that sustains itself via the subsidies of the state. The regime of corporate welfare for both local and foreign capital has taken away resources that could provide the basis for countercyclical policies that might offset or at least soften the economic downturn.

Estimates by a former secretary of the treasury point out that the potential revenue foregone by the government because of all the tax incentive scaffolds stands at $25 billion.[28] Even if we assume that in reality half of that total is actually needed for the survival of businesses, the remaining $12.5 billion is more than the total level of local investment ($8,608 for FY 2016). It also is more than the general fund of the government (around $9 billion). These two results point to the existence of what could be called a "rentier state" arrangement of corporate welfare, where the government practically guarantees the survival of firms that do not create jobs or economic activity on par with the help provided but that receive public benefits.

At the same time, there is a class-biased regime of austerity that seeks to balance a depleted budget by cutting important government expenditures (pensions, public employment, etc.) that directly affect the victims of the crisis while not touching the scaffold that provides all of these unexamined incentives.

That the tax incentive laws were *locally determined* by different governmental administrations, irrespective of status preference, within the relative autonomy of the state under the Commonwealth, gives credence to the perspective that the crisis was in important ways *self-inflicted*.[29] From a political economy perspective, the relevant questions then become, Which are the groups that have continuously benefited from the laws and policies enacted by the different governments and how do these extractive elites function to maintain the status quo?

Although a thorough analysis of the current class structure and its relation to the state is highly complicated and is yet to be produced, we can catch a glimpse of the main actors, given what we have discussed so far. Outcomes pertaining to income inequality, the class bias of the tax reforms enacted, the internal devaluation strategy for cutting labor costs, the increasing amounts of wealth extracted from the island, and the accumulation by dispossession and privatization of public assets all point toward the need to understand the crisis in terms of a colonial relationship not merely in which many Puerto Ricans are victims of the imperial cravings of the United States but where the looting of the public coffers is "rooted in [certain] coincidences of interest between local dominant classes and international ones" (Cardoso and Faletto 1979, xvi). One example of this is the recent labor reform law of January 2017 passed by the current government, endorsed by the Coalition of the Private Sector, and celebrated by multiple bondholder groups. This law basically increases the stress on the labor market conditions, which translates into an increase in the precarity of work and an added incentive for emigration, especially for those who are entering the labor market. Another example of the presence of extractive elites throughout the institutional scaffold of the island is apparent even when that scaffold seems, on a superficial level, to be fundamentally undermined. Specifically, the recent abolition of the relative autonomy of the government to control fiscal matters with the appointment of the FCB by the US Congress in August 2016 points to an apparent rupture with important elements of continuity. Former government officials under both main parties who have had direct connections with the financial sector now serve on a board that is supposed to balance the finances (i.e., pay a debt equal to 100% of GNP) of bankrupt Puerto Rico. This board, which can be seen as both a colonial imposition and the result of local lobbying from certain sectors within the island, reflects continuity with the local administrations in terms of the neoliberal structural adjustment that is seen as a solution and also in terms of the perpetuation of the failed economic model that we have discussed.[30]

Conclusion

The economic model of Puerto Rico is one where gains are privatized and costs are socialized for the benefit of local and foreign extractive elites. The class content of the relationship within the island and in relation to the United States can be clearly seen through the perpetuation of an economic model through locally determined policies that did not serve the needs of the majority of Puerto Ricans. Unfortunately, the emphasis on the colonial status of the island deprived of a class analysis has obscured the role that local governments, intermediaries, and economic elites have had in shaping economic policies that have reinforced local and foreign corporate welfare with no trickle-down effect on the rest of the population.

Even though the relative autonomy of the government of Puerto Rico has been put into question with the recent approval of the FCB, an important insight of the general analysis is that the current socioeconomic arrangement can potentially transcend an independent formula for Puerto Rico. This is an important dimension of a colonial legacy that transcends the colonial relationship between Puerto Rico and the United States that needs to be addressed in fundamental ways if the island is to escape its present state of socioeconomic catastrophe.

NOTES

1. Throughout the chapter we use the term "colonial" to refer to the juridico-political situation of Puerto Rico as a territorial possession of the United States. We focus on this narrow definition of the term given our interest in highlighting the relative autonomy of the government in fiscal manners, which for us is a fundamental variable for understanding the current political economy of the island.

2. The debates pertaining to what is "economic development" are beyond the scope of this chapter and are shared by the contributors of this book either explicitly or implicitly. For the sake of simplicity, we assume that capital accumulation is a precondition for economic development, even though we understand the limits of such an economistic outlook.

3. For a discussion of the abandonment of state-capitalist planning on the island for what became Operation Bootstrap, see Catalá (2013) and Dietz (1986).

4. The data presented in this section is based on Junta de Planificación (2016, 2018). In the economics literature, a "normal" level of consumption in relation to the size of the economy is usually around 75%. The relatively big size of consumption vis-à-vis internal investment in Puerto Rico is evidence of the meager size and anemic dynamism of the local private sector. Unfortunately, data for "foreign direct investment" by multinational firms in Puerto Rico is not available.

5. Agriculture accounts for less than 1% of GDP, and although it has experienced a resurgence in the last years, it experienced a major setback with the landfall of hurricane María, which destroyed around 80% of the harvest.

6. Measurements comparing the sectors in terms of productivity are difficult to make, given that a substantial amount of the profits reported in manufacturing are actually not created on the island but are the result of "transfer-pricing" strategies by multinational firms to evade taxes. For an analysis of Puerto Rico's place in the circulation of global profits, see Quiñones-Pérez (2006).

7. In September 2017, the island felt the effects of two hurricanes, Irma (category 4) and María (category 5). Then in December 2019, a series of earthquakes also shook Puerto Rico.

8. Author's calculations based on Junta de Planificación (2015, 2016).

9. Author's calculations based on Junta de Planificación (2015, 2016).

10. The year 2016 saw an increase of 21.6% in cases of mortgage foreclosures in comparison to 2015, which is the highest in a decade (Tellado-Domenech 2017).

11. According to the US Census Bureau (2015), the island's Gini index (a standard measure of income inequality) was measured at 0.559, higher than those of Washington, DC (0.535), and New York (0.514). When compared to World Bank data for other countries, these levels of inequality place Puerto Rico among the most unequal countries in the world.

12. In 2016, over 89,000 persons emigrated, while in the 10 years before, the average was 60,000 per year. This number is now spiking upward, even more after the onslaught of hurricane María.

13. Although official statistics for domestic violence are not very reliable, there has been an unquestioned rise in the cases reported and processed, especialy since

the hurricanes hit in the fall of 2017. The extreme pressure put on household finances has definitely shaped these outcomes.

14. See Quiñones-Pérez and Seda-Irizarry (2016b, 2020) for a discussion of concrete examples.

15. See Stiglitz (2016) for a general discussion of internal devaluation, specifically in the context of the euro crisis.

16. For a view that problematizes the discourse for shrinking the state versus the transformed functions of the state under neoliberalism, see Mirowski (2013).

17. See Shapiro (2012) for a review of arguments against austerity.

18. For a discussion of the implications of having sovereign debt while having monetary sovereignty (i.e., the ability to print money), see Wray (2016).

19. Chapter 9 is a section of the bankruptcy code of the United States that applies to insolvent local governments and their public utilities but not to territories like Puerto Rico.

20. For an analysis of this phenomenon, known as "transfer pricing," see Quiñones (2006). While Section 936 no longer exists, this mechanism still works via the "controlled foreign corporations" clause of the US tax system.

21. See Backiel (2015) for a recent example of this colonial-centric approach.

22. Authors' calculations based on Junta de Planificación (2015; 2016, table 11). Also of note is the fact that "payments to the rest of the world" had increased by 19% over the same decade.

23. It is important to note that one can still assign the last name of local families to different forms of capital operating on the island: the Fonalledas family as representatives of merchant capital, the Carrión family as representatives of financial capital, and the Ferré family representing productive capital in intermediary goods (i.e., cement, although now a subsidiary of the Mexican firm CEMEX) and owning the major media outlets in the country.

24. See Dietz (1986) and Catalá (2013) for a description of the expectations surrounding the application of this model of industrialization by invitation. See Quiñones-Pérez and Seda-Irizarry (2016a) for a historical overview of the performance of the economy.

25. See Tobin (1976) and Villamil (1976). In some senses, especially in terms of economic growth, the industrialization period 1947–73 could be considered the "golden age" of Operation Bootstrap.

26. It is interesting to note that the data for "foreign direct investment" of multinational firms stopped being collected by the government some decades ago. One would suppose that this information would be fundamental for analyzing the effectiveness of tax incentives.

27. Between 2006 and 2016, "payments to the rest of the world" increased by 18% (Junta de Planificación 2016, 2017). Author's calculations.

28. These numbers were publicly shared to the media in August 2016 by then secretary of the treasury, Juan Zaragoza.

29. See Quiñones-Pérez and Seda-Irizarry (2017).

30. For an analysis of the Fiscal Control Board, see Quiñones-Pérez and Seda-Irizarry (2016b).

REFERENCES

Backiel, Linda. 2015. "Puerto Rico: The Crisis Is about Colonialism, Not Debt." *Monthly Review* 67 (5): 11–18.

Cardoso, Fernando, and Enzo Faletto. 1979. *Dependency and Development in Latin America*. Berkeley: University of California Press.

Catalá, Francisco. 2013. *Promesa Rota: Una Mirada Institucionalista a Partir de Tugwell*. San Juan: Ediciones Callejón.

Dietz, James. 1986. *Economic History of Puerto Rico: Institutional Change and Capitalist Development*. Princeton: Princeton University Press.

The Economist. 2018. "The Fastest Growing and Shrinking Economies of 2018." https://www.economist.com/blogs/graphicdetail/2018/01/daily-chart-3

Harvey, David. 2003. *The New Imperialism*. New York: Oxford University Press.

Junta de Planificación. 2015. *Statistical Appendix, Economic Report to the Governor*. http://jp.pr.gov/LinkClick.aspx?fileticket=GuUCVHceco0%3d&tabid=228&portalid=0&mid=1405

Junta de Planificación. 2016. *Statistical Appendix, Economic Report to the Governor*. http://jp.pr.gov/LinkClick.aspx?fileticket=NyGfY4a9Ikw%3d&tabid=228&portalid=0&mid=1405

Junta de Planificación. 2018. *Resumen Económico de Puerto Rico* 2 (2). http://jp.pr.gov/LinkClick.aspx?fileticket=FiW62fqseN8%3d&tabid=262&portalid=0&mid=1592

Mirowski, Philip. 2013. *Never Let a Serious Crisis Go to Waste: How Neoliberalism Survived the Financial Meltdown*. London: Verso.

Quiñones-Pérez, Argeo T. 2006. "Ganancias Globales y la Economía de Puerto Rico." *Boletín Asociación de Economistas de Puerto Rico* 1 (3): 3–5.

Quiñones-Pérez, Argeo T., and Ian J. Seda-Irizarry. 2016a. "Wealth Extraction, Governmental Servitude, and Social Disintegration in Colonial Puerto Rico." *New Politics* 15 (4): 91–98.

Quiñones-Pérez, Argeo T., and Ian J. Seda-Irizarry. 2016b. "A Junta for Puerto Rico." Working Paper Series 1 (fall), Economics Department, John Jay College.

Quiñones-Pérez, Argeo T., and Ian J. Seda-Irizarry. 2020. "The Self-Inflicted Dimensions of Puerto Rico's Fiscal Crisis." *Journal of Latin American Perspectives* 47 (3): 87–102.

Shapiro, Nina. 2012. "Keynes, Steindl, and the Critique of Austerity Economics." *Monthly Review* 64 (3): 103–13.

Stiglitz, Joseph. 2016. *The Euro: How a Common Currency Threatens the Future of Europe*. New York: W. W. Norton.

Tellado-Domenech, Ruth. 2017. "Las Ejecuciones de Hipotecas Alcanzan la Cifra Más Alta en una Década." *El Nuevo Día*, March 5.

Tobin, James. 1976. *Informe al Gobernador del Comité para el Estudio de las Finanzas de Puerto Rico*. http://gis.jp.pr.gov/Externo_Econ/Programa%20de%20Planificaci%C3%B3n%20Econ%C3%B3mica%20y%20Social/1975.12-Informe%20al%20Gobernador%20del%20Comit%C3%A9%20para%20el%20Estudio%20de%20las%20Finanzas%20de%20Puerto%20Rico%20(Informe%20Tobin,%201976).pdf

US Census Bureau. 2015. *American Community Survey*. https://www.census.gov/programs-surveys/acs/

Villamil, José. 1976. "El Modelo Puertorriqueño: Límites del Crecimiento Dependiente." *Revista Puertorriqueña de Investigaciones Sociales* 1 (July–December): 3–14.

Wray, Randall. 2016. *Modern Money Theory: A Primer on Macroeconomics for Sovereign Monetary Systems*. London: Palgrave Macmillan.

CHAPTER 8

Sui generis

The Political Economy of the Philippines during the Spanish Colonial Regime

Alvin A. Camba and Maria Isabel B. Aguilar

This chapter[1] analyzes the Philippine political economy during the Spanish colonial regime (1571–1898). We argue that from the 16th to the 18th century, the Philippines' position in the Spanish colonial economy was unique, inasmuch as it departed from the conventional mercantilist relations that governed much of Spain's empire. However, at the end of the 18th century, the Philippines was eventually subsumed within the British world empire, converging to become an emerging cash crop exporter.

Our chapter will inevitably neglect some key nuances on the political, economic, and social features of the Philippines due to the focus on macroeconomic structures over 300 years, yet we suggest that our argument neatly characterizes the Philippines' political economy, paving the way for future comparative research with other Spanish and non-Spanish colonies. In the chapter, we discuss the social structures of precolonial Philippines; examine the Galleon trade, the main institution that governed the Philippines' political economy; and elaborate on the characteristics of the Philippines cash crop economy.

The Complexity of the Precolonial Philippines

The precolonial Philippines had complex and varied social structures, which somehow mimicked and concurrently departed from the larger

Maritime Southeast Asian polities. William Henry Scott (1994) estimated a political structure with approximately 40 to 100 families, called the barangay, with the *datu* serving as the leader.[2] These leaders combined some of the functions of modern state leaders today, such as the executive power to implement laws, the judicial power to adjudicate disputes, and the communal power to sanction traditions. Furthermore, the *datus* represented the barangay to their counterparts in matters of resource sharing, joint agricultural production, or alliance to preserve their autonomy from other barangays (Scott 1994, 24). There was also intense intra-barangay competition to become the *datu*, which was often decided by the strength of the coalition that the *datu* made with the various classes. In these situations, leaders exhibited power through their genealogical lineage, religious attributes, or even sheer charisma (32). In other situations, the control of economic resources to mobilize the military capacity to depose the existing *datu* decided the intra-barangay dispute.

Scott (1994, 35) additionally explains the upper, middle, and lower classes of Philippine polities, respectively, as Lakan, Maharlika, and Timawa. However, these social positions should not be held fixed, as their relative power and position to each other varied greatly across barangays, ethnic groups, and geographies. These structures can be found across the Philippines, though how they vary from the Ilocos region to the Visayas islands has yet to be studied systematically. In sum, the community structure was pyramidal yet flexible, competitive but survivalist.

A popular notion is that the Philippines and other Southeast Asian polities had slaves. However, the notion of "slavery" was different from the Western world: Specifically, slaves usually were the offenders or criminals of the community, temporarily serving their sentences as slaves under the guidance of the *datus* (Scott 1994, 56). Instead of enduring a permanent bondage and a status that was intergenerationally inherited, the criminals were treated as slaves for a limited period of time and mainly used to provide labor for the community. Other situations involved debt bondage, whereby people needed to work for a limited amount of time to pay off their debt. Indeed, these types of slaves reflect precolonial Philippines' relatively egalitarian structure and the population deficit that characterized much of Southeast Asia at that time.[3]

When the Spanish Empire arrived in the 16th century, the colonizers had to deal with these heterogenous social structures. In *Colonialism and Postcolonial Development* (2010), sociologist James Mahoney attempts to construct a comparative theory that can identify the main mechanisms that shape colonization. Mahoney argues that mercantilist colonizers prefer colonizing high-complexity indigenous institutions because of their already existing indentured labor force and population control mechanisms, while liberal colonizers concentrate on low-complexity indigenous institutions because they can be easily reengineered (2010, 20–21). However, Mahoney's concepts do not directly apply to the Philippines. There was variation of low-, medium-, and high-complexity communities across the Philippines. However, these structures did not affect Spain's decision to incorporate these polities into Spain's emerging colonial order, which meant that there was no direct link between the complexity of the precolonial polities and the decision of Spain to colonize.

Spanish government officials and religious entities were committed to the colonization of the Philippines: the earliest wave of migrants was made up of the religious orders eager to proselyte and place specific towns under their influence (Phelan 1959, 14; Scott 1994, 34). The government of Spain was mindful of the implications of holding territories in Asia, which they thought were important to Christianize Japan and China as well as to keep up with the Portuguese. As a result, Spain subsidized the Philippines and kept it running, but it never invested enough revenues on lands to build infrastructure and bolster production (Camba 2012; Phelan 1959).

Given this context, Spanish colonialism in the Philippines must be understood in terms of networks rather than fixed categories. The Philippine islands comprised decentralized polities that governed differently across geographies with their own histories, beliefs, and capacities rather than acting as a fully integrated colonial state. In some places, villages were spread across different areas, foraging and farming on shared plots. In others, like Manila, Vigan, and Cebu, more centralized polities had their own small armies and navies. When these places were put under Spanish rule, they were directly governed by the Spanish government in Manila.[4]

Colonization in the Philippines was a negotiation mediated by Spanish and Philippine actors with varying, compatible, and sometimes competing interests. On the part of the Spanish, the centralized power was held by the governor-general of Manila, who took broader orders from New Spain and Madrid. Military and government officials exerted their interests on governance, trade, and security. On the part of the religious orders, numerous groups—Jesuits, Franciscans, Dominicans—had an interest in spreading their interpretation over the colonized populace, taking the lead to Christianize and indirectly govern much of the peripheral areas in the Spanish Philippines (Camba 2012, 218). The Spanish Crown also had their own religious officials, who influenced much of Manila and competed with the decentralized religious orders (Phelan 1959, 78; Mehl 2016, 7).

Unlike Latin America, which imported members of the Iberian population to populate the recently defaced region, European colonialism in the Philippines was built on the backs of a moderately populous and relatively prosperous region. Spanish colonization systematized and standardized the social hierarchy in the Philippines. At the top of the structure were the Spanish, divided into the *peninsulares*, or the Spanish born in Spain, and the *insulares*, or the Spanish born in the Philippines. Among the colonized, the *principalia* were positioned next in the colonial hierarchy, represented by the Gobernadorcillos, or the former descendants of the *datus*, and the *Cabezas de Barangay*, or those who were given leadership after proving their loyalty to the Spanish. There were visitors and migrants before the waves of European colonization, which included Arabian merchants, Indian traders, and Chinese migrants. Some of these populations mixed with the various Filipino groups, forming the mestizo population, who were below the *principalia* but above the *indios*. At the lowest levels, the *indios* made up most of the population. The relative position of the Chinese population in the social hierarchy and economy varied (Mehl 2016, 34).

Spain's colonization of the Philippines experienced limitations caused by political interest, economic capital, and immovable geographies. There were simply more political and economic interests in Latin America during the 16th century. Though Spain attempted to influence its subject population to move to the Philippines, distance and travel time constrained migration from the "core" to the "periphery." Eva Maria Mehl (2016) estimates that, excluding the mestizos, there was an estimated 20,000 Spanish *peninsulares*, officials, and soldiers between the 16th and the 18th centuries in the Philippines. Demographic data on Spanish Philippines remains imprecise. However, Linda Newson's (2009) *Conquest and Pestilence in the Early Spanish Philippines* estimates the total number of tributary and non-tributary populations in the Philippines at 905,460 in 1600. This number declined from an estimation of 1,427,150 due to disease and conquest in the mid-16th century but eventually increased to 1,555,043 in 1800 (256–57).

The Galleon Trade and Property Relations

Previous works on the Philippine economy argue that the Spanish economic regime in the Philippines was built on "mercantilist" economic relations (e.g., Corpuz 1997; Phelan 1959; Scott 1994). We argue instead, following Merchant (2012), that the Spanish colonization of the Philippines did not fulfill three basic standards of mercantilist power: First, Spanish colonial officials relied on friars to govern places geographically distant from the capital, which means that the Spanish government of the Philippines was not centralized. Second, Spain provided the *situado*, or subsidy, to the Philippines, which was extracted from the import duties of Acapulco (Legarda 1999, 41). Legarda estimates that the average colonial subsidy was PhP 250,000 annually. And third, there was a clear absence of chartered companies until the British intervened in the Philippines in the 19th century. Instead, the Spanish regime relied solely on the galleon trade, which was estimated to be around 100–135 ships.[5]

In theories of colonialism, Mahoney (2010, 7) argues that the economic orientation of the colonizer shapes whether or not the colony becomes a mercantilist or liberal economy.[6] The Philippines ideally fits with mercantilism, whereby the colonizers rely on labor-repressive regimes, maximize short-term accumulation, and depend on rents to generate surplus. While the reliance on rents conforms to Mahoney's concept, the rest of the features do not neatly fit in the Philippines. Specifically, there was "preferential trade status" allotted to the Philippines, whereby every *vecino* or neighbor in Manila had a state-allotted space in the galleon to export goods to be sold in Mexico. The taxes on these products, called the *situado*, also added to the overall subsidy of the Philippines. In sum, the rents generated by having the reserved space to sell goods to Mexico and the taxes on goods subsidized the Philippines. By the end of the 18th century, the economy gradually became more self-sufficient through the government monopolies on cash crops. Furthermore, what is often underemphasized is how the economic colonial regime relied on a mixture of Chinese and *indio* labor. Merchant (2012) emphasizes the use of Chinese labor in the Philippine islands, while Legarda (1999) analyzes the accompanying goods—birds' nests, abaca, gold, spices and many others. While the galleon trade focused on exchanging goods across continents, Philippine polities and people also traded their goods with Latin American and Chinese merchants.

The Spanish colonial regime transformed the heterogeneous land relations across the islands into several distinct arrangements: (1) the friar lands, which were granted to the various Catholic orders due to their role in Philippine colonization, spanning 4,000 to 20,000 hectares; (2) the encomiendas, which were awarded to Spanish subjects in exchange for their service to the Crown in the 16th to the 18th century; and (3) the *pacto retroventa*, which allowed Filipinos and elites to own large swaths of land for export production (Cushner 1976).

While friar lands and the encomienda system were the most dominant arrangements from the 16th to the early 18th century, the *pacto retroventa* became more common with Spain's increasing need to bolster the colonial export economy in the middle of the 19th century. While historical sources give uneven and sometimes conflicting accounts about which forms of labor the three types of land arrangements employed (see Cushner 1976; Copeland 1908; Scott 1994), they concur that preexisting Philippine populations were incorporated into these land arrangements (Cushner 1976; Phelan 1959). Landlord-peasant ties became more common across these land arrangements, including inherited servitude with varying levels of fairness (Camba 2012). The most dominant one, called *servicios personales* (Cushner 1976), mimicked quasi-feudal relations from medieval Spain that required landlords to become "godfathers" of peasant children, provide capital for religious gatherings, and provision emergency measures at the time of droughts and disasters (Camba 2010, 2012; Cushner 1976). These benefits, in turn, ensured tenant political and cultural (religious) loyalties. The friar lands resembled the encomienda system (Phelan 1959).

Community Filipino norms were incorporated into the encomienda system, friar lands, and Spain's imperial ecologies (Camba 2012). At the broadest levels, peasant political and cultural loyalties were secured through this syncretic system of political, economic, and cultural obligations (Cushner 1976; Phelan 1959). However, the incorporation into and interaction with the colonial state varied depending on the Filipino actors' resistance to or participation in the regime, which varied across geographies. For example, Zamboanga del Sur developed *chabacano* at this time, a variant of the Spanish language with Southeast Asian characteristics. Manila and Cebu absorbed different Spanish characteristics in rituals, cultures, and language. Other places resisted these influences quite vigorously, partly also because of Spain's less intensive governance in these areas. Indeed, Stephanie Mawson (2013, 2016) challenges the prevailing assumption that Filipinos were simply incorporated into these social structures by highlighting the agencies, struggles, and resistance of communities to Spanish rule. In her "Philippine Indios in the Service of Empire" (2016), she demonstrates that the Spanish Empire employed thousands of Philippine soldiers whose loyalties were contingent on and shaped by the pre-Hispanic social norms: warfare or competition among ethnic groups and debt servitude to specific elites. Mawson shows how non-elites understood their conditions of existence as well as the constraints of their situation. Though Mawson sheds light on these issues, her research does not directly challenge the previous findings on the social structures of the Philippines. Instead, she complicates the relations of these actors using new data.

While the labor arrangement forms varied regionally, people became agrarian classes of labor that simultaneously depended on land and monetary relations. As Henry Bernstein (1994) argues, even though agrarian classes of labor lack access to the means of production, they are not entirely dispossessed. As they receive a combination of money and crops as payments, however, wage payments often fall below the market rate, which denotes the incomplete access to land, dependence on monetary payment, and reliance on commodity production to subsist. Indeed, this is what accounts for the subjugation of Philippine peasants on land and their capacity to barter with merchants tied to the galleon trade.

Transition to the British World Economy in the Mid-18th to 19th Century

The Spanish regime tied the Philippine economy to the galleon trade, though the economy slowly expanded to develop cash crops. At the end of the 18th century, the rise of Great Britain even before the turn toward large-scale industrialization led British capitalists to seek entrance to the Philippine economy as a consumption market and a source of cheap commodity inputs (Legarda 1999, 2). When Spain agreed to Great Britain's wish to establish merchant companies and production facilities in the Philippine islands, joint American-British trading companies like Russel & Sturgis or Kerr and Co. began to operate in the Philippines, investing in sugar, hemp, and indigo farms across the country (258).

The migration from China to the Philippines also changed population dynamics and ethnic relations in significant ways. Since the 9th century, the Philippines had been a recipient of vast numbers of Fukkien and Hakka migrants. Though the Spanish regime initially institutionalized discrimination based on Catholicism and race, the place of the Chinese in the Philippines changed in the 19th century when the Spanish needed to infuse new sources of capital into the colony. The Chinese population provided that window of opportunity (Camba 2017, 144; Wickberg 1965, 13), and the Spanish colonial regime allowed Filipinos, who were partial owners of land based on customary socioeconomic structures, and Chinese, who had capital from their migration, to intermarry and spur the Philippine economy. A Philippine-Chinese or Chinese mestizo elite emerged from the removal of these racial restrictions, leading to the creation of Filipino-owned firms such as J. M. Tuason and Company (Legarda 1999, 231).

Many Spanish, Chinese, and Filipino families subsequently intermarried and combined some of their businesses. Still, the rise of the British free trade regime in the 19th century and the subsequent response of the elites led to changes in the production relations in the Philippines. While the galleon trade was ongoing, landowners had no recourse but to trade in limited quantities tied to the Mexican companies and the Chinese merchants. When Latin America became independent, the galleon trade was discontinued, and it also forced Spain to develop other means of accumulating capital. After the galleon trade, these companies were finally able to offer their products on the broader export market. This led to the decision and impetus to upgrade their technological base in order to expand production. Landowners began importing draft animals to intensify work processes.

As an iteration of world systems theory, Giovanni Arrighi's *The Long Twentieth Century: Money, Power, and the Origins of Our Times* (1994) narrates the transformation of capitalist organizations and the world economy over time. Arrighi argues that cycles of accumulation among hegemons constitute the vacillation between "intensive regimes" and "extensive regimes."[7] In 19th-century Philippines, the British began incorporating parts of the world economy, which included the Spanish Philippines among other places, placing pressure on Manila to become part of the circuit of production.

Even with the emergence of these merchant companies and elites tied to the world market, however, the changes in the Philippine economy were still limited at best. Mahoney's (2010) theory would have expected the Spanish regime to become a liberal colonizer that enacts the free market, maximizes technological improvement, and follows the rule of law. An alternative explanation is the incorporation of the Philippine economy into the orbit of the British hegemony: The Philippines maintained its dependence on agrarian classes of labor but was more closely tied to the developments on the world market.

The integration of the Philippines into the British world economy was based on cash crops, such as abaca, hemp, tobacco, and many others. In this chapter, we focus on the case of sugar to demonstrate the changes that also occurred in these other areas. While sugar was integral in previous waves of capitalism from the 16th to the 18th century (Moore 2007), the crop was of marginal significance in the Spanish Philippines until the latter part of the 19th century (Insigne 1926). The entrance of British firms during the 19th century spurred the production of low-grade, muscovado sugar for global export, as the Spanish regime and the British investors never bothered to build centrifugal mills, expand irrigation, or increase fertilization (Waring and Dorfman 1937, 23). Indeed, John Foreman notes that in the "absence of proper banking facilities, certain commercial firms financed the business and production of sugar" (1906, 350), though in limited ways. Until the end of Spanish rule, the Philippine sugar sector was relatively uncapitalized and unmechanized compared to that of other sugar-exporting colonies.

Despite these limitations, sugar production expanded in the Philippines. While hemp was concentrated on the highlands and abaca occupied the lowlands, sugar was largely planted in the coastal areas of the islands of Iloilo, Negros, and Panay, where the fertility of the lands and the necessary nutrients provided the necessary environment for sugar plantations. Cuba and Hawaii, which provided similar conditions as the Visayas region, also became sugar centers at the end of the 19th century (Waring and Dorfman 1937, 23–34). It should be noted that numerous other companies and capitalists invested in abaca, tobacco, and hemp. Additionally, the Spanish maintained a monopoly of tobacco (Legarda 1999). When the Americans arrived, the role of all the other cash crops diminished in favor of coconuts (Camba 2018). Sugar and hemp became even more important sectors due to technological changes in the 20th century. Table 8.1 lists the average unit values of sugar, raw abaca, leaf tobacco, and coffee exports.

The types of ownership by European powers, Filipino capital, revenues of the Spanish government, and the work of Philippine agrarian laborers vary largely across these sectors.[8] As Legarda explains, land ownership ranged from the small peasants, who owned some small swaths of land, to the large hacendero landowners. As a result, the production of cash crops depended on these private individuals who either employed or used their own labor, subsidized by the Spanish government through a variety of programs (Legarda 1999, 201).

However, the way these commodities were incorporated into the market varied greatly. The Spanish government had a monopoly on tobacco, which began in the late 18th century, and placed production solely in the hands of the colonial government (Legarda 1999, 231). Sugar, abaca, and

TABLE 8.1. Major Philippine Exports (in Mexican Pesos per Metric Ton)

Year	Sugar	Raw Abaca	Leaf Tobacco	Coffee
1850	66.70	67.52	157.73	200.49
1865	64.83	105.75	332.78	220.97
1880	62.97	105.34	885.51	363.71
1895	34.58	118.23	215.06	141.15

Source: Legarda (1999, 120–21).

other commodities featured joint ventures between European and Filipino capital. However, the dominant feature was financing by the merchant houses, ranging from Russel & Sturgis to Martin Dyce & Co.

Conclusion

We conclude by reiterating the key argument: the Philippines were unique among the Spanish colonies from the 16th to the 18th century, yet this eventually changed from the late 18th century to the end of the regime. In other words, the colonial regime's low levels of centralization make the Philippines a different case from all the other Spanish colonies. There are three crucial features of Spanish Philippines that might have been reproduced as colonial legacies, persisted and continued on in some form until today. First are the unequal land relations started by the Spanish friar lands, encomienda system, and haciendas. While land was eventually commodified in the 19th century, unequal ownership and distribution led to the asymmetry of life outcomes among the Philippine population. Furthermore, the power of the landowners still subsumes numerous agrarian classes of labor or Philippine workers, shaping electoral outcomes, local politics, and personal subjugations. Put simply, provincial and local Philippine elites acquired political power in order to increase their capacity to accumulate economic capital. This means that the degree of centralization was not a prerequisite for these elites to believe that acquiring state power was necessary to increase their economic capacity, which departs from previous scholarship on the harmful effects of state centralization and underlies a different pathway of elite socialization. Second, the Philippines' position as a natural resource exporter in the world economy still remains. The chapter focused on sugar as the primary case of the cash crop. However, similar dynamics emerged in tobacco, hemp, and abaca. Though the Philippine economy created other sectors, agricultural exports—today, in coconut, sugar, and pineapples—remain an important part of the economy. And finally, a colonial legacy of stratification remains intact until today. Though these hierarchies began even before the Spanish arrived, low levels of centralization, which contrasted to Spain's colonial role in Latin America, limited the colonial regime's attempt to homogenize these social hierarchies. While Spain may not have shaped the direction of these hierarchies, it was relatively successful in molding some level of social stratification in the Philippines, which could be seen in religion (the Christian and Muslim divide), land, and markets. While many of these domains were "democratized" during the American period and eventually transformed via education, stratification today reflects land ownership, religion, and market positions. Some of these began with and were shaped by Spanish Philippines.

Our contribution to strengthening inductive category formation in postcolonialism was to empirically trace the formation and continuity of colonial processes that pervade in the Philippines up until today. We enumerated three colonial features of the Spanish Philippines: the unique and asymmetric land relations; the regional or global position as an exporter of natural resources; and the continuing effects of colonial stratification. Our claims rested on recent and innovative historical scholarship on Spanish Philippines as well as our understanding of current social science scholarship on American and contemporary Philippines. Because social science scholars still find the three features today, our chapter links historical and social science scholarship, highlighting the usefulness of focusing on macroeconomic structures while remaining contextually, sensitively, and comparatively cognizant of other Spanish colonies and the global economy. In doing so, we eschew the core peripheral relations that pervaded earlier world systems scholarship and forward postcolonial knowledge through systematic comparisons and grounded data.

We further highlighted the importance of an archipelagic perspective that forwards the mutual interconnections between the colonial and formerly colonized territories in a single analytical framework. Applying what other historians have said about the United States and its former colonies, our chapter finds interconnections in other Spanish colonies despite lacking the clear geographical contiguity yet reflecting deeper historical linkages. For instance, we argued that the Philippines' position within the Spanish colonial regime rejects the narrative of Spain's mercantilist relations with other former Spanish colonies. This unique position became possible due to the Philippines' geographic distance to Spain, the focus of the Spanish Empire and its migrants on the Latin American colonies, and the religious or ideological interests to proselytize China and Japan, which made the Philippines important to religious denominations. In other words, highlighting the Philippines' unique position revealed not only the limited economic role of the Philippines vis-à-vis other Latin American colonies in the Spanish Empire but also the heterogenous, non-economic, and religious interests of Spanish actors. In addition, the heterogeneity of state and nonstate Spanish colonizers in the Philippines gave further agency to Philippine elites to influence political and economic structures.

In other words, an archipelagic perspective highlights how non-economic interests and agents matter to the whole colonial and postcolonial process, rejecting the grand narratives put forward before.

Unfortunately, our chapter does not focus on the gender dimensions of the colonial process. Notably, Filipino scholars have examined the role of women in the Spanish regime. For instance, Ma. Luisa Camagay (1995) discusses Filipino women above and beyond the role of the housekeeper. Camagay discusses women as producers, buyers, and sellers across various industries, such as tobacco production, retail, agriculture, and clothing. She presents records of women during the Spanish regime, disproving the connotation of women as shy, timid, and subservient and showing that Filipino women "had a mind of their own, assertive, active and enterprising." Because Camagay's work only explains a small subset of women's stories in 19th-century Manila, further elaborating the role, position, and importance of women during the Spanish time requires more research.

NOTES

1. We would like to thank Kerby Alvarez, Kristie Flannery, and Ariel Lopez for conversations on the themes and ideas discussed in this chapter.

2. The other leaders were called the *rajah* or *lakan*. But for the sake of this chapter, we opted to use the term *datu*.

3. Across the Malay Peninsula during the Majapahit and Srivajayan empires, wars were waged not to acquire resources or conquer land but simply to acquire prisoners of war to be used for temporary labor in the communities. After serving their time, many of these were set free or were given the choice to join the community.

4. Governance, in this case, refers to the intensity of colonialism, pointing to the number of officials and troops and the amount of economic capital taken from New Spain.

5. What is unique about the Philippine case is Spain's reliance on the galleon trade, which could be summarized in the following terms: The New World or Spanish American galleon brings silver to East-Southeast Asia in exchange for Chinese silk, Indonesian spices, and South Asian ivory. Because East and Southeast Asia suffered from a silver deficit, the Spanish extraction of copper and silver from the mines at Potosi provided the payment for these various commodities, which were subsequently sent back to Europe. The Philippines, therefore, became a trading entrepôt for Spanish and Chinese merchants.

6. Mahoney (2010) argues that mercantilist colonizers seek inward-oriented economies with a preference for the extraction and export of commodities, relying on rents generated from these national monopolies and the repression of wages in the economy. Conversely, liberal colonizers seek to establish rules and institutions to open the economies characterized by free trade.

7. While intensive regimes include the Dutch and the United States, which consolidate newly acquired zones, the Genoese and the British are treated as extensive regimes because of their tendencies to expand the world economy.

8. Legarda's (1999) magnum opus summarizes these economic sectors.

REFERENCES

Arrighi, Giovanni. 1994. *The Long Twentieth Century: Money, Power, and the Origins of Our Times*. London: Verso.

Bernstein, Henry. 1994. "Agrarian Classes in Capitalist Development." In *Capitalism and Development*, edited by Leslie Sklair, 40–71. London: Routledge.

Camagay, Ma. Luisa T. 1995. *Working Women of Manila in the 19th Century*. Quezon City: University of Philippines Press.

Camba, Alvin. 2010. "Diskurso ng Siyensiya: Kolonyal na Diskurso sa mga Sakuna Mula sa Panahon ng Instrumentasyon Tungo sa Panahon ng mga Amerikano." *Daluyan: Journal ng Wikang Filipino* 16 (1): 119–33.

Camba, Alvin. 2012. "Religion, Disaster, and Colonial Power in the Spanish Philippines in the Sixteenth to Seventeenth Centuries." *Journal for the Study of Religion, Nature & Culture* 6 (2): 215–31.

Camba, Alvin. 2017. "The Patterns, Practices, and Direction of Philippine Mining." In *In China's Backyard: Policies and Politics in China's Resource Investments in Southeast Asia*, edited by Jason Morris-Jung, 129–53. Singapore: Institute of Southeast Asian Studies Press (ISEAS-Yusof Institute).

Camba, Alvin. 2018. "The Food Regime in Late Colonial Philippines: Pathways of Appropriation and Unpaid Work." *Journal of Agrarian Change* 19:101–21.

Copeland, Edwin Bingham. 1908. "Spanish Agricultural Work in the Philippines." *Philippine Agricultural Review* 1 (1): 307–18.

Corpuz, Onofre. 1997. *An Economic History of the Philippines*. Quezon City: University of Philippines Press.

Cushner, Nicholas P. 1976. *Landed Estates in the Colonial Philippines*. New Haven: Yale University Southeast Asia Studies.

Foreman, John. 1906. *The Philippine Islands: A Political, Geographical, Ethnographical, Social and Commercial History of the Philippine Archipelago, Embracing the Whole Period of Spanish Rule, With an Account of the Succeeding American Insular Government*. New York: C. Scribner's Sons.

Insigne, Manuel M. 1926. "The Plowman: Custodian of National Wealth Ignored. His Self- Improvement Still a Neglected Truth." *American Chamber of Commerce*. January.

Legarda, Benito Ed. 1999. *After the Galleons: Foreign Trade, Economic Change and Entrepreneurship in the Nineteenth Century Philippines*. Madison: University of Wisconsin Press.

Mahoney, James. 2010. *Colonialism and Postcolonial Development: Spanish America in Comparative Perspective*. Cambridge: Cambridge University Press.

Mawson, Stephanie. 2013. "Unruly Plebeians and the Forzado System: Convict Transportation between New Spain and the Philippines during the Seventeenth Century." *Revista de Indias* 73 (259): 693–730.

Mawson, Stephanie. 2016. "Philippine Indios in the Service of Empire: Indigenous Soldiers and Contingent Loyalty, 1600–1700." *Ethnohistory* 63 (2): 381–413.
Mehl, Eva. 2016. *Forced Migration in the Spanish Pacific World*. Cambridge: Cambridge University Press.
Merchant, Pranav. 2012. "Economic Effects of the Spanish Conquest of the Philippines and Mercantile Theory." *Stanford University Research Journal* 9:53–59.
Moore, Jason. 2007. *Ecology and the Rise of Capitalism*. Berkeley: University of California Press.
Newson, Linda A. 2009. *Conquest and Pestilence in the Early Spanish Philippines*. Honolulu: University of Hawai'i Press.
Phelan, John L. 1959. *The Hispanization of the Philippines Spanish Aims and Filipino Responses 1565–1700*. Madison: University of Wisconsin Press.
Scott, William Henry. 1994. *Barangay: Sixteenth-Century Philippine Culture and Society*. Quezon City: Ateneo University Press.
Waring, Frank, and Ben Dorfman. 1937. "Current Philippine Economics." *American Chamber of Commerce*.
Wickberg, Edgar. 1965. *The Chinese in Philippine Life, 1850–1898*. Ann Arbor: University Microfilms, University of Michigan.

CHAPTER 9

The Political Economy of Power in Contemporary Philippines

Patterns of Continuity and Change

Teresa R. Melgar

Continuity and change are important themes in the Philippines' contemporary political economy. Together, they provide a compelling optic, framing questions of power, voice, access, and contestation: Who has access to the state, and under what conditions are they able to wield institutional power? How do economic resources and political ties determine entry to political institutions? How has state power been used and for what purposes? What factors have allowed these trends to flourish, and to what extent have they changed in contemporary Philippines?

This chapter[1] explores these questions, using them to distill key trends in the political economy of contemporary Philippines. It takes the period following the demise of national authoritarian rule in 1986 as a key reference point, while invoking a much longer historical arc in elaborating key issues. The choice of the post-1986 period is purposive: politically, it marked the restoration of representative institutions, thus signaling the changing contours of the Philippine state. Yet, this period also crystallized much longer historical dynamics in the intersection of political and economic power in the country. The post-authoritarian era thus lends a fascinating window to both change and continuity on this issue.

In discussing such trends, this chapter also explores the relationship of some of the themes examined to postcolonial debates, with the term "postcolonial" understood here as an analytic perspective that is sensitive to the "diverse effects of the interaction between the colonizer and the colonized" (Ioakimidis 2015). The chapter concludes with some implications to the challenge of doing comparisons.

The Changing Philippine Economy: An Overview

To understand the political economy of contemporary Philippines, it is useful to begin with some broad economic trends. In terms of structure, the Philippine economy has undergone several changes in the last few decades (Krinks 2002, 58; Balisacan and Hill 2003). The contribution of agriculture to the gross domestic product (GDP) has been consistently declining, and in 2019, "agriculture, forestry and fishing"[2] as a sector was responsible for only 6.5% of the country's GDP (Philippine Statistics Authority 2020), as seen in table 9.1. The reasons for such decline are complex and include disparities in access to land, policy choices that depress agricultural productivity, and, in some cases, the conversion of cultivable land to industrial and residential use (David 2003; Balisacan and Hill 2003). Yet, some three-fourths of the country's poor can be found working in agriculture, a picture that has not changed much since the 1960s (Balisacan and Hill 2003, 32).

In contrast, industry's share of GDP has been relatively stable, contributing about 30% since the 1970s (Balisacan and Hill 2003, 14; Philippine Statistics Authority 2017). However, the manufacturing sector in the country is relatively small and concentrated only in a few areas. Accounting for 20–25% of the country's GDP since the 1970s (Balisacan and Hill 2003, 14), manufacturing is largely dominated by "food processing, beverages and tobacco" (Hill 2003, 228), while the production of capital goods such as machinery or transport equipment is almost negligible.[3] Resource extractive activities such as "mining and quarrying," which are classified under "industry," have contributed less than 1% to the country's GDP over time (Philippine Statistics Authority 2017, 2020), as seen in table 9.1. This suggests that mining and quarrying have not been historically extensive in the country,[4] even if serious environmental and social costs have characterized these activities in recent decades (Monsod 2012).

The service sector, however, has consistently grown since the 1990s, stimulated by liberalization measures that opened various areas such as telecommunications, banking, and retail trade to both foreign and domestic providers and investors (Abrenica and Llanto 2003, 257–59). In 2019, services accounted for almost half (49%) of the country's GDP, as seen in table 9.1. Given current trends, the service sector is projected to eventually absorb half of the total labor employment in the country (Balisacan and Hill 2003, 13). At the same time, overseas work has become a safety valve for households and the economy: in 2006, foreign remittances constituted some 12.2% of the per capita income of households, up from 6.9% in 1997, thus suggesting the increased importance of overseas work in sustaining local households (Asian Development Bank 2009, 24). This is consistent with findings that showed that some 12% of Filipino households had at least one member who had worked or was working abroad in 2018 (Philippine Statistics Authority and UP Population Institute 2019).

Notwithstanding these changes, some key characteristics of the Philippine economy have persisted, representing a major source of cleavages in contemporary times. Equity remains a pivotal issue, as a small economic elite has retained commanding control of important resources such as agricultural land, mining resources, real estate, or business capital (Riedinger 1995; Krinks 2002). These inequities, in turn, account for much of the disparities in income, life chances, and development prospects of the population (Asian Development Bank 2009, 46–48). Meanwhile, state provision of critical public goods in ways that strengthen inclusion has been minimal relative to public need (Balisacan 2003), as allocation decisions often get subsumed to the clientelist logic of Philippine politics.[5]

Such inequities provide a useful window into the intersection of political and economic dynamics in the country. As sections of the same economic elite dominate the policy-making arena, they often undermine reforms that seek to address these problems. Hence, Philippine economic trends cannot be understood separately from politics, and it is to these issues that we now turn.

Land, Power, and the Making of the Political Elite

As the previous discussion hinted, one of the most enduring characteristics of the Philippine political economy is the close intersection of economic and political power. In its most direct form, control of economic resources becomes the basis either for gaining political power outright or for influencing the direction of state policy.[6] Access to key resources gets parlayed into political power, as wealthy political aspirants are able to secure elective offices, often via an extensive campaign machinery and patronage. Thus, economic elites easily become political elites, their capture of elective offices giving them a pivotal role in shaping state policy.

TABLE 9.1. Philippine Gross National Income and Gross Domestic Product by Origin, 1998–2019 (in Percent) at Constant 2000 Prices

	Annual percent distribution							
SECTORS	1998	2001	2004	2007	2010	2013	2016	2019
Agriculture, forestry, and fishing	11.6	11.9	11.6	11.0	9.7	8.7	7.3	6.5
Agriculture and forestry	9.5	9.9	9.5	8.9	7.7	7.1	6.0	5.4
Fishing	2.2	2.0	2.1	2.2	2.0	1.6	1.3	1.1
Industry	31.0	28.6	27.9	27.6	27.1	27.2	28.3	28.4
Mining and quarrying	0.6	0.5	0.7	0.9	1.0	0.9	0.9	0.8
Manufacturing	21.5	20.7	20.1	19.5	18.5	18.9	19.3	19.2
Construction	5.7	4.3	3.9	4.2	4.8	4.7	5.3	5.7
Electricity, gas, and water supply	3.2	3.1	3.2	3.0	3.0	2.8	2.8	2.7
Services	45.1	44.2	45.4	47.0	46.4	46.9	47.7	49.0
Transport, storage, and communication	5.1	5.6	6.7	7.0	6.2	6.2	6.3	6.2
Trade and repair of motor vehicles, motorcycles, personal and household goods	12.8	13.7	13.9	14.5	13.8	13.8	14.0	14.5
Financial intermediation	4.7	4.5	4.6	5.4	5.5	5.9	6.0	6.5
Real estate, renting, and business activities	8.7	7.7	7.8	8.2	8.6	9.1	9.5	9.3
Public administration and defense, compulsory Social Security	4.9	4.3	4.2	3.8	3.7	3.5	3.3	3.8
Other services	8.9	8.4	8.2	8.1	8.5	8.5	8.6	8.8
Gross domestic product	87.7	84.7	84.9	85.6	83.2	82.8	83.3	83.9
Gross national income	100	100	100	100	100	100	100	100

Source: Adapted from Philippine Statistics Authority (2017, 2020).

But what kinds of economic resources become staging grounds for gaining political power via elective offices? Historically, ownership of land and other property was key to the economic elites' entry into elective positions in the Philippines. Under Spanish colonial rule, this interlocking of economic wealth with political power was already emergent as Spanish colonialists mobilized local village chiefs—then constituting the native "upper class"—to help administer the towns and villages (Simbulan 2005, 29–30).[7]

However, it was not until the early 20th century that economic wealth became especially pivotal to state entry, as US colonial rule set in place a "key institutional innovation" (Anderson 1988): the holding of regular elections, initially for municipal officials and provincial governors and later for national legislative positions and the presidency (Franco 2000, 76–77; Kramer 2006). Attracted by the opportunities they offered for political advancement, landed economic elites, including those engaged in an increasingly profitable export agriculture, contested such positions (Hutchcroft and Rocamora 2003; Anderson 1988; Corpuz 1989). Meanwhile, seeking to win over the elite to the colonial enterprise, the US colonial state also prescribed several property and literacy limitations that, in the process, narrowed the electorate and restricted mass political participation (Franco 2000). In addition, like most societies during this period where the public sphere was deemed a male domain, women did not enjoy the right to vote and run for public office until 1937 (Casambre and Rood 2012), or the latter part of US colonial rule. In this "controlled environment" (Franco 2000, 80), the economic elites who contested these elections were virtually assured of victories, as the small, predominantly propertied and educated male electorate were likely to vote for people from the same gender and class or economic origins. Indeed, as Kramer (2006) notes, this politico-institutional arrangement practically surrendered "local colonial politics" to the elite, "guaranteeing them control over municipal councils and provincial governorships and satisfying their desire for control of their constituents and labor forces" (173).

By the post–World War II period and up to the early 1970s, a pattern that started in the colonial era had become entrenched: landholding elites with economic bases in the provinces also became politically powerful as top municipal or provincial officials or as national legislators. In this sense, the province-based elites fused together economic and political power—and thus high social status and prestige—in a process often aided by the flow of patronage from national to local centers (McCoy 1994b). In the highly clientelist politics of the period, these elites typically acted as patrons, mobilizing plantation workers and other grassroots groups to vote for national state elites through various mechanisms of social control, including outright coercion and the extension of patronage (McCoy 1991, 1994b; Sidel 1999).

In return, local elites were rewarded with state funds, business or commercial opportunities, and other economic privileges that only the national state could bestow (McCoy 1994b), thus further strengthening their economic foothold in the local arena. But such patronage from the national state secured broader objectives as well. By ensuring the flow of resources to their localities and allocating them in clientelist fashion, these province-based elites also enhanced their social control over impoverished grassroots communities, which were often most dependent on such resources.

In this context, although the establishment of such virtual fiefdoms at the provincial or municipal level may have become more pronounced in the post–World War II period, it could be argued that its roots go all the way back to the colonial era. Land titling, export agriculture, and limited electoral competition under Spanish colonial rule provided a foundation for the accumulation of wealth and rudimentary political advancement of different factions of local elites (Franco 2000, 68; 2005, 118). But the opening of a broader range of elective offices to elite Filipinos under US colonial rule made the competition for local control—which was key to, and can be further accomplished by, electoral victory—fiercer and more widespread, thus facilitating the rise of local centers of power in the countryside. In the post–World War II era, the politico-economic elites at the heart of these local centers of power became pivotal to the entrenchment of patronage politics at the municipal, provincial, and national levels.

From a postcolonial perspective that, as noted earlier, is sensitive to the interactional effects of colonial processes and local societies, these encounters between initially Spanish and later US colonial rule and ambitious local elites underscore a particularly crucial moment. Out of this pivotal "interaction" (Ioakimidis 2015), one could trace the rise of politico-economic and institutional arrangements that further deepened these elites' increasingly privileged position in Philippine society, thereby motivating them to seek the long-term stability of such arrangements.

The Return of Representative Democracy

The 1986 democratic transition in the Philippines introduced a new terrain to the Philippine political economy. The demise of Ferdinand Marcos's national authoritarian rule (1972–86) saw the restoration of elections and representative institutions and a reinvigoration of civilian government. At the national level, this meant the establishment of a bicameral national legislature, while at the local level, this entailed the rebuilding of provincial, city, and municipal governments with their own elected executive and legislative officials.[8]

What did the return of representative democracy and its institutions mean for the historically interlocking relationship between wealth and political power in contemporary Philippines? The answer to this question can, in part, be gleaned by examining how most pre-1986 elites returned to political prominence in the country's restored institutions. Under Marcos's authoritarian rule, most of the province-based politico-economic elites found themselves politically marginalized, as the Marcos regime preferred to concentrate its patronage and political support to a narrow circle of its most loyal supporters—the so-called cronies—and their businesses (Hawes 1987; de Dios 1988). Thus, following the 1986 democratic transition, the province-based elites sought to reestablish their dominant positions in provincial or national politics. Ironically, the return of representative democracy provided the opportunity to do so, as these elites reactivated their interlocking economic, political, and social advantages in the new democratic arena.

Amid a democratic transition that mainly restored civil liberties, political rights, and representative institutions, but at the outset did not usher in broader redistributive measures, it was not difficult for most of these elites to rework their way into the new state institutions, especially, but not solely, the national legislature. By retaining significant control over local economic resources—as the Marcos regime did not undertake any considerable economic redistribution program—these elites could mount extensive national or provincial electoral campaigns, either independently or as part of the elite-led electoral vehicles that emerged during this period.[9] Indeed, in the post-1986 period, the huge expenses involved in running for elections in the Philippines as well as the lack of ideologically defined and socially rooted political parties not only posed significant barriers to those who had fewer resources to run for elective office. They also gave economic elites a strong advantage over other electoral challengers to the extent that they arose.[10]

Although there are no systematic analyses of the economic assets that the resurgent economic elites wielded during the immediate post-dictatorship period, individual case studies suggest that agricultural land remained an important source of wealth.[11] However, prefiguring future trends, these elites had also begun to diversify their economic holdings. This trend is captured in the early years of the post-Marcos national legislature, an institution that will be treated more extensively later in this chapter. In the second Congress (1992–95) of the post-dictatorship era,[12] the top economic areas in which members of the House of Representatives had "business and proprietary interests" were agricultural land (58%), property development and real estate (52%), trading (35%), and agricultural enterprises (32%) (Coronel et al. 2004, 38).[13] In this context, the wide-ranging economic interests of this early post-dictatorship batch of legislators reflect the increasingly diverse sources of wealth—aside from land—that supported the resurgent elites' bid for political power.

Most of these traditional elites, however, did not only regain state power via the electoral mobilization of economic resources. As in the post–World War II era, being a part of "political families" whose members previously held national, provincial, or local political offices was likewise pivotal to their national electoral success in the post-1986 period. Historically, such political families often served as a "socializing agent," enabling their members to build ties with other elites, develop valuable political and base-building skills, and generate a common worldview that sustained such interfamily alliances (Coronel et al. 2004; McCoy 1994b). The consolidation of such political families also had a gender component: in some cases, rising politicians were known to expand their networks by marrying prominent female members of political families (Coronel et al. 2004, 91–92). In the absence, once again, of political parties with relatively stable social constituencies, such families and their local patronage networks constituted a virtual political machinery that these traditional elites tapped to support their return to power.

Thus, in the post-1986 period, most of the attributes that structured access to, and control of, state power especially via elective positions remained highly salient. Together with a relatively high social status due to educational backgrounds in law or business (Coronel et al. 2004), these elites' political lineage and control of economic resources typically combined to facilitate access to state power, even if the sources of such wealth have become more varied and are no longer concentrated in land ownership.

The Philippine Congress: Change and Continuity

In the Philippines' post-dictatorship era, no other institution crystallizes the interlocking relationship between wealth, political lineage, and access to political power as strongly as the Philippine Congress, a bicameral body composed of the Senate (upper house) and the House of Representatives (lower house) that serves as the national legislature.[14] In an extensive study, Coronel et al. (2004) documented the economic, political, and social profile of the Congress's members over time, and this chapter draws on some of its finding to highlight key trends.

Tables 9.2 and 9.3 show the business and proprietary interests of two batches of legislators (1998–2001 and 2001–4) in the Senate and House of Representatives during the post-1986 period. It must be noted that a legislator may have business interests or properties in several categories, as the data for these economic sectors is not mutually exclusive.[15] As seen in tables 9.2 and 9.3, in both the Senate and the House of Representatives, post-1986 legislators had a variety of business interests and properties, reflecting the increasingly diverse sources of wealth of those elected to these positions (Coronel et al. 2004). Classifying these legislators' business or proprietary interests according to key Philippine economic sectors reveals another interesting dimension: by the early 2000s, members of both houses of Congress had predominant business interests in the growing "services" sector, followed only by "agriculture" and "industry."[16] Indeed, in contrast to the US colonial and post–World War II eras, agricultural land no longer constituted the main source of legislators' wealth. Instead, real estate, commercial enterprises, and industrial enterprises increasingly made up a significant share of these elites' economic assets and, consequently, their leverage for winning political office.

The Philippine Congress has not changed much in recent years. While no systematic study of legislators' sources of wealth has been done recently, some aggregate, though likely conservative, estimates of their economic status can be gleaned from their annual statements of "net worth."[17] For instance, in the Seventeenth Senate (2016–19), for which the most recent data is available, 2 (8.7%) of the 23 legislators had a net worth of at least 3 billion Philippine pesos (PhP); 19 (82.6%) had a net worth ranging from PhP 10.5 million to PhP 555.3 million; and only 2 (8.7%) had a fairly modest net worth of less than PhP 10 million by the end of December 2018 (Ramos 2019). In effect, multimillionaires and billionaires dominated the Seventeenth Senate, a characteristic that the preceding Sixteenth Senate (2013–16) likewise exhibited.[18]

TABLE 9.2. Profile of Business and Proprietary Interests in the Philippine Senate

	11th Senate (1998–2001) total = 22 senators[a]		12th Senate (2001–4) total = 24 senators	
Economic sector	Number of senators	%	Number of senators	%
Agricultural land	7	32	4	17
Agricultural enterprises	7	32	8	33
Fisheries	1	5	1	4
Banking	—	—	1	4
Financial services	2	9	4	17
Media, publishing, & telecommunications	6	27	6	25
Construction	1	5	3	13
Food manufacturing	3	14	4	17
Nonfood manufacturing	6	27	6	25
Trading	4	18	6	25
Transportation, shipping, and hauling	4	18	5	21
Property development and real estate	13	59	18	75
Hotel, restaurant, travel, and leisure	5	23	7	29
Mining, power, oil, and energy	4	18	4	17
Schools	1	5	1	4
Other sections	10	45	12	50
None declared	5	23	3	13

Source: Coronel et al. (2004, 34).

[a] Coronel et al. (2004) has data only for 22 out of 24 senators because two seats became vacant in the 11th Senate. During their terms of office, Marcelo Fernan passed away and Gloria Macapagal Arroyo vacated her seat to run for the vice presidency.

The Seventeenth House of Representatives (2016–19) was also dominated by the wealthy and propertied. Of the 291 legislators who filed their statements of net worth, 2 (0.7%) were billionaires; 6 (2%) had a net worth of PhP 500 million to PhP 999 million; 92 (31.6%) had a net worth of PhP 50 million to PhP 499 million; and 149 (51.2%) had a net worth of PhP 10 million to PhP 49 million by the end of December 2018. Only 36 (12.4%) legislators in the House had a fairly modest net worth of PhP 1 million to PhP 9 million, and 6 (2%) legislators had a net worth of less than PhP 1 million also by the end of 2018.[19] Hence, as in the Senate, an overwhelming majority of legislators in the lower house reported having extensive economic assets, savings, and incomes.

Political families have likewise retained their strong presence in Congress. In a study of the 297 members of the Seventeenth House of Representatives, Abao (2017a) notes that some 190 (64%) had "links" to political

TABLE 9.3. Profile of Business and Proprietary Interests in the Philippine House of Representatives

	11th House (1998–2001) Total = 220 representatives		12th House (2001–4) Total = 228 representatives	
Economic Sector	Number of representatives	%	Number of representatives	%
Agricultural land	92	42	89	39
Agricultural enterprises	63	29	63	28
Fisheries	24	11	18	8
Banking	33	15	29	13
Financial services	31	14	29	13
Media, publishing, & telecommunications	30	14	34	15
Construction	29	13	18	8
Food manufacturing	25	11	22	10
Nonfood manufacturing	37	17	32	14
Trading	75	34	71	31
Transportation, shipping, and hauling	32	15	33	14
Property development and real estate	115	52	111	49
Hotel, restaurant, travel, and leisure	62	28	58	25
Mining, power, oil, and energy	27	12	24	11
Logging and wood-based industries	13	6	13	6
Schools	13	6	9	4
Other sectors	55	25	53	23
None declared	34	15	38	17

Source: Coronel et al. (2004, 38)

families.[20] In the Seventeenth Senate, 13 (54%) out of 24 senators were identified with such families.[21] This is consistent with findings from earlier years. In 2004, some 135 political families were found to be historically "politically active" in the country's legislature (Coronel et al. 2004, 75). An overwhelming majority of these families had at least one member who occupied a seat in any of the Congresses from 1987 to 2004[22] and at least one member who served in the pre-1987 legislatures.[23] Moreover, of these 135 families, some 44 of them, or about one-third, had members who earlier occupied legislative posts under US colonial rule (Coronel et al. 2004, 75), thus underscoring their continued prominence in Philippine institutional politics.

Policy Making and Development in a Contested Arena

Thus far, this chapter has argued that in the Philippines' post-1986 era, elites who possess economic wealth and resources, a prestigious political lineage, and high social status via education have remained predominant actors in the political arena. But what happens once these economic elites become political elites as well, that is, when they gain access to state power via elections? How has this combination of economic wealth, social status, and political lineage interacted to shape the contours of policy making and development strategies in contemporary Philippines?

To examine how this dynamic has played out, it is crucial to locate the issue in the context of the changing institutional characteristics of the Philippine state. While the Philippine state was highly centralized with a strong executive throughout much of the post–World War II period (Wurfel 1988; Boudreau 2001) and especially under the Marcos regime, since the 1986 democratic transition, important changes have taken place in its institutional characteristics. For one, the executive and legislative branches of government came to play equally substantive roles in governance, with both branches having sufficient powers to steer state action on key issues.[24] Certainly, the Philippine state has also become more decentralized, as local governments assumed an increasing range of powers and responsibilities with the implementation of the 1991 Local Government Code, a decentralization law. But the national state remains a pivotal actor in governance, and its actions often reflect the articulation of older political trends with new or restored institutions.

In this context, while access to the presidency as a source of economic favors and political patronage remains important for traditional elites, winning a seat in the post-dictatorship legislature has become just as crucial. For most of these elites, a legislative seat opens the door to an array of powers and privileges (Coronel et al. 2004), including a platform from which to strategically mobilize the state in support of their interests either individually or as a group.

Not surprisingly, the palpably strong voice and dominant presence of such elites particularly in the legislature have often posed huge obstacles to reform-oriented or redistributive politics (Coronel et al. 2004). As state leaders and policy makers, these economic elites can set the parameters of state action in areas where they have enormous stakes, often leading to the creation of a political environment supportive of their interests. Thus, such elites have remained politically and economically dominant despite subsequent institutional changes in the Philippine state. In power, they have been able to mobilize the restored representative institutions, ironically, to weaken if not directly block any initiative that threatens their privileges, including measures to further democratize political representation and participation.[25]

Direct access to the state has enabled these economic elites to advance specific interests in development strategies as well, including those that underpin equity-enhancing efforts. For instance, reforming the country's regressive tax system to shift the burden of taxation to the top corporate and individual earners has constituted an important redistributive agenda in post-dictatorship politics. But through their legislative powers, economic elites in Congress get to shape such programs in ways that secure particularistic advantages, such as tax reform exemptions for sectors where they have specific business interests or political and financial supporters.[26] In the most recent round of tax reforms in 2017, senators with business interests in real estate and economic zones reportedly secured exemptions for these sectors from the restructured tax rates (Collas-Monsod 2017).

As will be discussed more extensively later in this chapter, Philippine development strategies in the 1990s followed a more liberalized, deregulated path, one anchored on the purported catalytic role of private capital and exports in stimulating economic growth. While the country's lawmakers did not invent this neoliberal development model—as it was the combined product of global shifts in economic thinking and the prescriptions of international lending institutions[27]–its adoption by Philippine economic managers, nonetheless, stood to benefit legislators with economic interests in export-oriented trade, manufacturing, and agribusiness. In this sense, aside from diluting equity-enhancing legislation to protect particularistic economic interests, sections of these elites are also invested in the same development model advanced by the country's top business magnates and corporations, thus making them less likely to act independently of such interests, as policy makers.

Finally, at the municipal or provincial level, economic elites have used their elective positions in the local state, as well as linkages with national government patrons who provide political and state-backed financial support, to gain control of lucrative economic activities and eliminate rivals (Sidel 1999). These coveted activities include resource-extractive ones such as logging, mining, and large-scale fishing; commercial and manufacturing ventures; and transport and property development; and, in some areas of the country, they even include illicit ones such as illegal gambling and smuggling (Sidel 1999; McCoy 1994a). Thus, these elites' access to state power has strengthened their local economic clout as well, in the process contributing to local monopolies and generating grassroots dependence.

Yet, at the same time, these economic cum political elites do not always get to completely wield the state—both national and local—according to their designs. The presence of reformers in other state institutions as well as civil society pressure from the outside can sometimes blunt the conservative thrust of elite dominance, making it possible to achieve a measure of change in some policy arenas. This dynamic is illustrated well by the issue of agrarian reform. In 1988, reformist officials pushed for a radical agrarian reform program that envisioned thoroughgoing land redistribution. But faced with stiff opposition from landed interests in Congress, legislators passed a moderate Comprehensive Agrarian Reform Program (CARP), which accommodated demands from landowners, agribusinesses, and peasant movements instead (Borras, Carranza, and Franco 2007). The program initially sought to redistribute 10.3 million hectares out of a total of 11.28 million hectares of agricultural land, both public and private (Borras 2001). In 1996, and with the availability of better data, the program's coverage was reduced to 8.064 million hectares, aimed at benefiting some four million rural poor households or about 80% of the agricultural population (Borras 2001, 2005).

While CARP had "loopholes" that clearly served elite, landed interests, it retained enough progressive features to advance "land rights claim making" (Borras, Carranza, and Franco 2007) on the ground. According to analysts, the period from 1992 to 2000 was particularly notable, as reformist agrarian reform officials worked closely with rural social movements to achieve "real redistribution" of land to small cultivators even in highly contentious areas (Borras, Carranza, and Franco 2007; Franco 2008; Borras 2001). By 2009, government records show that about 6.2 million hectares of land had been distributed under CARP (Adam 2013). Although these figures do not sufficiently reflect the depth of land tenure reform (Adam 2013) or its economic sustainability, they nonetheless help approximate the program's progress over time.

The extent to which the agrarian reform program has changed land ownership concentration is, however, less straightforward. In 1988, prior to CARP, less than 1% of all families was estimated to own 50% of "officially listed farm land" in the country, thus reflecting its highly skewed pattern of land ownership (Putzel 1992, 28–29).[28] While there has been no comprehensive study on how this picture has changed under CARP, the available data suggests that the program's impact on land ownership concentration is highly variable.[29] In some cases, land ownership has decidedly shifted in favor of peasants and small cultivators, particularly those better organized to press for substantive redistribution under the program (Franco 2008; Adam 2013). In others, landlords and corporate farm owners have been able to evade redistribution, retaining control over huge landholdings by availing of the so-called "landlord-friendly" provisions of the program (Borras, Carranza, and Franco 2007).[30] Yet, on the whole, the critical victories that have been achieved in land redistribution, despite a "compromise" agrarian reform law, illustrate how reformist currents can sometimes gain unexpected headway amid economic elites' overall dominance in national policy making.[31]

Economic elites in post-1986 Philippines, however, have not only sought to influence policy via their direct access to state power as elected officials. Indeed, some of the wealthiest economic elites in the Philippines—including business magnates, property developers, and media and bank owners—do not hold political office. The influence of such elites on state actions has thus been more indirect, though no less important, and is channeled in several ways. One is through the promotion of ideas and dispositions—or an overall political rationality—that embrace the importance of a "business-friendly" environment for growth and stability. Unlike during Marcos's authoritarian years when business leaders' efforts to influence state policies were often circumscribed by the regime's preference for its own cronies,[32] in the post-1986 era, Philippine state leaders have tended to approach business more coherently, seeking wide support for Philippine economic directions (de Dios and Hutchcroft 2003). Amid the state's constant need to sustain investments and "business confidence" in an increasingly globalized environment, these economic elites' dominant presence in key economic sectors provides them with leverage to insist on state support for private sector-led growth.[33]

Although accurate data is difficult to obtain due to the secrecy that often accompanies electoral campaign funding in the country, it is also well known in Philippine politics that these non-state economic elites contribute financially to the electoral campaigns of political candidates (Coronel et al. 2004, 27; Wurfel 1988, 58). In the Philippines' post-authoritarian yet still clientelist politics, such contributions become an implicit investment in a candidate's future policies. By supporting politicians perceived to be supportive of business, these elites seek to secure a favorable policy environment for their own economic interests and for the private sector more generally, in the event of their supported candidates' electoral victory.

State support for business is crucial to these non-state economic elites for several reasons that, when unpacked, also reflect the shifts in the economy since the 1986 democratic transition. As they diversified their economic holdings, most non-state economic elites moved into real estate, construction and property development, banking, commerce, telecommunications, mass media, transport, power generation, and infrastructure development, apparently attracted by their liberalization in the 1990s.[34] The enormous profitability of these sectors is reflected in *Forbes* magazine's list of the Philippines' wealthiest individuals in 2019. The majority of those who occupied the top 10 positions had a variety of business interests in the aforementioned sectors (Forbes 2019).

Since the late 1980s, the Philippine state has also removed most barriers to trade and the entry of foreign investments. While these liberalization measures introduced more competition in areas previously monopolized by some of these economic elites, such as telecommunications (Balisacan and Hill 2003, 27; Abrenica and Llanto 2003), they also opened profitable opportunities for joint ventures with foreign capital in the liberalized sectors (Krinks 2002, 210–11; Abrenica and Llanto 2003, 264). Reflecting the continuing geographically centralized character of Philippine economic activities, these increasingly profitable sectors have remained predominantly centered in Metro Manila, a large urban metropolis, and some "new growth centers" in the immediate surrounding provinces (Balisacan and Hill 2003, 34). Yet also as a sign of international integration, the non-state economic elites at the helm of such profitable sectors have become increasingly connected to the global economy via their expansion into foreign markets and partnership with foreign capital.[35]

The liberalization strategies favored by these non-state economic elites, however, are predicated on the availability of inexpensive, unorganized, and low- or semi-skilled labor. Indeed, the service sector is particularly characterized by non-regular, insecure work and low incomes (Herrin and Pernia 2003, 297), while much of the country's manufacturing—including the so-called export "success story," the electronics subsector—is dependent on inexpensive "unskilled and semi-skilled labor" (Hill 2003, 230, 234) to maintain profitability. In this context, policies that seek to improve working conditions by providing better job security, higher wages, and benefits to labor tend to be contentious in these sectors (Sicat 2009; McKay 2006).

Given the diversification of their economic interests in the post-1986 era, non-state economic elites in the Philippines have enormous stakes in a liberalized economic environment that facilitates further capital growth while controlling labor militancy. By politically and financially supporting state elites who uphold this vision, maximizing recent economic restructuring to prodigiously expand their business ventures, and leveraging their purported indispensability to growth to strengthen state commitment to market-friendly policies, these elites have sustained their dominant economic position in the Philippines' post-authoritarian era.

Concluding Remarks

This chapter has examined some of the critical trends that characterize the contemporary political economy of the Philippines, focusing on the changes and continuities that marked the post-1986 period following the demise of authoritarian rule. In so doing, it underscored the continuing, pervasive role of the control of economic resources, a prestigious and well-connected political lineage, and high social status in structuring access to the state, even if the sources of such wealth may have changed over the years. In the post-authoritarian era, these sources of power have remained highly salient, enabling the return of mostly province-based economic elites linked to political families into critical governance positions. Their control of key policy-making levers in the state has, in turn, created an environment highly skewed to the advancement of particularistic elite interests, thus accounting in large part for their continuing political and economic dominance. In the meantime, mostly urban-based non-state economic elites have expanded their sources of wealth as well, by taking advantage of recent economic restructuring while leveraging their economic power to consolidate state support for further capital growth.

The election of Rodrigo Duterte to the presidency in 2016 has not fundamentally disrupted this dynamic, even as it introduced new elements into this historic entanglement of political and economic power in the country. On the one hand, Duterte's base of power remains firmly rooted among factions of the politico-economic elite, including politicians who were marginalized under specific post-1986 administrations, the Marcoses, and some cronies associated with the Marcos regime, as well as business magnates (Teehankee 2017, 52–53; Claudio and Abinales 2017). His legislative base of support in Congress, and particularly in the House of Representatives, is likewise drawn from predominantly elite politicians identified with the traditional, patronage-driven practices of Philippine institutional politics (Abao 2017b). But Duterte has also buttressed this power base with the strong-arm tactics of an autocrat and a deep disdain for democratic rights, while seeking to appeal to a broad constituency. In this context, the rise to power of Duterte has rekindled an explosive combination of elite political and economic control with a state leader's readiness to quash dissent.

Yet the post-1986 period has not been completely devoid of changes. As elites tried to strengthen their privileges amid the Philippines' changing context, they had to contend with an increasingly politicized civil society and reformers in the state, who sought to change the historic "rules of the game" in the Philippine political economy. While the rise of Duterte may not bode well for democracy, the landscape of popular politics has not been static; civil society groups have remained key harbingers of change. In challenging the narrowing democratic spaces of Philippine politics, they can ignite broader debates on historic inequities in Philippine society, drawing attention to the urgency of deeper reforms that require more, not less, democracy.

This account of the political economy of power in the Philippines has also teased out broad dynamics from which comparisons with other cases may be made. As shown in this chapter, first Spanish rule and later on US colonial rule were foundational to the tight interweaving of political and economic power in the country. Many features of this arrangement have persisted, shaping contemporary state-society relations in ways that have prevented further democratization and equity. Yet, as this chapter has also shown, such deep intertwining of political and economic power has been partially reconfigured by elite choices, state policies, and the challenge posed by progressive social forces over time. When conceptualized as broad dynamics, they provide fertile starting points for pursuing innovative, even unexpected, comparisons with other cases, allowing us to unearth more deeply the historical construction of power and its consequences in different postcolonial settings.

NOTES

1. For helpful comments on earlier versions of this chapter, I am grateful to Hans-Jürgen Burchardt and Johanna Leinius. I also thank Jude Esguerra, Maureen Justiniano, Manuel Sapitula, Cynthia Bautista, and Teresita Melgar for various forms of support to this project.

2. The production and export of bananas, sugar, coconut, and other commercial crops in haciendas and plantations in the country are classified under "agriculture, forestry and fishing."

3. See Hill (2003, 228) for a breakdown of manufacturing output per industry from 1970 to 2000.

4. From 1970 to 1995, mining and quarrying contributed only some 1–2% to GDP. See Balisacan and Hill (2003, 14).

5. See, for instance, the case studies in Coronel (1998).

6. This insight is a running thread in many studies on the Philippine political economy. For an early articulation of this perspective, see Anderson (1988) and Simbulan (2005).

7. Simbulan (2005 16, 29) notes that prior to the coming of the Spaniards, these village chiefs controlled communal lands, trade, and fishing on behalf of the communities they governed. But as they gained privileged status in Spanish colonial society, they managed to enrich themselves by obtaining titles to previously communal lands and by benefiting from a system of forced labor ("*polo*") and the obligatory sale of agricultural produce to the government ("*vandala*").

8. This is provided for in the Constitution of 1987 and the 1991 Local Government Code of the Philippines.

9. See, for instance, the accounts of Turner (1991), Wolters (1991), and McCoy (1991).

10. Törnquist (1993) and Bevis (2006) speak to some of these issues.

11. See, for instance, the case studies in McCoy (1994a), as well as in McCoy (1991) and Coronel et al. (2004).

12. This is officially referred to as the Ninth Congress of the Republic of the Philippines. The Philippines had seven congresses beginning in 1946 as an independent republic, until Ferdinand Marcos abolished the institution with the declaration of martial law in 1972.

13. The House of Representatives had 199 members during this period. As will be noted in subsequent discussions, the categories reflecting these legislators' business and proprietary interests are not mutually exclusive; a legislator may have interests in several categories.

14. The Senate is composed of 24 members elected nationwide. The Philippine Constitution provides that the House of Representatives will be composed of a maximum of 250 members directly elected by plurality from single-member legislative districts, but as of 2016, the country only had 238 of these districts. An additional 20% of the existing membership of the House is reserved for winning candidates in the party list system, which operates via proportional representation and which was implemented beginning in 1998. Since not all parties that run under the party-list system are able to obtain the prescribed minimum 2% of all total votes cast in an election to obtain a seat, the said 20% of House seats may not get filled up in any given election year. Hence, total membership in the House may vary across election years.

15. See the database in the CD entitled "The Ties That Bind," which accompanies Coronel et al.'s (2004) study.

16. In this classification, agricultural land, agricultural enterprises, and fisheries will be categorized under "agriculture, forestry and fishing." Construction, food manufacturing, nonfood manufacturing, mining, power, oil, and energy will be classified under "industry," while logging and wood-based industries will have some

activities categorized under "agriculture, forestry and fishing," and others under "industry." Finally, banking, financial services, media, publishing and telecommunications, trading, transportation, shipping and hauling, property development and real estate, hotel, restaurant, travel and leisure, and schools will be classified under "services."

17. This is based on the "Statement of Assets, Liabilities and Net Worth" (SALN), a document that all Philippine government officials and employees are required to file annually covering the previous year. The "net worth" is computed from one's declared "assets" and "liabilities." It tends to provide a conservative estimate of net worth for at least two reasons: the valuation of "real properties" and "personal properties" is based on their "acquisition cost" and not on current prices and officials are widely believed to understate their assets or income. But while limited, these statements can still give a useful picture of government officials' economic wealth and standing.

18. The 24-member Senate only had 23 seats filled beginning on May 18, 2017, when Senator Alan Peter Cayetano left his seat to serve as secretary of the Department of Foreign Affairs. For an analysis of the SALN of the Sixteenth Senate, see Rappler (2016).

19. Computed from data in the House of Representatives (n.d.) using categories of "net worth" in Abao (2017a). One legislator in this database submitted his SALN only upon assuming office on March 5, 2019.

20. Abao (2017a) breaks down the 190 legislators as follows: 132 had relatives in another elective position; 38 succeeded a relative in the same legislative position; and 20 had a relative who occupied an elective position in the past. As Coronel et al. (2004) note, political families are especially likely to be prominent in the House of Representatives where legislators are elected from single-member districts nationwide that, in turn, tend to be dominated by individual families.

21. According to Abao (2017a), of the 13 senators, 8 had relatives in another elective position and 5 succeeded a relative in the same legislative position. Abao's study counted 24 senators because it included Alan Peter Cayetano, who left his Senate seat on May 18, 2017.

22. This period covers the Eighth (1987–92), Ninth (1992–95), Tenth (1995–98), Eleventh (1998–2001), and Twelfth (2001–4) Congress.

23. For a complete breakdown of these families' membership, see Coronel et al. (2004, 256–60). A small minority of these families had members who occupied legislative seats only in either the 1987–2004 period or the pre-1987 period, but not in both. These, however, were exceptions to the general trend. An overwhelming majority had family members who occupied legislative seats in both periods.

24. For useful discussions on the range of policy issues in which Congress was a key actor in the 1990s, see Wui and Lopez, eds. (1997). See Panao (2014) for an analysis of executive-legislative dynamics shaping the likelihood that Congress will pass a given bill.

25. This is exemplified by the fate of a number of bills in Congress that sought to implement the 1987 Philippine Constitution's prohibition on "political dynasties." None of these bills prospered in any post-Marcos dictatorship Congress due to strong opposition from their members, many of whom come from these political

dynasties. In the Philippines, the term "political dynasty" is often used interchangeably with "political families," in reference to a family or clan who has occupied a similar or a variety of elective positions, over successive generations. For the "anti-dynasty" bills in Congress, see Coronel et al. (2004, 46–52).

26. See, for instance, the account in Coronel et al. (2004, 126–27). Although this account focuses on the expanded value-added tax, which is generally not considered a progressive tax, it is illustrative of the efforts of legislators to secure particularistic advantages for specific sectors where they have business interests or enjoy political support.

27. See Broad (1988) on this issue.

28. Putzel (1992) based his computations on the initial reports of "Listasaka," a land registration program that the government launched in 1988 in preparation for CARP and that, at that time, covered some 80% of "officially listed farm area." He suggests, though, that this does not yet provide a complete picture since landowners may not have reported all their landholdings. See Putzel (1992, 28–29).

29. For a preliminary study on this issue in two rice growing villages, see Ballesteros (2007) and Ballesteros and dela Cruz (2006).

30. According to analysts, there are three "landlord-friendly" modes provided in CARP: voluntary land transfer (VLT), stock distribution option (SDO), and leaseback, which, they argue, have been subject to further manipulation by landowners. For instance, under the VLT mode, which allows landowners to directly sell ("transfer") land to beneficiaries such as tenants, some landowners have named family members as beneficiaries, thus avoiding redistribution beyond a given clan. In some cases, this "transfer" of land is tied to a "leaseback" option where the land is leased to its original owner at rates highly advantageous to the latter. The same is true in the case of the SDO, where corporate farm owners provide shares of stock instead to workers, thus exempting the land from redistribution; analysts have criticized these SDO arrangements for the disadvantageous terms they extended to workers. See Borras, Carranza, and Franco (2007); Borras (2005); and Adam (2013) for an overview of these issues.

31. In 2009, the Philippine Congress passed the Comprehensive Agrarian Reform Program Extension with Reforms (CARPER), a law that extended CARP for another five years, or until 2014. However, a provision of CARPER allows certain aspects of land distribution to continue even after 2014. See Department of Agrarian Reform (2014) on this issue.

32. See, for instance, de Dios (1988).

33. See Block (1987) for a theoretical discussion of some of these issues.

34. For a good overview of these liberalization efforts, see de Dios and Hutchcroft (2003) and Abrenica and Llanto (2003).

35. See Rivera (1994, 94–95) for developments on this issue in the mid- to late 1980s. For an overview of recent efforts of Ayala Corporation, one of the biggest business conglomerates in the country, to expand its overseas operations, often in partnership with foreign capital, see Schnabel (2017, 2018) and Rappler (2018).

REFERENCES

Abao, Carmela. 2017a. "Pluralism, Populism and Their Perversions: Congress in the Time of Duterte (Part 1)." *Rappler*, September 17. https://www.rappler.com/thought-leaders/182416-pluralism-populism-perversions-congress-duterte-part-1

Abao, Carmela. 2017b. "Pluralism, Populism and Their Perversions: Congress in the Time of Duterte (Conclusion)." *Rappler*, September 18. https://www.rappler.com/thought-leaders/182419-conclusion-pluralism-populism-perversions-congress-duterte

Abrenica, Ma. Joy, and Gilberto Llanto. 2003. "Services." In *The Philippine Economy: Development, Policies and Challenges*, edited by Arsenio Balisacan and Hall Hill, 254–80. New York and Quezon City: Oxford University Press and Ateneo de Manila University.

Adam, Jeroen. 2013. "Land Reform, Dispossession and New Elites: A Case Study on Coconut Plantations in Davao Oriental, Philippines." *Asia Pacific Viewpoint* 54 (2): 232–45.

Anderson, Benedict. 1988. "Cacique Democracy in the Philippines: Origins and Dreams." *New Left Review* 169 (May–June): 3–31.

Asian Development Bank. 2009. *Poverty in the Philippines: Causes, Constraints, and Opportunities*. Mandaluyong City, Philippines: Asian Development Bank. https://www.adb.org/sites/default/files/publication/27529/poverty-philippines-causes-constraints-opportunities.pdf

Balisacan, Arsenio. 2003. "Poverty and Inequality." In *The Philippine Economy: Development, Policies and Challenges*, edited by Arsenio Balisacan and Hall Hill, 311–41. New York and Quezon City: Oxford University Press and Ateneo de Manila University.

Balisacan, Arsenio, and Hall Hill. 2003. "An Introduction to the Key Issues." In *The Philippine Economy: Development, Policies and Challenges*, edited by Arsenio Balisacan and Hall Hill, 3–44. New York and Quezon City: Oxford University Press and Ateneo de Manila University.

Ballesteros, Marife. 2007. "Has Land Reform Improved on Ownership Inequality? Evidence from Philippine Rice Growing Villages." *Policy Notes* 2007–6:1–6. https://dirp4.pids.gov.ph/ris/pn/pidspn0706.pdf

Ballesteros, Marife, and Alma dela Cruz. 2006. "Land Reform and Changes in Land Concentration: Evidence from Rice Growing Villages in the Philippines." Discussion Paper Series No. 2006–21 (unpublished). https://dirp4.pids.gov.ph/ris/dps/pidsdps0621.pdf

Bevis, Gwendolyn. 2006. "Building Programmatic Parties in a Patronage Dominated System: Akbayan and the Liberal Party in the Post-1986 Philippines." PhD diss., University of Wisconsin–Madison.

Block, Fred. 1987. "The Ruling Class Does Not Rule: Notes on the Marxist Theory of the State." In *Revising State Theory: Essays in Politics and Post-Industrialism*, 51–68. Philadelphia: Temple University Press.

Borras, Saturnino, Jr. 2001. "State-Society Relations in Land Reform Implementation in the Philippines." *Development and Change* 32: 531–361.

Borras, Saturnino, Jr. 2005. "Can Redistributive Reform Be Achieved via Market-Based Voluntary Land Transfer Schemes? Evidence and Lessons from the Philippines." *Journal of Development Studies* 41 (1): 90–134. DOI: 10.1080/0022038042000276581.

Borras, Saturnino, Jr., Danilo Carranza, and Jennifer Franco. 2007. "Anti-poverty or Anti-poor? The World Bank's Market-Led Agrarian Reform Experiment in the Philippines." *Third World Quarterly* 28 (8): 1557–76.

Boudreau, Vincent. 2001. *Grassroots and Cadre in the Protest Movement*. Quezon City, Philippines: Ateneo de Manila University Press.

Broad. Robin. 1988. *Unequal Alliance: The World Bank, the International Monetary Fund, and the Philippines*. Berkeley: University of California Press.

Casambre, Athena Lydia, and Steven Rood. 2012. *Early Feminism in the Philippines*. March 7. https://asiafoundation.org/2012/03/07/early-feminism-in-the-philippines/

Claudio, Lisandro, and Patricio Abinales. 2017. "Dutertismo, Maoismo, Nasyonalismo." In *A Duterte Reader: Critical Essays on Rodrigo Duterte's Early Presidency*, edited by Nicole Curato, 93–110. Quezon City, Philippines: Ateneo de Manila University Press.

Collas-Monsod, Solita. 2017. "'Papa Bear,' 'Mama Bear,' 'Ice Queen.'" *Philippine Daily Inquirer*, December 2. http://opinion.inquirer.net/109165/papa-bear-mama-bear-ice-queen

Coronel, Sheila, ed. 1998. *Pork and Other Perks: Corruption and Governance in the Philippines*. Pasig, Philippines: Philippine Center for Investigative Journalism.

Coronel, Sheila, Yvonne Chua, Luz Rimban, and Booma Cruz. 2004. *The Rulemakers: How the Wealthy and Well-Born Dominate Congress*. Quezon City, Philippines: Philippine Center for Investigative Journalism (with CD database entitled "The Ties That Bind").

Corpuz, O. D. 1989. *The Roots of the Filipino Nation, Vol. II*. Quezon City, Philippines: Aklahi Foundation.

David, Cristina. 2003. "Agriculture." In *The Philippine Economy: Development, Policies and Challenges*, edited by Arsenio Balisacan and Hall Hill, 175–218. New York and Quezon City: Oxford University Press and Ateneo de Manila University.

de Dios, Emmanuel. 1988. "The Erosion of the Dictatorship." In *Dictatorship and Revolution: Roots of People's Power*, edited by Aurora Javate de Dios, Petronilo BN. Daroy, and Lorna Kalaw-Tirol. Metro Manila: Conspectus Foundation.

de Dios, Emmanuel, and Paul Hutchcroft. 2003. "Political Economy." In *The Philippine Economy: Development, Policies and Challenges*, edited by Arsenio Balisacan and Hall Hill, 45–73. New York and Quezon City: Oxford University Press and Ateneo de Manila University.

Department of Agrarian Reform (DAR). 2014. "Land Distribution to Continue Even after June 30, 2014." http://www.dar.gov.ph/national-news/795-land-distribution-to-continue-even-after-june-30-2014

Forbes. 2019. "Philippines' 50 Richest." *Forbes*. https://www.forbes.com/philippines-billionaires/list/

Franco, Jennifer Conroy. 2000. *Campaigning for Democracy: Grassroots Citizenship Movements, Less-than-Democratic Elections, and Regime Transition in the Philippines*. Quezon City, Philippines: Institute for Popular Democracy.

Franco, Jennifer Conroy. 2005. "On Just Grounds: The New Struggle for Land and Democracy in Bondoc Peninsula." In *On Just Grounds: Struggling for Agrarian Justice and Citizenship Rights in the Rural Philippines*, edited by Jennifer Franco and Saturnino Borras, 115–94. Quezon City, Philippines: Institute for Popular Democracy.

Franco, Jennifer Conroy. 2008. "Making Land Rights Accessible: Social Movements and Political-Legal Innovation in the Rural Philippines." *Journal of Development Studies* 44 (7): 991–1022. DOI: 10.1080/00220380802150763.

Hawes, Gary. 1987. *The Philippine State and the Marcos Regime: The Politics of Export*. Ithaca: Cornell University Press.

Herrin, Alejandro, and Ernesto Pernia. 2003. "Population, Human Resources, and Employment." In *The Philippine Economy: Development, Policies and Challenges*, edited by Arsenio Balisacan and Hall Hill, 283–310. New York and Quezon City: Oxford University Press and Ateneo de Manila University.

Hill, Hall. 2003. "Industry." In *The Philippine Economy: Development, Policies and Challenges*, edited by Arsenio Balisacan and Hall Hill, 219–53. New York and Quezon City: Oxford University Press and Ateneo de Manila University.

House of Representatives, Philippine Congress. n.d. *Summary Report of Declared Assets, Liabilities and Net Worth of Members of the House of Representatives as of 31 December 2018*. http://www.congress.gov.ph/download/

Hutchcroft, Paul, and Joel Rocamora. 2003. "Strong Demands and Weak Institutions: The Origins and Evolution of the Democratic Deficit in the Philippines." *Journal of East Asian Studies* 3:259–92.

Ioakimidis, Vasilios. 2015. "Neocolonialism and Social Work." In *International Encyclopedia of the Social and Behavioral Sciences, 2nd edition*, edited by James Wright, 456–61. Waltham, MA: Elsevier. https://www.sciencedirect.com/topics/social-sciences/postcolonia-lism

Kramer. Paul. 2006. *The Blood of Government: Race, Empire, the United States, and the Philippines*. Chapel Hill: University of North Carolina Press.

Krinks, Peter. 2002. *The Economy of the Philippines: Elites, Inequalities and Economic Restructuring*. London: Routledge.

McCoy, Alfred. 1991. "The Restoration of Planter Power in La Carlota City." In *From Marcos to Aquino: Local Perspectives on Political Transition in the Philippines*, edited by Benedict Kerkvliet and Resil Mojares, 105–42. Quezon City, Philippines: Ateneo de Manila University Press.

McCoy, Alfred. 1994a. *An Anarchy of Families: State and Family in the Philippines*, edited by Alfred McCoy. Quezon City, Philippines: Ateneo de Manila University Press and Center for Southeast Asian Studies, University of Wisconsin–Madison.

McCoy, Alfred. 1994b. "'An Anarchy of Families': The Historiography of State and Family in the Philippines." In *An Anarchy of Families: State and Family in the Philippines*, edited by Alfred McCoy, 1–32. Quezon City, Philippines: Ateneo de Manila University Press and Center for Southeast Asian Studies, University of Wisconsin–Madison.

McKay, Steven. 2006. *Satanic Mills or Silicon Islands: The Politics of High-Tech Production in the Philippines*. Ithaca: Cornell University Press.

Monsod, Christian. 2012. "Mining Is a Social Justice Issue." *Rappler*, March 4. https://www.rappler.com/thought-leaders/2065-mining-is-a-social-justice-issue

Panao, Rogelio Alicor. 2014. "Beyond Roll Call: Executive-Legislative Relations and Lawmaking in the Philippine House of Representatives." *Philippine Political Science Journal* 35 (1): 59–77. http://dx.doi.org/10.1080/01154451.2014.903554

Philippine Statistics Authority. 2017. "Table 6B: Gross National Income and Gross Domestic Product by Industrial Origin, 1998–2016 at Constant 2000 Prices." In *Annual National Accounts (1998–2016) at Current and Constant 2000 Prices*, April 6.

Philippine Statistics Authority. 2020. "Table 6B: Gross National Income and Gross Domestic Product by Industrial Origin, 1st Quarter 2017 to 4th Quarter 2019 at Constant 2000 Prices." In *National Accounts of the Philippines (1st Quarter 2017 to 4th Quarter 2019)*, January. https://psa.gov.ph/sites/default/files/Q4%202019%20NAP%20Publication-9ch3.pdf

Philippine Statistics Authority and University of the Philippines Population Institute. 2019. *2018 National Migration Survey*. https://psa.gov.ph/sites/default/files/2018%20NMS%20Final%20Report.pdf

Putzel, James. 1992. *A Captive Land: The Politics of Agrarian Reform in the Philippines*. London and New York: Catholic Institute for International Relations and Monthly Review Press.

Ramos, Pamela. 2019. "The Net Worth of Philippine Senators." *ABS-CBN News*, May 27. https://news.abs-cbn.com/news/multimedia/infographic/05/27/19/the-net-worth-of-philippine-senators

Rappler. 2016. "Cynthia Villar, Richest Senator; Escudero, Poorest." *Rappler*, May 17. https://www.rappler.com/nation/133334-villar-richest-senate-saln-2015

Rappler. 2018. "Ayala Land Takes Majority Control of Malaysian Construction Firm." *Rappler*, January 3. https://www.rappler.com/business/192777-ayala-land-majority-control-malaysia-mct-berhad

Riedinger, Jeffrey. 1995. *Agrarian Reform in the Philippines: Democratic Transitions and Redistributive Reform*. Stanford: Stanford University Press.

Rivera, Temario. 1994. *Landlords and Capitalists: Class, Family, and State in Philippine Manufacturing*. Quezon City, Philippines: UP Center for Integrative and Development Studies and University of the Philippines Press.

Schnabel, Chris. 2017. "Ayala's IMI Acquires British Electronics Manufacturer STI." *Rappler*, April 7. https://www.rappler.com/business/166339-imi-acquires-sti-ayala-group

Schnabel, Chris. 2018. "Manila Water Expands into Thailand." *Rappler*, February 19. https://www.rappler.com/business/196405-manila-water-expansion-thailand

Sicat, Gerardo. 2009. "Labor Policies and Philippine Companies: Analysis of Survey Opinions." *Philippine Journal of Development* 36 (2): 1–46.

Sidel, John. 1999. *Capital, Coercion and Crime: Bossism in the Philippines*. Stanford: Stanford University Press.

Simbulan, Dante. 2005. *The Modern Principalia: The Historical Evolution of the Philippine Ruling Oligarchy*. Quezon City, Philippines: University of the Philippines Press.

Teehankee, Julio. 2017. "Was Duterte's Rise Inevitable?" In *A Duterte Reader: Critical Essays on Rodrigo Duterte's Early Presidency*, edited by Nicole Curato, 37–56. Quezon City, Philippines: Ateneo de Manila University Press.

Törnquist, Olle. 1993. "Democratic 'Empowerment' and Democratization of Politics." *Kasarinlan* 8 (3): 22–57.

Turner, Mark. 1991. "Politics during the Transition in Zamboanga City, 1984–1988." In *From Marcos to Aquino: Local Perspectives on Political Transition in the Philippines*, edited by Benedict Kerkvliet and Resil Mojares, 13–35. Quezon City, Philippines: Ateneo de Manila University Press.

Wolters, Willem. 1991. "New Beginning or Return to the Past in Nueva Ecija Politics?" In *From Marcos to Aquino: Local Perspectives on Political Transition in the Philippines*, edited by Benedict Kerkvliet and Resil Mojares, 206–25. Quezon City, Philippines: Ateneo de Manila University Press.

Wui, Marlon, and Ma. Glenda Lopez, eds. 1997. *State-Civil Society Relations in Policy-Making (Philippine Democracy Agenda Vol. 2)*. Quezon City, Philippines: Third World Studies Center, University of the Philippines Diliman.

Wurfel, David. 1988. *Filipino Politics: Development and Decay*. Quezon City, Philippines: Ateneo de Manila University Press.

PART 3

The Past and Present of the Hierarchization of Difference and Power in Cuba, Puerto Rico, and the Philippines

CHAPTER 10

Spanish Colonization's Mark on Cuba

Javiher Gutiérrez Forte and Janet Iglesias Cruz

The colonial, as a defining feature of what makes a colony, can be understood as a network of relations, knowledges, and behaviors. Colonial relations do not end when the political and economic link with the metropolis is cut. Many of the features that characterized the colonial period, such as segregation, subordination, racism, sexism, poverty, and despotism, are an enduring part of that colonial legacy. Neither Cuba nor its colonizer Spain can escape it. One example may suffice: when studying the almost four centuries of Spanish colonialism in the Americas, it is necessary to keep in mind that the monarchy's social, political, and economic structures underwent several transformations during that time. One must not forget that the Spanish Empire and the Spanish state emerged at the same time. And it was in the midst of this process that the revolutions for independence and political changes occurred, which did not necessarily bring about radical transformations in the New World's societies.[1]

In Cuba, colonial relations were changing up until what is known as modern colonialism. The Spanish government could do little in regard to the modernizing transformation of its colonial empire. Its last colonies—Cuba, Puerto Rico, and the Philippines—in varying degrees, were those that went through this modernizing process in colonial relations, a process that was more a plan than a reality. For Cuba in particular, modernization was more an evolution of endogenous forging, against which the metropolitan authority maintained an often hostile attitude. In view of the peninsula's inability to develop modern colonialism, economic relations with

England, France, Holland, and the United States shaped the formation and consolidation of a Cuban economy that primarily produced raw materials for the global market.

But did colonial relations persist beyond the crumbling of the Spanish Empire in 1898? Our chapter aims to show that the answer to that question is unquestionably yes. To this end, emphasis is placed on the actions of the elite in the evolution and development of the Cuban state and society; on the link between the sugar industry, slavery, and racism; and on the role of the Catholic Church and the segregation of women.

In this chapter, we highlight the importance of studying the nearly 400 years of colonial rule in Cuba, since failing to recognize these years would make it impossible to understand the formation of Cuban society as it exists today. It is during the colonial stage that a profoundly unequal society—concerning skin color, place of origin, gender, and the appropriation of wealth—gradually established itself. By the same token, during the long colonial period, a political culture and a politico-administrative structure were established that have shaped Cuba until this day. Moreover, the island's environment also acquired its definitive traits.

Havana, Key to the New World

The geographic location of the largest Antillean Island in the middle of the Americas secured its importance in the Spanish colonial empire's development as an obligatory crossing point. For this reason, when Spanish ships packed with goods from the Americas were besieged by privateers and pirates and the Crown created a fleet system that would protect its riches, Cuba was the center from which the fleet left to collect revenue from the different ports of the Americas and where it then returned to gather for its return to Spain. This not only helped to invigorate the island's economy[2] but also allowed the island's inhabitants to stay well informed of the events that took place in the Americas as well as in Europe.

The island's progress was unequal, since only Havana, its port, and the residents closest to it benefited from these exchanges. This caused the west of the island to become the site of the greatest economic development. The rest of the island's residents often had to resort to ransom and contraband trade to survive. Island-wide, this generated great differences in development between Cuba's east and west. For example, in 1757, 50.93% of the archipelago's entire population was settled in Havana and its hinterland, and 87 of 95 sugarcane mills (*trapiches* and *ingenios*) and 2,205 of the 2,763 tobacco farms (*vegas*) were located there (Torres 1994, 276).

This regional differentiation deepened during the 19th century. By 1899, 424,804 of Cuba's 1,572,797 inhabitants were concentrated in Havana; that is, 27% of the total population lived in one single province out of an existing six. Continuing this trend, by the end of the 19th century, the capital housed 242,055 people, or 15.4% of the total number of islanders (DWD USA 1900, 10–15).

The ruthless exploitation of the island's land was on par with the increasing cruelty of the exploitation of slaves. A consequence of this was the disappearance of much of the island's woodlands, which existed upon the arrival of the Europeans. While sugar production increased through the exploitation of slave labor, the forest cover was likewise sacrificed to the steam boilers of the mills and locomotives. Out of the 80% of existing woodlands at the end of the 18th century, only 15% survived by the first quarter of the 20th century (Funes Monzote 2010, 21, 417).

Cuba's Population

It has been estimated that, at the time of the arrival of the Europeans, the indigenous population throughout Cuba's archipelago numbered between 60,000 and 100,000 people. In the wake of more recent archaeological investigations, this number has been raised to between 200,000 and 500,000 individuals (Domínguez, Febles, and Rives 1994, 7; Pérez de la Riva 1973, 2–24).

During the process of conquest and colonization, the first Europeans settled on the island, giving way to a new transculturation in which the native population was exterminated or absorbed by the colonizers. New diseases, a ruthless pace of work with no discernible end, and the invasion of their cultural universe contributed to the physical demise of many of Cuba's native inhabitants. Another large portion of the population intermarried with the colonizers, mixing in such a way that their subsequent presence was difficult to measure, beyond the existence of towns with indigenous names like Guanabacoa or Jiguaní. By 1550, fewer than 2,000–3,000 natives remained throughout the entire island (Domínguez, Febles, and Rives 1994).

Shortly after the arrival of the European colonizers, Africans were brought to Cuba—first gradually, then in larger numbers, generally against their will, and usually as slaves.[3] These groups of people formed the initial mix of what Fernando Ortiz (2002, 35) has labeled the "*ajiaco Cubano*" (Cuban stew), which later continued to expand and gave way to Cubanness (Iglesias Cruz and Gutiérrez Forte 2006) as the expression of Cuban culture's essence derived from these hybridizations.

According to the Cuban historian Juan Pérez de la Riva, between the beginning of the 16th century and the end of the 17th century, 225,000 immigrants, by choice or through slavery, arrived at the Cuban archipelago. In the 19th century, these numbers increased to 1,200,000, of which blacks constituted half. This differs from the migration in the first three decades of the 20th century, when 1,800,000 individuals came to the island, three-fourths of whom were Spanish.

Offering further information on these figures, Pérez de la Riva (1973) states that between 1511 and 1886, 700,000 Africans came to Cuba in successive waves. The massive enslavement of Africans has been described as "the most magnificent drama in the last thousand years of human history" (DuBois 1935, in Rediker 2016, 4). The cruel conditions in which people were packed together in the slave ships that crossed the Atlantic alone caused the deaths of an estimated 1,800,000 individuals (Rediker 2016, 4).

In the mid-19th century, following the signing of international treaties that sought to put an end to the African slave trade and replace it with other sources of labor, 125,000 Chinese laborers arrived in Cuba in an attempt to guarantee the workforce needed for the Cuban plantations (Pérez de la Riva 1973). At the end of Spanish rule in 1899, Cuba had 1,572,797 inhabitants, which is 9.2 times the 171,620 inhabitants reported in 1775. The Cuban population on the eve of independence is shown in table 10.1.[4] As can be noted in figure 10.1, in 1899 Cuba had 57,613 more men than women, with men accounting for 3.6 percent more of the population. The apparent imbalance between the two genders was due to the large waves of migration to Cuba made up of a majority of young men who were responding to Cuba's need for labor. The breakdown by skin color provided by the 1900 census is shown in figure 10.2.

Like most societies in the world, Cuban society was a patriarchal one, where women were subordinate to men. Women were destined to dedicate themselves to their families, tending to their marriage and the children's

TABLE 10.1. Cuban Population in 1899

Total	**1,572,797**
White	1,064,354
Female	486,547
Male	577,807
Colored	505,443
Female	267,545
Male	237,898

Source: Adapted from DWD USA (1900, 87–88).

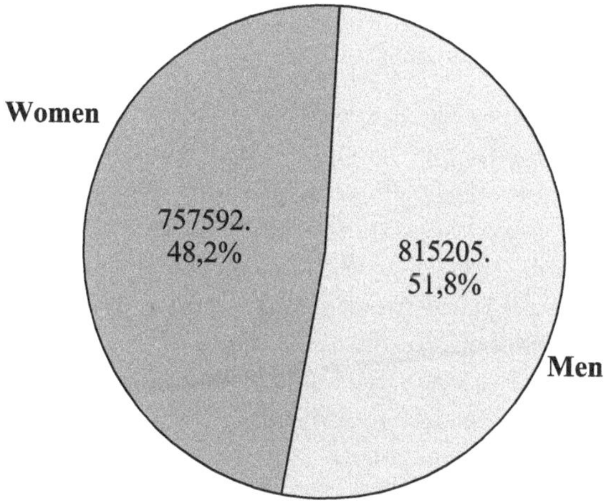

Fig. 10.1. Proportion of the Cuban population by sex in 1899
Source: Adapted from DWD USA (1900, 87–88).

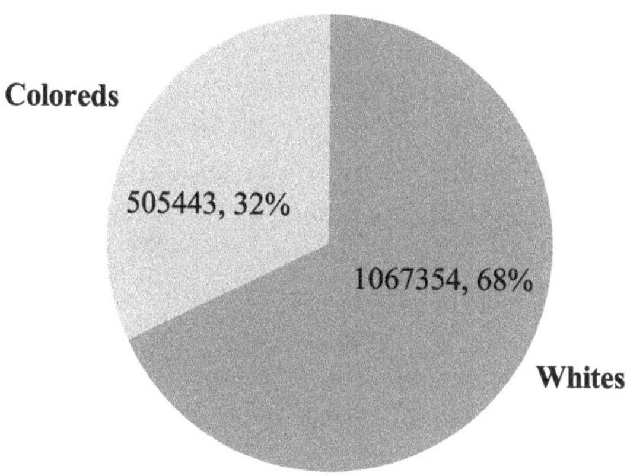

Fig. 10.2. Proportion of the Cuban population by skin color according to the 1900 census
Source: Adapted from DWD USA (1900, 87–88).

education. In the case of the elite, women were used as tools that, through marriage, facilitated the attainment of power and riches. Women's fight for their rights began to become visible at the end of the closing years of the 19th century. An example of this is found in the creation of the magazines *Minerva* and *La Armonia*, in which black and mixed-race women articulated their interests (Barcia Zequeira 2009, 85).

Women's subordinate position and the discrimination they faced, however, did not change with the end of colonial rule. Proof of this is found in the Cuban media's reaction to a Cuban politician's proposal in 1907 to extend the right to vote to women: such a suggestion was roundly mocked by the island's press (Gutiérrez Forte 2016, 61–62).

The Colonial Elites

Since the start of Cuba's conquest and colonization at the beginning of the 16th century, Creole elites emerged throughout the island. Generally, these groups were made up of white men, most of whom had settled in Havana and its hinterland. The possession of large expanses of land was another means of differentiation that served as a basis on which to organize the island's new society. Initial land distributions took into account what each of the colonizers had contributed to the conquest.

However, the large estates were not the result of these distributions, since the settlements and the haciendas created during the first two centuries of colonial rule did not extend inland into the island's territory but were instead kept along riverbanks and near the coast. Later, at the end of the 16th century, when the island's economic system of mineral extraction—gold and copper—was changed to one of livestock exploitation, the first large estates were established on the inner parts of the island. This led to the formation of the first powerful families, such as the Rojas and Recios, whose descendants played important roles in the economic and political life of the island during the 16th and 17th centuries (Sorhegui D'Mares 2010, 47–136; Barcia Zequeira 1998, 24–45). It is necessary to emphasize that during these initial years, agriculture primarily took the form of subsistence farming, though part of it was set aside for the colonizers' continental expeditions. Later, the planting and harvesting of tobacco led to production geared toward the external market. But it was the sugar industry that made the linkage to the global market more definitive.

The island's oligarchy, characterized by the possession of land, came to include prominent traders—many of whom had recently arrived from the Iberian Peninsula and some of whom were linked to the peninsula's nobility—who traded in the resources produced by the island and those that it needed. One of the island's needs was a workforce, whether slaves or otherwise. Many of these traders subsequently managed to become hacienda owners and even sugar producers. This process did not occur without opposition from the old colonizing elite. The intervention of the Crown's representatives was necessary for the acceptance of these new groups into positions of power, like the Havana town council (Sorhegui D'Mares 2010, 130–42). By the end of the 18th century and into the beginning of the 19th century, the immigrants dominated all aspects of sugar processing, from the agricultural side of the planting and harvesting of sugarcane, to its transformation into sugar, to its transportation to ports where it was shipped off to the global market. This converted these traders into landowners, as they assumed possession of land as an emblematic feature of the oligarchy (Moreno Fraginals 1978, 71–77; García Rodríguez 2007, 27–34). Members of the peninsular bureaucracy used the power they wielded in public office to acquire land as well, assimilating into the island's landowning oligarchy. Starting in the 16th and 17th centuries, traders and bureaucrats used marriage to increase their riches and enter into the powerful class of Creole elites, marrying the descendants of the Creole oligarchy's most important families.

These transformations coincided with the Spanish Crown's efforts to limit the influence of the island's landowning oligarchy formed by the colonizers' descendants, by creating incentives for the peninsular population to move to Cuba. We need to remember that, because Cuba was a settler colony,[5] town councils governed the first townships (Ayala 1988). These town councils were composed of the most prominent members of the colonizers' troops.[6] In many cases, their descendants continued the work of their forefathers in these government institutions. Once elected to the town councils, appointees saw to the island oligarchy's needs and aspirations, which were not always in line with the peninsular government's interests. These power structures became the primary tool through which the elites consolidated their hegemony. The composition of the local colonial government and its prerogatives changed over time, but they were always at loggerheads with the island's other two major powers: the governor and/or captain general, their representatives, and the Catholic Church.

The existence of a governor in Cuba, a position that later would become that of captain general, did not prevent the island's elite-run town councils from serving as the government's basis. It is also important to keep in mind that many of the families that belonged to these powerful groups had representatives in the peninsular court, which allowed for the further strengthening of the island's town councils. Starting in the 19th century, various steps were taken to diminish the town councils' power, which tipped the scale of power in favor of the captain general. The monarchy won this struggle for power when it endowed its highest representative, the captain general, with major powers, thus contributing to the centralization of Cuban politics and administration. In spite of this, it cannot be omitted that the island's captain general always governed in concert with the island's various elite groups—and always with a preference for those of peninsular origin—which is why the island's elite always played an important role in political, social, and economic life. An example of this is found in the fact that many Cuban-born men held important political positions at both the regional and imperial levels.[7]

Even though traders and bureaucrats joined the town council at the end of the 16th century and the beginning of the 17th century, in the inland townships, these two sectors did not attain the same political influence that they had achieved in the Cuban capital. In Havana's town council, these sectors managed to occupy key positions in the governing body, such as in the treasury and accounting, which opened up the possibility of entering into the oligarchic landowning class. The inclusion of traders and bureaucrats in the island's oligarchy put an end to the former hegemony of the families of the colonizers' descendants, who found themselves obligated to share power.

The Catholic Church and Colonial Development

In the townships and villages where town councils were being formed, churches were also being erected to provide residents with the necessary religious services. Since Cuba was a settler colony, the Catholic kings Fernando and Isabel deemed it unnecessary to send religious orders to Christianize the region, as was done in continental America. Instead, church personnel were sent to lead services for a population made up of the Spanish subjects who inhabited the island and who were understood to be practicing Catholics. In the first years of colonial rule, it was a requirement that everyone who set off to the New World be baptized, including slaves (Torres Cuevas and Leiva Lajara 2007, 85–92).

This requirement did not impede the arrival of a variety of monastic orders, like the Franciscans and the Dominicans, who were the first to arrive in Cuba. In fact, the Dominicans were granted permission to fund a university, which was established in the order's convent on January 5, 1728, and remained the only Cuban university during the colonial period. At the end of the 17th century, several authorities on the island, such as the bishop of Compostela, endeavored to attract the Jesuit order due to its renowned teaching quality. It was hoped that inviting them to Cuba would compel them to take charge of the island's educational development.[8]

Since the beginning of Spanish colonization, the Catholic Church tried to control Cuban inhabitants' life—birth, education, marriage, all the way through to death. This could not be completely achieved, as is evidenced in the first diocesan synod, which attempted to reform the island's church due to the population's and prelates' licentious customs (Torres Cuevas and Leiva Lajara 2007, 262–74).

One of the characteristics of Spanish colonization in the Americas was the Catholic Church's subordination to the Spanish monarchs in the *patronato* system (Torres Cuevas and Leiva Lajara 2007, 51–82). This led to the church's establishment as one of the pillars of the monarchy's consolidation. Unlike the church in other Latin American nations, the Cuban church was not a major landowning economic power. Though it owned lands, these lands were not as sizeable as those in other locations in the Americas. This meant that the church was, to a large extent, a tool of the sugar-producing elite (Torres Cuevas 1994, 290). All the same, the church ended up supporting slavery, owning slaves, and becoming an efficient agricultural producer. What was produced on their lands served for their subsistence needs as well as the global market, and they had estates for livestock as well as for sugar and tobacco production (Leiva Lajara 2007, 289–93). Proof of the Catholic Church's complicity in slavery (at least during the 18th century) was the Society of Jesus's ownership of four sugar mills equipped with 128 slaves. The Convent of Saint Catherine of Siena, for its part, owned a sugar mill worked by 24 slaves (García Rodríguez 2007, 336–45). In addition to dictating and regulating the island residents' morals, the Catholic Church played an essential role in the population's education, which prioritized basic literacy. It was also in charge of health and charitable organizations (Torres Cuevas and Leiva Lajara 2007, 312, 330–40, 428–37).

Black and mixed-race men (and most certainly women) were barred from attending the Dominican order's university and the seminary schools in Havana or Santiago de Cuba. To access the knowledge imparted there, one had to be male, and applicants had to provide documents that proved the purity of their blood, which entailed not being the descendant of Moors or Jews, converts or not, and having proof, at least four generations back, of a lineage of white Catholic ancestors.

Toward the end of the 18th century and the beginning of the 19th century, the island's elite succeeded in forming a Creole clergy who attended to their interests and not to those of the monarchy. This changed with the advent of the continental Americas' independence and the arrival of Spanish clergy who were driven out of these regions. Furthermore, the secularization that began in Spain, which stripped the church of much of its property, meant, among other things, that the church lost leadership of the university. This, along with other factors, led to the weakening of the Creole Catholic Church's influence in the island community. Nonetheless, this religious organization continued to wield significant power in what remained of the colonial dominion in Cuba by means of its religious schools, like the Colegio de Belén, or through control of the media, like the *Diario de la Marina*. However, the Catholic Church's support of the colonial government and its repudiation of Cuban independence would end up greatly impinging on the social influence it held in the final stages of Spanish colonialism in Cuba (Torres Cuevas 2005, 185–90).

Perhaps one of the most evident ways the Catholic Church shaped Cuban society's stratified nature was through the separation of whites and blacks in various religious services. This led to the registration of baptisms and deaths in different books, marked by skin color. A catechism for recently arrived slaves was even created, which sought to explain the fundaments of the Christian religion through comparisons with life at the sugarcane mill (Moreno Fraginals 1978, 116).

Conclusion

With the demise of the indigenous population, the path was cleared for the creation of a "new people," whose cultural core would be Spanish mixed with the various groups from distinct latitudes and cultures who were being added to colonial society. The inequalities and injustices caused by slavery were presented by the hegemonic ideology as necessary evils on Cuba's path to progress. The island's hegemonic groups managed to maintain a degree of cohesion and reproduction by means of the transmission and inculcation of the dominant ideology. This dissemination was carried out through schools, the Catholic Church, the laws, the government, and the press—what Althusser (2003) referred to as "ideological state apparatuses."

As was previously noted, political authority was not only in the hands of the Spanish. It is important to keep in mind that the term "Spanish" is itself modern. The residents of the empire were all subjects of the Crown. Depending on the time period, different groups held the reins of political and economic power, as was the case in Cuba. This led to clashes among a diverse set of elites. Just as the social, political, and economic structures were transforming in the Spanish mainland, the island elite was being reconstructed over the years, passing from the first colonizers to their descendants to new groups coming from the other side of the Atlantic. This replacement process only came to a close with the end of Spanish rule on the island.

Once independent, Cuba inherited from its colonial legacy an unequal distribution of property and riches. This situation is evident in the large 19th-century latifundia. The independent island also inherited a tradition of centralist government lacking in participatory practices. To add to this, there existed an imbalance in regional development that disproportionately favored the capital, Havana. Furthermore, despite the fact that universal voting rights were put into effect in 1901, effective political participation was a privilege accorded to a small group of professional politicians. This situation was exacerbated by the prevalence of illiteracy on the island. The island's ecosystem was also profoundly altered over the 387 years of Spanish colonization, a process that is evident in the disappearance of the original woodlands that existed when the Europeans arrived.

Beyond the establishment of economic, political, and sociocultural institutions, the colonial period in the Americas, and particularly in Cuba, built a cultural legacy created and sustained by a structural framework of different strata of social relations, which shared the common structure of a centralized society and the disproportionate control of a small group. These features fostered the development of an ideology that would stretch beyond colonial society, marked by discriminatory formations fundamentally based on raciality. It is this cultural inheritance, transformed into "common knowledge," that has outlived Spanish colonialism and its institutions.

NOTES

1. For these matters, a summary comparison between what we now call Spain and its former colonies in the continental Americas suffices. There are numerous authors who go into detail on this topic; see Barcia Zequeira and Torres Cuevas (1994).

2. A broad services economy network was set up in Havana to supply for the fleet. This put Havana's territory and its hinterland to work producing to supply for the needs that a given quantity of ships and people required, not only during their stay in the Great Antilla's capital but also in preparation for voyages to come. Cattle was brought from the central townships, like Sancti Spíritus, to trade in Havana's market.

3. Not all of the blacks that arrived in Cuba came as slaves; some accompanied the colonizers from the Iberian Peninsula and lived freely on the island.

4. We are employing the denominations used at that time, such as "colored," which encompasses all non-whites.

5. A settler colony is a colony characterized by the relocation of a significant number of the metropole's inhabitants to the occupied territories. As its name indicates, the intention is to settle. In the case of the Crown of Castile-Aragon, the process of "colonization through settlement" began in 1502 with the arrival of Nicolás de Ovando to what was known as the New World. This caused substantial changes in the form of land occupancy. The number of townships increased, and a residency system was introduced. This opened access to land, an indigenous workforce, and

the ability to elect and be elected as a member of the town council (cabildo). (Rey Betancourt and García del Pino 1994, 76–87).

6. The municipal or town council was in charge of governing the townships. It was made up of two mayors, the first of which presided over the town council's sessions and, in case of absence, would be filled in for by the second mayor. They also performed administrative functions regarding both civil and criminal matters. The mayors worked in concert with a governing council that was responsible for regulating all matters relating to life in the township. These councillors were elected by residents. Along with the resident-elected councillors, there were also councillors designated by the Crown who held lifetime appointments (Rey Betancourt and García del Pino 1994, 87; Ots and Capdequí 1943).

7. For more on the presence of Cuban-born individuals in high regional and imperial political positions, see Iglesias Cruz (2012, 33–43) and Gutiérrez Forte (2012, 44–55).

8. For more information on the Catholic Church during this period in Cuba, see Torres Cuevas and Leiva Lajara (2007, 325–57) and Leiva Lajara (2007, 116–44).

REFERENCES

Althusser, Louis. 2003. *Ideología y Aparatos Ideológicos del Estado, Freud y Lacan*. Buenos Aires: Nueva Visión.

Ayala, Manuel Josef de. 1988. *Diccionario de Gobierno y Legislación de Indias*. Vol. 2. Madrid: Ediciones de Cultura Hispánica.

Barcia Zequeira, María del Carmen. 1998. *Elites y Grupos de Presión*. Havana: Editorial de Ciencia Sociales.

Barcia Zequeira, María del Carmen. 2009. *Una Sociedad en Crisis, La Habana a Finales del Siglo XIX*. Havana: Editorial de Ciencia Sociales.

Barcia Zequeira, María del Carmen, and Eduardo Torres Cuevas. 1994. "El Debilitamiento de las Relaciones Sociales Esclavistas. Del Reformismo Liberal a la Revolución Independentista." In *La Colonia: Evolución Socioeconómica y Formación Nacional Desde los Orígenes Hasta 1868*, edited by Instituto de Historia de Cuba, 1:401–63. Havana: Editora Política.

Domínguez, Lourdes, Jorge Febles, and Alexis Rives. 1994. "Las Comunidades Aborígenes de Cuba." In *La Colonia: Evolución Socioeconómica y Formación Nacional Desde los Orígenes Hasta 1868*, edited by Instituto de Historia de Cuba, 1:5–57. Havana: Editora Política.

DWD USA. 1900. *Census of Cuba*. Washington, DC: Government Printing Office.

Funes Monzote, Reinaldo. 2010. *De los Bosques a los Cañaverales*. Havana: Editorial de Ciencias Sociales.

García Rodríguez, Mercedes. 2007. *Entre Haciendas y Plantaciones*. Havana: Editorial de Ciencias Sociales.

Gutiérrez Forte, Javiher. 2012. "Entre Despotismo y Constitución: La Habana y su Cabildo entre Julio y Noviembre de 1814." *Debates Americanos* 3 (January–June): 44–55.

Gutiérrez Forte, Javiher. 2016. "El Debate sobre la Ley Electoral en la Prensa Habanera Durante la Segunda Intervención (1906–1909)." Master's thesis, Universidad de La Habana Facultad de Filosofía e Historia, Havana.

Iglesias Cruz, Janet. 2012. "La Aristocracia Habanera en las Cortes de Cádiz." *Debates Americanos* 3 (January–June): 33–43.

Iglesias Cruz, Janet, and Javiher Gutiérrez Forte. 2006. "Ensayo Introductorio." In *En Busca de la Cubanidad*, 1:7–21. Havana: Editorial de Ciencias Sociales.

Leiva Lajara, Edelberto. 2007. *La Orden Dominica en La Habana (1578–1842)*. Havana: Ediciones Boloña.

Moreno Fraginals, Manuel. 1978. *El Ingenio, Complejo Económico y Social Cubano del Azúcar*. Vol. 1. Havana: Ciencias Sociales.

Ortiz, Fernando. 2002. "Los factores humanos de la cubanidad." In *Perfiles de la Cultura Cubana*, May–December: 1–15.

Ots y Capdequí, José María. 1943. *Manual de Historia del Derecho Español en las Indias y del Derecho Propiameiannte Indo*. Buenos Aires: Talleres Gráficos de A. Baiocco y Cia.

Pérez de la Riva, Juan. 1973. "Poblamiento y Ciclos Económicos en Cuba." *Cahiers des Ameriques Latines* 8. Paris: Institut des Hautes Etudes de l´Amerique Latine.

Rediker, Marcus. 2016. *El Barco de Esclavos. Una Historia Humana*. Havana: Imagen Contemporánea.

Rey Betancourt, Estrella, and César García del Pino. 1994. "Conquista y Colonización de la Isla de Cuba." In *La Colonia: Evolución Socioeconómica y Formación Nacional Desde los Orígenes Hasta 1868*, edited by Instituto de Historia de Cuba, 1:58–106. Havana: Editora Política.

Sorhegui D´Mares, Arturo. 2010. *La Habana en el Mediterráneo Americano*. Havana: Ediciones Imagen Contemporánea.

Torres Cuevas, Eduardo. 1994. "La Sociedad Esclavista y sus Contradicciones." In *La Colonia: Evolución Socioeconómica y Formación Nacional Desde los Orígenes Hasta 1868*, edited by Instituto de Historia de Cuba, 1:265–313. Havana: Editora Política.

Torres Cuevas, Eduardo. 2005. *Historia de la Masonería Cubana, Seis Ensayos*. Havana: Imagen Contemporánea.

Torres Cuevas, Eduardo, and Edelberto Leiva Lajara. 2007. *Historia de la Iglesia Católica en Cuba. La Iglesia en las Patrias de los Criollos (1516–1789)*. Havana: Ediciones Boloña.

CHAPTER 11

Race, Gender, and Social Structure in Contemporary Cuba

Between Colonial Legacy and Current Structural Transformations

Jenny Morín Nenoff

"For blacks in Cuba, the Revolution hasn't begun," affirms the poet Roberto Zurbano (2013), sparking controversy in Cuba on the topic of race. Zurbano notes that racial exclusion, the legacy of over three centuries of slavery during the Spanish colonial era, which continued after Cuba's independence in 1902, has not been overcome in the half century since the 1959 revolution.

When analyzing the racial divide in social equality in Cuba, it is important to highlight the fact that the issue of racial identification and belonging is extremely thorny among Cuban and foreign researchers. While the majority of Cuban researchers residing on the island use the concept of "skin color" as a racial trait and one of the pillars of the cultural construction of race in Cuba (Espina Prieto 2008, 185), foreign researchers tend to use the concept of "race,"[1] whose anthropological definition describes it as a social construction (Hansing and Hoffmann 2019, 21). The essence of the controversy seems to lie in the different scientific purposes that, on the one hand, draw attention to social problems, often overlooked and omitted in policy, that continue to be linked with racial origins and historical inequality in Cuban society and, on the other hand, highlight unity among all Cubans regarding the revolution's social project while still recognizing the structural disadvantages and problems associated with the persistence of racist practices and attitudes in contemporary Cuban society. Taking into account this controversy, this chapter uses the term "race" in its sociocultural sense to refer to the racial stereotypes and prejudices that are unjustifiably attributed to people bearing the physical attributes of black or brown skin. In this sense, the concept of skin color is used as an indicator of enduring structural disadvantages, such as access to material assets like decent housing in residential neighborhoods, which can be attributed not solely to the vestiges of a neocolonial, slave-owning society but to a great extent to the dramatic socioeconomic effects of the collapse of the socialist bloc, such as the loss of importance of state employment as a principal path to well-being, the drastic devaluation of state wages, and unequal access to income not related to work, like remittances, due to the unbalanced ethnic composition of the Cuban diaspora. However, an analysis of transformations in contemporary Cuban society's social structure would be incomplete if we failed to take into account both the disadvantages that Cuban women face and the territorial inequalities.

Undeniably, the Cuban Revolution legally dismantled institutionalized racism through the prohibition of discrimination based on race or skin color in the Constitution of 1976 (article 42). Also, the political measure was taken to eliminate private property, replacing latifundios and private companies owned by the descendants of slave owners with (collective) state-owned[2] property administered by the revolutionary government. This measure, along with the eradication of the exploitation of the working class, composed mostly of descendants of African slaves and Chinese immigrants, was intended to structurally alter the social and legal foundation of racial inequality that was the hallmark of colonial society. However, since the revolutionary government did not directly address the racist culture deeply rooted in the Cuban population's collective imagination, racial stereotypes and prejudices persist to this day without being officially acknowledged.

In his speech delivered on March 22, 1959, Fidel Castro addressed the issue of racism:

> There are two types of racial discrimination: one is found in recreation and cultural centers and the other, which is the worst, the one we must fight first, is racial discrimination in work places. (Castro 1959)

However, in the same speech, Fidel Castro claimed that racial discrimination can be overcome "without the need of enacting any law or sanctions . . . by carrying out a campaign to put an end to this hateful and repugnant system" (1959). According to the Cuban researcher Esteban Morales, in 1962, the race problem was proclaimed to have been resolved, which was then followed by a long period of silence until the issue resurfaced in the late 1980s (2007).

According to Zurbano, the first step to tackling and overcoming cultural racism would be to have an official count of Cubans with black and brown skin, given that the practice of racial self-identification applied in the census has hidden the real extent to which the population has African origins. According to the official 2012 census, allegedly 64.1 percent of the Cuban population is white, 26.6 percent is mixed-race, and only 9.3 percent is black (ONEI 2016). Keeping in mind the massive expansion of slave trade and smuggling in the mid-1800s, which dramatically increased blacks' presence in Cuba, it is evident that this ethnic distribution does not reflect Cuban society's true composition. The poet Zurbano describes this paradox as "numeric fraud" or a "tragicomedy" that reveals the lack of ethnic consciousness and identity among black and mixed-race Cubans (2013).

Colonial Legacy

This tendency among Cubans to "whiten" their skin color is unquestionably related to the colonial legacy of the ethnic and cultural "whitening" of "colored races." It was a strategy targeting both slaves and freed slaves promoted by José Antonio Saco, who was convinced that this tactic would serve as a counterweight to the growing number of "black *bozales*," the young male slaves who were abducted and taken to Cuba between 1820 and 1840 during the period of rampant smuggling of slaves. Saco's political position was fed by the conviction that "whitening" would form the ethnic basis of Cuban nationality, which prior to the abolition of slavery in 1886 was solely attributed to the white criollo elite (Zeuske 2004, 335–36). The popular phrase "advance the race" (Booth 1976), still very common in Cuba today and frequently used as praise, is closely related to the concept of "whitening." This racist compliment brings to light the belief present in the popular imagination that descendants of interracial couples are considered fortunate simply because they have managed to lighten their skin tone.

Conditioned by the late abolition of slavery and independence, the Cuban slave society differed in its internal structures from those of other colonial societies that were economically dominated by large plantation systems. The late development of an economy of large-scale plantations run with slave labor made it possible in the preceding period for a relatively large group of blacks and mixed-race freed men to live alongside and mix among whites in similar or neighboring social strata (Núñez 2015, 136).

The colonial social structure was characterized, on the one hand, by an unequal relationship between the black and white population and, on the other hand, by the relationship between the enslaved and free population (Zeuske 2004, 315). In 1792, following the successful slave rebellion in Saint-Domingue, Cuba embarked on large-scale sugar production, which reached its peak in 1840. This coincided with the expansion of slavery facilitated by the Spanish Crown under the Bourbon Reforms, which aimed to maintain Cuba as a Spanish colony, since the other American colonies were in the process of being emancipated (Zeuske 2016, 74–75).

This economic change toward a productive model that was almost exclusively focused on sugar transformed the Cuban colonial society's economic composition and social structure: while slaves remained a negligible part of the Cuban population until 1740, their numbers grew to make up a considerably larger proportion of the population in 1774, constituting 26 percent of a total of 171,620 inhabitants when the first census was conducted. The number of slaves continued to grow rapidly, reaching 37 percent of over half a million people in 1817 (Zeuske 2004, 114). According to the 1841 census—notwithstanding its inaccuracy—the population had reached around 1 million inhabitants, with 43 percent slaves, 15 percent freed mestizos, and close to 42 percent white (Zeuske 2004, 208). As a result, black and mixed-race Cubans made up close to 60 percent of the population, clearly constituting the majority in colonial society.

In spite of slavery's abolition in 1886 and Cuba's independence in 1898, the colonial social structure remained intact. Skin color continued to be the principal marker of social inequality in Cuban society during the period of the neocolonial republic. It is worth noting that the first census carried out after the independence, in 1899, indicated a drastic increase of 25 percent in the number of white Cubans compared to the 1841 census, now suddenly constituting 67 percent of the population (ONEI 2016, 17), something that cannot be explained solely in relation to a general population increase and miscegenation (*mestizaje*).

Regarding territorial inequalities, it is also important to keep in mind the regionally differentiated features of ethnohistorical and socioeconomic development: the west (Havana), the area with the greatest sugar plantation development, held a large concentration of slaves and was the principal destination of Chinese people; the center (Santa Clara) was primarily devoted to ranching, and the population was predominately made up of white farmers, mainly descendants of immigrants from the Canary Islands; and the east (Santiago de Cuba) was the location with the greatest number of freed black and mixed-race people, indigenous people, and French and French Haitians who had settled following the Saint-Domingue rebellion (Núñez 2015, 138).

The Elimination of Structural Racism and the Continuation of Cultural Racism

Finally, in 1959, the Cuban Revolution raised the possibility of overcoming the structural inequalities inherent in the capitalist mode of production as well as the patriarchy and slavery system.

Some of the political measures the revolutionary government implemented to guarantee basic universal rights and to facilitate structural mobility for lower socioeconomic status groups largely made up of people of color included alphabetization; the nationalization of occupation, which led to the almost absolute predominance of the state sector in terms of employment; the application of a uniform and centralized wage system; and the universalization and expansion of a state supply network of highly subsidized and state-controlled goods and services, which ensured wider access to consumption and equal distribution. Regarding the nationalization of employment, the information provided by the 1981 Population and Housing Census revealed that between the years 1953 and 1970, the occupational structure was altered: the number of state workers rose from 8.8 percent to 87.5 percent, and private wage earners dropped from 63.3 percent to 1.3 percent (Espina Prieto 2008, 117). Despite the fact that the data does not directly address skin color, it can be concluded that 88 percent of state workers were made up of a high percentage of blacks and mestizos. Until the crisis of the 1990s, certain careers proved to be reliable pathways for social mobility among slave descendants, particularly the professional military career in the Revolutionary Armed Forces,[3] political careers, and careers in arts and sports. The drastic drop in private wage earners is due to the Revolutionary Offensive of 1968, which spurred the nationalization of over 57,000 businesses in the small urban commercial production sector (Granma 1968).

With the implementation of the General Salary Reform (1983), the definition of the qualification-pay scale was fixed on a spectrum of thirteen groups, allowing for a difference between maximum and minimum salaries of 4.5 to 1. Keeping in mind that the state was the sole employer until the 1990s, 95 percent of income came from state work (Espina Prieto et al. 2003, 33–34). Nonetheless, it is important to clarify that these measures, rather than achieving the objective of creating social equality, served to reproduce inequalities, given that the state failed to implement "policies known as affirmative action, or positive discrimination, which aim to stop the reproduction of social disadvantages by offering better opportunities to the most vulnerable groups" (Espina Prieto 2008, 172). Equal opportunities had not automatically translated into racial equality, given that a universal social policy was applied that did not take into account the fact that baseline differences between racial groups needed to be addressed differently.

In the absence of a differentiated approach for addressing them, these differences persisted and were reproduced from generation to generation, silenced or ignored until the process of social homogenization was abruptly interrupted by the crisis, which destroyed the economic base that undergirded the country's social progress toward a society with high rates of equality and social justice.

Unlike racial inequalities, the gender gap received targeted treatment, since social policy had explicitly included differential treatment of women on a strategic planning level and through numerous programs. Furthermore, the Federation of Cuban Women was established, a family code was implemented as a legal instrument addressing equality between men and women, and the Commission on Children, Youth, and Women's Rights and Equality was formed within the Parliament (Espina Prieto 2008, 186). The following indicators offer evidence of Cuban women's socioeconomic advancement until the 1990s: a female presence of 42.5 percent in the civil state sector's labor force, 64 percent of whom reached the category of professionals and technicians and 30 percent of whom held positions as managers (186).

The Crisis's Impact and Reforms in Current Social Structure

With the collapse of the European socialist bloc in general and the Soviet Union and COMECON in particular, Cuba found itself abandoned overnight and suddenly exposed to an international market that its economic system was neither designed nor prepared for. Faced with this situation, the

Cuban head of state, Fidel Castro, decreed the so-called Special Period on August 29, 1990, which essentially consisted of a set of rationing measures intended to ensure the survival of the Cuban people and the Cuban socialist model.

Due to Cuba's high economic dependency, the cancellation of advantageous commercial agreements with the Soviet Union, which represented an immense source of economic subsidies, marked a severe crisis in external commercial relations for Cuba that quickly transformed into a multidimensional economic crisis. This multidimensional crisis encompassed a macroeconomic crisis reflected in a 43.1 percent per capita drop in gross national product caused by a sudden decline in the country's productive capacity due to a loss of capacity to import goods of all types; by an energy crisis due to a decline of imported oil from 13 million to 6 million tons; and a food crisis, principally caused by the loss of imported food supplies (Espina Prieto 2008, 127). This multidimensional crisis brought the economy to the brink of collapse. Industries were closed or temporary halted, which simultaneously caused scarcity in the internal market and increased unemployment, which in turn led to a drastic drop in personal consumption.

In addition, the Cuban government contributed to an accelerated expansion of monetary liquidity by printing money without material backing (causing inflation to rise by 183 percent in 1993) in order to continue paying salaries and wage guarantees. This had the negative impact of drastically increasing prices and provoking the devaluation of average nominal salaries, which resulted in a dramatic drop in purchasing power. Real wages can be used as an indicator to quantify state salaries' purchasing power, which, in contrast to the nominal salary, is adjusted for inflation (consumer price index) and takes as a reference point the average salary in 1989, the year prior to the crisis. According to this calculation, in 2016, the real wage was 74 Cuban pesos (CUP), taking the nominal wage of 188 CUP in 1989 as a reference point, which differs substantially from the average nominal wage of 740 CUP. In other words, in 2016, the real state salary was still 39.3 percent of what it was in 1989, which means that, currently, despite a slight recovery, purchasing power remains contracted by 60.7 percent (Mesa-Lago 2018). These calculations are based on wages in CUP and do not include wages paid in Cuban convertible pesos (CUC), since that statistic data is not published.

Facing this situation, Cuban political leaders were forced to implement measures that entailed the liberalization of the economy, ultimately leading to the adoption of a dual economy or "mixed socialism model." This duality cannot be exclusively defined by ownership of the means of production (state/non-state) but above all in terms of monetary duality (foreign/national currency). This double duality materialized in the emerging sector that operated in foreign currency. Since commercial companies can operate in exclusively Cuban, foreign, or even mixed capital, the new economic actors in the emerging sector can classify in both property sectors (Figueroa Albelo 2009, 372–78).

The urgent need to access foreign currency in order to join the international market and thus obtain goods for basic public consumption, in conjunction with the drastic devaluation of national currency against the dollar, compelled the Cuban government to approve Decree Law Number 140 in 1993, at the height of the crisis, which simultaneously legalized Cuban citizens' possession of foreign currency and family members' remittances from outside the country. It is precisely this measure, colloquially termed the "dollarization" of the Cuban economy, that caused the major undesired side effect of dividing the society into winners and losers. The second fundamental measure was an opening up to foreign capital through joint ventures (Law Number 77 of 1995), establishing a parallel sector subject to market logic but controlled by the Cuban planning system. The third fundamental measure, the expansion of self-employment through the Decree Law Number 141, approved in September 1993, was implemented with the intention of legalizing all illegally exercised economic activities. As a result of the almost complete paralysis of the national economy, which materialized in severe scarcity, conditions were created for the proliferation of the black market, where an increasing number of clandestine workers began to operate, temporarily replacing the state in its function of securing supplies for the population. Finally, the fourth significant measure was the division of large state farms into lots to create Basic Units of Cooperative Production (UBPC) (Decree Law Number 142 of 1993).

In a nutshell, the profound economic and social transformations of the 1990s can be seen in the following four developments: the expansion of the market as a (partial) distributor of goods of basic necessity, the introduction of foreign capital, the expansion of small urban and rural commercial property, and the parceling of state farms.

The inequalities marked by skin color are fundamentally manifested in the social and labor structure of today's Cuba (Izquierdo Quintana and Burchardt 2017), in the alternative forms of economic income, and in the occupation of urban space and housing.

In this context of crises and reforms, Cuban social classes changed substantially: the state sector's loss of space as employer constitutes the first element of re-stratification since it diversified "socio-structural locations by their link with property, their place in the social division of work, their sources and types of income" (Espina Prieto 2008, 162). Since 1988, state employment, which made up 94 percent of the economically active population, diminished considerably until it stabilized at 78 percent in 1999. During this same period, the non-state sector increased from 6 percent to 22 percent, including cooperatives, joint ventures, private farmers, and self-employed workers. Among these subgroups, a notable increase is found among private farmers (Credit and Service Cooperatives [CCS]), agricultural cooperatives (UBPC and Agriculture Production Cooperatives [CPA]), and, to a lesser extent, self-employed workers. However, starting in the early 2000s, the cooperatives began to decrease in number, while the private farmers continued to increase, reaching 11.2 percent of the workforce in 2006, or half of the non-state sector. Self-employment, in contrast, remains stable between 3 percent and 4 percent (Espina Prieto 2008, 161–62).

Unlike the 1990s, the current expansion of the Cuban non-state sector (private and cooperative), which includes 28.9 percent of all employees, is part of a long-term process of change in the economic and social model. The group of self-employed workers currently includes nearly 540,800 people, representing 11.8 percent of all workers. One-fifth of the self-employed are privately contracted workers. The private farmers mainly associated with CCS make up 13 percent of employees, while the CPAs and UBPCs make up 2.9 percent, and the non-farming cooperatives constitute 0.2 percent of workers in the non-state sector (ONEI 2017, 11).

One of the approaches for addressing the phenomenon of change in the social class structure was developed and popularized by economists: the inverted pyramid (Guzmán 1995). This approach presumes the existence of a former structure, where social positions are defined by a directly proportional relationship between cultural capital and economic capital. The development of new economic spaces (joint ventures and foreign companies, the expansion of the private sector and cooperatives) gives rise to mobility processes that are incompatible with the norms of socialist equality. As a nominal salary does not satisfy basic needs, distortions were introduced into the work-income relationship. Social position related to qualifications was devalued, resulting in the exodus of professionals from the state sector to the private sector, often carrying out work unrelated to their vocation or academic profile (doctors and teachers being among the most notable examples), and making it increasingly common to see surgeon/gardeners, professor/candy makers, cardiologist/taxi drivers, historian/weavers, and gynecologist/programmers, among others.

According to the norm of socialist equality and equity, the inequalities associated with the quantity, quality, and complexity of individual and collective work (not exploitation) are considered legitimate in socialism, "and in any case, the inappropriate feature of this asymmetry is due to the inability of the state sector to remunerate workers in relation to the magnitude and relevance of their work" (Espina Prieto et al. 2003, 35).

According to the Cuban sociologist Mayra Espina, this norm was distorted as much by excess as by defect. She argues that prior to the crises and reforms of the 1990s, this norm was left equally unfulfilled due to the exercise of an exaggerated form of egalitarianism that did not recognize legitimate social differences linked to work contributions, which was detrimental to the social mobility of Cubans who had very good professional preparation. On the other hand, the norm was distorted due to the crisis's negative social effects, which materialized in Cuban society's social stratification and the resurgence of poverty, which are considered to be incompatible with the humanist aspirations of Cuban socialism.

The Reforms' Undesired Effects: Re-Stratification

The process of socioeconomic re-stratification driven by the crisis unleashed by the collapse of the socialist bloc developed along ethnic, gender, and territorial lines. This development was the result of multiple interrelated factors, such as the ethnic composition of the remittances-issuing diaspora, the racial barriers preventing access to lucrative employment that is paid in hard currency, and inferior economic capacities and worse living conditions, which make it difficult to obtain initial investments and have access to a domestic space where it would be possible to launch a private business.

The economic reforms of the 1990s, which included the legalization of the dollar as a second currency, led to the undesired effects of creating social differences not derived from labor, such as differences caused by remittances and the unequal distribution of the possibilities and routes of accessing them. While it is calculated that around 50 percent of the population had access to foreign currency in 1997, now the figure is estimated to be close to 60 percent.

Regarding migration, it is important to take into account the fact that the first wave of exiles was almost exclusively composed of members of the bourgeoisie and white elite, who had supported Fulgencio Batista's dictatorship. Although subsequent waves of migration were less homogenous in terms of ethnicity, they still were predominantly white (Hansing and Optenhögel 2015, 11). Conversely, the number of black emigrants until the end of the 1990s made up 7 percent of total emigration (Aja and Milán 1997). In this regard, it is not surprising that recipients of remittances on the island are white families who not only can afford the higher consumption of a variety of goods and services but are also able to invest in businesses like restaurants (*paladares*) and private guesthouses (in private homes).

Adding legal and illegal emigration, between 1994 and 2012, Cuba registered a negative migration balance totaling 637,513 during this period, an annual average of 33,553, reaching a maximum of 47,844 in 1994 and increasing from over 20,000 in 1996 to 46,662 in 2012. According to data provided by the Cuban Ministry of Foreign Affairs, Cubans reside in 148 countries, with the highest concentration, nearly 80 percent, living in the United States (Domínguez, Machado Cajide, and González Delgado 2016, 118).

It is important to highlight that, since the relaunching of the private sector in 2011, remittances are used not only for consumption but as start-up capital, in other words, as investments in freelance businesses, which are mostly small- and medium-sized enterprises. According to a recent study of family members receiving remittances in Havana, access to material well-being is limited for those who receive remittances for consumption in contrast to those who receive start-up capital, given that on average the total annual remittances received by this second group are 11 times higher than remittances received for consumption (Delgado 2016, 27).

In regard to racial and gender gaps, this same study concluded that the recipients of remittances for start-up capital fit the following profile: men, between the ages of 31 and 60, white, with a high school education, with private businesses, who are residents of Havana's central upper-middle-class neighborhood Plaza de la Revolución. In contrast, the majority of the recipients of remittances for consumption are women, under 30 or over 60 years old, mixed-race, with higher-education degrees, working in the state sector, and residing in the low-income neighborhood Centro Habana, which is considered a precarious residential area (Delgado 2016, 27). Consequently, remittances influence family strategies, allowing some to improve the satisfaction of basic needs, while helping others to improve their social status by setting up a successful private business.

In terms of access to lucrative jobs paid in hard currency (CUC), two Cuban anthropologists, Rodrigo Espina and Pablo Rodríguez, established a direct relation between the economic crisis and the greater visibility of racial inequalities. They confirm that black and mixed-race Cubans have a smaller proportional presence in the emerging sector that operates in foreign currency, which includes the tourism sector, joint ventures, foreign companies, and Cuban trading companies (Espina Prieto and Rodríguez 2006). Statistical data reveals that employees in the emerging sector represent 1 percent of the total economically active population, with white employees making up between 50 percent and 72 percent, depending on the type of business; black employees constituting between 9.7 percent and 12.2 percent; and mixed-race employees making up between 19.1 percent and 37.6 percent (ONEI 2016, 39).

The self-employment sector, which at the time of the 2012 census had reached 7.7 percent of the economically active population, also reflects a predominance of white people, who make up 68.1 percent of self-employed workers, followed by 22.9 percent mixed-race and 9 percent black workers (ONEI 2016, 39). The racialized construct of "pleasant appearance" implies the belief that blackness is ugly and that blacks lack appropriate social behavior, thus representing a good example of the concrete manifestation of racial barriers to better-paid work in the private and emerging state sectors. However, the data also shows that, when adding the urban and rural private sector to the emerging sector, these sectors only make up one-third of the total number of employees, compared to the over 70 percent that still work within the state sector. Nonetheless, the statistical overrepresentation of blacks stands out in state employment, representing 83.5 percent in comparison to white and mixed-race employees (38).

There is a notably greater presence of whites in residential neighborhoods with better living conditions, while black and mixed-race individuals tend to be more represented in poor neighborhoods, mainly in slum-like housings (*solares*) and abandoned mansions subdivided into family rooms (*ciudadelas*) (Núñez 2015, 140). The statistical data available clearly indicates an unequal distribution: out of the total homes built before 1959, that is to say, those located in residential neighborhoods, 69.5 percent were inhabited by whites, 10.9 percent by blacks, and 19.7 percent by mixed-race individuals (ONEI 2016, 48).

Since most of the black population continues to live in precarious living conditions in outlying low-income neighborhoods, they are unable to reap the benefits of the current economic opening, since they lack the private homes that could be used to launch successful businesses, a position that the majority of the descendants of the former middle- and upper-class whites can avail themselves of. It is also evident that, in general, only people who have foreign financial support (remittances) and are part of solid social networks go on to have successful business ventures (Echeverría León and Díaz Fernández 2017). Self-employed workers who neither manage to join an informal network of entrepreneurs and/or successful suppliers nor have close ties to the tourism sector do not form part of Cuban entrepreneurs with high and stable incomes.

A concrete manifestation of territorial inequalities can be found in the irregular populations called *llega y pon* (come and put), spontaneously formed by migrant citizens, primarily coming from the country's eastern provinces, who arrive in the capital in search of better living conditions and construct their homes without state permission, not adhering to basic regulations for urban housing planning. As a result, these zones are characterized by an absence of sewage systems and by buildings of poor construction quality.

In the early 1990s, territorial inequalities were gradually reduced through policies of universal access to basic goods and services, while, at the same time, new inescapable inequalities were superimposed upon previous ones through economic reform measures (adjustments) intended to alleviate the crisis. The greatest impact on the country's territorial inequalities was caused by the decision to concentrate investments in prioritized productive sectors like tourism, mining, metallurgy, and biotechnology, among others. As a result, the implementation of development plans and programs was carried out in selected spaces that failed to spread the advantages attained by these developments to nearby territories. In this way, the country was reconfigured into "luminous and opaque spaces" (Iñiguez Rojas 2015, 216). This territorial inequality is also expressed in the distribution of socioeconomic actors: while joint ventures and state companies with a strong presence of workers and leaders are predominant in Matanzas, Santiago de Cuba, and the Isla de la Juventud, companies with 100 percent foreign capital and a strong presence of intellectuals and employees are more numerous in Havana. Conversely, the rural provinces with the largest presence of CPA and UBPC are Artemisa, Mayabeque, Ciego de Ávila, and Cienfuegos, while private farmers, the majority of whom are associates in the CCS, predominate in Pinar del Rio, Sancti Spíritus, Granma, Villa

Clara, Las Tunas, Camagüey, Guantánamo, and Holguin (Espina Prieto et al. 2003, 36–37).

Another factor that granted privileges to white Cubans is dual Cuban and Spanish citizenship, which can be acquired thanks to the Historical Memory Law, also known as the "grandchildren's law," in force since 2007, which accords Spanish citizenship to anyone who can present evidence proving that their parents or grandparents were Spanish. As of 2018, over 110,000 Cubans have acquired Spanish citizenship, and 70,000 applications are still being processed (Hansing and Hoffmann 2019, 22). Given the fact that black and mixed-race Cubans do not tend to have direct kinship links with Spanish citizens in the last two generations, this route does not offer a possibility for attaining a European passport, which would facilitate international mobility and other advantages associated with dual citizenship. As a result, marriage to foreigners offers the most viable route for attaining European or North American passports, which would present the possibility of traveling without a visa to almost all the countries of the world.

Due to this range of factors, the majority of black and mixed-race Cubans are not able to reap the benefits of the advantages offered by the transformations connected to a mixed economy model. Lacking viable alternatives, many remain trapped in the traditional state sector without access to CUC, adversely affected by a salary that never recuperated its purchasing power.

Conclusion

Under the mandate of Raúl Castro (2008–18), the issue of the racial and gender gap, at least in political representation, had regained importance, which is proven by a sustained increase of both women and black and mestizo members in the State Council and the National Assembly of People's Power. Currently, 22 percent (7 out of 31 members) of the State Council and 40.5 percent of the 605 deputies are black and mestizo individuals, while females represent 48 percent and 53.2 percent of the respective legislative bodies (Cubadebate 2018). In comparison to the 1960s and 1970s, when the black and mixed-race population was politically represented by the Commander Juan Almeida, who was part of the Political Bureau of the Community Party of Cuba, and by Lázaro Peña, the president of the Cuban Workers' Union, today's statistics can be seen as progress.

This representation, above all, has symbolic importance, since it remains to be seen if it will materialize in proactive policies that guarantee equal access to well-paid jobs in the economy's emerging sector, like tourism, joint ventures, and self-employment (de la Fuente 2011), a challenge that is within reach for the Cuban government. In contrast, the ethnic composition of the Cuban diaspora and unequal access to remittances and dual citizenship as well as international mobility patterns are beyond the Cuban government's scope of action and political responsibility.

In 2011, the year declared by UNESCO as the International Year for People of African Descent, the results of a research project entitled "Racial Relations in Cuba" that was carried out between 1990 and 2003 with the aim of identifying racial gaps in social equality in Cuba were published (Colectivo de Autores 2011). The main results, on the one hand, reflect high levels of ethnic integration achieved by the essentially "Indo-Afro-Hispanic" Cuban national culture (Núñez 2015, 144), which is expressed in the common features of food, clothing, music, and dance, as well as in socio-normative elements like values and codes of conduct. On the other hand, there is a greater racial differentiation regarding housing, spiritual culture, and intimate relationships, which are mainly intraracial rather than interracial (ONEI 2016, 32).

The persistence of a racist culture in Cuba, manifested in the existence of stereotypes ("advancing the race"), racial prejudice, and discrimination ("pleasant appearance"), can be explained to a certain extent by the white ideology developed during the times of slavery. The inequalities linked to the interrelation of class and race that became visible in the context of the crisis of the 1990s, in turn, give evidence of structural problems not explicitly addressed politically that place blacks and mixed-race Cubans in situations of comparative disadvantage to face the crisis's adverse effects and to prevent them from taking advantage of the opportunities that the Cuban non-state sector offers in the context of the reforms ("updating").

It is understandable that in an adverse socioeconomic context, such as the one Cuba faces today, the policy of the Cuban government emphasizes the unity of all Cubans around the social project of the revolution. However, it is also urgent to develop and implement policies aimed at vulnerable groups such as women, blacks and mestizos, and residents of economically disadvantaged municipalities and provinces. What is at stake is the sustainability of the revolution's achievements that constitute the legitimizing foundation of this unique socioeconomic model.

NOTES

1. In Cuba's National Statistics Office's (ONEI) recent publication, the terms "race" and "of African descent" are deemed inappropriate. Regarding the term "race," it is argued that "due to the *mestizaje* that occurred, both biologically and culturally," it has lost its true meaning, a statement that genetic studies also seem to support. The term "of African descent" is considered inappropriate for the Cuban context because "this denomination is associated with marginalization and open recognized discrimination" more characteristic of North and South America (ONEI 2016, 8–9).

2. Following two agrarian reforms in 1959 and 1963, the 1960s were marked by the foundation of Credit and Service Cooperatives for small farmers, the majority of whom were beneficiaries of the revolutionary government's first and second Agricultural Reform Laws, which reduced land ownership to 400 hectares in 1959 and to 63 hectares in 1963 and, in this manner, redistributed land owned by latifundistas among dispossessed farmers. In the 1970s, Agricultural Production Cooperatives were founded by small farmers. Aiming to increase productivity, they relinquished their private means of production to the cooperative, in other words, transferred them to collective ownership. One of the many reform measures of the 1990s that affected the Cuban cooperative sector was the structural redistribution of the large state agricultural companies into small Basic Units of Cooperative to make the production of food more efficient and thus mitigate the effects of the food crisis (Fernández Peiso 2012). The reduction of private business was due to the "Revolutionary Offensive" of 1968, which led to the nationalization of over 57,000 businesses in the small urban commercial production sector (Granma 1968).

3. Pedro represents one such case. Pedro, who was born in 1949 in Santiago de Cuba, was the second child of an Afro-Cuban family who fit the description of "poor." As a black child who had lived through "a little bit of capitalism" for 10 years, it is understandable that he identifies as a communist and revolutionary, since the Cuban Revolution gave him the opportunity to reach the position of lieutenant colonel in the Armed Revolutionary Forces (FAR) and to graduate as an engineer in the Soviet Union. This made his mother proud, who before 1959 only harbored the hopes that her children would attain the modest work of pharmacy courier. Unconditional support of the revolution is an integral part of Pedro's identity, whose profile matches the majority of poor Cubans who have benefited from revolutionary policies and achievements. In 1993, after 30 years of service in the FAR, Pedro retired as lieutenant colonel at the age of 42. His retirement coincided with one of the worst epochs in revolutionary Cuba, called the Special Period. Due to drastic devaluation of the national currency, the Cuban peso, immediately following the country's economic crisis, his good pension suffered a drastic decline in its purchasing power. Since his pension was no longer enough to meet his family's basic needs and Pedro was still of working age, he set out to work on his own, taking advantage of the reinstatement of permits for certain professional activities (Morín Nenoff 2018).

REFERENCES

Aja Díaz, Antonio, and Guillermo Milán Acosta. 1997. "El Flujo Migratorio Externo de Cuba en la Década del Noventa." *Universidad De La Habana* 247:41–61.

Booth, David. 1976. "Cuba, Color, and the Revolution." *Science and Society* 40 (2): 129–72.

Castro Ruz, Fidel. 1959. "Discurso Pronunciado Por El Comandante Fidel Castro Ruz, Primer Ministro Del Gobierno Revolucionario." In El Palacio Presidencial, March 22. http://www.cuba.cu/gobierno/discursos/1959/esp/f220359e.html

Colectivo de Autores. 2011. *Relaciones Raciales en Cuba. Estudios Contemporáneos.* Havana: Fundación Fernando Ortiz.

Cubadebate. 2018. *Integrantes del Consejo de Estado de la República de Cuba.* http://www.cubadebate.cu/cuba/consejo-estado/

de la Fuente, Alejandro. 2011. "Race and Income Inequality in Contemporary Cuba." *NACLA Report on the Americas* 44 (4): 30–33.

Delgado Vázquez, Denisse. 2016. "Efectos del Uso Diferenciado de las Remesas en la Desigualdad Social. Un Estudio en la Capital Cubana." Buenos Aires: CLACSO. http://biblioteca.clacso.edu.ar/clacso/becas/20160401090229/denissedelgado.pdf

Domínguez López, Ernesto, Landy Machado Cajide, and Dalia González Delgado. 2016. "Nueva Inmigración y Comunidad Cubana en Estados Unidos en los Albores del Siglo XXI." *Migraciones Internacionales* 8 (4): 105–36.

Echevarría León, Dayma, and Ileana Díaz Fernández. 2017. "Política de Empleo en Cuba 2007–2015: Desafíos a la Equidad." *Miradas a La Economía Cubana.*

Espina Prieto, Mayra Paula. 2008. *Políticas de Atención a la Pobreza y la Desigualdad. Examinando el Rol del Estado en la Experiencia Cubana.* Buenos Aires: CLACSO.

Espina Prieto, Mayra Paula, Lucy Martín Posada, and Lilian Núñez Moreno. 2003. "Reajuste Económico y Cambios Socioestructurales." In *Los Cambios en la Estructura Socioclasista en Cuba*, edited by Manuel Menéndez Díaz, 10–50. Havana: Editorial de Ciencias Sociales.

Espina Prieto, Rodrigo, and Pablo Rodríguez. 2006. "Raza y Desigualdad en la Cuba Actual." *TEMAS* 45:44–54.

Fernández Peiso, Avelino. 2012. "Notas Características del Marco Legal del Ambiente Cooperativo Cubano." In *Cooperativas y Socialismo*, edited by Camila Piñeiro Harnecker, 366–96. Havana: Editorial Caminos.

Figueroa Albelo, Víctor. 2009. *Economía Política de la Transición al Socialismo: Experiencia Cubana.* Havana: Editorial de Ciencias Sociales.

Granma. 1968. *Resumen de la Nacionalización del Sector Privado.* April 15.

Guzmán, Antonio. 1995. "Redimensionamiento y Reestructuración de la Economía Cubana." Paper presented at the Seminario por el Primer Aniversario del Sindicato de las Ciencias, Havana.

Hansing, Katrin, and Bert Hoffmann. 2019. "Cuba's New Social Structure: Assessing the Re-Stratification of Cuban Society 60 Years after Revolution." *GIGA Working Papers* 315.

Hansing, Katrin, and Uwe Optenhögel. 2015. "Cuba: las Desigualdades se Tornan

Visibles: Consecuencias de la Economía de Escasez y Reformas." *Nueva Sociedad* 255:4–18.

Iñiguez Rojas, Luisa. 2015. "Trayectorias y Transformaciones Territoriales en la Cuba Actual." *Geousp—Espaço e Tempo* 19 (2): 212–27. https://www.revistas.usp.br/geousp/article/download/102773/pdf/

Izquierdo Quintana, Osnaide, and Hans-Jürgen Burchardt. 2017. *Trabajo Decente y Sociedad. Cuba Bajo la Optica de los Estudios Socio Laborales*. Havana: Editorial Universidad de la Habana.

Mesa-Lago, Carmelo. 2018. "Una Apostilla Sobre Salarios, Pensiones y Asistencia Social en Cuba." *El Estado Como Tal*, March 20. https://elestadocomotal.com/2018/03/10/carmelo-mesa-lago-una-apostilla-sobre-salarios-pensiones-y-asistencia-social-en-cuba

Morales, Esteban. 2007. *Desafíos de la Problemática Racial en Cuba*. Havana: Fundación Fernando Ortiz.

Morín Nenoff, Jenny. 2018. "Biografías Laborales de Actores Socioeconómicos del Sector no Estatal Cubano y su Contribución a una Transformación Innovadora." PhD diss., Cologne University.

Núñez González, Niurka. 2015. "Inequidades Raciales ante el Proceso de Actualización del Modelo Económico Cubano." In *Retos para la Equidad Social en el Proceso de Actualización del Modelo Económico Cubano*, edited by Zabala Argüelles, Maria del Carmen, Dayma Echevarría León, Marta Rosa Muñoz Campos, and Geydis Elena Fundora Nevot, 135–46. Havana: Editorial de Ciencias Sociales.

Oficina Nacional de Estadísticas e Información (ONEI). 2016. "El Color de la Piel según el Censo de Población y Viviendas 2012." http://www.one.cu/publicaciones/cepde/cpv2012/elcolordelapielcenso2012/PUBLICACI%C3%93N%20%20COMPLETA%20color%20de%20la%20piel%20.pdf

Oficina Nacional de Estadística e Información (ONEI). 2017. *Anuario Estadístico 2016. Edición 2017: Empleo y Salarios*.

Zeuske, Michael. 2004. *Schwarze Karibik. Sklaven, Sklavereikultur und Emanzipation*. Zürich: Rotpunktverlag.

Zeuske, Michael. 2016. *Kleine Geschichte Kubas*. München: Verlag C.H. Beck.

Zurbano Torres, Roberto. 2013. "Para los Negros en Cuba la Revolución No Ha Comenzado Aún," April 17. http://www.rebelion.org/noticia.php?id=166862&titular=para-los-negros-en-cuba-la-revoluci%F3n-no-ha-comenzado-a%FAn-

CHAPTER 12

The Perpetual Colony

Historical Memory and Inequalities in Puerto Rican Society

Milagros Denis-Rosario

From Borikén to Puerto Rico: Vestiges of the Colonial System

This chapter will discuss the Spanish colonial system's features in, implementation in, and impact on Puerto Rican society. The following analysis is grounded in a sociohistorical reevaluation that emphasizes the ways in which economic, plantation, and slave systems, and to a lesser extent military service, were used by African descendants to rise in the social hierarchy. To develop this argument, I will use the oil painting entitled *Plaza del Quinto Centenario* by the Afro–Puerto Rican artist Ramón Bulerín to explore the colonial system and its social ramifications and discriminatory consequences on contemporary society. This work offers a means for examining the discourse of Hispanic nationality elites constructed as a mechanism to impose and perpetuate their ethnic and racial hegemony while excluding African elements.

Christopher Columbus and his crew arrived at Borikén, or Borinquén, as the Taino Indians called the island, on November 19, 1493. The island endured the consequences of Spanish conquest and colonialism, such as Columbus changing its name from Boriken to San Juan Bautista, which Juan Ponce de León changed again in 1509 to its current name. During the first decades of the 16th century, the governorship was very unstable, since, according to historians Aida Caro Costas (1983, 25–26) and Loída Figueroa (1979, 81), Christopher Columbus's heirs decided to sell their rights to the territories of the viceroyalty of the Indies in 1536 (Figueroa 1979, 77, 78), and, as a result, the Crown evaluated different proposals for governing the island, ultimately establishing it as a *presidio militar*, or fortified military settlement (Brau [1904] 2000, 76).[1]

After a number of attacks by pirates and European enemy nations, the island's military strategic position—as well as its vulnerability—was recognized. Therefore, the military government was created for its management. In 1580, King Charles V created the position of *gobernador general*, or captain general (a professional military officer who ran the island as a *sitio militar*, or military site, for which San Juan was the operations center), which existed up until 1898 (Caro Costas 1983, 26; Picó 1988, 56; Brau [1904] 2000, 89). This was a five-year position, and whoever held it had absolute authority, represented the king of Spain, and even exercised control over *partidos*, or districts.[2] With the island as a military site, civilian participation was limited and the administrative focus was on protecting riches coming from other territories, like the Mexican *situado* (remittance issued to the colony by the Crown). In legal terms, with the Treaty of Granada, the Crown declared that the island's settlers were its subjects (Picó 1988, 56).[3]

The captain general was in charge of the community's well-being and acted as a judge. Caro Costas (1983, 27) mentions that the governor general, lacking judicial knowledge, availed himself of legal advisers from the Santo Domingo *audiencia* (court of justice). The 19th-century historian Salvador Brau ([1904] 2000, 89) noted that, starting in 1599, an ordinance excused the captain general from reporting to the *audiencia*. Additionally, the governor general presided over the town council (*cabildo*), using the laws of the police and good governance proclamations (*Bandos de la Policía y Buen Gobierno*) to govern.[4] These legal mechanisms were modified over different periods and used to control certain population sectors such as poor farmers, women, and black slaves and freedmen. Later, the phenomenon of the foundation of towns began and gave rise to the assignment of lieutenants (*tenientes de guerra*), who were named by the governor and were usually members of prominent Puerto Rican or Spanish families. This was a two-year position, and those who held it were in charge of enforcing laws and safeguarding against smuggling (Caro Costas 1983, 29).

The church's involvement in administrative and legal decision-making is rooted in the island's colonization. This function was sanctioned by the 1508 papal bull passed by Pope Julius II, in which he authorized the Catholic monarchs to evangelize the new territories at their own expense and granted them the right to designate prelates and erect dioceses as they pleased. For instance, in 1511, King Ferdinand ordered the establishment of a diocese, which Bishop Alonso Manso, the first bishop of the Indies, led. He was also the first inquisitor (chief of the Inquisition in the Americas, 1533–88). Meanwhile, Puerto Rico became part of an archdiocese that extended throughout the lesser Caribbean islands (Figueroa 1979, 72, 74; Abbad y Lasierra [1788] 1970, 255; Brau [1904] 2000, 33). Furthermore, the founding of Puerto Rican towns followed a pattern associated with religious zeal; people who could not attend religious services established hermitages in the name of the Virgin or a saint, which, in turn, became the test for establishing a town or village.[5] This practice consisted of a group of residents submitting a petition to the head of the town council requesting the town's creation, and, afterward, the official and priest evaluated the petitioners' zeal to decide whether to rubber-stamp the request (Brau [1904] 2000, 96). In fact, many of the cities were founded over the blueprint of Taino villages. Today a significant number of the municipalities in Puerto Rico are Hispanized versions of Taino names.

As previously mentioned, the church and the state acted together in regard to both conquest and colonization (Figueroa 1979, 71). These events were consequential for the populations marginalized by the Spanish and the whites. Clearly, black individuals did not exercise the same degree of influence in the foundation of towns, given their lack of resources. Evidence indicates that the village Piñones was founded by the Piñón brothers, but this is more a neighborhood in Loíza than a town (Sued Badillo and López Cantó 1986). When Loíza was registered as a town in 1719, a group of Spanish-Irish property owners proposed that a chapel be established in the name of Saint Patrick, leading to the town's establishment as well as the designation of Saint Patrick as its patron saint. However, the zone's black population were followers of James the Apostle, the saint of blacks from Loíza and of the mulatto militia (*milicia de pardos*), and while James was more popular and his name day was celebrated on July 25, the town's registers recognized Saint Patrick as Loíza's patron saint (Alegría 1954; Giusti 1994).

Puerto Rico's Social and Economic Profile

During the first decades of the 16th century, the colonial system developed a method for obtaining an indigenous workforce, or repartimiento. It consisted of dividing up Indians into encomiendas, or groups, where they were forced to work and remunerate the colonists with gold or other services.

The encomienda, which originally was managed by the settlers, had devastating effects on the indigenous population and led to the establishment of a social class within the colony.[6] Many suffered illness and physical exhaustion, while others fled and settled in the mountains or nearby islands. As a result, the Dominican missionaries made a plea to the monarchy demanding more humane treatment of the Tainos. After a series of measures created to regulate the encomienda system, the Burgos Laws (1512) became the standard regulation. They basically gave the church jurisdiction over the encomienda system. These stipulations also established the teaching of Catholic instruction to the Tainos and separated their villages from the settlers (Jiménez 1998, 38–41). One could suggest that the separation of the Indian villages is very similar to the establishment of the Indian reservations in the US. The church's administration over the encomiendas also gave the institution a prominent role in the economic system. Since the clergy was in charge of the Indian labor and the land, this put them in control of the production revenues. Besides, it occasioned the combination of the tithes collected and other taxes to help complete the *situado*. The indigenous population was exponentially diminished and was almost at the point of extinction when they gathered in the San Germán jurisdiction, according to the 1799 census, which reported a total of 2,000 Indians (Picó 1988, 55).[7]

Since mining had not yielded results, the colony was obliged to expand its economic production. Ranching and the plantation system, or haciendas, had been the main sources of income for the colony. However, it wasn't until the development of the island's sugar production that the colony came to rival its Caribbean counterparts.[8] This new dynamic played a part in the acquisition of slave labor and the growth of haciendas devoted to sugarcane crops.[9] Consequently, Africans were brought to the island to work in plantations and urban environments (Picó 1988, 32; Negrón Portillo and Mayo Santana 2007, 137). As a result, starting in the 1530s, the population of free and enslaved blacks surpassed the number of Creoles and Spaniards.

Table 12.1 shows the demographic characteristics of Puerto Rican society at different periods in Spanish colonization up until the 18th century. As the table reveals, whites were in the minority during Spanish settlement. Despite initiatives to control the flight of white Spaniards from the continent by implementing austerity measures and by bringing black settlers from other islands outside of Spanish territory, the black and indigenous populations surpassed the colonizers. Picó (1988, 98) notes that 200 families were brought from the Canary Islands during this period to increase

TABLE 12.1. Population Numbers for Puerto Rico (Select Years)

Year	Total	Whites	Free Blacks	Slaves
1530	2,988	724	—	2,264
1673[a]	1,791	820	304	667
1700	6,000	—	—	—
1765[b]	44,883	—	—	5,037
1776	72,916	30,640	34,530	7,746
1795	110,053	43,330	48,667	18,056

Source: Adapted from Abbad y Lasierra ([1788] 1970, 153); Brau ([1904] 2000, 53, 131); Figueroa (1979, 103).

[a] The 1673 census was taken only in the district of San Juan.

[b] In the 1765 census, whites and blacks are counted together.

the white population and to facilitate trade. This demographic feature combined with attacks on the island in the 16th, 17th, and 18th centuries and the revolutionary climate in the Caribbean at the end of the 18th century—that is, the Haitian Revolution and the Latin American wars for independence—served as a pretext for implementing means of social and economic control over the black (freed as well as enslaved) population.[10] In particular, freed blacks were prohibited from congregating, and slaves were monitored when they moved from plantation to plantation. They were also prohibited from engaging in social activities during their days off (Sundays), among other things (Díaz Soler 2000), out of fear that they would find out what was happening in other colonies and try to organize escapes and rebellions.

Ergo, following colonial society's settlement pattern, the Spanish occupied the highest position in society. Following the Spanish were Creoles, then poor whites, free people of color (called mulattos, or *pardos*), the few remaining indigenous people, and, finally enslaved African blacks.[11] By the 18th century, San Juan was shaping up to be typically colonially structured, with class and race stratified accordingly. The friar Iñigo Abbad y Lasierra ([1788] 1970, 99) noted San Juan's class-related activities in his visit to the island at the end of the 18th century, observing that "[l]a construcción de las casas varían como las castas o clases de sus habitantes" (house construction varies depending on the caste or class of its inhabitants). The friar went on to describe how Spaniards and citizens had the best houses, which were made of lime and had roofs built with rafters and tile. Meanwhile, the homes of "mulattos" were made of flat boards, and their roofs were covered with palm leaves. Abbad y Lasierra (100) also noted that the housing for blacks and poor people was very similar to that of the mulattos, "aunque más groseras y reducidas" (more rustic and smaller).

Education on the island was left to the church. The encomienda system that had been set up immediately following Spanish settlement stipulated that the Indians in the system receive a Catholic Christian education. According to Salvador Brau ([1904] 2000, 203), during the so-called liberal period (1812–14), various schools opened that were financially sustained by students' parents. Clearly, this system limited education to members of the privileged class. Later, a Lancasterian system of mutual and free teaching was developed. Members of the moneyed class sent their children to Europe to acquire formal and university-level schooling, which strengthened the hegemonic class's grip on the reins of political, economic, and intellectual power. In this way, members of this class reaffirmed their control and superiority as Creoles of Spanish descent. Nonetheless, it is worth noting exceptions like the siblings Cordero Molina, Celestina and Rafael. Rafael, a free black tobacco farmer, and his sister, Celestina, are credited with pioneering free education for boys and girls of both races (Nieves 2016; Alverio Ramos 2017). The absence of an education system would be the direct cause of the island's high level of illiteracy at the turn of the 20th century.

Women from the colonial period, on the other hand, lived in accordance with the guidelines set by a patriarchal society. They were expected to take care of household tasks as well as the nuclear family. They also did not have a right to education, and the esteem they were granted depended on their race and social class, practices that the Catholic Church reinforced. Félix Matos Rodríguez (2001), in his study on women in San Juan, established that white Spanish or Creole women were under the protection of their husbands. In the event that they were widowed, class and race were determining factors in their acceptance as heads of household. Matos Rodríguez points out that these women, in order to survive as widows, became innkeepers or took on other businesses in accordance with their status. For free black women, racial stigma made single motherhood or widowhood more difficult than it was for white Spanish or Creole women. Free black women supported themselves as, for example, saleswomen, seamstresses, maids, nannies, and washerwomen. However, jobs like food vendors, which required women to be in the street, exposed them to criticism and harassment.[12] The case of women in San Juan certainly wasn't unique and also applied to the rest of the island.

Colony and Reform

During the Spanish colonial period, reforms were introduced that changed the organization of the colony. The first were the Bourbon Reforms (1730s–1780s), which were an attempt to organize—militarily and administratively—the Spanish colonies. This resulted in the military's reorganization following racial parameters and the creation of slave codes, both of which perpetuated class and race hierarchies. Consequently, the Spaniards and Creoles used slave labor as economic manpower to maintain the colony and their way of life. Finally, there was a prevailing concern in these reforms to eliminate smuggling. This initiative compelled the Crown to take care of its colony and propelled the dismantling of the illegal trade.

In the early 19th century, Spain introduced another series of colonial reforms in response to political instability in the American colonies, which granted subjects greater political participation. The Constitution of Cadiz was very important in the sense that it established who was a Spanish citizen. To receive this denomination, it was ruled, an individual had to prove that he was the descendant of Spanish parents, was educated, was of legal age (21 years old), and was a landowner.[13] Proof of these requirements accorded them the authority to participate in parliament and vote for representatives. In Puerto Rico, representatives were first chosen to advocate for the colony in the Cadiz Cortes in 1812. Ramón Power y Giralt, who belonged to the Creole class, represented Puerto Rico and presented recommendations that were generally written up by town council leaders. The immediate result was better fiscal management and the formation of councils whose members were exclusively white men—blacks and individuals of color were not accepted (Picó 1988, 129). As mentioned earlier, the island's status as a military base (*presidio*) influenced the management style and decisions made in regard to its budget, particularly Mexico's *situado*, which was used to pay the soldiers' salaries. In Puerto Rico, budgetary decisions were made based on the island's needs and priorities as a strongpoint. In the same manner, San Juan's architectural planning followed a grid pattern in which the plaza, where soldiers conducted their military demonstrations, was the central point in the urban design. Military organization also reflected racial structures; it was a black company that carried out their patriotic duty during the English attack of 1797, thus heading off the island's conversion to an English colony through military strategy and courageousness.

Napoleon's wars in Europe created an instability in the monarchic sys-

TABLE 12.2. Puerto Rico's Population (Select Years)

	1820	1834	1846	1869
Total	236,622	358,836	443,914	600,233
Number of whites	102,432	188,869	216,023	323,454
change			+27,216	+107,371
Number of free blacks	106,460	126,399	102,946	237,710
change			+49,392	+61,919
Number of slaves	21,730	41,818	51,264	39,069
change			+9,447	–12,196

Source: Jiménez (1998, 149).

tem. As a result, the Constitution of 1812 was annulled. Financial crisis and the king's return to the throne led to the creation of the quartermaster general's post and the decree of 1815, also known as the Decree of Graces. This decree encouraged Spanish citizens (from the Canary Islands, Catalonia, and Corsica, among other places) to immigrate to Puerto Rico. Ironically, these last reforms promoted blacks' exclusion from the island's political sphere while opening it up to Haitians and Louisianans of color (de Hostos 1966, 78). By 1869, the free black population had stabilized and the slave population had diminished (see table 12.2). Historian Olga Jiménez (1998, 150) noted that, during this period, the population of those designated whites or free blacks grew the most.

José Luis González (1980, 49, 51) in his text *El País de Cuatro Pisos y Otros Ensayos*, in turn stated that the migration wave to Puerto Rico was part of an effort to "whiten" the island's culture, adding that what was in fact achieved was only "a posponer la posibilidad de que Puerto Rico cuajara una sociedad predominantemente afroantillana como las colonias inglesas y francesas" (the postponement of the possibility Puerto Rico would settle into a predominantly Afro-Antillean society like the English and French colonies). In Puerto Rico's case, hundreds of individuals arrived to the island and received land incentives, primarily in the mountainous region where they became farmers.

This region had very unequal land distribution. Hacienda owners or colonial administrators constituted the majority, while the rest of the population were landless or lived as laborers. In turn, there was a great deal of unclaimed properties or royal property, much of which the Decree of Graces determined should be conceded to Spanish and foreign emigrants (Picó 1988, 132).[14] These lands were almost entirely used for coffee and tobacco crops and other export products.

Following the different stages that affected the Spanish Crown, the Creole class participated in liberal reform in the second half of the 19th century. During this period, the abolition of slavery was being debated; Puerto Rico and Cuba held opposing positions regarding the slavery system and relations with Spain. Cuba's hacienda owners were enjoying a boom in sugar production and depended heavily on slave labor. Puerto Rico, on the other hand, had relatively few slaves, and slave trade had been banned in 1840, making acquiring slaves costlier (Morales Carrión 1978, 198; Figueroa 1979, 309–14). Furthermore, the Creoles ensured free labor through compulsory initiatives like the *régimen de la libreta* system. Established in 1849 during Juan de la Pezuela's rule, this system, which demanded that day laborers have their own land or cultivate the land of someone else (an *agregado),* lasted until 1870. The day laborer, who could be chosen from among unemployed males age 16 and above, carried a notebook in which the employee wrote down the place and hours worked, and observations his employer made.[15] Those who did not meet these demands were subject to fines or prison sentences or were forced to work for half pay on public work projects (Jiménez 1998, 144). To top it all, demographic expansion led to competition over access to arable land among commercial hacienda owners. This spurred an increase in the price of *cuerdas* (Puerto Rico's land unit measurement), which restricted day laborers' options for acquiring land. With this backdrop, freed slaves entered into the labor force.

Puerto Rico abolished slavery on March 22, 1873, a decade before Cuba. The newly freed men and women faced difficulty integrating into the emerging working class and resentment from the slave-owning class, since their group status was wrested from them with slaves' liberation. However, other documents discuss how the hacienda owners who had slaves were, in some manner, compensated for their "losses" through Moret Law's apprentice system, which enacted "freedom of wombs," which freed slaves over age 60 and those in the custody of the state.[16] Additionally, when slavery was abolished, the freedmen who entered into the labor force were at a disadvantage when it came to integrating into society and supporting themselves. First, they weren't going to be recognized as free by the plantation owners. Second, as free workers, they lacked the tools for negotiating contracts and had to accept what they were offered. The freedmen who lived in urban centers were at an advantage since they worked as artisans and earned better salaries. Yet these urban freedmen also were disadvantaged in comparison to the white population.[17]

During this period, the Creole class—made up of merchants, politicians, and plantation owners—matured and launched new initiatives, like petitioning for greater autonomy and more flexible trade rules. In the political realm, Spain granted the Cuban and Puerto Rican islands autonomy in 1897. The new autonomous government gave the Creole class control over commerce laws as well as other benefits. Nonetheless, the Creoles' managerial capabilities were curtailed due to the Spanish-American War in 1898. Spain lost the war against the United States as well as its control over Cuba, Puerto Rico, the Philippines, and Guam. From that point on, a colonial system was instated, which replaced the Autonomous Council with a tutelage system, initially under American military governors, and later, in 1900, named civil governors, who were American as well. The Americans implemented similar patterns of colonial government to what the Spanish did to the Tainos—for instance, establishing a military government, changing the name of the island from Puerto Rico to Porto Rico, and imposing the English language for the administration and education of the island. Various series of changes typical of the colonial system suggest that the island entered a new phase of colonialism. The creation of several political parties (Republican, Autonomist, Nationalist, and Popular) from 1900 to the 1940s reflects the different political ideologies of Puerto Ricans in relation to the US presence. In 1938, with the rise and triumph of the Partido Popular Democrático (PPD), or Popular Democratic Party, Puerto Ricans seemed to negotiate their colonial status. Finally, on July 25, 1952, the island was turned into a Commonwealth, a political status that made Puerto Rico an unincorporated US territory.[18] In summary, it could be said that Puerto Rican society had developed a sense of nation and identity by the end of the 19th century. The social classes were composed of a Spanish minority, Creoles, and, last, the poor classes, made up of both whites and people of color. Many in this last group were aware of the labor movements taking place in the United States and Latin America and adapted rhetoric from the workers' movement as a vehicle for fighting for their rights.

At the beginning of the 20th century, despite a close political and economic relationship with the United States, local political parties emerged in opposition to or in support of the new regime, depending on their interests regarding the island's American administration. Many party alliances were established, and the labor movement flourished as a political alternative to the new regime. It was during this period that the question of national identity became a divisive issue. The political and intellectual elite, particularly those who were descendants of hacienda owners who were supplanted by new American economic interests, did all that was in their power to reaffirm their Spanish and European heritage. The intellectual debate sought to reconstruct Puerto Rican identity through the exaltation of the *jíbaro* (the white countryman of Spanish heritage), the romanticization of the Taino Indian, and the "folklorization" of Africans/blacks (González 1980, 43–56; Godreau 2015, 221–26). This debate coincided with the rise to power of the PPD and its founder, Luis Muñoz Marín, a member of the political elite. The PPD led Puerto Rico's modernization efforts; the party and its followers subscribed to their generation's social conception of Puerto Rican identity, which was reflected in the PPD's political campaigns in which the *jíbaro* was adopted as the essence of Puerto Rican national identity.

An important strategy in reaffirming the island's Spanish heritage was to procure tangible evidence. Specifically, by the 1940s, intellectual groups like the Foro were established that debated the role that higher education institutions should play, such as the University of Puerto Rico and, later, the Institute of Puerto Rican Culture, when it was established in 1955. These two government entities had a decisive voice in regards to articulating a patriotic discourse. At the end of the 1940s, a commission was created to preserve Old San Juan as a historic area. This in turn went along with different efforts to reclaim indigenous heritage. In 1972, more areas were added to the US's National Register of Historic Places, and, in 1983, UNESCO declared Old San Juan a World Heritage Site (US National Park Service 2018; UNESCO 2018). This declaration gave the island an enviable and advantageous position. On the one hand, it attracted many tourists and adventurers. On the other hand, this new status connected the island with its Spanish heritage and with the rest of the Americas; ironically, at the same time, it distanced the island from its Antillean or black/African context. The geographer and Latin American scholar Joseph L. Scarpaci (2004) observed in his study on the restoration of colonial plazas and neighborhoods that this tendency to validate colonial spaces was mirrored elsewhere in Latin America. Puerto Rico, it could be argued, was not exempt from these trends.

Recovering the Spanish Memory: *Plaza del Quinto Centenario*

The artwork *Plaza del Quinto Centenario* (fig. 12.1) portrays the plaza that was constructed to commemorate the 500th anniversary (1492–1992) of the so-called discovery of the Americas. Puerto Rico played an active role in the celebrations that were organized throughout the year and also cel-

Fig. 12.1. *Plaza del Quinto Centenario* (Ramón Bulerín, oil on canvas, 2007).

ebrated the 500th anniversary of the island's discovery (1493–1993). The plaza was inaugurated on October 12, 1992, at the same time as the opening of the Museum of the Americas. It should be noted that, in April 1991, Governor Rafael Hernández Colón signed Law No. 4, which declared Spanish the island's official language (Hernández-Colón 1991, 2). The governor himself reiterated that Spanish was part of Puerto Rican identity and recognized the legacy of Taino Indians, Africans, and Spaniards. The inclusion of these three cultural heritages could be considered very progressive, but the architectural works and policy proposals did not focus on this element. The government's participation and the allocation of funds suggest the imposition of a patriotic discourse that institutionalized the Spanish–Puerto Rican connection. Governor Hernández-Colón was presented with the Prince of Asturias Award in 1992. In this context, the posture taken by Hernández Colón's government suggests that language not only was used as a vehicle to affirm Puerto Rican identity among the Puerto Rican people, but also could be considered as a signal to the Anglo-Saxon colonial system that Puerto Rican society held on to its Iberian roots.[19]

With this cultural and political background, the event's official catalog called upon Puerto Ricans to come together to celebrate 500 years of "la evangelización de nuestros países, la restauración del español como lengua oficial de la isla" (our countries' evangelization, the reinstatement of Spanish as the island's official language) (Comisión del Quinto Centenario 1992, 4), actions that, according to the executive director, "son parte de la realidad y el perfil de los puertorriqueños y los ibéricos" (are part of Puerto Ricans' and Spaniards' reality and profile) (5).

In the center of a photo of the plaza (see fig. 12.2), we see a sculpture made by the artist Jaime Suárez, entitled *Totém telúrico*. The totem, located at the plaza's highest part, is 40 feet high. The staircases leading to the lower level are flanked by two sculptures on each side (the lamb, symbol of the city and of Catholicism). The totem's base is made of black granite, and the centerpiece is made of ceramic, which is a medium commonly used by the Taino Indians. Suárez indicated in a statement that this color and material combination represented the Americas' historical roots (Gutíerrez Viñuales 2005, 7).

It comes across as ironic that this sculpture would celebrate the Americas' cultural heritage, since it is erected within an old Afro–Puerto Rican neighborhood—an unknown fact to most people. According to historian Adolfo de Hostos (1966, 79), in the early 19th century, Ballajá was the extension of what is currently San Sebastián Street and consisted of a few streets and blocks that made up one of San Juan's poorest and most underdeveloped areas, which, in 1853, was officially converted into a neighborhood. This space that today is referred to as the Plaza del Quinto Centenario is not part of the Spanish colonial complex. The contemporary architect Edwin Quiles Rodríguez (2003) noted that Ballajá was where the families of black Puerto Rican soldiers (also known as *milicianos de morenos* or *pardos*) lived. Over time, the Spanish soldiers who participated in the wars for independence and were expelled from other territories settled in

Fig. 12.2. *Puerto Rico, San Juan, Plaza del Quinto Centenario, View of El Totem in Plaza del Totem* (Danita Delimont / courtesy Alamy Stock Photo).

this zone, displacing the black families and forcing them to relocate to the areas known today as La Perla, La Marina, Puerta de Tierra, and Cangrejos (Quiles Rodríguez 2003, 39, 56). Kinsbruner (1996, 142) asserted that whites' properties were larger than those of free blacks, despite the fact that both had nuclear families of the same size. He added that whites enjoyed better economic conditions that allowed them to maintain these properties. In summary, Kinsbruner concluded, San Juan's free black population faced economic limitations due to racial discrimination (143). This observation confirms that the social structure favored certain racial groups over others; although black soldiers' families had a historic presence in the Ballajá area, they were discounted due to racial considerations.

As was previously mentioned, at the dawn of the 19th century, Spain implemented a series of constitutional reforms that granted greater political participation to the Creole class, using Spanish descent as a test of eligibility. It also promoted Spanish immigration to Puerto Rico. In both circumstances, class and race differences were widened and the marginalization of people of color was institutionalized. De Hostos (1966, 78), for his part, noted that under Miguel de la Torre's government (1823–37), the proclamation of good governance (*Bando de Buen Gobierno*) was announced. This proclamation, among others, promulgated the restoration of the city and made it necessary to obtain a government license for the construction of new houses. Additionally, a new construction code was created that prohibited the erection of shacks, wood homes, and straw roofs and required that houses be brick with tile roofs. It could be argued that, with these new regulations, the lower classes (blacks and single mothers, who made up a large part of San Juan's population) were victims of gentrification, given that the majority of their homes were made of materials that had been made obsolete. Materials like brick and tile were very costly, which discouraged marginal sectors. According to de Hostos (1966, 79), the poor homeowners had to face authorities on various occasions, given that the police order gave them six years to rebuild their houses, which, if not carried out within this period, would be demolished. Another pretext used to evict residents was to bring up the danger they posed to public health. Quiles Rodríguez points to these urban changes as the cause behind many families moving away and the destruction, and then reconstruction, of their homes under new construction laws (Quiles Rodríguez 2003). As a result, well-off families began to live in neighborhoods that were traditionally black, events that historical memory overlooks.

By establishing a new narrative for this controversial space, Bulerín, in his oil painting *Plaza del Quinto Centenario*, shifted the focus from the totem to the people. The work's layout is divided into four scenes, and a combination of images—such as stairs, floating anthropomorphic figures, and a series of rectangular niches—stand out. The plaza at issue was strategically constructed to offer a space to enjoy the view of the Atlantic Ocean and the Castillo San Felipe del Morro, which is another attraction featuring Spanish colonial architecture. This historical background goes unnoticed today. However, Bulerín, in his painting, reconstructs a new iconography in his framing of the plaza's center and the people ascending and descending the stairs, which shifts attention away from the plaza itself. In an interview, Bulerín indicated that he sought to capture in this painting, through a more contemporary lens, "el perfil de los residentes de la ciudad, en lugar de resaltar los elementos que normalmente se asocian con la arquitectura de San Juan" (the city residents' profile, rather than highlight elements normally associated with San Juan's architecture) (Bulerín 2015). His interpretation reveals class, gender, and race dynamics that the friar Iñigo Abbad y Lasierra had observed several centuries earlier.

It could be argued that the artist's interpretation provides an alternative to the political-cultural discourse of the time. That is to say, the PPD's administration devoted its efforts to restoring San Juan's historic zones and many points of interest that would go down in history as one of the wins for the Puerto Rican people by the Commonwealth's administration (*Guía oficial* 1995, 19–21). With many projects underway (the Paseo de La Princesa, wall restorations, and street restorations), Old San Juan was converted into a local and international tourist mecca. The commission's agenda was successful, and, from that moment on, the island's collective memory would accentuate Spanish-American principles. Cultural reaffirmation was once again intertwined with modernizing and commemorative thinking, overlooking the place's centuries of history.

In the work's aesthetic conceit, the artist engages in a social analysis of people who coexist and inhabit the old city. This coexistence is part of a dynamic that originates from the same colonial structure that underscores the imposition of one group over another and, to some extent, subjugation. In the case of San Juan, this gave way to negotiations and led to consensuses in the name of Puerto Rican-ness.

This modernizing tendency contrasts with the function of the artist and work being discussed. *Plaza del Quinto Centenario* is an attempt to recover Old San Juan's cultural and historic memory in a more inclusive manner; the artist presses the observer to inquire into the past. If the plaza wasn't part of the original colonial layout, in renovating and cementing this part of San Juan, part of its historical and urban memory is erased. A new urban recreation space is built that excludes black Puerto Ricans from the discourse on national identity, since what is emphasized is a Spanish legacy, with all its colonial complexity. It could be argued that the analysis generated by the oil painting and its connection to a colonial legacy reflects what Colombian artist and writer Virginia Villaplana Ruiz identified as the "post-memory" element in the production of a "biographic medium" (2010, 91). This interpretation validates one of this chapter's premises: that historic memory and the artist's background as an Afro–Puerto Rican influence the creation of the oil painting. In other words, Bulerín recreates the plaza without relying on the immediate reference: the *tótem telúrico* or the staircases. On the contrary, in his creative process, the artist reclaims San Juan's residents and lays the foundations for different spatial interpretations while encouraging observers of the work to see beyond the plaza's iconography. The spectator is invited to call upon the historical memory of "aparentemente no se ve, pero si se busca se encuentra" (what to all appearances isn't seen, but if one looks for it, will be found) (Bulerín 2015).

Conclusion

The case of Puerto Rico discussed in this chapter brings into line one of the postulations in Burchardt's and Leinius's pieces in this volume: that there are contemporary patterns of Spanish colonialism in the society. Postcolonial legacy is evidenced in the perpetuation of a Hispanic identity. The recreation of a Hispanic discourse became an intellectual project and catapulted with the celebration of the 500th anniversary of the so-called discovery of the Americas. This chapter uses the artwork *Plaza del Quinto Centenario* to illustrate how the artist takes over this exclusionary discourse and nuances its rhetoric. In addition to the colonial nuances, the complex political relationship between the island and the US exacerbated and reproduced the preexisting colonial structures.

Urban and colonial spaces establish, and can perpetuate, race, class, and gender hierarchies. Ever since Puerto Rico was established as a colony, the Spanish created an unequal system on all these levels, and the city of San Juan clearly reflected these hierarchies. Even as a minority, the Spanish were in charge of military and political functions, and the island's position as a military site greatly delayed its economic development. Creoles, for their part, who voiced their discontent on many occasions, took advantage of their class privilege to challenge colonial rule. On the other hand, they copied mechanisms of oppression and applied them to people of color, limiting their education access, decreasing their economic mobility, and perpetuating a system of racial and spatial segregation that disadvantaged blacks. Males of African descent used military service to climb the social ladder and, even in the face of limitations, managed to establish communities that continue to exist today.

As was alluded to earlier, free blacks fought for access to education, and only groups who lived in urban areas possessed some type of education. This feature would persist until the beginning of the 20th century, when Americans introduced educational reforms.

Creole, enslaved, and free black women played a dominant role in San Juan's urban economy, as well as in other towns, by providing domestic services and acting as breadwinners, mothers, and wives. The economic system established did not just depend on slave labor, and free blacks also contributed to social and economic development. At the end of the 20th century, these hierarchies were reproduced through the continuation of a pro-Spanish discourse centered on the exaltation of a class. The elite class's discourse has been fostered in a variety of different ways, one being through partisan political rhetoric.

As this chapter has shown, San Juan's old city underwent a transformation when it was "restored" to attain national heritage status and promote Puerto Rico as a world-class example of Spanish colonial architecture. This national project is an example of how the government and Puerto Rican society allegorically took part in the "national identity races" with the aim of reclaiming Spanish ancestry as part of its national pride and distancing itself from Antillean attributes. As a result, framing the capital's space by exalting race, class, and gender hierarchies ensured the perpetuation of Creoles' and Spaniards' prominence. Free blacks, who also made their mark in this structure, developed ways of surviving and producing in these circumstances. When the colonial legacy is considered in this light, it can be argued that a socioeconomic imbalance, difficult to uproot, has been perpetuated and, in one form or another, intensified under the American neocolonial system.

NOTES

1. Once Puerto Rico acquired strategic military importance, King Charles V reorganized the government by appointing *alcades-ordinarios*, or magistrates, who exercised their functions in the San Juan and San Germán town councils. Another administrative body was subsequently created, called *alcaldes-gobernadores*, who acted as political and judicial directors. This position was dissolved in 1545 and replaced by the *alcaldes letrados*, who were named by the king or the Santo Domingo *audiencia* and whose duties were limited to legal and political affairs. This position lasted until 1564. During their incumbency, the *alcaldes letrados* maintained the peace and boosted the island's economy.

2. It is worth making a comparison here to the colonial/territorial system established in 1898 by the United States in Puerto Rico, where a military governor was named by the US president to govern the new territory.

3. This legal uncertainty rooted in the colonial period is repeated under American rule when Puerto Ricans are kept as "subjects of the Congress of the United States" from the invasion until 1917, when they are granted American citizenship.

4. These proclamations regulated land use for agriculture and livestock and ensured the supply of meat. The proclamation of good governance (*Bando de Buen Gobierno*) was a mechanism used to regulate social activities, including cockfighting, gambling, and patron saint days.

5. Only six villages were founded in the 16th century: San Juan/Caparrra (1509), San Germán (1506), Coamo (1518), Arecibo (1515), and Aguada (1592) (Brau [1904] 2000, 96–97; Santana and Torrech 1988, 34). It is worth noting that the boom in new towns would begin in the 19th century, corresponding to a general rise in population.

6. The management of the Indians and the activities they were assigned were decreed by the Crown. The document, commonly known as the "Orders of Queen Isabella," gave instructions on how to organize the workday (see Wagenheim and

Jiménez 1996, 18). It also stipulated that the Indians be treated well, that they be given six workdays, and that, on the seventh day, they be taught the Catholic doctrine. The Indians had supporters among the Dominican missionaries, who denounced the encomenderos for their abuse of Indians to the government and the Crown.

7. This fact would influence the decision to import more African slaves. From that time forward, the island's demographic profile would shift toward a black population, including both free and enslaved blacks. In this sense, it could be argued that, with the fall of the indigenous population, the black population became the majority and the Spanish the minority.

8. The sugar industry was part of the island's economy since the 16th century. However, the industry would suffer losses between 1580 and 1640. It wouldn't be until the beginning of the 18th century that the sugar industry would experience growth following Spanish and European market demand (see Jiménez 1998, 137–44).

9. A plethora of literature exists on the impact of the sugar industry on 19th-century Puerto Rican society. See the work of Pedro Luis San Miguel (1989) and Luis A. Figueroa (2005), among others.

10. This took place under the governance of Toribio Montes (1804–9), Miguel de la Torre (1823–37), and Juan de Prim (1847–48), who established a proclamation against the black race. According to historian Guillermo Baralt (1981, 156–57), 55 attempted slave uprisings were registered between 1795 and 1848.

11. However, despite this marginalization, Africans and their descendants greatly contributed to the island's cultural and social fabric. Creoles, for their part, tired of the colonial system's injustices, expressed their discontent through policy proposals that included greater participation in the colonial government, as was mentioned earlier.

12. This type of situation transpired throughout the island. See Suárez Findlay (1997).

13. In the case that this was in doubt, parish books could be used to check. For the black population, this resulted in a type of exclusion, given that their mixed-race status automatically disqualified them.

14. These immigrants would be praised for their economic contributions; they also would become stigmatized for their agrarian way of life. At the same time, the intelligentsia would start to designate this class as *jibaros*, or country people, in the 19th-century Creole literary movement, since they considered them to be ingenuous and, at the same time, to symbolize the essence of Puerto Rican identity. For example, Manuel Alonso's work entitled *El Gíbaro* (1849) immortalized the Spanish farmer who immigrated to Puerto Rico. One could say that it was starting at this point that the discussion over what was considered "Creole" versus "Spanish" would permeate intellectual debates (see González 1980, 56).

15. This led to the abuse of peasants and the extension of a system that perpetuated dependence on the hacienda or landowner, not only in terms of providing work but also in creating an additional socioeconomic level in which the poor peasants would develop their own identity and way of life, which would be the subject of empathy and solidarity among intellectuals and politicians.

16. See the seminal work of Raúl Mayo Santana, Mariano Negrón Portillo, and Manuel Mayo López (1997) and Luis M. Díaz Soler (2000, 349–69).

17. For works on the post-emancipation period, see Rosa E. Carrasquillo (2005); Mariano Negrón Portillo and Raúl Mayo Santana (2007); and Luis A. Figueroa (2005), among others.

18. According to *La Gran Enciclopedia de Puerto Rico* (The Great Encyclopedia of Puerto Rico), a Commonwealth is defined as "la Carta Magna que establece los fundamentos legales del gobierno de Puerto Rico desde el 25 de julio de 1952. Este documento histórico es el resultado de la lucha del Partido Popular Democrático (PPD) y sus líderes por obtener mayores poderes políticos dentro del control norteamericano. Fue y continúa siendo objeto de fuertes debates sobre la identidad, estatus y definición política de la isla" (the Magna Carta that, as of the 25th of July in 1952, establishes Puerto Rico's government's legal foundations. This historic document is the result of the Popular Democratic Party [PPD] and its leaders' fight for greater political power under North American rule. It was, and continues to be, the subject of heated debate regarding the island's identity, status and political definition) (Mota Maldonado 2017).

19. It is important to note that the Spanish spoken in Puerto Rico is not the same as Spanish in Spain, or Castilian, and has acquired characteristics from the groups that make up Puerto Ricans' ethnic core. Álvarez Nazario's (1974) compelling study highlights how the Spanish spoken in Puerto Rico is enriched by African words, which he terms "Afro-Spanish."

REFERENCES

Abbad y Lasierra, Fray Agustín Iñigo. [1788] 1970. *Historia Geográfica, Civil y Natural de la Isla de San Juan Bautista de Puerto Rico. Estudio Preliminar de Isabel Gutiérrez del Arroyo*. Editorial de la Universidad de Puerto Rico.

Alegría, Ricardo. 1954. *La Fiesta de Santiago Apóstol en Loíza Aldea*. Madrid: ARO, Artes Gráficas.

Alonso, Manuel. 1849. *El Gíbaro. Cuadro de las Costumbres de la Isla de Puerto Rico*. Barcelona: Juan Oliveres.

Álvarez Nazario, Manuel. 1974. *El Elemento Afronegroide en el Español de Puerto Rico*. San Juan: Instituto de Cultura Puertorriqueña.

Alverio Ramos, Zulmarie. 2017. *La Gran Ausente: La Maestra Celestina Cordero Molina*. Río Piedras: Ediciones EDP.

Baralt, Guillermo. 1981. *Esclavos Rebeldes. Conspiraciones y Sublevaciones de Esclavos en Puerto Rico (1795–1873)*. Río Piedras: Ediciones Huracán.

Brau, Salvador. [1904] 2000. *Historia de Puerto Rico*. New York: D. Appleton.

Bulerín, Ramón. 2015. Telephone interview. May.

Caro Costas, Aida R. 1983. "The Organization of an Institutional and Social Life." In *Puerto Rico: A Political and Cultural History*, edited by Arturo Morales Carrión, 25–40. New York: W. W. Norton.

Carrasquillo, Rosa E. 2005. *Our Landless Patria: Marginal Citizenship and Race in Caguas, Puerto Rico, 1880–1910*. Lincoln: University of Nebraska Press.

Comisión del Quinto Centenario. 1992. *Puerto Rico Summer '92. Guía Oficial de los Eventos Conmemorativos del Quinto Centenario.* New York: R. Paniagua.

de Hostos, Adolfo. 1966. *Historia de San Juan Murada. Ensayo Acerca del Proceso de Civilización en la Ciudad Española de San Juan Bautista de Puerto Rico, 1521–1898.* San Juan, Puerto Rico: Instituto de Cultura Puertorriqueña.

Denis-Rosario, Milagros. 2012. "Expresiones de Inclusividad: Análisis Socio-histórico de 'Mi Viejo San Juan,' Serie de Pinturas de Ramón Bulerín." *Delaware Review of Latin American Studies* 13 (2). http://www.udel.edu/LAS/Vol13-2Denis-Rosario.html

Díaz Soler, Luis M. 2000. *Historia de la Esclavitud Negra en Puerto Rico.* Rio Piedras: Editorial de la Universidad de Puerto Rico.

Figueroa, Loida. 1979. *Breve Historia de Puerto Rico Desde sus Comienzos Hasta el 1892.* Vol. 1. Rio Piedras: Editorial Edil.

Figueroa, Luis A. 2005. *Slavery, Sugar and Freedom in Nineteenth-Century Puerto Rico.* Chapel Hill: University of North Carolina Press.

Giusti, Juan. 1994. "Labor, Ecology and History in a Caribbean Sugar Plantation Region: Piñones (Loiza), Puerto Rico, 1770–1950." PhD diss., State University of New York, Binghamton.

Godreau, Isar. 2015. *Scripts of Blackness: Race, Cultural Nationalism, and U.S. Colonialism in Puerto Rico.* Champaign: University of Illinois Press.

González, José Luis. 1980. *El País de Cuatro Pisos y Otros Ensayos.* Rio Piedras: Ediciones Huracán.

Gutiérrez Viñuales, Rodrigo, ed. 2005. "Barro y Conmemoración en Puerto Rico. El Tótem Telúrico de Jaime Suárez." In *Arte Latinoamericano del siglo XX. Otras historias de la Historia*, edited by Rodrigo Gutiérrez-Viñuales, 167–89. Prensas Universitarias de Zaragoza, España.

Hernández Colón, Rafael. 1991. "Mensaje del Gobernador del Estado Libre Asociado Honorable Rafael Hernández Colón en Ocasión de la Firma del Proyecto de Ley que Declara el Español Como Idioma Oficial de Puerto Rico." April 5, San Juan, Puerto Rico.

Jiménez de Wagenheim, Olga. 1998. *Puerto Rico: An Interpretive History from Pre-Columbian Times to 1900.* Princeton: Markus Wiener.

Kinsbruner, Jay. 1996. *Not of Pure Blood: The Free People of Color and Racial Prejudice in Nineteenth-Century Puerto Rico.* Durham: Duke University Press.

Matos Rodríguez, Félix V. 2001. *Women in San Juan, 1820–1868.* Princeton: Markus Wiener.

Mayo Santana, Raúl, Mariano Negrón Portillo, and Manuel Mayo López. 1997. *Cadenas de Esclavitud . . . y de Solidaridad. Esclavos y Libertos en San Juan, Siglo XIX.* Rio Piedras: Centro de Investigaciones Sociales.

Morales Carrión, Arturo. 1978. *Auge y Decadencia de la Trata Negrera en Puerto Rico (1820–1860).* San Juan: Centro de Estudios Avanzados de Puerto Rico y el Caribe / Instituto de Cultura Puertorriqueña.

Mota Maldonado, Yanelba. 2017. "Operación Estado Libre Asociado." *Gran Enciclopedia de Puerto Rico en línea.* https://enciclopediapr.org/encyclopedia/operacion-estado-libre-asociado/

Negrón Portillo, Mariano, and Raúl Mayo Santana. 2007. *La Esclavitud Menor: la*

Esclavitud en los Municipios del Interior de Puerto Rico Siglo XIX. Estudio del Registro de Esclavos de 1872: Segunda Parte. Río Piedras: Centro de Investigaciones Sociales / Universidad de Puerto Rico.

Nieves, Bethsaida. 2016. "Cordero Molina, Rafael." In *Dictionary of Caribbean and Afro-Latin American Biographies*, edited by Franklin W. Knight and Henry Louis Gates Jr. New York: Oxford University Press. https://doi.org/10.1093/acref/9780199935796.001.0001

Picó, Fenando. 1988. *Historia General de Puerto Rico*. Rio Piedras: Ediciones Huracán.

Quiles Rodríguez, Edwin R. 2003. *San Juan Tras la Fachada. Una Mirada Desde Sus Espacios Ocultos (1508–1900)*. San Juan: Editorial del Instituto de Cultura Puertorriqueña.

San Miguel, Pedro Luis. 1989. *El Mundo que Creó el Azúcar: las Haciendas de Vega Baja (1800–1873)*. Río Piedras: Ediciones Huracán.

Santana, Arturo, and Rafael A. Torrech. 1988. *Atlas de Historia de Puerto Rico. Desde Sus Orígenes Hasta Finales del Siglo XIX*. San Juan: Editorial Cordillera.

Scarpaci, Joseph L. 2004. *Plazas and Barrios: Heritage Tourism and Globalization in the Latin American Centro Historico*. Tucson: University of Arizona Press.

Suárez Findlay, Eileen. 1997. *Imposing Decency: The Politics of Sexuality and Race in Puerto Rico, 1870–1920*. Durham and London: Duke University Press.

Sued Badillo, Jalil, and Ángel López Cantó. 1986. *Puerto Rico Negro*. Rio Piedras: Editorial cultural.

UNESCO. 2018. "La Fortaleza and San Juan National Historic Site in Puerto Rico." *UNESCO*. http://whc.unesco.org/en/list/266

US National Park Service. 2018. "San Juan National Historic Site." *National Park Service*. http://www.nps.gov/saju/index.html

Villaplana Ruiz, Virginia. 2010. "Memoria Colectiva y Mediabiografía Como Transformación de las Narrativas Culturales." *Artes y políticas de identidad* 3:87–102.

Wagenheim, Kal, and Olga Jiménez. 1996. *The Puerto Ricans: A Documentary History*. New Jersey: Markus Wiener.

CHAPTER 13

Postcolonial Colonialism in Puerto Rico

Inequality, Capital, and Social Transfers

Miguel A. Rivera Quiñones

The United States occupied Puerto Rico in 1898 and since then has had colonial control of the country. In 2016, the US Supreme Court reiterated that the source of sovereignty in Puerto Rico resides in the US Congress.[1] Given this particular situation, some have called Puerto Rico the "oldest colony in the world" (see Trias Monge 1997). The presence of the United States as a colonial power has certainly changed the economic and social landscape of the country. In the second part of the 20th century, Puerto Rico experienced an important economic expansion that increased the per capita income of the country far above that of other countries in the region (see fig. 13.1). Nevertheless, the paradox of this economic expansion is that the inequality level has followed a less consistent path (Sotomayor 2004, 1403). Income inequality increased during the early stages of economic expansion (1948–60), declined during 1969–89, and from the 1990s onward increased again (Sotomayor 2004; Segarra 2006). The postwar colonial economy produced high unemployment, which is central to these socioeconomic inequality patterns. Nevertheless, something particular about US colonialism is that in order to withstand its political dominance, it has incorporated some sectors of the population into its colonial project from the beginning by providing material benefits (Matos-Cintrón 1988, 21). Considering that Spanish colonialism left mostly a social legacy of poverty in Puerto Rico, American postcolonial colonialism was able to depict its control over Puerto Rico as "benevolent imperialism" (62).

This chapter provides a reflection on how postwar American colonialism has shaped inequality[2] in Puerto Rico and how the US government has consolidated its dominance by providing social transfers. It will uncover how the postwar foreign direct investment (FDI)-led model played an integral role in shaping socioeconomic inequalities and how the United States extended to Puerto Rico some social safety nets to diminish the ills generated by this economy. The first part of this chapter presents how Spanish colonial legacies offered the conditions for fostering popular support for American colonialism on the Island (Matos-Cintón 1988, 62). The second part explores how the postwar FDI-led model impacted Puerto Rico's labor regime and how this played an essential role in shaping economic inequalities. The third part investigates the role of US transfers to low-income families as a policy for managing inequalities from the 1970s onward. The last part concludes that, to assure extraordinary corporate profits, the US government has provided social transfers in order to maintain inequality and poverty levels on the brink of toleration.

The Postcolonial Transition

The "postcolonial" as a concept describes the broad historical fact of decolonization and the realities of nations emerging into new forms of economic and political subordination (Young 2001, 57). In the case of Puerto Rico, the end of Spanish colonialism was not the result of decolonization but instead the beginning of re-colonialization. The "postcolonial" also specifies a transformed historical situation and the social formations that have ascended in response to changes in the political circumstances (57). The response to the end of Spanish colonialism in Puerto Rico was a different system of colonialism under the United States. The sweeping change that Puerto Rico's economic structures experienced with its integration into American capitalism typically obscured how Spanish colonial legacies provided the conditions for the American practices to incorporate sections of the general population into their colonial project by providing some material benefits (Matos-Cintrón 1988, 21–39). The 19th-century forced labor economy and the lack of civil rights and public goods under Spain offered a positive foundation on which America could establish their postcolonial colonialism.

For instance, education and schools were at the center of the US imperial intentions in Puerto Rico. Under the banner of "benevolent imperialism," the US government funded new public schools and trained Puerto

Rican teachers (del Moral 2013, 8). In 1898, the last year of Spanish colonialism, only 9 percent of school-age children were attending school. By 1920, the US imperialist actors raised this figure to 48 percent (Torres 2017, 44). While teachers and families rejected the cultural assimilation tenets of the "Americanization" that came with these investments in education, such as English-language instruction, they also appropriated others to their benefit to increase literacy and skills required for better occupations (del Moral 2013, 10). In addition, in 1903 the University of Puerto Rico became the first higher education institution in the history of the country. In contrast to Cuba, where the University of Havana was established during Spanish rule, in Puerto Rico higher education began under the auspice of American imperialism.

The working class also experienced an improvement in conditions with the end of Spanish colonialism. Under Spanish rule, the popular classes in Puerto Rico experienced slavery, serfdom, and suppression of trade unions (Matos-Cintron 1988, 27). The labor movement, in its struggle against the legacies of Spanish colonialism, became the promotor of the incomplete "bourgeoisie revolution" experienced after the American invasion (28). In 1899, the new colonial power allowed the foundation of the Free Federation of Labor (FFL), which by 1901 was accepted as a member of the American Federation of Labor (AFL) (Sanabria 2005, 150). The AFL promoted the basic ideals of their trade unionist ideology in Puerto Rico by emphasizing the organization of workers into trade unions and the use of collective bargaining to improve wages and the conditions of the working class (144). The FFL fought for the right of workers to organize trade unions and to have higher wages, shorter hours of work, free speech, free press, and freedom of assembly (158). In 1904, 43 trade unions existed in Puerto Rico. By 1909, this number had increased to 120, with a total membership of 55,000 workers (154). However, this was part of the US imperialist actors' method to consolidate popular support for American colonialism (Matos-Cintrón 1980, 63). The leadership of the AFL was explicit about their support of the American presence in Puerto Rico, and they did not antagonize the presence of the US Sugar Corporation on the island (63). These concessions generated support for US colonialism because it granted rights that were denied under Spanish colonialism. However, the new colonialism also weakened the pro-independence motivation that could have arisen from friction between the workers and the sugar corporations (63).

It is important to stress that even though some public goods and rights were granted at the beginning of US rule, Puerto Rico was still a poor rural society until the late 1950s. The American invasion had a significant influence on the local economy. Agricultural, estate-based coffee production was the main economic activity during 19th-century Spanish colonial rule. It was rapidly replaced by industrial sugar production (Quintero-Rivera 1986, 70–71), which only represented 20 percent of exports when the United States first invaded Puerto Rico. Three years later, however, sugar represented 60 percent of exports (70–71). By 1910, American corporations owned 62 percent of the agricultural land dedicated to sugar production, which enforced the proletarization of rural labor under precarious work conditions (70–71). Yet, in comparison with Spanish colonialism, US colonialism appeared as "benevolent" because it was willing to provide some benefits to the general population. This was reinforced when in 1917 the US Congress granted second-class American citizenship to Puerto Ricans and the professionalization of the female labor force as trained teachers, which provided opportunities to women that were not previously possible under Spanish rule (Matos-Cintrón 1988, 36). The practice of providing material benefits to foster support for American colonialism became part of the governance method under US rule and remains into the present. When the postwar model was at risk during the 1970s, social transfers became the new mechanism for encouraging support for colonial rule.

Inequality, US Capital, and Unemployment

The sugar economy crisis throughout the Great Depression in the 1930s transformed the economic landscape of Puerto Rico. During the 1940s, Puerto Rico briefly embarked upon a "state-led" development plan under the governorship[3] of Redford Tugwell and the emergent Popular Democratic Party (PPD) (Dietz 2002, 203–7). From 1941 to 1946, the government implemented a land reform, founded "state-owned" industrial corporations, nationalized the electricity and water supply, and created a Board of Planning, a Government Development Bank and a Corporation for Industrial Promotion (203–7). The brief attempt to build a national economy ended with Tugwell's removal as governor and the electoral victory of the PPD in 1948. Under the leadership of Luis Muñoz Marín, the industrialization plan known as Operation Bootstrap promoted US industrial firms' direct investments by offering generous tax incentives, public subsidies, and cheap labor.

The foreign direct investment (FDI)-orientated industrialization program had a notable economic impact. Due to this program, a total of 272

American industrial firms started operations in Puerto Rico from 1947 to 1953 (Dietz 2002, 230–31). By 1957, over 37,000 industrial jobs had been created, and by 1962, industrial output had increased by 300 percent (230–31). American capitalists' eagerness for investing in Puerto Rico was founded on the fact that, under US and local laws, they were exempt from paying taxes (227). Under these conditions, US firms transformed Puerto Rico into an exporting platform to trade light industrial goods, such as textiles and processed foods, in US markets. Per capita income growth over this period was drastic by any standards. In 1969, per capita income in Puerto Rico was 30.7 times higher[4] than in 1950 (see fig. 13.1). The poverty rate dropped by 23 percent, and the country transitioned from a rural to an urban society in 20 years (Sotomayor 2004, 1397).

Nevertheless, the industrial expansion did not reduce economic inequalities (Sotomayor 2004, 1403). In 1969, Puerto Rico's Gini coefficient, used to measure inequality, was 0.550. It was a markedly important increase from the 1953 Gini coefficient of 0.440 (1403). The process of dependent industrialization experienced in Puerto Rico transformed the labor regime and the composition of the working class. There was increased employment among industrial operatives, professionals, semiprofessionals, and craft and service workers up until 1970 (Toro 2014, 108). One of the effects of this transformation was a decline in seasonal employment and an increase in take-home pay in most areas (108). In manufacturing, for instance, hourly wages tripled from 1940 to 1960 (Dietz 2002, 278). However, while by 1962, production in manufacturing tripled in value, agriculture still employed 19 percent of the labor force (278). Ninety percent of the increases in household income experienced during this period can be associated with changes in earned incomes (Sotomayor 2004, 1403). This suggests that wage differences between agricultural workers and sectors of the emergent working class were an important factor in rising inequalities over this period.

Nonetheless, the central factor in rising inequalities during this period was the chronic unemployment rate (Irizarry-Mora 2001, 196). The unemployment rate in Puerto Rico in 1950 was 12.9 percent, and in 1968, after the economic boom, it was 11.6 percent (Dietz 2002, 294). By the mid-1960s the unemployment situation continued to worsen, because companies began to close their operations and relocate to other countries. From 1962 to 1967, for firms organized under Operation Bootstrap, the average number of workers per factory declined from 80 to 55 (Dietz 1976, 10). The crisis of Operation Bootstrap produced a policy response from

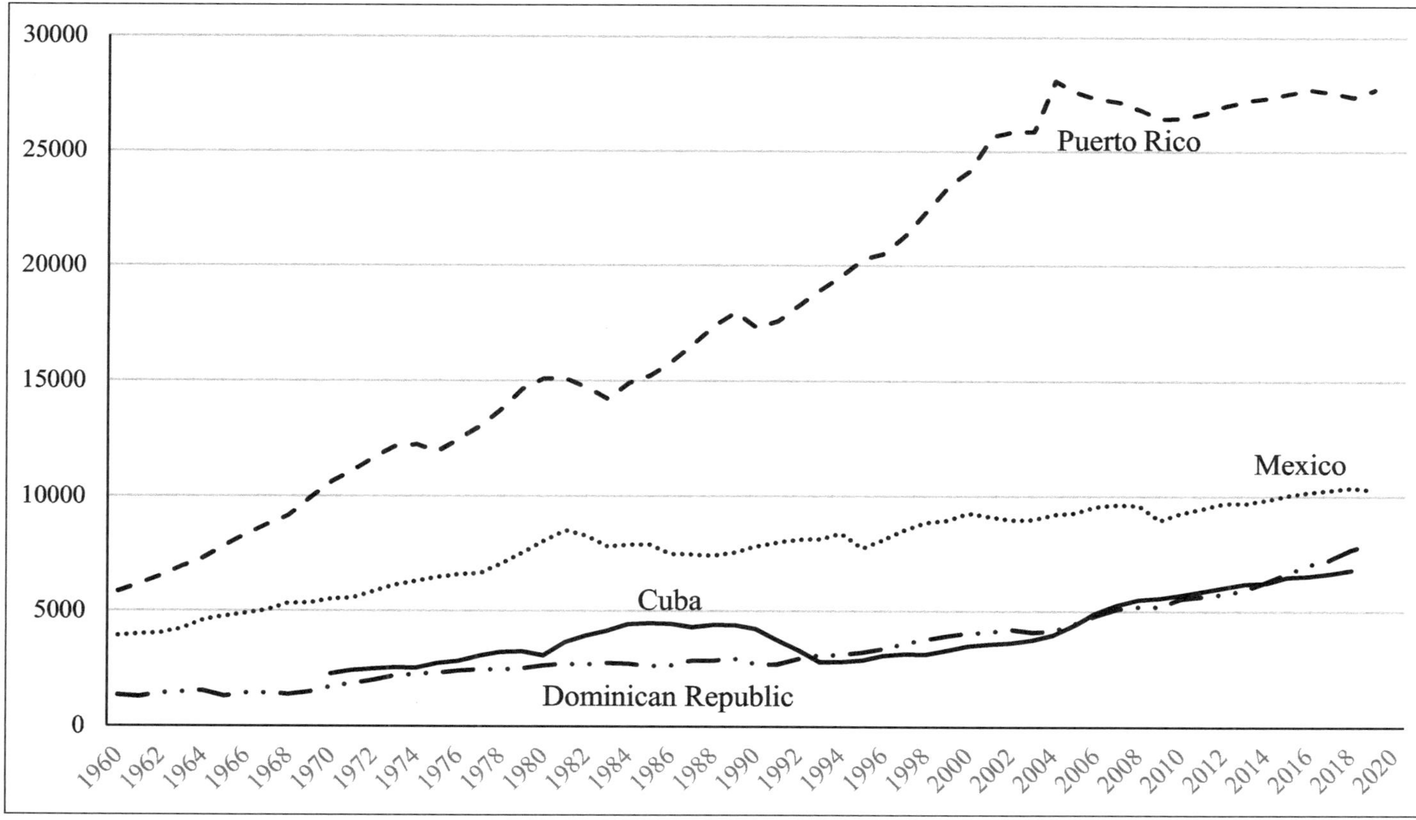

Fig. 13.1. Puerto Rican GDP per capita in US dollars, 1960–2015
Source: Data from World Bank (2019).

the US government and local elites. The aim of the new economic policy was to attract investments from US firms in the petrochemical sectors to transform Puerto Rico into an exporting platform for the US market. This short-lived project ended with the oil crisis in the 1970s. It is worth noting that these corporations only created 7,700 new jobs, even before oil prices rose (10). The incapacity to generate enough jobs has been a key structural limitation of dependent industrialization (Irizarry-Mora 2001, 196). In 1953, the labor participation rate reached its peak with a very weak 53.1 percent (Dietz 2002, 294). Although labor protection laws were introduced and wages increased over this period, the colonial economy could not create enough jobs. The structural imbalances generated by an economy centered on the maximization of profit for foreign transnational firms created a social structure that benefited some sectors in the postwar economy, but not all (Dietz 1976, 12). In addition, 605,000 people migrated to the United States from 1950 to 1970. This figure was equivalent to 27 percent of the population in 1950 (Rivera-Ramos 1998, 9). In 1969, the richest 10 percent of families received more of the total income than the poorest 60 percent of the families (Dietz 1976, 12).

In the early 1970s, economic stagnation along with a severe fiscal crisis and increasing oil prices were clear indications that the FDI-led export-oriented economy was running out of steam. In 1976, the US government introduced Section 936 of the Internal Revenue Code in the tax reform. Section 936 was the central building block of the last phase of the postwar economy. Under Section 936, US transnationals could repatriate dividends to the United States from their subsidiaries in Puerto Rico without paying federal taxes. This attracted dozens of capital-intensive manufacturers to Puerto Rico, mainly from the pharmaceutical sector. Pharmaceutical product exports increased from $630 million in 1978 to $3.3 billion in 1987 (Santiago 1989, 66). In 1988, 85 factories from 18 global pharmaceutical corporations were operating in Puerto Rico (61). In terms of the economic impact of this scheme, capital-intensive manufacturing protected against the collapse of industrial production and greater job losses. It also injected financial liquidity into the banking system because subsidiaries had to deposit dividends in local banks for several years before repatriating them to the United States to avoid the payment of a "tollgate tax" to the local government (68). Yet, although capital-intensive manufacturing sustained industrial activity, it did not stop the severe growth of unemployment. In 1983, the unemployment rate rose to 23.4 percent and the labor participation rate was 41 percent (Dietz 2002, 294). The adverse impact of capital-intensive manufacturing was reduced by huge inflows of economic transfers paid by the US government to low-income families. Although unemployment worsened, these transfers had the effect of decreasing inequality, as shown by a Gini coefficient of 0.4999 in the 1980s (Sotomayor 2004, 1403).

During the 1990s, the Gini coefficient rose to 0.558. Thus, inequality was yet again on the rise (Sotomayor 2004, 1403). While the 1990s was a period of economic growth, the US Congress cancelled the "936" incentives. They initiated a phase-out transition in 1996 and ended it in 2006. The absence of Section 936 corporations had a severe impact on employment. Puerto Rico lost 64,000 industrial jobs from 1996 to 2010 (Department of Labor and Human Resources of Puerto Rico 2012, 43). In addition, in the 1990s, laws were passed that made workers' labor contracts more "flexible," having the impact of deteriorating the private sector workers' employment conditions. One of the social paradoxes of the 1990s was that although factories were closing down, labor rights were reduced, and US economic transfers were not increasing, the country experienced a personal credit–driven growth in retail sales: retail sales increased from $11.7 billion in 1992 to $17.1 billion in 1997 (Rivera 2005, 30). Retail sales growth was accompanied by more American megastores entering the Puerto Rican market. American megastores went from generating 41 percent of retail sales in 1997 to making up 72 percent in 2012 (Caraballo 2016, 4). The increase in megastores in Puerto Rico had the effect of encouraging jobless economic growth because of their "self-service" business model (4). Consequently, in 2000, the unemployment rate was 10.1 percent and the income share of the richest 10 percent was 40 percent higher than in 1970 (Segarra 2006, 5).

The end of the "936" tax incentives in 2006 marked the beginning of the economic depression that the country has been experiencing since then. The US government did not replace Section 936 with any other new incentives that could revive the FDI-led export-oriented economy, and the local government has not been able to introduce an alternative economic model. The issuing of bonds was a short-term solution to the economic crisis. This solution ended in the current debt crisis and the reestablishment of "direct rule"[5] by the US government under the Puerto Rico Oversight, Management, and Economic Stability Act (PROMESA) in 2016. The Fiscal Control Board, created under PROMESA, has a clear neoliberal agenda for assuring bondholders' interests. The local government's main economic initiative has been to provide foreign investors with

4 percent tax rate if they establish their residence in Puerto Rico. It is estimated that under this incentive scheme[6] 13,000 jobs have been created by 2015 (Estudios Técnicos 2015, 43). However, the cumulative job loss between 2007 and 2015 was 137,000 (43). Even before the present debt crisis, the postwar colonial economy could not bring about an adequate labor market. From 1970 to 2000, the share of the population living in households headed by economically inactive individuals rose from 37 percent to 59 percent and those living in households with no income earners rose from 19 percent to 29 percent (Sotomayor 2004, 1403). In 2013, the highest wage earners worked in professional-technical services and managerial services, with average yearly wages between $39,000 and $49,000 (Estudios Técnicos 2015, 43). While this income level is decent for the local standard of living, jobs in these sectors did not exceed 42,000 workers (25).[7] As a result of the economic crisis, 597,000 people migrated from 2006 to 2017. This is equal to 15.7 percent of the population in 2006 (Mora 2018, 213).

The 2018 Human Development Report for Puerto Rico presented the latest data on inequality. The Gini coefficient in 2016 was 0.547,[8] which is among the highest in Latin America (Instituto de Estadísticas de Puerto Rico 2018, 185). The report indicates that from 2000 to 2012, the median income of the 20 percent of the poorest households in Puerto Rico declined by 33 percent (188). It also estimates that 21.3 percent of the working class in Puerto Rico live under the US poverty line (198).[9] In 2012, the income of the richest 10 percent was 34 times higher than that of the poorest 10 percent. This is a notable increase from 2000, when the richest 10 percent income was 25 times higher than the poorest 10 percent (187). The report also shows that after four decades of US transfers to low-income families, female-headed households are still the poorest, youth unemployment has worsened, and the black and female population is more affected by poverty and discrimination. In 2016, it was estimated that in San Juan, the richest city in the country, 53.7 percent of black people lived in poverty, while the poverty rate in the city was 39 percent (206). In 2010, the unemployment rate in the age group of 25–34-year-olds was at a disturbing 60 percent. In 1970, the unemployment rate for this age group was 18 percent (Department of Labor and Human Resources of Puerto Rico 2012, 20). In 2013, 69 percent of female-headed households with children lived in poverty (Instituto de Estadísticas de Puerto Rico 2018, 200). In 2020, the wage gap between men and women with undergraduate studies was $6,000 and with postgraduate studies was $12,000 (Tellado 2020, 2).

The paradox of the postwar colonial economy is that, although social conditions were deteriorating, earnings from FDI between 2001 and 2014 were at an average of $29 billion per year (González and Alameda 2017, 16). FDI yields totaled $406 billion during this period. This amount is equal to 7.6 times the noncontributory transfers to poor families received from the US government during this period.[10] This is a clear indication of how only some have truly benefited from the postwar colonial economy.

Federal Transfers and Social Stability

The disbursement of federal funds to Puerto Rico reflects the interest of the US government and US corporations (Pantojas-García 2007, 220). Federal funds from the 1970s onward sustained the economy, enabling dividend repatriation of American firms while maintaining socioeconomic stability (220). During the 1970s, federal transfers to Puerto Rico increased by an annual rate of 20 percent (210). Federal transfers, using current prices, increased from $720 million in 1970 to $10.8 billion in 2000 (211). Despite the myth that Puerto Ricans live off federal handouts, in 1980 only 35 percent of federal disbursements were noncontributory transfers,[11] and in 2000 this share declined to 23 percent (214). Nonetheless, these welfare transfers to poor families have played an important role in decreasing inequality and poverty throughout the decades (Sotomayor 2004, 1403). Even though federal transfers were not a charitable donation but actually a manifestation of American corporate and political interests, social transfers to poor families have served as a "social cushion" to stabilize the colonial economy crisis and its incapacity to generate jobs.

In 2013, federal welfare programs providing subsidies for food, housing, and education disbursed $3.8 billion (Instituto de Estadísticas de Puerto Rico 2018, 190). In Puerto Rico, some 80,000 homes are recipients of rent subsidy, 51,000 families live in social housing, and a third of the population receives food subsidies (209). These programs, to some extent, have generated a degree of tolerance of existing inequality and poverty levels among the poor. In 2014, a study published about poverty in Puerto Rico revealed that poor people there do not consider themselves poor (Rodríguez 2014, 4). Since poor people in Puerto Rico can eat almost every day and have a place to live, 56 percent of the informants from poor areas who participated in the study identified themselves as being part of the "middle class" (139). This can be an indication of how federal transfers have played a role in diffusing political instability and generating some sense of welfare among the most vulnerable segments of society by enabling some degree of consumption. One particularity of American colonial rule in Puerto Rico is that, even if colonialism is at the heart of the economic and social crisis, the United States has provided a minimum social safety net to reinforce its political dominance. The authorization of social transfers to Puerto Rico is a prerogative of Congress. Puerto Rico, as an unincorporated territory, is not fully covered by the Bill of Rights even though Puerto Ricans are US citizens (Venator 2015, 4). Only when the 1970s crisis became worse did Congress decide to allow social transfers to Puerto Rico. To guarantee corporate profits, the US government has, since then, provided social transfers to maintain tolerable inequality and poverty levels.[12]

Conclusion

American colonialism has had a considerable influence on economic inequality in Puerto Rico. The structural imbalances caused by a colonial economy that was focused on the profit maximization of transnational corporations created a permanent unemployment crisis in Puerto Rico. The incapacity to create enough jobs due to following an FDI-led economic model has contributed to fluctuating inequality levels. In every decade since Operation Bootstrap, unemployment has been one of the most critical issues in the local economy. Although some sectors of Puerto Rican society have substantially benefited from the postwar colonial economy, the working class's living conditions have been declining for decades. Yet, US federal transfers to Puerto Rico have helped to keep the poverty level in Puerto Rico above regional averages. The US policy of incorporating sectors of the population into the colonial project by providing some material benefits, which began with the end of Spanish colonialism, became part of the colonial governance dynamics in Puerto Rico.

The main legacies of American colonialism are an economy of increasing yields from FDI, chronic unemployment, decreasing wages, and increasing social transfers. All these factors have impacted Puerto Rico's inequality dynamics. It is likely that the debt crisis will worsen inequality. The Fiscal Control Board's austerity adjustment will be a crucial determinant of inequality dynamics in the following years. Therefore, even though the postwar economic model is virtually over, the colonial relationship with the United States is still a determining factor in Puerto Rico's inequality dynamics.

NOTES

1. See the US Supreme Court decision *Commonwealth of Puerto Rico v Sánchez Valle*, No. 15–108, 2016.

2. "Inequality" in this chapter is understood as economic and income inequality as measured by the Gini coefficient (see Sotomayor 2004).

3. From 1898 to 1947, the US President appointed the governors of Puerto Rico. In 1947, a Puerto Rican was appointed as governor for the first time, and in 1948, Luis Muñoz Marín became the first elected governor of the country (see Scarano 1993).

4. Net gross domestic product per capita in 1950 was USD 289 (see Dietz 2002, 223).

5. From 1952 to 2016, local political parties controlled Puerto Rico's public administration, local tax policy, and the administration of the local budget. Under PROMESA, the Fiscal Control Board reserves the right to reverse any policy of the local government that interferes with their fiscal plan.

6. The incentive regime was established under Act 22 of 2012.

7. The latest figures show that Puerto Rico's labor force is around 851,000 workers (Department of Labor and Human Resources of Puerto Rico 2018).

8. That the Gini coefficient declined in comparison to 1999 can be explained by the fact that during the current crisis the income of the richest 1 percent declined by 14 percent (Instituto de Estadísticas de Puerto Rico 2018).

9. Poverty in Puerto Rico is measured by the standards of the United States, which establishes the poverty line at $12,140 per year for a family unit of one person (US Department of Health and Human Services 2017).

10. This has been calculated on the bases of the disbursement in 2013 ($3.8 billion) (Instituto de Estadísticas de Puerto Rico 2018).

11. Federal transfers to Puerto Rico are divided into three groups: contributory transfers as Social Security pensions, unemployment benefits, pensioner medical benefits (Medicaid), and war veteran benefits; grants to the government of Puerto Rico; and noncontributory transfers as nutritional, housing, and educational benefits (Pantojas-García 2007).

12. Although the poverty rate in Puerto Rico is 45 percent, poverty is measured by the American poverty line of $12,140 per year for a family unit of one person. In the Dominican Republic, the poverty rate is 30 percent but measured by the World Bank's poverty line of $5.50 a day (Instituto de Estadísticas de Puerto Rico 2018; World Bank 2019).

REFERENCES

Caraballo Cueto, José. 2016. "Deindustrialization with Higher Productivity, Higher Tax Compliance, and Jobless Growth in Megastores." *Perspectivas* 23 (5): 4–7.

del Moral, Solsiree. 2013. *Negotiating Empire: The Cultural Politics of Schools in Puerto Rico, 1898–1952*. Madison: University of Wisconsin Press.

Department of Labor and Human Resources of Puerto Rico. 2012. *Estadísticas de Empleo por Ocupación*. Estado Libre Asociado de Puerto Rico, San Juan.

Department of Labor and Human Resources of Puerto Rico. 2018. *Encuesta de Empleo Asalariado No Agrícola.*

Dietz, James. 1976. "The Puerto Rican Political Economy." *Latin American Perspectives* 3 (3): 3–16.

Dietz, James. 2002. *Historia Económica de Puerto Rico.* San Juan: Ediciones Huracán.

Estudios Técnicos. 2015. *Act 20 and 22 Economic Impact Study.* Instituto de Estadísticas de Puerto Rico, December 18. https://estadisticas.pr/files/BibliotecaVirtual/estadisticas/biblioteca/DDEC_Act_20_22_Economic_Impact_Study_2015.pdf

González Alfredo, and José Alameda. 2017. "El Estancamiento Económico, la Desigualdad del Ingreso y la Financiarización en Puerto Rico." In *Ensayos Para una Nueva Economía.* San Juan: Ediciones Callejón.

Instituto de Estadísticas de Puerto Rico. 2018. *Human Development Report for Puerto Rico.* San Juan: Instituto de Estadísticas de Puerto Rico.

Irizarry-Mora, Edwin. 2001. *Economía de Puerto Rico: Evolución y Perspectivas.* Ciudad de México: Thompson Learning.

Matos-Cintrón, Wilfredo. 1980. *La Política y lo Político en Puerto Rico.* Ciudad de México: ERA.

Matos-Cintrón, Wilfredo. 1988. "La Formación de la Hegemonía de Estados Unidos en Puerto Rico y el Independentismo: Los Derechos Civiles y la Cuestión Nacional." *El Caribe Contemporáneo* (16): 21–56.

Mora, Maire. 2018. "Migration, Geographic Destination and Socio-economic Outcomes of Puerto Rican During La Crisis Boricua." *El Centro Journal* 30 (3): 208–29.

Pantojas-García, Emilio. 2007. "Federal Funds and the Puertorrican Economy: Myths and Realities." *Centro Journal* 19 (2): 207–23.

Quintero-Rivera, Ángel. 1986. *Conflictos de Clase y Política en Puerto Rico.* San Juan: Ediciones Huracán.

Rivera, Ricardo. 2005. *Informe de Ventas al Detalle en Puerto Rico.* San Juan: Compañía de Comercio y Exportación de Puerto Rico.

Rivera-Ramos, Efrén. 1998. *Hegemonía y Legitimidad en el Puerto Rico Contemporáneo.* Serie Working Papers (149). Barcelona: Institut de Ciències Polítiques i Socials.

Rodríguez, Norma. 2014. *Pobreza en Puerto Rico: Una Mirada desde las Experiencias de las Personas que Habitan Sectores Empobrecidos.* San Juan: Publicaciones Puertorriqueñas.

Sanabria, Carlos. 2005. "Samuel Gompers and the American Federation of Labor in Puerto Rico." *El Centro Journal* 17 (1): 140–61.

Santiago, Carlos Ala. 1989. "La Reconversión Industrial en Puerto Rico: el Caso de la Industria Farmacéutica." *Revista de Administración Pública* 21 (2): 61–89.

Scarano, Francisco. 1993. *Puerto Rico: Cinco Siglos de Historia.* San Juan: McGraw Hill.

Segarra, Eileen. 2006. "What Happened to the Distribution of Income in Puerto Rico during the Last Three Decades of the XX Century? A Statistical Point of View." *División de Investigaciones Económicas* 13:1–20.

Sotomayor, Orlando. 2004. "Development and Income Distribution: The Case of Puerto Rico." *World Development* 32 (8): 1395–1406.

Tellado, Ruth. 2020. "A Mayor Nivel de Educación Más Grande es la Brecha Salarial Entre Mujeres y Hombres." *Revista Negocios*, March 8.

Toro, Harold. 2014. "Economic Change and Occupational Stasis: Puerto Rico as a Case Study of Stratification and Development." *Research in Social Stratification and Mobility* 36:101–19.

Torres, Roame. 2017. "Trasfondo Histórico de la Educación Básica en Puerto Rico, 1898–1980." In *Educación Básica en Puerto Rico: Política Pública y Trasfondo Histórico, Legal y Curricular*, edited by Consejo de Educación de Puerto Rico, 33–69. San Juan: Consejo de Educación de Puerto Rico.

Trias Monge, J. 1997. *Puerto Rico: The Trials of the Oldest Colony in the World*. New Haven: Yale University Press.

US Department of Health and Human Services. 2017. *U.S. Federal Poverty Guidelines to Determine Eligibility for Federal Programs*. https://aspe.hhs.gov/poverty-guidelines

Venator Santiago, Charles R. 2015. *Puerto Rico and the Origins of the US Global Empire*. New York: Routledge.

World Bank. 2019. *Poverty Headcount Ratio at National Poverty Lines (% of Population): Puerto Rico*. https://data.worldbank.org/indicator/SI.POV.NAHC?locations=DO

Young, Robert. 2001. *Post-Colonialism: An Historical Introduction*. London: Blackwell.

CHAPTER 14

Colonial Government and Social Organization in the Spanish Philippines

Interactions and Ruptures

María Dolores Elizalde

The Philippine archipelago was part of the Spanish Empire for 333 years, from 1565 to 1898. During this time, the metropolis established different colonial models and economic regimes depending on the domestic state of affairs, the international context, economic circumstances, and the utility that the Philippines was deemed to have within the imperial structure. This necessarily influenced the political, economic, social, and cultural reorganization of the islands' inhabitants, conditioned by the new governmental and organizational norms imposed by the colonizers. All of this was clearly reflected in the archipelago's social organization and the formation of different and changing population groups.

Much depended on the policies pursued by the colonizers, as well as the reactions experienced and provoked by the autochthonous population. The metropolis designed an organizational and relationship model in accordance with its own standards and imposed its own terms of power, organization, hierarchy, and separation. The colonized societies in turn acted in response to these impositions and contributed in shaping their future. One cannot consider the actions taken by the colonizers without contemplating the reactions of the colonized. The Philippines should not be considered only divided and characterized by these two vectors of the colonizers and the colonized. The reality was far more complex, and we can't disregard the processes nor the reasons behind the collaboration and conflict among various groups, the hybridizations and blends that took place, the impact of other external influences, and the initiatives that came from the islands' population, all of which contributed to shaping the development of the Philippines.

In any case, the colonial relationship held undeniable weight in the Philippines' evolution and left an unquestionable legacy, which will be analyzed in the following pages.[1] The chapter seeks to answer a series of questions: What colonial models did the Spanish establish in the Philippines? How was the exercise of power and participation in political and economic life organized? To what extent did the established models shape the formation of elites and the organization of the population? How were relations between distinct groups codified?

Political Models and Economic Regimes during the Spanish Governance of the Philippines

The First Centuries: Pact, Governance, and Imposition

The Spanish arrived in the Philippines while exploring new routes to the East Indies and Spice Islands. In 1521, the expedition led by Ferdinand Magellan took possession of the islands in the name of the then king of Spain, Charles I, during the voyage that became the first circumnavigation of the world, completed by Juan Sebastián Elcano. This expedition was followed by various others directed at measuring the riches that these archipelagos could offer, studying the possibility of a Spanish settlement in the area, and exploring maritime routes that would allow for communication among the viceroyalties of the Americas, the Pacific islands, and the Asian coasts. In 1565, these efforts culminated in Miguel López de Legazpi's voyage to the Philippines with King Philip II's explicit mandate to establish a stable settlement on the archipelago. After examining several islands, the Spanish decided to settle in Manila, the head of the archipelago's principal island, Luzon, which was already the commercial center where Chinese, Indian, and Japanese merchants and other peoples traded with Filipino residents. The island also had a well-protected bay that could serve as a secure refuge when facing a possible external attack, a constant fear in these early times (Cabrero 2000).

To settle in this spot, Legazpi negotiated the signing of a peace and friendship treaty with the two main population groups. On one side, the Muslims, from the converted Islamic communities in the south of the archipelago, established on both banks of the mouth of the Pasig River. And, on the other side, the populations of Malay descent organized in autonomous barangays—decentralized, scattered groups made up of between 30 and 100 families, headed by a hereditary *principalía*, or noble class.[2]

In the early days of its colonization, the Philippines was believed to be the coveted platform that would lead to Spanish presence in Asia, promote commercial trade, and facilitate the evangelization of the area. The actual capabilities and power of the neighboring populations, Spain's scarce resources, and the end of the rivalry between Spain and Portugal following the union of the two Crowns in 1580 led to the abandonment of plans for greater conquests and the decision to concentrate energies in the Philippine archipelago, endowing it with a meaning and utility for the Spanish Empire as a strategic border against Asia and a defensive bastion in the Americas (Ollé 2000).

Following this approach, it was decided that the Philippines would be integrated into the Spanish monarchy as an additional territory of the Crown, administratively connected to the viceroyalty of New Spain. A basic colonial administration was established, made up of soldiers, civil servants, and clergy, who delegated most of their duties to the encomenderos, religious orders, and indigenous authorities (Fradera 2005; Elizalde 2003, 2009; Sánchez 2010). The Spaniards established their administrative seat in the walled city called Intramuros, located at the mouth of Manila's harbor. This was the residence of the islands' principal authority, the governor-general, and the officials in charge of the different official institutions—political, military, economic, judicial, educational, and religious—that the provincial delegates depended on. In these early days, there would have been no more than 3,500 Spaniards, in addition to the religious missionaries.

A work and farming system was organized based on the encomienda, which required the limited presence of the Crown's representatives and the Spanish metropolis. The encomienda model established that the encomenderos had to provide a return on the land that they had been accorded, committing them to protecting and evangelizing the inhabitants in exchange for receiving the taxes paid by that territory's residents. The encomenderos put the indigenous *principalía* in charge of organizing work among its own subjects and collecting fees that would eventually end up in the pockets of the encomenderos. In this way, a limited number of Spanish representatives were sufficient for the supervision of this procedure (Hidalgo 1995).

Among the Spaniards who resided throughout the archipelago, the religious orders—primarily Augustinians, Franciscans, Jesuits, Dominicans, and Recollects—were of particular note. They spread through the native towns in accordance with the territorial distribution of different geographic, ethnic, and linguistic areas. To facilitate their mission, instead of spreading Spanish, they learned the autochthonous languages. Through living together daily and their evangelizing and educational work, they acquired a great degree of influence over the Christianized indigenous population. They became advisers in local governments, acting as spokespeople and intermediaries between the islands' inhabitants and the colonial authorities, and thus became an important instrument for the maintenance of order and control over the population (Elizalde and Huetz de Lemps 2015).

To defray the costs of management, defense, and evangelization of the islands, once the existence of spices and precious ores—gold and silver—was ruled out, agricultural production was boosted, the cultivation of lowlands was increased, and the irrigated cultivation of rice, which didn't require large extensions of fallow land, was encouraged. Taxes were also imposed on the population, and Filipinos were required to offer their personal labor. This encouraged the concentration of the population in towns under the rule of those who wielded greatest control.[3]

In this manner, facing extensive terrain where colonial regulation was unknown, colonial authorities established a concerted partnership with leading local groups that accepted the Spanish administration. In the spots where the new regime was recognized and new population associations were formed, local politics was left in the hands of the traditional rulers, respecting the original power structure. A *gobernadorcillo*, or captain, elected from among the hereditary barangay heads that made up the *principalía*, was appointed head of every town. These *gobernadorcillos* held political and judicial power. They also enjoyed great economic power, given that they controlled the land, distributed the workforce, meted out *bandalas*, organized the provision of obligatory personal labor—the zones and services—and charged taxes, from which they could reserve a part for themselves. Furthermore, these authorities were themselves exempt from taxes and were not required to provide their own personal services.

This incorporation of the indigenous *principalía* into the colonial administration consolidated Spanish presence in the archipelago. Thanks to the new colonial authorities' collaboration and the recognition they gave to the role the *principalía* played, the power of the indigenous elites over their subjects was reinforced. The system also favored the preservation of Filipino political, social, and economic structures, since, within the colonized areas, the majority of the population, despite having to adjust to the Spaniards' requirements and tax payment, were able to maintain their traditional organization and way of life, still in function of the native elites' directives.

Since the early period of colonization, a Chinese population also had settled on the island. Originally associated with trade, little by little they took over other economic activities until they became a fundamental pillar of island society. Relations between the Chinese emigrants and colonial authorities—and at times also with the autochthonous population—weren't easy, as evidenced by frequent uprisings, repressions, and expulsion orders. However, their presence became a fixed feature on the islands to the point of requiring legislation and taxes specific to the Chinese and the Chinese mestizos, who were continually growing in number (Wickberg 2001; Wilson 2004; Chu 2010; Félix 1966).

The Manila Galleons: Transpacific Trade and the Rise in Inequalities

The last decade of the 16th century witnessed a decline in agricultural production in the Philippines (Alonso 2003). This favored a rise in the inflow of Chinese food products, which came with other valuable Asian commodities. The Spanish realized that these articles held far greater value than the old Filipino export goods—textile fibers, cotton blankets, and wax—and could generate large profits if they were brought back in the galleons that regularly connected New Spain and the Philippines. In this way, commercial trade began in which products from China, Japan, India, and Southeast Asia, brought to Manila by Chinese junks (the only ones authorized to do so), were exchanged for silver from the Americas, which was in high demand in the Chinese economy and ended up becoming the fundamental exchange value. Commercial traffic was thus organized through the galleons, which linked Manila with Acapulco, from which products were then redistributed to the rest of the world. In this manner, the Philippines was transformed into an intermediary economy between Asia, the Americas, and Europe at an essential stage in this new transpacific trade route, and Manila acquired concrete relevance as a port and bridge for trade with Asia.

This consolidation of the Philippines as the central point of commercial intermediation between Asia and the Americas was made possible thanks to the island economy's capacity to provide the necessary infrastructure for the galleons' operation, even if it was secured through fiscal coercion. Thanks to obligatory labor and the forced sale of food, the provinces supplied the ships with a workforce; with wood for the construction and repair of hulls and masts; with cotton fabric and abaca needed to make sails and rigging; with cord to wrap around merchandise sent to Acapulco; or with food and various essential supplies for the crossings and also for sustaining the growing floating population—Spanish, New Spanish, and Chinese—who worked in Manila for the galleons. In this process of intermediation between the capital and the provinces, essential for the system's organization, the work carried out by the colonial authorities was of key importance, as was the role played by the indigenous *principalía* that was in charge of organizing the Filipinos' obligatory personal services. There was thus a close relationship and interdependence between the internal and external economy (Alonso 2000).

In this manner, a strictly regulated economy was organized around the galleons and the transpacific exchanges, which largely benefited the traders involved, generally Spanish residents of the Philippines, who were theoretically the only ones able to participate in this traffic, as well as the traders and storekeepers in New Spain, who were in charge of the sale and distribution of the incoming products. The Manila galleons also allowed for custom duties that contributed to the colonial administration's upkeep for a long period of time. It also gave the colony new prosperity and interest and the Philippines a new status within the Spanish Empire. It advanced the archipelago's insertion in international trade and its integration into the global economy. However, it did not strengthen the islands' internal development, given the limited presence of the native population in this trade, nor did it drive the islands' production, given that that it was generally not based on the trade of goods produced in the archipelago. Furthermore, the main beneficiaries of this commercial traffic were the Spanish residents of the islands and the sectors with whom they maintained close relations for guarantee of the correct functioning of the system, while the islands' population—with the exception of those directly involved in the galleons' operations—obtained few benefits, thus increasing inequalities among the different groups that lived in the Philippines. Even so, the galleons' commercial traffic persevered until 1815, and efforts were even made by private traders to prolong it through budgets promoting free trade that the islands' population could participate in until the independence of the Americas' republics made it unfeasible (Schurtz 1939; Yuste 1984; Bernabéu and Martínez Shaw 2013; Pérez Lecha 2014).

The Bourbon Reforms Era: Reorganization and Resistance

In 1700, a new dynasty succeeded the Habsburgs who were in charge of the Spanish Crown. The Bourbons, originating in France and from a different political culture based on more centralist and interventionist directives, promoted a deeply reformist policy during the time of the Enlightenment, in accordance with the requirements of the time.

The colonial authorities in the Philippines had been warning for years that the territorial organization through encomiendas, mayors, *gobernadorcillos*, and religious orders entailed an excessive delegation of powers and frequently led to abuses and resulted in a large part of the Philippines' taxes and output never reaching the Crown, which hurt the interests of the metropolis. In addition to this, new international circumstances required the strengthening of the Philippines' defenses against British ambitions—since in 1762 the English invaded Manila, as well as Havana, as part of the Seven Years' War. The taking of Manila demonstrated Spain's weak position in the Pacific and made clear the indispensable need for undertaking urgent reforms in the archipelago.

Since the middle of the 17th century, the governors-general, alarmed by frequent conflicts, had begun to reconsider the advantages of changing the provincial, municipal, and native towns' organization. To this end, they drew up successive ordinances on good governance to better coordinate colonial society's relations, revive economic activities, enable Spanish settlement in indigenous towns, improve the state of the provinces, and promote the teaching of Spanish to make direct dialogue possible between the islands' population and the colonial authorities.

In the last decade of the 18th century, the reforms process was implemented with particular success. At the political level, this was reflected in the adoption of a centralized government model, in which the governor-general's prominence was reinforced and the archipelago's local administration was transformed in order to get rid of the old imperial practices of delegated powers. At the military level, new regulations focused on the reorganization of the army, the growth of the navy, and the strengthening of Manila's defenses and the archipelago's most strategic points. At the economic level, income generation was considered fundamental in order to undertake the reforms and secure Spanish presence in the islands without having to seek help from the metropolis. To this end, the indigenous tax was extended and increased and new control mechanisms were created, like the Intendencia de Hacienda, which, from that moment on, was in charge of the direct collection of taxes. It was also decided to establish a state-run monopoly over the cultivation and selling of tobacco and the local nipa and coconut liquors that in the following decades came to provide important support to the colonial administration (see Fradera 2005, 439–533; De Jesús 1980; García de los Arcos 1983). A charter company, la Real Compañía de Filipinas, was also created with the aim of boosting the islands' agriculture and, for the first time, of driving direct trade between the Philippines and the peninsula.

The smooth operation of a strong, centralized government model, the tobacco monopoly, and the thorough collection of taxes imperatively required a more complex government apparatus than the one developed up until that point, as well as greater control of certain parts of the archipelago in which the Spanish administration had little more than theoretical sovereignty. In this context, a powerful colonizing offensive was launched into the country's interior. This entailed the transition from a lax government system, which did not demand direct control over the provinces or their inhabitants beyond tax collection and a few obligations that the indigenous *principalías* took charge of, to a new model in which Spanish officials' control of territory and population was indispensable, which created resistance among the different colonial administrative agencies as well as within the Filipino population.

19th-Century Transformations: Changes, Collaborations, and Conflicts

Nevertheless, the Bourbon Reforms led to the successful handling of a delicate juncture. In the first decades of the 19th century, when the republics of the Americas were gaining independence, the Philippines maintained an administration and economy capable of guaranteeing the colonial regime's continuation and sustaining the archipelago´s financing. This allowed relations between Spain and the Philippines, carried out from then on across the Indian Ocean, to survive the breakdown of the empire in the Americas and to be upheld another 100 years longer.

This shift in position coincided with new international demand for tropical products that could be cultivated in the Philippines, such as sugar, cotton, indigo, tobacco, and abaca. The Filipino economy progressively transformed into an agro-exporting economy geared toward international markets. Producers, industrialists, traders, and investors from different backgrounds were involved in this economy: Creole and peninsular Spaniards, native and mixed Filipinos, and Chinese, British, and other foreigners (Legarda 1999; Larkin 1993; Owen 1984).

In 1789, a partial opening of Manila's port took place. It was officially opened to international traffic in 1834. Years later, it was followed by the opening of other ports and the adoption of increasingly pro–free trade policies. In 1863, the state-run tobacco monopoly was abandoned, since the operating costs came to exceed the profits that were generated (Fradera 1999). This led to significant increases in taxes, trade, business creation, and investments in the archipelago, within the larger context of growing international interest in the Pacific, Western penetration into Asian markets, and the forced opening of China and Japan. It also was a time marked by the opening of new communication routes—particularly the Suez Canal in 1869—and of technological advances. All this favored the Filipino economy's progress (see Legarda 1999; Elizalde 1998, 2017a; Rodrigo 2003; Delgado 1996).

These economic transformations were accompanied by the continued rethinking of forms of government. In the Cortes de Cádiz (1810–14), the Trienio Liberal (1820–23), and the period of the Royal Statute (1834–37), the Philippines and the other overseas territories were given parliamentary representation, in accordance with the Spanish Constitution of 1812, which established political and civil equality for Spaniards in both hemispheres. This fostered increased Creole control of the levers of power in the Philippines, the assertion of indigenous *gobernadorcillos* in local politics, and the growing prominence of Chinese-Filipinos and the rise of new sectors that demanded greater participation in the archipelago's political life. In 1837, however, the metropolitan government, overwhelmed by the numeric weight the overseas territories could reach in parliament, curtailed their capacities, put an end to their representation in the Cortes, and remitted them to special laws adapted to the circumstances of each territory. Cuba and Puerto Rico regained parliamentary presence in the century's final decades, but the Philippines remained forever excluded from the representative chamber. To promise equality and then take it away inevitably had severe repercussions in the archipelago's evolution. This change also led to a painful reprisal process, first, to the creation of alternative national projects and, later, ultimately, to an unstoppable independence movement (Fradera 2016; Llobet 2011).

Despite these circumstances, activity was still taking place on the political level. Since the 19th century, the colonial authorities were conscious that, in order to maintain sovereignty over the archipelago in the face of imperial pressures, other powers, and internal unrest, it was necessary to invest energy into introducing reforms and modernizing the administration. It proved not to be an easy road, due to the dissent it provoked among the colonial regime's representatives regarding the reforms' reach and the prominence it gave to the Filipinos in the process, which led to complications in the islands' development. The government wanted to reform and modernize the administration, while at the same time reinforce the mechanisms of colonial control and avoid secessionist movements. As such, the modernizing process of the administration and economy was applied by the colonial authorities following highly restrictive guidelines for fear of encouraging pro-independence movements. Some reforms were implemented: governance mechanisms were modernized; the provincial and local regimes were modified; education and a new sanitary policy were promoted; new professional bodies were created; and infrastructures were renovated in accordance with the new era's requirements of technical and economic progress. All this permitted a slightly greater opening of the political playing field and a rise in the population's expectations. But these efforts led above all to reinforcing the metropolis's position, keeping Filipinos as far away as possible from the political and economic power structure, only giving them responsibility over determined advising or local administration assignments, which over time exacted a heavy cost.

The tension between the measures put in place by the metropolis and the strength of the Filipino population eager to take on political power and end secular abuse brought about a growing number of protests and grievance demands. The proliferation and deepening of discontents resulted in the organization of different types of movements from various origins against the colonial regime. These movements increasingly radicalized their positions until they came to consider the fight for independence the only possible formula through which they could attain their aspirations, leading to the 1896 revolution.

Social Structure and Population Groups

The Population's Legal Division

The Laws of the Indies, which also extended to the Philippines, divided imperial society into a *República de Españoles*, on one side, and, on the other, a *Republic de Indios*, each with its own institutions and governance mechanisms. Respecting a strict social and ethnic hierarchy, each group had different duties but also rights guaranteed by the Laws of the Indies and the possibility to request protection from the monarch, a commonly used measure throughout the centuries.[4]

Following this setup, during the colonial period, the Philippines' population was divided into four basic categories, according to legal status and racial differentiation: first, the Spanish, which included those of peninsular origin and those of Spanish descent on their father's side, who didn't pay taxes or provide free obligatory labor; second, the "Indios" or native Malayo inhabitants, who paid a reduced tax and were required to offer their personal services; third, the Chinese-Filipino mestizos, who paid around double the indigenous tax rate, based on their perceived greater ability to generate wealth, and who also had to provide their personal labor services; and fourth, the Chinese, who paid the highest tax rate for the same perceived reason but were not obligated to carry out any type of work, given the difficulty of forcing this population to comply with this last obligation. This highlights the importance the Chinese world had in the Philippines, to the point of meriting two levels in the population's classification system.

In addition to these four categories, two others existed on the margins of colonial society. First were the infidels, who were Moors—Muslim residents who inhabited the archipelago's southern islands—as well as the blacks or "savages," who had gone up into the mountains to free themselves from the Spanish and who, whether enslaved or not, lived outside the colonizers' rules or were in constant battle with them. For many years, it was understood that the colonizing process was incapable of assimilating these populations and commanding their respect to comply with certain laws and pay taxes. In the second position was the foreign population (excluding the Chinese). Up until the first decades of the 19th century, subjects from other countries could not officially settle on the islands. However, once they received authorization to do so, they had a notable impact on the archipelago's evolution, particularly in respect to economic activity.

Each of the categories outlined, in addition to differential tax rates and personal work obligations, implicitly designated different rights to participate in colonial institutions, local governments, choice and change of residency, the purchasing of land, the ability to carry out certain activities, or the application of different laws. In this manner, the colonial taxonomy imposed on the archipelago's inhabitants assigned a certain hierarchical position to each individual, imposed obligations, and established certain limits on non-Spaniards' rights and aspirations, reinforcing inequality among the different population groups. However, while this division was never completely overturned in the Filipino archipelago, with time, it came to be blurred, opening up new directions for social classification.

Social Structure

In the 19th century, colonial Filipino society was formed by different groups, all of whom contributed to the archipelago's evolution. The first group of note was the peninsula-born Spaniards, who generally were on the islands due to their posts in the colonial administration. They were officials in different administrative branches, military men in the army and navy, members of religious orders, professionals in different technical and sanitary bodies, partners and representatives of investor companies and businesses, small-business owners engaged in carrying out necessary activities for the colony's proper functioning, and employees. In many cases, they only stayed for the time their post stipulated, enough to complete the duties they were entrusted with or to obtain desired administrative and economic advantages.

Then there were the Spanish Creoles and mestizos, who had a peninsular background but had been born in the Philippines, many of whom would remain forever in the Filipino archipelago, becoming part of its population. As Spanish descendants, they held the same legal status as Spaniards and thus the same rights and privileges. The difference between Spanish Creoles and mestizos was founded on the theoretical basis that the former were peninsular descendants on both their father's and mother's sides, while the latter were of mixed blood, usually from a Spanish peninsular origin father and a native or Chinese mestiza mother. Nonetheless, the differences between the two did not always depend on strictly racial criteria; rather, in many cases, the determination of a person's status was influenced by more arbitrary factors like belonging to certain social or family networks, levels of wealth, or duties performed (Elizalde 2017a, 2017b; Huetz de Lemps 2017).

Together with the population of peninsular origin, throughout the 19th century the contours of the new Filipino society would come to be defined. It was an especially complicated task, given that the population was made up of more than 50 ethnicities and different languages, cultures, and religions. Among the native population, pride of place was held by the indigenous *principalía*, which, thanks to its secular control of the levers of political, economic, fiscal, and legal power in local government, maintained its superior position at the top of native society. Once the post of *gobernadorcillo* ceased to be hereditary in 1789, confrontations took place between the old representatives and the new sectors that aimed to gain power, at times with the support of a Spanish administration representative, like the friars who lived in the villages (Inarejos 2015). Throughout the 19th century, the Filipino population did not let up in their demands for greater capacities in political and economic areas. They also expressed an increasingly critical position against the religious orders' interference in community life.

On the other hand, among the autochthonous elites, differences were accentuated between rural *principalías*, nearly always indigenous; the provincial elites, natives, and mestizos, who governed important towns or provincial heads and held important rural properties; and the urban elite of Manila, Cebu, or Iloilo, mainly mestizos, Creoles, or those of multiethnic heritage, who were often involved in the agro-export economy, hacienda and urban property owners, and were increasingly involved in trade in collaboration with traders and investors from different backgrounds (McCoy and De Jesús 1982; Cullinane 2003).

Alongside these often interwoven groups, an educated class was forming who attended Filipino universities and often completed their education in Spanish peninsular or foreign institutions. This group played an essential role in the formation of a Filipino national consciousness. Initially, its demands did not question relations with Spain, but the lack of answers in response to their claims gradually led to the call for self-governance and independence (see Schumacher 1997; Mojares 2006; Thomas 2012).

Throughout the 19th century, a class of Filipino farmers was also reaffirmed. They were less economically powerful but equally aware of the need for the recognition of their rights in the face of the colonial administration, the religious orders, and the native and mestizo owners of land who hired them under harsh work conditions. Alongside these classes, an incipient working class emerged in the cities, who worked in the growing number of factories, trading houses, and service enterprises.

Another fundamental sector in the formation of a Filipino identity was the native clergy, who clashed with the colonial administration. This was due to the administration's attempts, since the first decades of the 19th century and at the insistence of religious orders, to counter the influence the native clergy could have on the population, progressively limiting the parish action that it could develop (Schumacher 1981; Blanco 2013). Various populist native religious movements were also of importance and played a valuable role in certain contexts in defending the most disadvantaged Filipino populations (see Ileto 1979; Blanco 2009; McCoy 2017).

Ruptures and Interactions in the 19th Century

The 19th century was a time of ruptures and the opening of new channels in the social structure. It was clear that the Filipino society was subject to a colonial regime, in which the colonial authorities determined the policies and the rules of the game. There were laws that established different population categories and determined their respective rights, obligations, and opportunities. Inequality among the different population groups was evident and deliberate (Kramer 2006; Thompson 2010, 2017; Anastacio 2016).

However, several factors led to the blurring of these divisions. On the one hand, it was necessary to reach a level of equilibrium and provide compensation to ensure acceptance of the colonial regime in order to maintain power and avoid rebellions in different local environments, which meant that some benefit went to the oppressed and checked uprisings. On the other hand, the barriers proved more permeable than had been imagined. In numerous occasions the established limits were transgressed. There were arbitrary and subjective features that united different population types and facilitated their integration, such as the level of Hispanization; family; marriage and inclusion within different family dynasties; the instruction received; the practice of Catholicism; social status and belonging to distinguished networks; economic status; shared business and interests; responsibilities and participation in associations and organizations; social traditions; and the possession and visibility of certain phenotypic traits susceptible to assimilation to fit standard features. All these traits could open pathways to inclusion and permeability between distinct population groups.

Additionally, in the final decades of the 19th century, categorization among different population types was affected by different circumstances. First, in 1884, the implementation of a new personal documents model was approved that marked the elimination of the old system of ethnic and physical categories for tax payment. From then on, it was ruled obligatory that personal documents be acquired that corresponded to the individual's class—first, second, third, and so on, until fifteenth, depending on their activities—for all individuals living in the Philippines, "regardless of race, nationality, or sex, starting at the age of 18,"[5] even if they were Spanish—including all categories, from peninsular Spaniards to "Indios"—or foreigners with over a year of residency. In this way, from that moment on, distinctions were made among the population at the time of paying taxes that were based not on ethnic or national origin, which was only underscored in censuses or in certain official documents, but on wealth, the income received, and the economic activities carried out.

Furthermore, in these final decades of the 19th century, a somewhat more assimilative policy was adopted and the application of new laws was approved in the Philippines, such as the extension of the peninsula's civil and penal code to the archipelago; a greater separation between executive and judicial power; the adoption of a new code of trade; the approval of new taxes on economic activities; and the modification of provincial and local governments, which spelled the end of *alcaldes mayores* and led to the creation of civil or political-military governors in the provinces and the formation of new local governments that opened up new possibilities for upward mobility for natives and mestizos. None of these things made the differences between the different population groups disappear—native, Chinese mestizo, and sangley courts remained, for example—but they opened up a broad and continuous debate over which laws applied to whom and who was exempt from these regulations (always according to the metropolis's and colonial authorities' interests), which enabled greater discretion when the time came to decide each person's place, relaxing in some cases the boundaries between the population categories (Huetz de Lemps 2017).

Additionally, the relative frailty of the Spanish colonization's administration, economy, and migration allowed for the emergence and ascent of autochthonous elites—"Indios" and mestizos—as well as the settling of foreign communities, who played a more active role than in other European colonies.

What's more, the possibility that existed in the Philippines of the 19th century to receive primary-, secondary-, and university-level instruction on the islands themselves allowed for the formation of population groups with an advanced educational level, which enabled their upward social and professional mobility and their inclusion in a shared Hispanic culture, blurring certain barriers. In this manner, the emergence of economic and professional solidarities that transcended the old colonially imposed categories was assisted. There was thus a certain margin of maneuvering in mobility among population groups.

A complementary factor also influenced the Spanish Philippines' social classification, which was the practice of Catholicism, to the point that the indigenous population was divided into believers and infidels, with the unbelievers remaining on the fringes of colonial society. Religion and the fact of sharing the same faith became essential elements for acceptance in colonial society. A properly baptized "Indio" or Chinese mestizo, Hispanized in customs and traditions and with good economic and social standing, could be more easily assimilated if there were the interest and reasons to do so. Catholicism was always a powerful instrument not only for evangelization but also for Hispanization.

In the Philippines of the 19th century, there were frequent interactions among population groups that went beyond legal status and racial traits. To keep power in the hands of peninsular officials and the like and to remove groups from posts that could allow them to challenge Spanish sovereignty, the political level was where the different population categories were most strictly marked. On the social level, the line between differentiation and assimilation was somewhat arbitrary due to the malleability of the criteria used for social acceptance, ascent, or exclusion. On the economic level, synergies were of particular importance. Alliances, clashes, and the formation of interest groups did not depend on ethnic or national background or on legal status but instead on the existence of common interests and strategy plans that would enable profit, as was reflected in businesses like the San Miguel brewery, the Tramway Company of the Philippines, the Maritime Company and other shipping lines, sugar haciendas, abaca and textile fiber enterprises, construction, oil and alcohol companies, numerous loan agreements, and the multitude of small businesses made up of multiple stakeholders (Legarda 1999; Elizalde 2017a).

Conclusion

It is clear that more than 330 years of colonial relations between Spain and the Philippines without a doubt left its imprint on the archipelago. In that sense, a series of traits can be highlighted that are linked as much to the colonial legacy as to the islands' subsequent evolution: first, the persistence of a population structure presided over by several political and economic elites who continue to shape the archipelago, the importance of a limited group of families and family dynasties that controlled important levers of power, the existence of a vast gulf between these main elites and the rest of the population, and the worsening of inequality; second, a clear differentiation and imbalance between life in the cities and life in the rural world of the provinces; third, the continued relevance of the Catholic religion in Filipino society, alongside the existence of significant autochthonous religious movements; fourth, the magnitude of the Chinese influence and the population of Chinese descent, which has now become an essential and unbreakable pillar of Filipino society; fifth, the consolidation of an open, inclusive, mestizo society, which was the product of multiple influences; sixth, although it appears to contradict the previous point, the persistence of the view of Muslims as a world apart, largely withdrawn to the archipelago's south and possessing very specific characteristics; seventh, a country with an Asian makeup but in which influences from Europe and the Americas could be perceived, as well as Hispanic cultural traits, which accord special consideration to the islands throughout Asia; eighth, the weight of various successive colonial administrations in the archipelago, each of which left its own legacy and exerted an influence on the previous administration's decisions in order to justify its own existence—and, finally, as a result of all this, the formation of a Filipino society that fights to defend its own identity, resolve its contradictions, reach more egalitarian conditions, and claim, in the face of all this, national independence with support from the regional organization ASEAN, or the Association of Southeast Asian Nations, which contributes to its international relevance, always navigating between Asia, the Americas, and Europe.

NOTES

1. The work was conducted as part of the research project "La modernización de Filipinas, 1868–1898" (HAR2015–66511-P), financed by the Plan Nacional de Investigación (Spain, MINECO-FEDER). It is also part of the shared work carried out by the Unidad Asociada CSIC-UPF "Estudios sobre Asia y el Pacífico."

2. As specialists have highlighted, once having acquired firsthand experience in the Americas, the metropolitan authorities insisted that the Philippines be settled by avoiding violence to the greatest degree possible and seeking peace accords and pacts with the autochthonous population in which Spanish presence would be accepted in exchange for a number of benefits, such as defense against foreign attacks or rival tribes. As Luis Alonso, for example, stated: "Legazpi ended up choosing a distinct conquest model from the American one, in which violence was largely substituted for peace accords and pacts with the natives" (Legazpi acabó optando por un modelo de conquista distinto al americano en donde la violencia fue sustituida, en gran medida, por acuerdos y pactos con los naturales) (Alonso 2000, 190–91).

3. Additionally, a "situado" was sent from New Spain to provide financial assistance when necessary (see Alonso 2009).

4. Of the many examples of this type that have taken place throughout the centuries, I will just mention two cases that I have directly studied: first, the missive that the Creole Domingo Roxas wrote to the kingdom's regent in 1842 after having

been accused of participating in the unrest at the Cofradía de San José and the riot in Tayabas (National Historical Archive, Madrid [AHN], Ultramar, leg. 2153, exp. 39); and second, the letter sent in 1888 to the Queen Regent María Cristina by 476 liberal-leaning Filipinos, including many *gobernadorcillos*, requesting the protection of Emilio Terrero in the wake of conflicts that took place after various reforms were introduced during his time of governance (Archivo Histórico Nacional [AHN], Madrid, Ultramar, leg. 5258, exp. 53).

5. The quote is taken from an official booklet collecting information on the "tax on personal identity cards" (El Faro Administrativo 1894).

REFERENCES

Alonso, Luis. 2000. "Repartimientos Forzosos y Economía en las Islas Filipinas Bajo Dominio Español, 1565–1815." In *El Repartimiento Forzoso de Mercancías en México, Perú y Filipinas*, edited by Margarita Menegus, 170–215. México: UAM.

Alonso, Luis. 2003. "¿Qué Nos Queréis, Castillas? El Tributo Indígena en las Islas Filipinas en los Siglos XVI y XVIII." *Jahrbuch für Geschichte Lateinamerikas* 40:13–42.

Alonso, Luis. 2009. *El Costo del Imperio Asiático. La Formación Colonial de las Islas Filipinas Bajo Dominio Español, 1565–1800*. México: Instituto Mora-Universidad de A Coruña.

Anastacio, Leia Castañeda, 2016. *The Foundations of the Modern Philippine State: Imperial Rule and the American Constitutional Tradition, 1898–1935*. New York: Cambridge University Press.

Bernabéu, Salvador, and Carlos Martínez Shaw, eds. 2013. *Un Océano de Seda y Plata: el Universo Económico del Galeón de Manila*. Sevilla: CSIC.

Blanco, John D. 2009. *Frontier Constitutions. Christianity and Colonial Empire in the Nineteenth-Century Philippines*. Berkeley: University of California Press.

Blanco, Roberto. 2013. *Entre Frailes y Clérigos. Las Claves de la Cuestión Clerical en Filipinas*. Madrid: CSIC.

Cabrero, Leoncio, ed. 2000. *España y el Pacífico. Legazpi*. 2 vols. Madrid: Sociedad Estatal de Conmemoraciones Culturales.

Chu, Richard T. 2010. *Chinese and Chinese Mestizos of Manila: Family, Identity, and Culture, 1860s-1930s*. Leiden: Brill.

Cullinane, Michael. 2003. *Ilustrado Politics: Filipino Elite Responses to American Rule, 1898–1908*. Quezon City: Ateneo de Manila University Press.

De Jesús, Edilberto. 1980. *The Tobacco Monopoly in the Philippines: Bureaucratic Enterprise and Social Change, 1766–1880*. Quezon City: Ateneo de Manila University Press.

Delgado, Josep M. 1996. "Bajo Dos Banderas (11881–1910). Sobre Cómo Sobrevivió la *Compañía General de Tabacos de Filipinas* al Desastre del 98." In *La Nación Soñada: Cuba, Puerto Rico y Filipinas Ante el 98*, edited by Consuelo Naranjo, Miguel Ángel Puig-Samper, and Luis Miguel García Mora, 293–304. Aranjuez: Ed. Doce Calles.

El Faro Administrativo. 1894. *El Impuesto de las Cédulas Personales*. Manila: Imprenta de D.J. Atayde y Compañía.

Elizalde, María Dolores. 1998. "Filipinas, Fin de Siglo: Imágenes y Realidad." *Revista de Indias* 213:307–39.

Elizalde, María Dolores, ed. 2003. *Las Relaciones Entre España y Filipinas, Siglos XVI-XX*. Madrid: CSIC-Casa Asia.

Elizalde, María Dolores, ed. 2009. *Repensar Filipinas. Política. Identidad y Religión en la Construcción de la Nación Filipina*. Barcelona: Editorial Bellaterra.

Elizalde, María Dolores. 2017a. "Interacciones Empresariales Entre las Elites Urbanas Filipinas: Barcos, Tranvías, Cervezas y Aceites." In *Filipinas, Siglo XIX. Coexistencia e Interacciones Entre Comunidades en el Imperio Español*, edited by María Dolores Elizalde and Xavier Huetz de Lemps, 63–98. Madrid: Ed. Polifemo.

Elizalde, María Dolores. 2017b. "Navegando Entre Comunidades: El Caso del 'Español-Filipino' Pedro P. Roxas y su Entorno." In *Filipinas, siglo XIX. Coexistencia e Interacciones Entre Comunidades en el Imperio Español*, edited by María Dolores Elizalde and Xavier Huetz de Lemps, 247–94. Madrid: Ed. Polifemo.

Elizalde, María Dolores Elizalde, and Xavier Huetz de Lemps. 2015. "Un Singular Modelo Colonizador: El Papel de las Órdenes Religiosas en la Administración Española de Filipinas." *Illes i Imperis* 17:185–220.

Félix, Alfonso Jr., ed. 1966. *The Chinese in the Philippines, 1570–1770*. Manila: Solidaridad.

Fradera, Josep M. 1999. *Filipinas, la Colonia Más Peculiar. La Hacienda Pública en la Definición de la Política Colonial, 1762–1868*. Madrid: CSIC.

Fradera, Josep M. 2005. *Colonias Para Después de un Imperio*. Barcelona: Ed. Bellaterra.

Fradera, Josep M. 2016. *La Nación Imperial (1750–1918). Derechos, Representación Y Ciudadanía en los Omperios de Gran Bretaña, Francia, España y Estados Unidos*. 2 vols. Barcelona: Edhasa.

García de los Arcos, María Fernanda. 1983. *La Intendencia en Filipinas*. Granada: Ediciones Universidad de Granada.

Hidalgo, Patricio. 1995. *Encomienda, Tributo y Trabajo en Filipinas (1570–1608)*. Madrid: Ed. Polifemo.

Huetz de Lemps, Xavier. 2017. "El Ayuntamiento y la Comunidad Española de Manila en el Siglo XIX." In *Filipinas, siglo XIX. Coexistencia e Interacciones Entre Comunidades en el Imperio Español*, edited by María Dolores Elizalde and Xavier Huetz de Lemps, 173–226. Madrid: Ed. Polifemo.

Huetz de Lemps, Xavier. 2018. "Los Criollos en las Filipinas del Siglo XIX: una elite Discreta." In *Redes Imperiales. Intercambios, Interacciones Y Representación Política Entre Nueva España, las Antillas y Filipinas, Siglos XVIII y XIX*, edited by María Dolores Elizalde and Carmen Yuste, 185–203. Madrid: Consejo Superior de Investigaciones Científicas.

Ileto, Reynaldo. 1979. *Pasyon and Revolution: Popular Movements in the Philippines, 1840–1910*. Quezon City: Ateneo de Manila University Press.

Inarejos, Juan Antonio. 2015. *Los (Últimos) Caciques de Filipinas. Las Élites Coloniales Antes del 98*. Granada: Editorial Comares.

Kramer, Paul. 2006. *The Blood of Government: Race, Empire, the United States and the Philippines*. Chapel Hill: University of North Carolina Press.

Larkin, John A. 1993. *Sugar and the Origins of Modern Philippine Society*. Berkeley: University of California Press.

Legarda, Benito, Jr. 1999. *After the Galleons: Foreign Trade, Economic Change and Entrepreneurship in the Nineteenth-Century Philippines*. Quezon City: Ateneo de Manila University Press.

Llobet, Ruth de. 2011. "Orphans of Empire: Bourbon Reforms, Constitutional Impasse, and the Rise of Filipino Creole Consciousness in an Age of Revolution." PhD diss., University of Wisconsin–Madison.

McCoy, Alfred. 2017. "Formación de Élites y Revolución Social en las Filipinas del Siglo XIX." In *Filipinas, siglo XIX. Coexistencia e Interacciones Entre Comunidades en el Imperio Español*, edited by María Dolores Elizalde and Xavier Huetz de Lemps, 137–70. Madrid: Ed. Polifemo.

McCoy, Alfred, and Edilberto De Jesús. 1982. *Philippine Social History: Global Trade and Local Transformations*. Manila: Ateneo de Manila University Press.

Mojares, Resil. 2006. *Brains of the Nation*. Quezon City: Ateneo de Manila University Press.

Ollé, Manel. 2000. *La Invención de China. Percepciones y Estrategias Filipinas Respecto a China Durante el Siglo XVI*. Wiesbaden: Harrassowitz Verlag.

Owen, Norman. 1984. *Prosperity without Progress: Manila Hemp and Material Life in the Colonial Philippines*. Berkeley: University of California Press.

Pérez Lecha, Manuel. 2014. "Los Últimos Años del Galeón. El Ocaso de un Modelo Colonial Hispano en el Pacífico, 1785–1821." PhD diss., Universidad de Castellón.

Rodrigo y Alharilla, Martín. 2003. "Los Intereses Empresariales Españoles en Filipinas." In *Las Relaciones entre España y Filipinas, siglos XVI–XX*, edited by María Dolores Elizalde, 207–20. Madrid: CSIC-Casa Asia.

Sánchez, Luis Ángel. 2010. "Gobierno y Administración del Territorio en Filipinas, 1565–1898." In *Poblar la Inmensidad: Sociedades, Conflictividad y Representación en los Márgenes del Imperio Hispánico, siglos XV-XIX*, edited by Salvador Bernabéu. Madrid: CSIC-Ed. Rubeo.

Schumacher, John N. 1981. *Revolutionary Clergy and the Nationalist Movement, 1850–1903*. Quezon City: Ateneo de Manila University Press.

Schumacher, John N. 1997. *The Propaganda Movement: 1880–1895. The Creators of a Filipino Consciousness, the Makers of the Revolution*. Quezon City: Ateneo de Manila University Press.

Schurtz, William. 1939. *The Manila Galleon*. New York: Dutton.

Thomas, Megan. 2012. *Orientalists, Propagandists, and Ilustrados: Filipino Scholarship and the End of Spanish Colonialism*. Minneapolis: University of Minnesota Press.

Thompson, Lanny. 2010. *Imperial Archipelago: Representation and Rule in the Insular Territories under US Dominion after 1898*. Honolulu: University of Hawai'i Press.

Thompson, Lanny. 2017. "Colonial Governmentality in Puerto Rico and the Phil-

ippines: Sovereign Force, Governmental Rationality, and Disciplinary Institutions under US Rule." *Political Power and Social Theory* 33:21–56.
Wickberg, Edgar. 2001. *The Chinese in Philippine Life, 1850–1898*. Quezon City: Ateneo de Manila University Press.
Wilson, Andrew R. 2004. *Ambition and Identity: Chinese Merchant Elites in Colonial Manila*. Honolulu: University of Hawai'i Press.
Yuste, Carmen. 1984. *El Comercio de la Nueva España con Filipinas, 1590–1785*. México DF: INAH.

CHAPTER 15

Social Inequalities and Political Organization in the Philippines

Cristina Cielo

In the Philippine islands, inequalities—local, national, and global—are inscribed into the nation's landscapes and into its peoples' subjectivities. And these, in turn, are lived through the bodies of the Filipino people. In rural areas, where poverty is highest and agricultural work is disappearing, unemployed men's "tenuous masculinities" (Hill 2011, 237) increase along with their dependence on women's development-supported livelihood ventures. And in cities just waking to the day, young professionals finish their call center jobs at dawn, as morning rises over more dead bodies of the urban poor suspected to be drug dealers or addicts, victims of President Rodrigo Duterte's brutal war on drugs.

Because of its extremes, the Philippines lends itself to descriptions in stark contrasts. Extravagant casinos compete with those in Macau, with an average of more than $6 million wagered at slot machines in just one day at the City of Dreams casino, for example.[1] In 2015, meanwhile, more than a quarter of Filipinos fell below the poverty line, with 12.1% of the Philippine population classified as extremely poor, without the income needed to meet basic food needs (Philippines Statistics Authority 2016). Another conspicuous disparity: the traffic in the country's capital city of Metropolitan Manila is infamous. So, for a price, its wealthier inhabitants can travel on skyways that allow them to sail over the standstill mayhem on the streets, or take the "point-to-point" air-conditioned buses with Wi-Fi that cost 10 times the price of the sweaty, open-air jeepneys. How to comprehend the coexistence and co-constitution of such intensely divergent worlds?

Of course, Philippine society is not unusual for being unjust and unequal. As in other postcolonial societies, its hierarchical differences are powerfully defined and legitimated by political cultures rooted in a historically dependent economic system. In the Philippines, inequalities have been shaped not only by the global aspirations of its modern nation and workers but also by state institutions traditionally dominated by powerful landowning families. A postcolonial perspective allows us to examine socioeconomic configurations as emergent outcomes (Byrne 2005) of a palimpsest of interacting events and institutions, including those inherited from colonial histories. For example, the domestication of the gendered Philippine labor force studied by McKay (2006) requires workers' subjective, material, and political dependence. This dependence is enabled by the intersection of national liberalization and international development efforts, on the one hand, and political legacies of colonial property regimes, on the other.

Both stable employment opportunities and effective political participation for the vast majority of Filipinos continually slip out of reach, particularly in rural areas where chronic poverty is experienced by households headed by farmers, forestry workers, and fishermen (Bayudan-Dacuycuy and Lim 2014). Poor households are increasingly sustained by women's paid work, as we will see below, yet social mobility is elusive. This chapter examines three interrelated elements critical to sustaining the country's persistent inequities: the globalization of Filipino labor, the privatization of basic services, and the undermining of subaltern political cultures. Social and economic disparities are intensified by continued elite dominance over the political system, paving the way for the rise of a popular discourse that obscures these inequalities in its promise of a shared prosperous future for all, once the dangerous, drug-trafficking "Others" are eliminated.

Workers of the World

Through the democratic institutions it established in the Philippines, the US colonial government legitimated the political power of the landed elite, in exchange for their acceptance and loyalty. In his comparison of American tutelage in Puerto Rico and the Philippines, Julian Go (2008) shows how early Filipino leaders of this period were educated and groomed to take on stabilizing roles as modernizing representatives indebted to the American presence. This elite's economic power, based on agricultural goods, was buoyed by US congressional acts that gave preference to Philippine products in the American market, transitioning its colonial dependence on the exportation of primary commodities into an equally dependent place in the international capitalist system (Bello et al. 2005). Americans also bought church estates to resell them back to both local families and US corporations (Corpuz 1997). The formalization of Philippine land during the US colonial period led to land-grabbing by those who could access courts, to the detriment of peasant and indigenous communities (Borras 2007).

Territorial displacement was accompanied by cultural displacement. Central to US contributions to Philippine political culture was the establishment of liberal institutions such as the public education system. Widespread public schools transported American meritocratic values to young Filipinos and paved the way for the comparative advantage of the Philippine labor force's high levels of education (Maca and Morris 2015). Yet it was also this generation of students arriving in Manila in the 1950s that brought to cities resistance brewing in the hinterlands. The Hukbalahap Rebellion of the 1940s brought together peasant movements united against exploitative tenant-landlord relations. Once the movement was brutally defeated by military operations in 1954, its struggle was carried on by the Communist Party of the Philippines (CCP). The CCP articulated rural resistance with urban and university movements to challenge social inequalities and the country's systemic dependence.

These movements protested against the political and economic policies of Ferdinand Marcos, first elected president in 1965. Early in his presidency, Marcos began to extravagantly invest public monies in infrastructural development in a bid to convert Manila into a global city for an international public, with little regard for the Filipinos living there (Shatkin 2005). In 1972, Marcos cited increasing political turmoil and the need for a "New Society" to justify martial law, pointing to the economic successes of authoritarian South Korea, Taiwan, and Singapore. He promised anti-feudal and modern nationalism through his centralized government (Hutchcroft and Rocamora 2011). To the US, Marcos assured the security of their investments in the country; he liberalized conditions for foreign investment. In 1974, his administration nullified a Supreme Court ruling that ordered all lands in possession of American nationals turned over to Filipinos upon expiration of the 1955 Laurel-Langley Agreement.[2] Marcos's sights were equally aimed at placing the Philippines on the global cultural stage, hosting international gala events and building the spectacular

Cultural Center of the Philippines (Lico 2002), despite destructive consequences for Filipinos.[3]

A less flamboyant but far more enduring Marcos decree was the 1974 Labor Code, a central piece in his program to develop export-oriented industrialization. Marcos sought to attract transnational investors through the strict discipline of militant labor and strikes in export manufacturing (McKay 2006). The Labor Code also established a short-term employment program to address rising unemployment, its accompanying social unrest, and the need for foreign currency. The first state forays into organizing the export of Filipino workers were to the Middle East and North Africa, as Philippine labor was integrated into efforts to secure strategic relations with oil-rich countries in the context of rising energy consumption, embargo-induced prices, and petrodollars (Gonzalez 1998). Encouragement of overseas workers, however, has since mushroomed far beyond state regulation into a lucrative billion-dollar industry in which supply continually outstrips demand.

In 2013, more than 10 million Filipinos lived and worked abroad in close to 200 countries, and the country continues to deploy a little less than 4,000 overseas Filipino workers per day on average (David 2016). This globalized labor force includes over 400,000 Filipinos who work on the seas; the Philippines has been the main supplier of the world's seamen since 1987 (Choudhury 2010). Migrant Filipino workers, including these "sea-based migrant Filipino workers," send home remittances amounting to about $2 billion a month. This tremendous influx of $26.6 billion sent home by overseas Filipino workers in 2016 accounted for 9.8% of the country's gross domestic product (de Vera 2017). As we will see below, these remittances have had a profound impact on the shaping of a consumption-driven society not dependent on national productivity.

Filipino workers, in fact, are increasingly dedicated to sustaining not only their own but also global consumer cultures through the direct provision of services to transnational companies. The business process outsourcing (BPO) industry[4] is now the largest organized employer in the country, generating 1.3 million jobs (Lazo 2017). The Philippines is the world leader in providing BPO services, surpassing India in 2010, with earnings from the outsourcing service of $21.3 billion, second only to remittances sent by overseas workers (Business Inquirer 2017). Employment in this sector is expected to grow further, contingent on the availability of a disciplined professional and educated class with full command of the English language.

The ability to communicate in English allows for opportunities of employment in the most lucrative labor sectors, particularly overseas work and transnational business servicing. There are officially 134 Filipino languages across the archipelago, though only 12 of them are considered major national languages, each with over 1 million speakers. Decades of disinvestment in public services has deteriorated the widely accessible though very uneven educational system (Toh and Floresca-Cawagas 2003). While the Philippines' literacy rate of 96.9% is second only to Singapore's in Southeast Asia and more than two-thirds of Filipinos speak English (Pennington 2017),[5] levels of both education and English knowledge reflect social and economic disparities (Tupas and Salonga 2016). From 1993 to 2008, the proportion of Filipinos ages 15–24 considered "educationally poor"—that is, with less than four years of education—increased, with the largest increase in "educational poverty" affecting rural youth; 8.5% of rural youth have less than two years of schooling, compared to 2.7% of urban youth (Albert, Dumagan, and Martinez 2015). English-speaking ability, reported by 63.7% of Filipinos, is thus also highly skewed by region, with by far the highest percentage of English speakers found in urban areas and in Metropolitan Manila (Carpenter 2016). Beatriz Lorente describes the Philippines' uneven educational system as having produced a "hierarchy of labor" with a "multi-tiered skills-oriented population whose proficiencies in English [are] ordered accordingly" (2012, 193).

Rural areas also suffer from negative consequences of national policies aimed at globalizing the Philippine workforce. Over the last decades, there has been a devaluation and steady decrease in agricultural work, a field that men have traditionally dominated (Estudillo, Quisumbing, and Otsuka 2001). The share of Filipinos employed in agriculture has fallen from 52% in 1980 to 27% in 2016, while service jobs have increased from under 26% to 56% of total employment in that same period (World Bank 2017; Park and Noland 2013; Briones 2017). Rural men, as a result, have faced increasing difficulties fulfilling their traditional roles as providers for their families (Alipio 2013).

It is in this context that Kathryn Hill writes of poor Filipinos' "tenuous masculinities" (2011, 237). Local development projects and the insertion of Philippine labor into global flows of mobility have opened more jobs for women than for men, as development policy rhetoric and global care chains favor women's essentialized caretaking roles (Resurreccion 2006). State and development programs support women's "alternative livelihood sources" through microcredits and income-generating projects. Along with the feminization of migration, this means that the range and financial importance of women's work have increased, even as male employment, especially in rural areas, has contracted (Kajisa 2007). The "cultural caricature of [men's] irresponsibility with money" has further impeded their access to formal financial support (Hill 2011, 238), heightening susceptibility to usury. Rural families are more likely to leave land to their sons, while they invest in their daughters' schooling (Estudillo, Quisumbing, and Otsuka 2001); given labor and economic transformations, this puts rural poor men at a distinct disadvantage in the contemporary labor market.

Yet despite women's increased economic power, gender roles are still clearly defined in Philippine society. Researchers have found that both men and women devalue women's work as temporary, unskilled. and supplementary, even if it represents the main household income (Collantes 2016). Service sector work also relies on and reinforces the care work expected of women; one study (McKay 2006) showed that tech companies employ strategies such as hiring eldest daughters, whose family responsibilities mean they are less likely to quit or make risky employment demands. Thus, the globalizing workforce in the Philippines provides opportunities at the same time that it consolidates inequalities.

Given the availability of primary education, widespread knowledge of English, and migrant labor opportunities, class borders in the Philippines may seem porous and mobility possible. At the same time, however, differential access to education and skills reinforces class distinctions. This is characteristic not only of the meritocratic society established under the tutelage and ideals of American liberalism but also of a society in which consumption defines status. Consumer culture is materialized in the abundant shopping malls found not only throughout Philippine cities but also beside *palenkes*, local town markets, or next to fields in which water buffalo graze (Collantes 2016). *Malling* is something of a national pastime for both urban and rural Filipinos; 80% of Filipinos go to malls at least once or twice a month. The importance of malls in the Philippines cannot be overstated,[6] and their contribution to social and economic inequalities is evident in the privatization of public spaces and development priorities, as we will see below.

The enormous and enormously important commercial spaces of malls have undoubtedly played a role in shaping the political and economic structures of the country. Construction began for the country's first shopping mall in the midst of martial law, by Chinese-born Henry Sy, the richest man in the Philippines for the last 10 years (Rivera 2013). Among other international and transnational economic actors, Chinese businessmen have benefited from the liberalizing economic policies that began during the Marcos period. Through an executive order in 1975, Marcos facilitated the mass naturalization of Chinese immigrants, enabling a generation of important ethnic Chinese businessmen to come to the fore of the Filipino economy. Amy Chua (2004) notes that Chinese Filipinos of pure Chinese descent make up 1% of the Filipino population but control 60% of its economy. Of the 10 richest Filipinos, 8 are of Chinese descent; 3 of these 10 have made their wealth from building malls.

Chinese Filipinos number about 2.5% of the Philippine population and have higher average incomes and education than other Filipinos (Reyes, Mina, and Asis 2017). The three other distinct population groups in the Philippines are characterized by their spatial, ethnic, and religious identification (Abanes, Scheepers, and Sterkens 2014; Girardin et al. 2015): Muslim Filipinos live mostly in the southern provinces of Mindanao and make up about 5.5% of the Filipino population; indigenous peoples who inhabit communities in the highland areas constitute about 8.6% of Filipinos; and the broadest category, with over 50 other ethnicities grouped together as "Christian lowlanders," make up over 82% of the Philippine population (Abanes, Scheepers, and Sterkens 2014). Muslim Filipinos and highland indigenous Filipinos are the populations with the highest levels of poverty and the least access to education and labor opportunities (Reyes, Mina, and Asis 2017). Among the more than 80 million lowland Christian Filipinos, however, racial and ethnic divisions are less salient than other markers of socioeconomic hierarchies, which we continue to explore below.

Privatizing Social Life

The harsh inequalities in the Philippines are reinforced by the lack of effective public services to mitigate them. Community, social, and citizen relations, instead, often take place in spaces defined by private interest. Such a privatization of social life is vividly expressed in the importance of malls, long declared the public spaces of Philippine cities and towns (Connell 1999; Rafael 2003). Not only are theaters and health clubs found in malls, but so are government agencies, community activities, and religious services. With high levels of pollution and overcrowding in Manila (Andong and Sajor 2017), heat that can reach 32 degrees Celsius, and the highest energy prices in Asia (Rico and de Leon 2017), mall air-conditioning "has almost become a public good" (Murphy and Hogan 2012, 13). In a country where the average monthly wage is approximately $220 a month (Philippine Statistics Authority 2017a),[7] malls reflect an aspirational consumer society in which the privatized administration of social spaces exacerbates political and consequently socioeconomic inequities.

The Philippines was an early and remains a faithful implementer of economic neoliberalism, receiving one of the first structural adjustment loans from the World Bank in 1980 (Mosley 2005). With the structural adjustment program, tariff rates were reduced from 43% in 1980 to 28% in 1986 (Borras 2007, 150). From that point through to the present, the Philippine government has continued to deregulate both businesses and trade and legislate growth measures to increase manufacturing zones for investment and exportation (Brillo 2015; Ortega et al. 2015). Even the first widely supported post-dictatorship president, Corazon Aquino, conceded to international pressures to liberalize the economy and repay debts acquired by Marcos instead of responding to the social demands of the multi-sectorial populace that had elected her. The Aquino government directed more than 40% of the country's budget between 1987 and 1991 to paying the national debt (Borras 2007) rather than investing in much-needed public infrastructure and services.

Saturnino Borras (2007) argues that these political and economic decisions have deepened and modernized the elitist agrarian structures that have long beset the Philippine countryside. He likens current conditions in Philippine rural areas to Latin American agrarian structures, since the development of hacienda workforces have led to semi-proletarianization, tenancy arrangements in favor of landlords, and widespread practices of usury (Borras 2007, 150). Latin American land inequalities are the highest in the world, with 16 Latin American countries among the top 20 most unequal countries in land distribution (Frankema 2006, 8). Though less extreme than most Latin American countries, Philippine land inequality is among the highest in Asia, as measured by the land Gini index; other countries in the region have decreased their land inequality,[8] but in the Philippines the land Gini index actually increased from .48 in 1950 to .55 in 1991 (Frankema 2006; You 2014; World Bank 2008).

Though it aimed to transfer productive agricultural land from landlords to tenants, the Comprehensive Agrarian Reform Law of 1988 resulted in increased conversion of productive land to nonagricultural uses, as landlords sought to avoid redistribution (Borras, Kay, and Lahiff 2013; Kelly 2003). Decentralization measures such as the 1991 Local Government Code allowed municipal and local elite (Yilmaz and Venugopal 2013) to reclassify agricultural lands to their advantage for real estate speculation and industrial and commercial enclaves. With increasing poverty and precarity in rural areas, Filipinos began moving to cities in droves; urbanization in Philippine cities exploded in the last decades of the 20th century. Metro Manila grew from less than 7 million inhabitants in 1980 to more than 12 million, as of the 2015 census. In 2015, more than a quarter of the total population of Filipinos lived in the Greater Manila Area, the urban area contiguous with Metro Manila (Philippines Statistics Authority 2016). Similar dynamics of urban growth and sprawl are found in other major Philippine cities (Ofreneo 2013; Sajor 2003).

Beginning in the last decade of the 20th century, Philippine cities have positioned themselves as global cities designed to attract foreign investments. With extensive redevelopment and rising property values, lower-income urban residents have increasingly been unable to afford housing. As private investment in urban development has increased, so have informal settlements, in both absolute and percentage terms (Shatkin 2016). A full third of the urban population in the Philippines lives in slums. In Metro Manila, more than 4 million people live in informal settlements, which is projected to reach 9 million by 2050 (Porio 2009).

Unregulated private investments in cities such as Manila disproportionately affect the poor through the rise of property values beyond their reach. The poor are then hit hardest with increased distances between employment and residence and suffer the most from the deterioration of the urban environment. Edsel Sajor (2003) examines these dynamics in Cebu, analyzing the local equity outcomes of globally linked property development. For Sajor, the problem only begins with lower-income urban residents' inability to compete with the increasing demands for land due to international investments. In the context of weak state and municipal bureaucracies and strong local bosses, these residents are further disenfranchised by their inability to impact urban policies. Powerful families often control public decisions, at both the state and the local levels and in both urban and rural areas (Coronel 2004; Lange 2010; Cruz, Labonne, and Querubin 2017).

In addition, the paucity of public funding for infrastructural investments means that private sectors and groups linked to economic globalization are granted inordinate power over development agendas (Kleibert 2017). The result has been the privatization of infrastructural, urban, and development planning. Those profiting are mainly the families who originally benefited from the concentration of land in the region, as their territorial domination was transformed into political power and now, through private control of public goods, into financial prowess. The Ayala family, for example, once owners of more than half the land that is now Metro Manila, established the Makati Business District in the 1950s (Garrido 2013). This mixed-use zone, which includes residences, offices, and commercial areas, is the most important business zone in the country. Ayala Land, Inc. planned, built, and benefits from the rents of this zone as it implements its vision of urban development within its perimeters (Shatkin 2011).

The government mainly acts as the facilitator of private investments for the construction of the city by providing transportation and services, although even such infrastructure is increasingly privatized. Accommodating private interests trumps tackling intractable fiscal and political urban problems. The majority of city residents do not benefit from the privatized city but rather experience it through its resulting pollution, traffic, and spatial and environmental degradation. The tendency for private sector actors to take charge of central functions of urban planning is not limited to the Philippines. Gavin Shatkin (2011) traces the growth of integral urban megaprojects in the Asian region, examining these large-scale self-contained residential and commercial projects, built at the scale of a city or district primarily with the aim of profitability.[9] The Ayala Land now seeks to develop several integral urban megaprojects in the outskirts of Manila. The company also maintains that it needs to develop infrastructure networks to increase the efficiency of their planned districts or cities, as the ineffective or inexistent state provision of basic services is an obstacle to business growth (Shatkin 2011).

In 1997, Ayala Land competed for and won the concession to service potable water with the Manila Water Company, which serves almost half the population of Metro Manila (Chng 2012). This represents the largest private water service in the world (Hall et al. 2004). Ayala Land has also developed plans to construct a regional system of transport to connect its development areas and has even sought to enter the energy sector. When public infrastructure is privately owned and managed, social organization can be capitalized for corporate profitability (Gago and Mezzadra 2017), as we see in studies on Manila Water. Most of Manila Water's clients are low-income inhabitants of informal settlements. They buy mass access to the water service through what is called a mother meter, and neighbors oversee supervision and billing within the micro-network system in their neighborhood (Wu and Malaluan 2008). The risk and the responsibility for paying the water that enters the mother meter are assumed by the neighborhood group. In this model, they shoulder unpaid bills. They collect monthly fees and find leakages more quickly than the centralized company ever could, so the water company lowers its costs and its water losses. Since the implementation of mother meters, the water that enters the distribution system but remains unpaid for has been lowered from 63% in 1997 to 16% in 2009 (Cheng 2013). The privatized water company working through neighborhood groups effectively profits from their social relations and organization.

Survival strategies of marginalized citizens are converted into virtues of efficiency, and local participation is channeled into individual or collective accountability. As we will see in the next section, these dynamics are part of a tendency that began with international development efforts in the 1970s and have become central elements of Philippine political cultures.

Political Cultures and Interlocking Divisions

The divides that so severely characterize social and economic inequalities in the Philippines are reflected in the country's political culture, in which patronage plays an important role in state institutions and civil society (Hodder 2013; Hutchcroft and Rocamora 2011). The interconnected nature of economic and political power of the elite characterizes Filipino political relations, in the context both of a majority of Filipinos' economic precarity and dependence and of elites' decentralized power over local and municipal decisions (Lange 2010). Analysts have highlighted the warlords and political dynasties that have traditionally reigned over resource distribution in the archipelago (Coronel 2004; Tadem and Tadem 2016). John Sidel, for example, writes that local "bosses" are "predatory power brokers who achieve monopolistic control over both coercive and economic resources within given territorial jurisdictions or bailiwicks" (1999, 19). Filipinos disparagingly call these "traditional politicians" *trapos*, the term in Spanish for "old rags," yet have been hard-pressed to do away with them.

Collective challenges to these institutionalized structures of domination were brutally suppressed at a national level during Marcos's dictatorship, but grassroots organizing did find outlets in functional community organizations. Pre-Marcos state support for 4-H clubs, farmers' associations, and cooperatives (Bankoff 2012) emulated the US Alliance for Progress's promotion of rural development as a counterinsurgency strategy in Latin American countries (Grandin 2006). But as opposition to Marcos grew, nongovernmental organizations (NGOs) collaborated with these community organizations to focus first on education and primary care and then on the promotion and protection of civil and political rights (Bankoff 2012). In the years following the end of Marcos's rule, these groups exploded (Racelis 2005). Kent Eaton discusses the enormous hope placed by international observers on NGOs in the democratic transition after martial law, noting their fundamental role in fostering "the emergence of a robust civil society, unknown in the previous democratic period" (2003, 469–70). In fact, through the 2000s, the term "civil society" in the Philippines referred almost exclusively to the country's influential nongovernmental sector, described at the time as "one of the most dynamic NGO communities in the world" (Aldaba 2002, 179).

In the heady post-Marcos period, NGOs' vibrant activity was incorporated into institutional political processes. A 1999 Asian Development Bank report observed that the Philippines had the "most open and enabling legal framework for NGOs in Asia," with their role institutionalized in the Constitution of 1987, the 1988 Comprehensive Agrarian Reform Law, the 1991 Local Government Code, and the 2004–10 Medium Development Plan, which "all recognize and highlight the role of NGOs and define rights and opportunities for NGOs to participate in the country's development" (Racelis 2005, 4). As sectoral NGOs were allocated seats on municipal government boards, they took on responsibilities in local development, housing, and education; thus, "civil society" attention shifted from the national policy arena to local government needs (Hutchison 2007).

Led mostly by professional and middle-class activists, these organizations became de facto representatives of marginalized populations. A decade into the restored democracy in the Philippines, there were some 80,000 NGOs in the country, but only about 6% of these were grassroots-oriented NGOs (Fisher 1997). While NGOs may certainly have provided benefits to marginalized populations, this appropriation of representation finally weakened people's organizations, debilitating their autonomy and depoliticizing their demands (Constantino-David 1995). A vicious circle of the urban population's dependence on NGOs was thus encouraged, where NGOs participated in social service delivery while "the inclusion of the urban poor in formal decision-making processes . . . remain[ed] more apparent than real" (Etemadi 2000, 72). Represented by elites or, in the best of cases, by organizations that lobby for them without an organic proximity to their interests, informal and popular sectors have lacked forceful and articulated political organization. Such limited political engagement by the Philippine poor has inhibited their contestation of the very frameworks of legitimacy that lead to their marginalization (Velasco 2007).

This is also the case in rural areas, where chronic poverty is three times more likely than in urban households, and vulnerability to poverty[10] more than doubles (Bayuducan-Dacuycuy and Lim 2014). James Eder shows that "despite the ubiquitous 'community organizing' of government and NGO project sponsors" (2005, 165), the political participation of rural fishermen and women he studies in the province of Palawan remains nominal and passive. In addition, "women, the poor and other local community members [are] most at risk of subordination by local-level and possibly 'top-down' political processes" (165). The gendered transformations of labor examined in the first section complicate and aggravate the dependent subjectivities of disadvantaged Filipinos (Salazar 2008), with men disempowered economically and women's work essentialized and devalued.

Even the prominence of women in political positions throughout the country has not necessarily translated into their autonomy (Niu 1999). Researchers widely acknowledge that the two female presidents and many other national and local female politicians in the country are products of the patriarchal "kinship politics" of the country and have helped to reinforce rather than challenge these politics (Roces 2002). Both Corazon Aquino and Gloria Macapagal Arroyo rose to the presidency because of the political dynasties they represented (Thompson 2007), and many female politicians take over posts from male relatives whose terms have ended (Reese 2010). Thus, social inequalities and elite dominance have persisted post-Marcos, despite transformed gender, labor, and class dynamics.

Increasingly disillusioned Filipinos began venting their frustrations and shaping a new political culture in the medium provided by television. Through the 1990s, English was the preferred language for news and public affairs programs. Public political discussions took place in English, as reflected in the print media. As remittances grew in the 1980s, however, more Filipinos could afford household electronics and televisions, and national stations began to air sitcoms and variety shows in Filipino, Tagalog, and other regional languages. It was not long until political discussions were also taking place in the media in Philippine languages. As Philippine sociologist Randolf David notes, "Because serious opinion need no longer be made in English, the *masa* have recovered the power of public speech" (2016, 239). The *masa* are the lower middle classes identified by pollsters as making up 60–75% of the nation's voting population.[11]

One of the first political victories on a national scale of this demographic was the election of action-movie-actor-turned-president Joseph Estrada in 1998, whose anti-elite discourse united this lower stratum (Hedman 2001).

When accusations of his corruption surfaced, it was mostly middle-class and not lower-income Filipinos who took to the streets in protest. They styled themselves another revolution by and for the people, calling their mobilization EDSA2 after the famous site—Epifanio de los Santos Avenue (EDSA)—where the 1986 People's Power movement brought down the Marcos dictatorship (Rafael 2003). We have seen in this section, however, that such a liberal middle-class civil society's presumed representation of the Filipino "people" is precisely one of the ways that class differences are legitimated and reproduced (see Spivak 1988). The forms in which contestations to structures of power are channeled are a fundamental element of those very structures. Though interrelated and interdependent, the differentiation and hierarchies in spaces of work, language use, and political cultures anchor socioeconomic inequalities in the Philippines today.

The widespread popular support of current strongman president Rodrigo Duterte can be understood as a challenge to these distinctions. Duterte's populist portrayal of a "dangerous Other" blames the country's problems on the drug trade that his campaign promised to clean up. During his campaign, Duterte vowed to "fatten the fish in Manila Bay" by dumping into it a hundred thousand bodies of drug users and pushers (Guardian 2016). Until this became one of his central campaign promises, however, the country's drug problem was of low priority in public opinion. His adversaries ran on platforms to end corruption, bring about more employment, reform taxes, and improve government programs for the poor, all elements of a "class politics of dignity" (Schaffer 2005). Duterte's campaign was anything but dignified. Instead, he promised ruthless measures and forceful changes to a long-frustrated citizenry. Rather than attempt to combat corruption through a highly ineffective justice system, Duterte pledged, "If you are corrupt, I will fetch you using a helicopter to Manila and I will throw you out. I have done this before. Why would I not do it again?" (Reuters 2016).[12]

Duterte was wildly popular as a mayor who "made Davao safe," both for the city's inhabitants and for investors, although certainly not for those targeted by his Davao Death Squad (McCoy 2017). He served as mayor from 2001 until 2016, replaced by his daughter Sara Duterte for three years from 2010 to 2013 to skirt term restrictions and again in 2016 when he became president. Duterte's more than 80% cross-class approval rating is astonishing to international analysts, who cite up to 27,000 extrajudicial killings in his war on drugs (Human Rights Watch 2020). But Filipinos see in Duterte hope for their stalled country, whose important national position in the Southeast Asian regional economy in the 1950s has since faltered (Harris 2016).

Drug dealers and users have become an expedient target of blame, particularly in the context of the privatization of social life and the majority of Filipinos' lack of access to political power. In her ethnographic study in a provincial city, Nicole Curato (2016) found that before Duterte's war on drugs, Filipinos she interviewed did not view the "drug problem" as a pressing national issue. They felt, instead, that drug use was a common aggravation similar to petty thievery, carried out by delinquents who added more stress to their already difficult workday. Duterte's discourse responded to these everyday anxieties with the aspiration of a shared future for class-divided Filipinos. His supporters feel that politics under Duterte may be "within the realm of [their] control rather than something that is left solely in the hands of elites" (Curato 2016, 102). At a 2016 Duterte campaign rally "filled with infectious optimism," an elderly supporter enthused, "It's like People Power all over again" (Syjuco 2017).

Conclusions

Rodrigo Duterte declared martial law in his home province of Mindanao in May 2017, in response to an ISIS-related faction that succeeded in occupying Marawi City. Despite the government's victory in Marawi in October 2017, martial law was extended in Mindanao through the end of 2019. The most vocal critics of martial law's extension—who recall the brutal and violent period under Marcos—are Duterte's elite political opponents in Manila, whom he replaced and whom he infuriates (Casiple 2016). In contrast, historically marginalized Filipinos such as the inhabitants of Mindanao continue to enthusiastically support Duterte, believing that his strongman tactics may finally improve their living conditions in ways that their political system has not (Reyes 2016). Despite a promising shift to democracy after Marcos, high hopes in work opportunities, geographic mobility, and education, and an increase in women's economic and political power, the country continues to have the highest income inequality rate in Southeast Asia and the smallest decrease in inequalities since 1990 (Jain-Chandra et al. 2016).

As we have seen in this chapter, the structures of these social inequalities are shaped by elements of Philippine colonial history that continue to influence contemporary political and economic configurations of power. Spanish colonialism's exclusive control of land produced elite agrarian structures, leading to uncertain subsistence for rural populations and, eventually, significant migration and urbanization. Elite families established in the Spanish colonial period have benefited immensely from the unplanned and unequal development of Philippine cities, while other economically dominant groups—such as the Chinese businessmen mentioned above—rose with the liberalization that sought to improve the Philippines' peripheral position in a postcolonial political economy. Another response to this subjectively incorporated position has been the globalization of labor that has weakened the collective political power of lower- and working-class Filipinos.

The post-Marcos Philippine state wagered its economic growth on the export and marketing of the country's educated and English-speaking workforce. To ensure the availability of this comparative advantage, it has secured labor's weak market position through such means as the isolation and private regulation of workers in export processing zones (Lu 2014) and its more general lack of enforcement of labor protection (Kelly 2001). The privatization of public decisions, policies, and services has reinforced the differentiation and policing of the spaces, times, and languages that structure Philippine society. In this context, poor Filipinos see in their president's severity a response to their precarious positions and lack of access to political power. Duterte promises a future that might also be theirs, a cleansed nation unified by the elimination of newly identified scapegoats. But it is a treacherous future, refusing as it does to recognize its continuity with past sacrifice of the islands' inhabitants to a "greater good," whether that be a disciplined nation under Duterte, a globalized and competitive national economy, or colonial estates under king and god.

In the face of such relentless reproduction of injustice, this volume aims to contribute to questioning its inevitability. Colonial histories are not givens. They transform along with the understandings, actions, institutions, and structures that we forge from their legacies. The archipelagic approach proposed by the editors of this volume may do more that brings to light "interconnected (post-)colonial histories [and] subterranean networks not easily visible from the surface and yet vital for their functioning" (Leinius and Burchardt, this volume). Archipelagos are also political constructions. Bringing analyses of the Philippines, Puerto Rico, and Cuba into dialogue reconfigures alliances. I hope that such collaborative and comparative analyses may help locate the contingencies of historically reinforced structures of power and open possibilities for widening their rifts.

NOTES

1. This number reflects the gaming machine handle of $2.23 billion for 2016, divided by the days of the year (Francia 2017).

2. This agreement gave US citizens equal economic rights as Filipinos in the Philippine economy (Batalla 2010).

3. With martial law, Marcos could initiate development projects and employ orders with no oversight or opposition. In preparation for the first event in the CCP, the Miss Universe pageant in 1974, some 100,000 people in Manila were evicted from their homes, and during the IMF and World Bank meetings in 1976 in the expanded Cultural Center Complex, 60,000 more lost their places of residence (Berner 2000). The most infamous building of the imposing complex on Manila Bay was the Manila Film Center, hurriedly built in 1981 to host the Manila International Film Festival. Four thousand workers were required to work in shifts 24 hours of the day to complete the structure, and there was no time to stop when scaffolding fell on some 170 construction workers. Instead of stopping construction for rescue operations, local lore has it that concrete was poured over workers' bodies and the building was finished in the hour before the international guests, including Brooke Shields, Jeremy Irons, and Robert Duvall, stepped on the red carpet (Severino 2005).

4. Eight subsectors make up the BPO industry: call centers, knowledge process outsourcing, back offices, animation, software development, game development, engineering design, and medical transcription.

5. Both Filipino and English are the official languages of the Philippines, as established in the country's Constitution of 1987. Most Filipinos are at least familiar with English, in a way that they never were with Spanish, though Spanish names and words are integrated into the Malay structure of the Philippine languages.

6. In SM City North Edsa, the country's first shopping mall, average daily foot traffic is estimated at 350,000 to 400,000 (Flores 2010). Currently, SM Prime Holdings, the Philippine's largest mall developer, has opened 67 malls in the country, and its malls cover a total gross floor area of 9.3 million square meters (SM Prime n.d.).

7. The monthly wage of $220 is the average for employment in the Philippines. Families with remittances receive an average of about $240 more per month (Philippine Statistics Authority 2017a).

8. In Indonesia, the land Gini index decreased from .53 in 1963 to .45 in 1993, and in Korea it decreased from .73 in the mid-20th century to .38 in 1990.

9. Integral urban megaprojects often have areas for offices and industries and even include schools, universities, hospitals, hotels, and convention centers. They provide the efficiency that is supposedly necessary to attract investors and to shape conditions for corporate entities. In Jakarta, for example, 13 planned districts have been constructed and established through the private sector. Each of these districts covers an area of more than 750 hectares (Skatkin 2008).

10. Vulnerability to poverty is a dynamic and multifaceted concept that "consists of economic insecurity based on exposure and risk to poverty in the present and the future" (Bayuducan-Dacuycuy and Lim 2014).

11. Pollsters define these classes as those households that live in precarious living conditions, whose heads have no greater than high school education, and are in unskilled or rural occupations, and with family incomes of about USD 200 a month or below.

12. His brutal (if effective) tactics as mayor of the Mindanao city of Davao, in the marginal and war-torn province of Mindanao, included killing criminals and opponents (Lamb 2017).

REFERENCES

Abanes, Menandro, Peer Scheepers, and Carl Sterkens. 2014. "Ethno-religious Groups, Identification, Trust and Social Distance in the Ethno-Religiously Stratified Philippines." *Research in Social Stratification and Mobility* 37:61–75.

Albert, Jose Ramon, Jesus C. Dumagan, and Arturo Martinez Jr. 2015. "Inequalities in Income, Labor, and Education: The Challenge of Inclusive Growth." Discussion paper no. 2015–01. Manila: Philippines Institute for Development Studies.

Aldaba, Fernando. 2002. "Philippine NGOs and Multistakeholder Partnerships: Three Case Studies." *Voluntas: International Journal of Voluntary and Nonprofit Organizations* 13 (2): 179–92.

Alipio, Cheryll. 2013. "Young Men in the Philippines: Mapping the Costs and Debts of Work, Marriage, and Family Life." *Annals of the American Academy of Political and Social Science* 646 (1): 214–32.

Andong, R. F., and E. Sajor. 2017. "Urban Sprawl, Public Transport, and Increasing CO2 Emissions: The Case of Metro Manila, Philippines." *Environment, Development and Sustainability* 19 (1): 99–123.

Bankoff, Greg. 2012. "'For the Good of the Barrio': Community Associations and the State in Rural Philippines." In *Beyond Empire and Nation; The Decolonization of African and Asian societies, 1930s-1960s*, edited by Els Bogaerts and Remco Raben. Leiden: Brill.

Batalla, Eric Vincent. 2010. "Entrepreneurship and Philippine Development." *Canadian Journal of Development Studies/Revue canadienne d'études du développement* 31 (3–4): 341–65.

Bayudan-Dacuycuy, Connie, and Joseph Anthony Lim. 2014. "Chronic and Transient Poverty and Vulnerability to Poverty in the Philippines: Evidence Using a Simple Spells Approach." *Social Indicators Research* 118 (1): 389–413.

Bello, Walden, Marissa De Guzman, Mary Lou Malig, and Herbert Docena. 2005. *The Anti-Development State: The Political Economy of Permanent Crisis in the Philippines*. London: Zed Books.

Berner, Erhard. 2000. "Poverty Alleviation and the Eviction of the Poorest: Towards Urban Land Reform in the Philippines." *International Journal of Urban and Regional Research* 24 (3): 554–66.

Borras, Saturnino, Jr. 2007. "'Free Market,' Export-Led Development Strategy and Its Impact on Rural Livelihoods, Poverty and Inequality: The Philippine Experience Seen from a Southeast Asian Perspective." *Development and Class* 14 (1): 143–75.

Borras, Saturnino M., Jr., Cristóbal Kay, and Edward Lahiff, eds. 2013. *Market-Led Agrarian Reform*. New York: Routledge.

Brillo, Bing Baltazar. 2015. "A Path-Dependent Explanation of the Philippines' Debt-Driven Development Strategy." *UPLB Journal* 8 (1): 47–54.

Briones, Roehlando. 2017. "Characterization of Agricultural Workers in the Philippines." Discussion paper no. 2017–31. Manila: Philippines Institute for Development Studies.

Business Inquirer. 2017. "BPO Revenues vs OFW Remittances 2017." *Business Inquirer*, 22 January. http://business.inquirer.net/223299/bpo-revenues-vs-ofw-remittances

Byrne, David. 2005. "Complexity, Configurations and Cases." *Theory, Culture, Society* 22 (5): 95–111.

Carpenter, William. 2016. "Philippines: A Friendly Country for English Speakers." *Investopedia*, 25 January. https://www.investopedia.com/articles/personal-finance/012516/philippines-friendly-country-english-speakers.asp

Casiple, R. C. 2016. "The Duterte Presidency as a Phenomenon." *Contemporary Southeast Asia: A Journal of International and Strategic Affairs* 38 (2): 179–84.

Cheng, Deborah. 2013. "(In) Visible Urban Water Networks: The Politics of Non-Payment in Manila's Low-Income Communities." *Environment and Urbanization* 25 (1): 249–60.

Chng, Nai Rui. 2012. "Regulatory Mobilization and Service Delivery at the Edge of the Regulatory State." *Regulation & Governance* 6 (3): 344–61.

Choudhury, Perla Aragon. 2010. "Filipino Seamen Still Rule the Seas, For Now." Planet Philippines, 2 February. http://planetphilippines.com/migration/filipino-seamen-still-rule-the-seas-for-now/

Chua, Amy. 2004. *World on Fire: How Exporting Free Market Democracy Breeds Ethnic Hatred and Global Instability*. New York: Anchor.

Collantes, Christianne. 2016. "Reproductive Dilemmas, Labour and Remittances: Gender and Intimacies in Cavite, Philippines." *South East Asia Research* 24 (1): 77–97.

Connell, John. 1999. "Beyond Manila: Walls, Malls, and Private Spaces." *Environment and Planning A* 31 (3): 417–39.

Constantino-David, Karina. 1995. "Community Organizing in the Philippines: The Experience of Development NGOs." *Community Empowerment: A Reader in Participation and Development*, edited by Gary Craig and Marjorie Mayo, 154–67. London: Zed Books.

Coronel, Sheila. 2004. *The Rulemakers: How the Wealthy and Well-Born Dominate Congress*. Pasig City: Philippine Center for Investigative Journalism.

Corpuz, Onofre. 1997. *An Economic History of the Philippines*. Quezon City: University of Philippines Press.

Cruz, Cesi, Julien Labonne, and Pablo Querubin. 2017. "Politician Family Networks and Electoral Outcomes: Evidence from the Philippines." *American Economic Review* 107 (10): 3006–37.

Curato, Nicole. 2016. "Politics of Anxiety, Politics of Hope: Penal Populism and Duterte's Rise to Power." *Journal of Current Southeast Asian Affairs* 35 (3): 91–109.

David, Randolf. 2016. *Understanding Philippine Society, Culture, and Politics*. Manila: Anvil Publishing.

de Vera, Ben. 2017. "OFW Remittances Hit Record High in 2016." *Business Inquirer*, 16 February. http://business.inquirer.net/224635/ofw-remittances-hit-record-high-2016

Eaton, Kent. 2003. "Restoration or Transformation? Trapos versus NGOs in the Democratization of the Philippines." *Journal of Asian Studies* 62 (2): 469–96.

Eder, James. 2005. "Coastal Resource Management and Social Differences in Philippine Fishing Communities." *Human Ecology* 33 (2): 147–69.

Estudillo, Jonna, Agnes Quisumbing, and Keijiro Otsuka. 2001. "Gender Differences in Land Inheritance, Schooling and Lifetime Income: Evidence from the Rural Philippines." *Journal of Development Studies* 37 (4): 23–48.

Etemadi, Felisa. 2000. "Civil Society Participation in City Governance in Cebu City." *Environment and Urbanization* 12 (1): 57–72.

Fisher, William. 1997. "Doing Good? The Politics and Antipolitics of NGO Practices." *Annual Review of Anthropology* 26 (1): 439–64.

Flores, Wilson Lee. 2010. "The Mall That Started It All: Celebrating 25 years of SM City North EDSA." *Philstar Global*, 4 August. https://www.philstar.com/lifestyle/sunday-life/2010/08/15/602978/mall-started-it-all-celebrating-25-years-sm-city-north-edsa

Francia, Arra. 2017. "Revenues of City of Dreams Manila Surge." *BusinessWorld Online*, 4 April. http://www.bworldonline.com/content.php?id=143207

Frankema, E. H. 2006. "The Colonial Origins of Inequality: The Causes and Consequences of Land Distribution." Growth and Development Centre Paper. Groningen: University of Groningen.

Gago, Verónica, and Sandro Mezzadra. 2017. "A Critique of the Extractive Operations of Capital: Toward an Expanded Concept of Extractivism." *Rethinking Marxism* 29 (4): 574–91.

Garrido, Marco. 2013. "The Ideology of the Dual City: The Modernist Ethic in the Corporate Development of Makati City, Metro Manila." *International Journal of Urban and Regional Research* 37 (1): 165–85.

Girardin, Luc, Philipp Hunziker, Lars-Erik Cederman, Nils-Christian Bormann, and Manuel Vogt. 2015. *GROW UP—Geographical Research on War, Unified Platform: EPR Atlas*. ETH Zurich. http://growup.ethz.ch/

Go, Julian. 2008. *American Empire and the Politics of Meaning: Elite Political Cultures in the Philippines and Puerto Rico during US Colonialism*. Durham: Duke University Press.

Gonzalez, Joaquin. 1998. *Philippine Labour Migration: Critical Dimensions of Public Policy*. Singapore: Institute of Southeast Asian Studies.

Grandin, Greg. 2006. *Empire's Workshop: Latin America, the United States, and the Rise of the New Imperialism*. New York: Metropolitan Books.

The Guardian. 2016. "Philippines President Rodrigo Duterte Urges People to Kill Drug Addicts." *The Guardian*, 1 July. https://www.theguardian.com/world/2016/jul/01/philippines-president-rodrigo-duterte-urges-people-to-kill-drug-addicts

Hall, David, Violeta Corral, Emmanuele Lobina, and Robin de la Motte. 2004. *Water Privatisation and Restructuring in Asia-Pacific*. London: Public Services International Research Unit, University of Greenwich.

Harris, Richard. 2016. "Critical Perspectives on Politics and Development in the Philippines." *Journal of Developing Societies* 32 (3): 209–19.

Hedman, Eva-Lotta E. 2001. "The Spectre of Populism in Philippine Politics and Society: Artista, Masa, Eraption!" *South East Asia Research* 9 (1): 5–44.

Hill, Kathryn. 2011. "'Male Providers' and 'Responsible Mothers': Gender and Livelihood Politics in the Rural Philippines." *Gender, Technology and Development* 15 (2): 223–47.

Hodder, Rupert. 2013. *High-Level Political Appointments in the Philippines: Patronage, Emotion and Democracy*. Berlin: Springer Science & Business Media.

Human Rights Watch. 2020. *World Report 2020: Events of 2019*. New York: Human Rights Watch. https://www.hrw.org/world-report/2020/country-chapters/philippines

Hutchcroft, Paul D., and Joel Rocamora. 2011. *Patronage-Based Parties and the Democratic Deficit in the Philippines*. New York: Routledge.

Hutchison, Jane. 2007. "The 'Disallowed' Political Participation of Manila's Urban Poor." *Democratization* 14 (5): 853–72.

Jain-Chandra, Sonali, Tidiane Kinda, Kalpana Kochhar, Shi Piao, and Johanna Schauer. 2016. "Sharing the Growth Dividend: Analysis of Inequality in Asia." Working Paper 16/48. Washington DC: IMF Asia and Pacific Department.

Kajisa, Kei. 2007. "Personal Networks and Nonagricultural Employment: The Case of a Farming Village in the Philippines." *Economic Development and Cultural Change* 55 (4): 669–707.

Kelly, Philip. 2001. "The Political Economy of Local Labor Control in the Philippines." *Economic Geography* 77 (1): 1–22.

Kelly, Philip. 2003. "Urbanization and the Politics of Land in the Manila Region." *Annals of the American Academy of Political and Social Science* 590 (1): 170–87.

Kleibert, Jana. 2017. "Exclusive Development(s): Special Economic Zones and Enclave Urbanism in the Philippines." *Critical Sociology* 44 (3): 471–85.

Lamb, Kate. 2017. "Thousands Dead: The Philippine President, the Death Squad Allegations and a Brutal Drugs War." *The Guardian*, 2 April. https://www.theguardian.com/world/2017/apr/02/philippines-president-duterte-drugs-war-death-squads

Lange, Andreas. 2010. "Elites in Local Development in the Philippines." *Development and Change* 41 (1): 53–76.

Lazo, Kristyn Nika. 2017. "BPO Revenues to Outpace OFW Remittances by 2018—ING Bank." *Manila Times*, 27 January. http://www.manilatimes.net/bpo-revenues-outpace-ofw-remittances-2018-ing-bank/309043/

Lico, Gerard. 2002. *Edifice Complex: Power, Myth and Marcos State Architecture*. Quezon City: Ateneo de Manila University Press.

Lorente, Beatriz. 2012. "The Making of 'Workers of the World': Language and the Labor Brokerage State." In *Language in Late Capitalism: Pride and Profit*, edited by Alexandre Duchêne and Monica Heller, 193–216. New York: Routledge.

Lu, Jinky Leilanie. 2014. "A Discourse on the Convergence of Information Technology, Women's Work, and Global Capital in Export Processing Zones in the Philippines." *International Journal of Sociology Study* 2: 82–87.

Luc Girardin, Philipp Hunziker, Lars-Erik Cederman, Nils-Christian Bormann, and Manuel Vogt. 2015. *GROW UP—Geographical Research on War, Unified Platform: EPR Atlas*. ETH Zurich. http://growup.ethz.ch/

Maca, Mark, and Paul Morris. 2015. "Education, National Identity and State Formation in the Modern Philippines." In *Constructing Modern Asian Citizenship*, edited by Edward Vickers and Krishna Kumar, 125–48. New York: Routledge Studies in Education and Society in Asia.

McCoy, Alfred. 2017. "Philippine Populism: Local Violence and Global Context in the Rise of a Filipino Strongman." *Surveillance & Society* 15 (3–4): 514–22.

McKay, Steven. 2006. *Satanic Mills or Silicon Islands? The Politics of High-Tech Production in the Philippines*. Ithaca: Cornell University Press.

Mosley, Paul. 2005. "Structural Adjustment: A General Overview, 1980–9." In *Foreign Trade Reforms and Development Strategy*, edited by Jean-Marc Fontaine, 29–43. New York: Routledge.

Murphy, Peter, and Trevor Hogan. 2012. "Discordant Order: Manila's Neo-Patrimonial Urbanism." *Thesis Eleven* 112 (1): 10–34.

Niu, Greta Ai-Yu. 1999. "Wives, Widows, and Workers: Corazon Aquino, Imelda Marcos, and the Filipina 'Other.'" *NWSA Journal* 11 (2): 88–102.

Ofreneo, Rene. 2013. "Precarious Philippines: Expanding Informal Sector, 'Flexibilizing' Labor Market." *American Behavioral Scientist* 57 (4): 420–43.

Ortega, Arnisson Andre, Johanna Marie Astrid E. Acielo, and Maria Celeste H. Hermida. 2015. "Mega-Regions in the Philippines: Accounting for Special Economic Zones and Global-Local Dynamics." *Cities* 48:130–39.

Park, Donghyun, and Marcus Noland. 2013. *Developing the Service Sector as an Engine of Growth for Asia*. Manila: Asian Development Bank.

Pennington, John. 2017. "Education, Inequality, Poverty—a Paradox in the Philippines." *Asean Today*, 22 March. https://www.aseantoday.com/2017/03/education-inequality-poverty-a-paradox-in-the-philippines

Philippine Statistics Authority. 2016. *Results from the 2015 Family Income and Expenditure Survey*. 24 October. https://psa.gov.ph/content/results-2015-family-income-and-expenditure-survey

Philippine Statistics Authority. 2017a. *2016 Occupational Wages Survey*. Reference no. 2017–112, 15 September. https://www.psa.gov.ph/content/2016-occupational-wages-survey-ows

Philippines Statistics Authority. 2017b. *2016 Survey on Overseas Filipinos*. Reference no. 2017–112, 4 May. https://psa.gov.ph/content/2016-survey-overseas-filipinos

Porio, Emma. 2009. *Urban Transition, Poverty, and Development in the Philippines: A Preliminary Draft*. London: International Institute for the Environment and Development.

Racelis, Mary. 2005. "Civil Society, Populist Politics and the State—Philippine Democracy Today." Presented at Humboldt University, the Institute for Foreign Cultural Relations, and the University of Hamburg, 29 April.

Rafael, Vicente. 2003. "The Cell Phone and the Crowd: Messianic Politics in the Contemporary Philippines." *Philippine Political Science Journal* 24 (47): 3–36.

Reese, Niklas. 2010. "'Still Working on It': An Overview on the Current State of Public Activism of Women in the Philippines." *Austrian Journal of South-East Asian Studies* 3 (2): 136–50.

Resurreccion, Bernadette. 2006. "Gender, Identity and Agency in Philippine Upland Development." *Development and Change* 37 (2): 375–400.

Reuters. 2016. "Philippine Leader Says Once Threw Man from Helicopter, Would Do It Again." *Reuters World News*, 29 December.

Reyes, Celia, Christian Mina, and Ronina D. Asis. 2017. "Inequalities of Opportunities among Ethnic Groups in the Philippines." Discussion paper no. 2017–42. Manila: Philippines Institute for Development Studies.

Reyes, Danilo Andres. 2016. "The Spectacle of Violence in Duterte's 'War On Drugs.'" *Journal of Current Southeast Asian Affairs* 35 (3): 111–37.

Rico, Jore-Annie, and Kim Robert de Leon. 2017. "Mall Culture and Consumerism in the Philippines." In *State of Power* series. Amsterdam: The Transnational Institute.

Rivera, Temario. 2013. "The Leading Chinese–Filipino Business Families in Post-Marcos Philippines." In *Ethnic Business: Chinese Capitalism in Southeast Asia*, edited by Brian Folk and K. S. Jomo, 106–18. New York: Routledge.

Roces, Mina. 2002. "The Gendering of Post-War Philippine Politics." In *Gender and Power in Affluent Asia*, edited by Krishna Sen and Maila Stivens, 305–30. New York: Routledge.

Sajor, Edsel. 2003. "Globalization and the Urban Property Boom in Metro Cebu, Philippines." *Development and Change* 34 (4): 713–42.

Salazar Parreñas, Rhacel. 2008. "Transnational Fathering: Gendered Conflicts, Distant Disciplining and Emotional Gaps." *Journal of Ethnic and Migration Studies* 34 (7): 1057–72.

Schaffer, Frederic. 2005. "Clean Elections and the Great Unwashed." *Vote Buying and Voter Education in the Philippines*. MIT Center for International Studies Paper no. 21. https://www.sss.ias.edu/files/papers/paper21.pdf

Severino, Howie. 2005. *The Manila Film Center Mystery: Ghostly Place or Urban Legend?* Documentary produced by i-Witness, Manila.

Shatkin, Gavin. 2005. "Colonial Capital, Modernist Capital, Global Capital: The Changing Political Symbolism of Urban Space in Metro Manila, the Philippines." *Pacific Affairs* 78 (4): 577–600.

Shatkin, Gavin. 2011. "Planning Privatopolis: Representation and Contestation in the Development of Urban Integrated Mega-Projects." In *Wording Cities: Asian Experiments and the Art of Being Global*, edited by Ananya Roy and Aihwa Ong, 77–97. Oxford: Wiley.

Shatkin, Gavin. 2016. *Collective Action and Urban Poverty Alleviation: Community Organizations and the Struggle for Shelter in Manila*. New York: Routledge.

Sidel, John. 1999. *Capital, Coercion, and Crime: Bossism in the Philippines*. Redwood City: Stanford University Press.

SM Prime. n.d. *SM Prime Corporate Profile*. http://www.smprime.com/corporate-pro file

Spivak, Gayatri Chakravorty. 1988. "Can the Subaltern Speak?" In *Marxism and the Interpretation of Culture*, edited by C. Nelson and L. Grossberg, 271–315. Champaign: University of Illinois Press.

Syjuco, Miguel. 2017. "Is Populism a Problem?—a Story for the World Forum for Democracy 2017." *Open Democracy*, 20 November. https://www.opendemocracy.net/miguel-syjuco/is-populism-problem-story-for-world-forum-for-democracy-2017

Tadem, Teresa S. Encarnacion, and Eduardo C. Tadem. 2016. "Political Dynasties in the Philippines: Persistent Patterns, Perennial Problems." *South East Asia Research* 24 (3): 328–40.

Thompson, Mark. 2007. "Presidentas and People Power in Comparative Asian Perspective." *Philippine Political Science Journal* 28 (51): 1–32.

Toh, Swee-hin, and Virginia Floresca-Cawagas. 2003. "Globalization and the Philippines' Education System." In *Globalization and Educational Restructuring in the Asia Pacific Region*, edited by K. Mok and A. Welch, 189–231. London: Palgrave Macmillan.

Tupas, Ruanni, and Aileen Salonga. 2016. "Unequal Englishes in the Philippines." *Journal of Sociolinguistics* 20 (3): 367–81.

Velasco, Djorina. 2007. "Marginalized Groups and Political Participation: Perspectives from the Philippines." *Development* 50 (1): 117–21.

World Bank. 2008. *World Development Report 2008: Agriculture for Development*. Washington, DC: World Bank.

World Bank. 2017. "Philippines: Employment in Agriculture." *The Global Economy*. https://www.theglobaleconomy.com/Philippines/Employment_in_agriculture/

Wu, Xun, and Nepomuceno A. Malaluan. 2008. "A Tale of Two Concessionaires: A Natural Experiment of Water Privatisation in Metro Manila." *Urban Studies* 45 (1): 207–29.

Yilmaz, Serdar, and Varsha Venugopal. 2013. "Local Government Discretion and Accountability in Philippines." *Journal of International Development* 25 (2): 227–50.

You, Jong-sung. 2014. "Land Reform, Inequality, and Corruption: A Comparative Historical Study of Korea, Taiwan, and the Philippines." *Korean Journal of International Studies* 12 (1): 191–224.

PART 4

The (Post-)Colonial Legacies of Puerto Rico, Cuba, and the Philippines

A Comparative View

CHAPTER 16

Legacies of Slavery and People of African Descent in Cuba, Puerto Rico, and the Caribbean

Michael Zeuske

There's not just one "legacy of slavery" (Zeuske 2013, 146–80) but various ones, both in Cuba and in the Caribbean, as well as in other parts of the Atlantic World. During the nearly 200 years between 1822 (the definitive abolition of slavery in Santo Domingo), 1873 (in Puerto Rico), 1886 (in Cuba), and 2021, the understanding of the legacy of slavery has changed. Until today, cultural instead of structural changes have almost always been addressed. But it is important to stress the fundamental nature of these changes.[1]

Many of the problems defined today as "postcolonial" come from, in one way or another, the time of slavery and the ways in which emancipation was brought about—how slavery and the colony as well as discrimination and racial inequality were brought to an end (the first two anyway). The issues that have been addressed to a lesser extent, at least in "post" times (postmodern and postcolonial, more or less between the 1970s and the early years of the 21st century), are structural changes: is it because they did not happen or because there was only minimal structural change? But there are historical structural legacies (demographic, land, political, economic, cultural) and problems regarding the perception of what was at times not even called "slavery's legacies." Thc problem with structural legacies—that is, people in the demographic sense, landownership, hard and enduring institutions, and material features—is the question of whether there were fundamental changes or not.

I would like to address "the first legacies" of slavery in Cuba and, in a general manner, of the Spanish Caribbean, namely, Puerto Rico and Santo Domingo (ca. 1880–1920) (Zeuske 1998, 65–84; 2004a, 59–99). I would also like to explain some of their consequences up until today, among them the total absence of the concept of or simply the word "legacy" in combination with "slavery" or "ex-slaves" in Caribbean societies until the advent of postcolonialism in the 1990s.

What Happened to the Former Slaves?

Slavery's most important legacy are the women, men, and children who were former slaves. Some of these former slaves were the subjects of the final abolition in 1886 (Scott 2000). What stands out, at first glance, in the context of this newfound "freedom" (Scott 2005) is a profound "silence" on past slavery. In the debate over this "silence" and former slaves' actions regarding the recently abolished slavery, there is a tendency to highlight the wish to "forget it."

Another trend, which the majority of the black Cuban press and the famous Directorio Central de Sociedades de la Raza de Color (Central Directorate of Societies of Color) in Cuba subscribed to, was not to forget it but to distance themselves from it and use the memory of slavery as a form of pressure against colonialism. There is also evidence of hatred against former slave owners (Schmieder 2018, 423–42)[2] and Cuban society's tendency to suppress the memory of slavery altogether (symbolically José Martí: "olvidar la esclavitud" [forget slavery] [(1893) 1975, 298–300]). The same thing occurred in Puerto Rico and, in a rather particular way, in Santo Domingo, only in very conflictive situations, like in the case of the propaganda and counterpropaganda that took place during the Second War of Independence in Cuba (1895–98), where this memory was used in its totality by both sides to debilitate their respective opponents (in truth, the "icon of fear," "Guarico," and "Haiti" were more often used by the Spanish side, but they were also used clandestinely among the revolutionaries themselves) (Ferrer 1999; Sartorius 2014, 158–86). In general, there was also debate and discourse about abolitionism and anti-abolitionism, as well as "freedom," throughout the anti-colonial process between 1866 and 1902 (Ferrer 1999). Those were the "uses of history" of that time. During this period, real former slaves and their real-life problems disappear from almost all the texts of published opinion to make way for constructions based on the ideological rules of the time ("civilization vs. barbarism," "blacks from Africa," poor "barbarians," "uncivilized people," witches and sorcerers, etc., with a nod to Cesare Lombroso; inventing "afro" [F. Ortiz]).

On the other hand, slavery itself is treated as a "Spanish institution." In reality, we know that slavery and, to an even greater extent, human trafficking after the formal abolition of the slave trade (1820) was in fact a "Cuban-Spanish" or "Porto Rican-Spanish" institution. In actuality, it was an institution controlled by the criollo elite (who, until around 1860, called themselves "Spanish") with respect to its ground operations and by mainland Spaniards, as well as naturalized foreigners, many of whom acted in and from Cuba and Puerto Rico, with respect to the transportation and trade of slaves (mainly maritime and partially by land) (Zeuske 2015a, 280–301). In his "Ensayo sobre la isla de Cuba" (Essay on the Island of Cuba) (1826/27), Humboldt treated slavery as an elite local institution, in other words, run by Cubans (Zeuske 2008, 257–77). But the pro-independence, anticolonial, and anti-Spanish movement in Cuba, which took place between 1880 and 1895, leading up to the Second War of Independence, won the discursive victory by presenting slavery as a "colonial-Spanish" institution. The tip of the iceberg in this sense is José Martí's "cubano sin color" (colorless Cuban) (Ferrer 1999).

This silence, up until today and in spite of many investigations in recent years, means that, first, we have almost no self-representations of slaves (*in* slavery [Sanz and Zeuske 2017, 9–21]), and, second, we don't have a clear idea about *who* defined themselves as a former slave[3] or *how many* "former slaves" there were in 1886; in other words, we don't know with certainty who felt themselves to be part of this group and who didn't.

I think that this subjective membership was a changing one, ambiguous and hybrid, but at times tacitly decisive for political and electoral dynamics, as well as for upward social and economic mobility. We also don't know if former slaves acted as a group and, if so, at what level. Just locally or temporarily? And, finally (and due to the aforementioned problems), we don't know or we know very little about the problem of *where* they ended up staying (Zeuske and Finzsch 2011, 285–318).

In large part, the answers depend on more general problems related to the cultural history of slavery and post-emancipation, on prevailing theories (both during the time periods that are investigated and today),[4] and on the emancipation in the Atlantic World (Zeuske 2002a; Scully and Paton 2005). Above all, they depend on the definition of who is encompassed in the term "former slave." For example, does it mean all those who've passed through the institution and were shackled and emancipated (and their descendants) between 1511 and 1886 (until 1873 in Puerto Rico; until 1794/1802–3 in Saint-Domingue/Haiti; until 1822 in Santo Domingo)? Does it mean only the "*bozales*" (slaves recently brought from Africa) or also "criollos"? Or only the "emancipated generation" (1868–86, 1868–73) or only the *patrocinados* (children of slaves under the *patronato* in Cuba and Puerto Rico) and the slaves emancipated between 1880 and 1886? Or does it mean only the slaves emancipated in 1886 (Scott 2000)? If we only consider those who were slaves between 1880 and 1886, we soon run into the problem of the "freed" children of enslaved mothers, one of the sociopolitical problems central to the Second War of Independence. If we don't recognize the large groups of "blacks" and "browns" already freed and free before 1880, we'll never understand the problem that many Cubans of color have with "afro" (Rubiera Castillo and Martiatu Terry 2011), nor will we understand the cultural dynamics behind the anti-colonial battles that took place from 1860 to 1898 or, in terms of life stories, the career dynamics of personalities like the black generals Pedro Díaz and José González Planas or, also, of Antonio Maceo, all representatives of freed slaves ("pardos" and "morenos") who organized themselves in groups (*clientelas*), along with their comrades and workers, according to their relation with slavery (Zeuske 2002b, 2005; Scott and Zeuske 2004).

The thesis can certainly be upheld that former slaves did not express a collective identity but that they were identified as a group, to say it in a slightly mechanical manner, from outside, according to the interests of the person constructing the discourse.

I won't enter into a discussion here about the number of ex-slaves. For our purposes, we can consider a maximum number of slaves of more or less 500,000 women, men, and children in Cuba (which is a low estimate)[5] out of a total population of around 2 million (1899 census, [US War Department 1990]), which is to say, at least a fourth of Cuba's population. There are reliable estimates, however, that in 1890 a minimum of more or less 13,000 slaves came directly from Africa[6] during the last period of slave transports from Africa to Cuba during the clandestine trade (the famous hidden Atlantic) (Zeuske 2018, 103–35) and were emancipated between 1880 and 1886.

There were Afro-Cubans and former slaves who, by the end of 1898, with the transfer of Cuba's sovereignty from Spain to the United States, tried to organize themselves as a "particular people," which was a consequence of the cultural policy of African "nations" (*negros de nación*) that Spain developed in its colonies. Various individuals' requests (in some cases, it could have been men of color in the United States or Jamaica) included demands that they be given the right to represent as consuls all of Cuba's "Africans" or African nations—a minority position, practically treating former slaves as "another people" (very far removed from the discourse of "Cubanidad" [Cubaness]).

The town councils' and partnerships' organizers, often former slaves and their criollo children, had gone from the different rural zones of sugar production (such as the interior of Matanzas or Cienfuegos) to work in a port-centered and urban economy. With a basis in the cultural nuclei of "*reglas*" (slave cults, from the councils and from the cultural amalgam made up of runaway slaves), they set up at least five cultural-religious systems as part, though first as a "shadow," of the Cuban identity under construction.[7] The important thing to note is that these identities surrounding the slave "cults" (if they were left only in this dimension, they would be something like a historical "preserve") grew out of former slaves' fights for integration into society and for the construction of a "Cuban" cultural identity and a respective "citizenship" (with status and property) (Scott 2005; Bronfman 2002, 2004).

A fundamental feature of this process was a network of interrelations on a social and cultural level, which, as a whole, Fernando Ortiz called "black sorcerers" in 1906 and between 1930 and 1940 began to call by cultural activism's concept "transculturation," coinciding with the Constitution of 1940, which also legally resolved the "slave name" question (Ortiz 1940, 273–78; Iznaga 1989; Zeuske 2011b, 51–80). The meaning of Ortiz's concept of "transculturation" had been exactly that: to recognize, to an extent imposed by Cesar Lombroso's racist theories (racial psychopathology, but also "witchcraft," spread of disease [Zeuske 2015b, 177–205]), early forms of biometric control, and lack of "civilization"), the "African races" of Cuban culture and to use those features to organize and integrate former slaves "from above," a policy that was made official between 1920 and 1940, after apparently failed attempts to redefine the "nation."[8] In broad strokes, almost all the politicians (the majority of whom were then defined as "liberals" but in some parts also as "conservatives") did the same thing with local differences throughout Cuba following a policy of interracial alliances in the war of 1895–98.

Based on old conflicts (Ferrer 2002, 141–62; García Martínez 2001, 163–92), there was already the very early development of a group of (primarily) young black and mixed-race officials who did not want to take the path of Fernando Ortiz ("understanding as authentically belonging to the 'black class,'" as conceptualized during the colonial period [Arango 1811, in Zeuske 2016, 353–57) as only "African blood" or the old "African" tradition, identified first as "sorcery" and later as the basis for transculturation). As the children of ex-slaves, they initiated a discussion of Cubanness based on modernity and black and mixed-race protagonists. Here we have the seeds of the Partido Independiente de Color (PIC) movement (Portuondo 2002). On a national level, this discourse and PIC's policies were seen as dangerous to certain groups of the national elite (first to the conservatives, then to American occupiers in 1906–9, and then, starting that year, to liberal followers of the liberal president José Miguel Gómez), because the PIC began to come together to gain control over the hybrid, not clearly bounded, majority of men of color and former slaves. They also began to wrest control of the vision of "slavery's legacy," in other words, history (which, for these officials and young politicians of color, again, did not have to be only the controversial marginal culture of blacks from Africa, but American modernity, as defined by the criteria of the period).

The important political break in the process of the construction of what was "Cuban" between 1899 and 1902 was the establishment of universal male suffrage in the Constitution of 1901 (and the rejection of a racial policy of the state, which is to say, apartheid). This allowed the new Cuban elite of liberators to make use of their relations with their black former soldiers (or officials), which were sometimes very personal in nature (at times they were also relations between former masters and slaves), and at the same time hide them under the political language of the upper echelons of the political sphere. The "colorless and neutral Cuban"[9] had become discursive and textual reality. In any case, this "new Cuban" would have to maintain racial etiquette in a "racial democracy," one of the first formations, following Thomas Holt, of what could be called "new nations" in the Americas (Fuente 2003, 23–53; Holt 2003).

We do not know either how many former slaves were political activists, nor do we know what the thousands of people listed as "no-other-surnames" in provincial archives thought (the majority[10] of whom accepted or at least did not protest against their "slave name" after the abolition of slavery). For this reason, we put forward the hypothesis that the majority of former slaves, independently of the size of the group and their location, attempted to stay silent about slavery but not about the nation.

The major problem was that parts of society and the majority of former property owners and personnel involved in slavery did not allow it to be forgotten. There were many restrictions (the structural problems stemming from the lack of work and the lack of land will be addressed later in the chapter) affecting former slaves and the attempt to keep intact the group's "slave name." Soon after 1886 (the official abolition of slavery), there were also complaints of the slavish nature of the work former slaves were given, despite contracts and discourses about legalism and "free work." The mass participation of the black and mixed-race *mambises* in the war of 1895 in this context was a massive attempt to break out of their marginal positions and gain equal status in a new republic free of colonialism; this attempt was repeated in 1906 (and, as we've seen, in 1912) (Zeuske 1999, 127–56). What emerged from these serious conflicts was a false calm and something that could be called "a group with a slave name" as the nucleus of marginal classes between 1886 and 1940 (and until 1960).

The mainstream ("white") press, the published majority opinion (there were exceptions in the "black" press; see Schmieder 2018, 423–42), and science used this forgetting and silence about conflicts to construct something like a mentality of shame in order to manipulate the sense that "white Cubans had given blacks their freedom." In regards to forgetting and discourses of shame and the "generosity of the whites," there are important exceptions, particularly in the electoral process, with the objective of the foundation of the Cuban state and constitution between 1899 and 1902, which was practically a failure for the official policy of the United States and, especially, for Leonard Wood. At the end of these battles, universal male suffrage was imposed essentially from below (particularly on the municipal level) (Scott 2005), with strong influence from transracial *clientelas* from the war but also from what Rebecca Scott calls the "rural wage labor force" (2005).

The Structures

It is definitively clear that structures, particularly the rural structures of landownership and sugar production and the slavish nature of work, continued to exist (becoming centralized after the wars); the economic and technological dynamism also continued—along with the ecological destructions it brought (Ayala 1999, 183–230; Dye 1998; Santamaría García 2002; Santamaría García 2011, 149–75; Funes Monzote 2001, 2008; Tomich and Funes Monzote 2002). This momentum grew, beginning in 1899, with Cuba and Puerto Rico opening their doors to the United States, in other words, their *Americanization*. The political pressure exerted by sugar manufacturers and investor groups also deepened the cultural debate surrounding the "legacies" of slavery: for example, the famous debate over whether "racism" in Cuba is endogenous or exogenous or the no less famous decision, spurred by American pressure, to clear a path for the immigration of "necessary hands," which is to say, sugarcane cutters from the non-Cuban Caribbean (in Cuba, mainly Haitians and Jamaicans), against the interests of sugar workers (many of them former slaves, as we saw). Starting in 1910, with the newfound predominance of American sugar companies in the east of the country (Camagüey and Oriente), a new wave of Haitian and Jamaican immigrants, with their own legacies of slavery in Jamaica and in Saint-Domingue (which, in many respects, made up a significant part of a "Caribbean type"), started to arrive (Knight 1985, 84–114; Naranjo Orovio and García González 1995).

As for sugar work and the sugarcane workers' daily life itself, as Esteban Montejo points out, not much had changed; that is to say, freedom was always precarious due to the harsh character of the work, and "the work was exhausting" (Montejo and Barnet 1966, 63; Zeuske 2014, 77–99). What had changed was the fact that, after 1880, there were wages (and, since there was a lack of workforce, there was a little more pay starting in 1899, sometimes in American dollars). In any case, beginning in the 1880s, the division of labor changed in the sugar sector. The former female slaves "lost" their work in the sugarcane fields (female work was an "improvement" that existed since around 1790, after Arango y Parreño's projects). Women continued to work the "*conucos*," the small land plots or the urban lots (sometimes with notary protocols and property titles) (Zeuske 2005, 181–98), and educated their children. They also began to work in another very dynamic sector, that of domestic and urban services (washers, ironers, servants, at times in relations of civil clientelism that continued from the time of slavery). What was new in the post-emancipation period was a clearer division of work in regard to gender. "Poor" neighborhoods of people of color and former slaves began to grow and develop around the cities (also rural cities, like Lajas, Palmira, Cruces, Artemisa, or Güines). Many former slaves became social and economic elements in the dynamic urban economies, in the sector of services, port economies, and the transportation and construction sector, as well as prostitution (Rubiera Castillo 2000, 71–74) and the first tourist economies (starting in the 1920s).

The mobility of the rural workforce rose, to the point where it's almost possible to talk about a new nomadism of men and sugarcane workers.

First a "whitening" of the rural workforce developed, especially between 1880 and 1910, due to the seasonal migration between Galicia and Cuba ("Para Vigo me voy"), as well as the re-emigration and emigration of many poor Spaniards to Cuba starting in 1902 (such as Fidel Castro's father) (Naranjo Orovio 1994, 121–36). Between 1895 and the first years of the 20th century, this large group of rural workers formed a relatively stable transracial body (Scott 2005, 181). Beginning in 1910, there was a sort of "re-enslavement" of rural work and the sugarcane workforce due to the above-mentioned pressure exerted by large American companies. As a result, a strong anti-American and anti-imperialist sentiment emerged, even among the Spanish-Cuban elites, along with anti-black xenophobia and racism (particularly against Haitians and Jamaicans). This began a type of subphase in the debate over slavery's legacies (Naranjo Orovio and Puig-Samper 1998, 12–23; Naranjo Orovio and Puig-Samper 2003, 311–47; Fuente 2002, 235–69; Araquistáin 1961).

In Puerto Rico, the phases of these processes—based in lasting structures and social classes, with the same contents but quantitatively smaller and in more concrete spaces (especially in Ponce and the west of the island)—are approximately the same. The discrepancies, if we wish to call them that, come from the early crisis of Second Slavery[11] in Puerto Rico (dating from the 1850s and its temporary revival around the 1870s, when Puerto Rico reaffirmed its status as the second producer in the Caribbean [Zanetti Lecuona 2012a, 31]). Other differences include the fact that Puerto Rico never had as many enslaved individuals from Africa (called *bozales*, in colonial slang) as Cuba (which is to say that the cultures were more creolized and transculturized); that they had a practically "imported" coastal, slave-owning elite and, furthermore, the earlier formal abolition of slavery due to the fact that rural slave owners were not as powerful as they were in Cuba in 1873 (Zanetti Lecuona 2012b, 48); the near total failure in implementing a rural middle class; tenant farming (which in Cuba was not a failure and in the Dominican Republic was not widespread); and, of course, the United States' early and more direct neo-colonization (Morales Carrión 1978; Moreno Fraginals, Moya Pons, and Engerman 1985; Moya Pons 2007, 235–36; Cabrera Salcedo 2010; Ayala 1999, 183–230).

The new imperial power's control of the Caribbean brought about a spectacular boom in export production on the three islands and even greater control over the "hard" large structures of landownership: clearly in Cuba (with a few exceptions in the mountainous zones like Escambray and Oriente); in Puerto Rico there was a spatial structure between the mountainous interior (primarily subsistence farming and coffee) and the flat coasts; and in Santo Domingo, mainly between northwest and southeast Cibao. Since formal slavery had already been abolished in the Dominican Republic for many years (since 1822) and the majority of the rural population were *conuqueros* (small farmers without titles), the principal owners ran into difficulty finding agricultural workers. All the same, between 1900 and 1930, the three islands' sugar production rose from 7% to reach almost half of the world's sugar production (Zanetti Lecuona 2012c, 69–145).

In short, we have very strong dynamics in these post-slave societies, which, in some form, also was the legacy of slavery. After a political crisis of formal slavery (1870–95), the great structures of slavery were built up to new heights in the 20th century in Cuba. In Puerto Rico, after a near fiasco in 1860–1900, sugar production boomed in the 20th century. This also happened in the eastern and southeastern parts of the Dominican Republic. These structures were accompanied by a high degree of poverty on one side and wealth on the other, but with relatively high per capita profits (e.g., compared with societies where slavery was less entrenched in 1830, like Venezuela or Colombia, or more impoverished, like Haiti and Jamaica) in a cosmopolitan society in large cities and an open economy. The centers of societies with slave and post-slave economies would form the first seeds of a globalized and slave-capitalist society.

Structural Inclusiveness, Racism, and Slavery's Enduring Legacies

To conclude, I don't know if there was a culture of shame (with nuances) in Cuba, Puerto Rico, and the Dominican Republic concerning slavery's legacies. There was, however, a relation between the enduring legacies, like structures and strong asymmetrical dependencies, the silences and the forgotten past, as widespread feelings of the Cuban population and the development in Cuba of open racism until 1959 (following which, new forms developed) (Zeuske 2011a, 105–21)—perhaps in Puerto Rico, where relatively more poor whites existed and transculturation was stronger, not in the original sense of Ortiz's term ("the elite must accept former slaves' culture") but in the sense of a common, popular mix distanced from the elite. In the Dominican Republic, the "forgetting of the past" (which was more of an eradication due to its temporary duration) is the strongest among the three territories.

Due to the pressures of racism, silence also had some very positive outcomes, for example, with respect to the alliances formed within the labor movement. It was only regarding political control of the population (the multitude of whom—again, mainly in rural areas of sugar production—were former slaves in Cuba and Puerto Rico and were "new" salaried workers in Dominicana) and the important urban centers, as well as the nation's symbolic dimension (that is, particularly in Havana), that major movements against black "sorcery" were put into motion (especially between 1902 and 1909).[12]

Racism is one of the great legacies of slavery, with ancient roots and international actors that influenced Cuba's, Puerto Rico's, and the Dominican Republic's post-emancipation situations. But Cuba, especially due to its inclusive anti-colonial battles, was a special case. Ever since the tradition established by the *Ejército Libertador Cubano* (one of the few transracial armies in the Americas, with very high-ranking "black" generals and mixed-race leaders like Antonio Maceo), continuing during the more local clientelism up until legal and theoretic nationalism (constitution), there were strong currents of inclusion, though internally accompanied by many conflicts. This was the same case with the large sugarcane production structures and the rural proletariat who worked within them (Dumoulin 1974, 1981, 2000).

What can be referred to as "written racism" developed most strongly in Cuba between 1910 and 1930, along with political conflicts and debates about the past and the values of the future (Pruna and García González 1989; García González and Álvarez Peláez 1999).[13] It was above all the combination of society's basic pro-slavery posture (making up the bulk of published opinion) of pro-slavery individuals, former owners, and "modern" science at the end of the 19th century and the beginning of the 20th that played a role in the symbolic prolongation of slavery (Zeuske 2002c, 2011). "Racial science" operated and developed against the backdrop of slavery's written administration's tradition of control techniques and values. Notaries, for example, until around 1870–80 (earlier, in Puerto Rico) gained most of their income through the establishment of protocols regarding the buying and selling of slaves. Beginning in those years, they started to earn a large part of their income through both protocols regarding slaves' "freedom"; they used the same words (Zeuske 2011b) both in the buying and in the selling of slaves and through the business done by former slaves as "agents of their own freedom" (Aguirre 1993). In "high" written culture, the official historiography, sociology-criminology, and medicine all played an important role in the circulation of "scientific racism" without mentioning colors.[14] After the intellectual debates over abolitionism or anti-abolitionism (which ended in the 1880s [Vila Vilar and Vila Vilar 1996]), the most important sector where the silence on slavery was broken was the "battle for the past." In this battle for the past, the institutionalized and free scholars, influenced by the flourishing of Darwinism, Lombrosianism, and international racism, opened the door for "scientific" racism in Cuba. There was a heated debate, not only among intellectuals in the humanities but also among doctors, anthropologists, and intellectuals in the natural sciences (including psychologists and psychiatrists) (Pruna and García González 1989; García González and Álvarez Peláez 1999). The result was scholarship's symbolic appropriation of slavery's legacy, politicizing and, in a certain sense, "racializing" (and psychologizing) its history.

Conclusion

Between 1902 and 1920, there was a policy of what Alejandro de la Fuente calls "racial democracy" in Cuba, Puerto Rico (though less so), and the Dominican Republic that installed a theoretical equality in the population and constitution that in practice discriminated against *negros*, "black Haitians" (Fuente 2002, 2013), and Jamaicans. Meanwhile, there existed—above all, in the hierarchized culture of the *clientelas* but in a deeply transracial tradition (inherited from the *clientelas*, which were the tactical entities behind the great movements of the time)—an empirical and everyday mentality of inclusiveness within the political system of universal male suffrage, both before and after 1912. After 1912, this was particularly found in local and regional *clientelas*, in labor forces, movements and organizations, in journalism, and in literature (Scott 2005, 252). Despite the common foundation of transracial patriotism, in most of the institutionalized sciences, the official public culture, family rights (and certainly in the prisons and the state's criminal system), and the bureaucracies, a "second-class citizenship" was constructed under the blanket of silence on the history of slavery, as well as the use of "afro" for them. This second-class citizenship principally applied to the poor, rural, "uncultured"—lacking a second surname—former slave (Palmié 2002b, 186–88).

To sum up, the "hard" foundation of all this was the prolongation and extension of large plantation structures (especially the control of good, flat land) in Cuba, along with the calcification of the "Roman" law of private property, salaried work, and the structure of an exportation economy. Inevitably, with the creation of classes tied to different types of work, the class of former slaves and the poorest white emigrants (Galicians and Canary Islanders) were left with the hardest jobs in the mills and in transportation.

Puerto Rico followed the same pattern, but with more volatility and crises and with a hard nucleus of resistance as well, concentrated in the mountainous interior. In Dominicana, there was the construction of large properties in parts of the country and the creation of salaried work (with minimum wages), in some cases, with military intervention. This was the most important legacy of colonialism in the Spanish Antilles.

What an enduring legacy!

NOTES

1. To give just one example: today, what is considered "modern" music, which grew out of what we call "afro" (Afro-Cuban and other Afro-Americanisms) rhythms, was presented as savage noise by writers, travelers, and opinion leaders between 1800 and 1920. In 1800, for the renowned figure Humboldt, it was something even worse: he almost always speaks of the monotonous shouting of "black'" music (1991, 263), while the Cuban hacienda owner Francisco Suárez y Romero alludes almost directly to the religious function of African rhythms: "Dos negros mozos cogieron los tambores y, sin calentarlos siquiera, comenzaron a llamar, como ellos dicen" (Two black lads picked up the drums and, hardly even warming them up, began to call, as they say) (Suárez y Romero 1974, 109). And slaves themselves, in an inquiry sponsored by the Military Commission in Cuba on a "vaile de tambor hecho del dia treinta al primero del actual [octubre de 1837] p.r cinco negros de la propiedad de D Benito Rodrig.z" (drum dance done by five blacks on D Benito Rodriguez's property from the thirtieth to the first of the current month [October 1837]) (Suárez y Romero 1974, 109), let it be known that they simply did it to entertain themselves during the rough times of the sugar harvest or on the coffee plantations.

2. As in the legal case of Andrea Quesada and her allies (Scott 2005, 216–52) or the case of María de los Reyes Castillo Bueno, 1902–97. Reyita explains how the Revolutionary War of 1895–98 was the origin of the right to choose your own surname, which is to say, to define one's own identity as a family in opposition to the despised former owner's last name (see Rubiera Castillo 2000, 18, 171).

3. For a social and institution history of *patrocinados* and former slaves, see "Patrocinados: Obstacles and Initiatives" (Scott 2000, 141–71) and "Former Slaves" (Scott 2000, 227–54).

4. As for the United States' urban sociology, which unfortunately focused almost only on the concept of "race," see Baldwin (2004, 397–450).

5. Given that there were already 200,000 slaves in 1877; approximately 100,000 in 1883; 53,382 in 1885; and around 25,000 in 1886 (Scott 2000, 140, 141–97, 194).

6. Exactly 12,897 (Pérez de la Riva 1979, 17).

7. Palo Monte or congas reglas; santería or regla de ocha or regla Ifá; reglas arará (also as the basis for the *tumba francesa*), Oggunismo, Voodoo; carabalí or Abakuá reglas (Ñáñigos), openly mixed with forms of popular Catholicism and different forms of Protestantism/spiritualism and, clandestinely, with Islamic and

Chinese features (see Millet and Alarcón 1998; James Figarola 1999; Palmié 2002a, 2002b; Fuentes Guerra and Schwegler 2004; Zeuske 2004b).

8. One of the first and best-known openly racist images of slavery and the legacy of slavery is found in the paradigmatic book previously mentioned, *Hampa-afrocubana* (the second edition of *Black Sorcerers*) by Fernando Ortiz. Ortiz was the first to use "Lombrosian" racism, as a "scientist," to break the silence on slavery and to also "scientifically" explain Cuban society's post-abolitionist but not post-slavery problems. But he was also one of the first to drop this concept after 20 years (more or less in the mid-1920s). Instead of excluding former slaves and slavery's legacies, starting in 1925, Ortiz proposed the inclusion of former slaves, their culture, and slavery's legacies in Cuba. It was clearly a patriarchal inclusion, under the control of scientists (who even today are predominately "white"), but Ortiz also was one of the first to coin and use the notion of Afro-Cubans, the precursor to the concept of African descent that we use today. Ortiz broke the silence regarding the future of former slaves. And Ortiz was the one who, as a result of debates (and, of course, real history) about slavery's legacies, introduced the highly important concept of *transculturation* previously mentioned, without which, as Fernardo Coronil observed, there would not have been postcolonialism.

9. For more on the beginnings of these processes, see Ferrer (1999, 117–23).

10. One exception is found in Reyita's memoirs (see Rubiera Castillo 2000).

11. *Second Slavery* is a concept that defines modern slavery in the south of the United States, Cuba, and the south of Brazil as part of global capitalism. Slavery in other territories, like small islands, only shows dichotomist and partial dimensions of Second Slavery, such as is the case in Puerto Rico, which had a small number of slaves in the workforce from 1840 to 1870 (Tomich 1988, 2004, 2018; Tomich and Zeuske 2008).

12. One of the early results of this was Fernando Ortiz's first edition of *Black Sorcerers* (the "Lombrosian edition") (1906).

13. See, for example, Israel Castellanos's (1929) and Alejandra Bronfman's (2004) work.

14. For example, Figueras ([1907] 1959); for a critique of Ortiz's "objectivity," see Quiñones (1999).

REFERENCES

Aguirre, Carlos. 1993. *Agentes de su Propia Libertad. Los Esclavos de Lima y la Desintegración de la Esclavitud, 1821–1854*. Lima: Fondo Editorial de la Pontificia Universidad Católica del Perú.

Araquistáin, Luis. 1961. *La Agonía Antillana. El Imperialismo Yanqui en el Mar Caribe*. Havana: Editorial Lex.

Ayala, César J. 1999. "The Twentieth-Century Plantation." In *American Sugar Kingdom: The Plantation Economy of the Spanish Caribbean, 1898–1934*, edited by César J. Ayala, 183–230. Chapel Hill: University of North Carolina Press.

Baldwin, Davarian. 2004. "Black Bells and Ivory Towers: The Place of Race in U.S.-Social Thought, 1892–1948." *Critical Sociology* 30 (2): 397–450.

Bronfman, Alejandra. 2002. "Plena Libertad y Democracia: Negros Brujos and the Social Question, 1904–1919." *Hispanic American Historical Review* 82 (3): 549–87.

Bronfman, Alejandra. 2004. *Measures of Equality: Social Science, Citizenship, and Race in Cuba, 1902–1940.* Chapel Hill: University of North Carolina Press.

Cabrera Salcedo, Lizette. 2010. *De los Bueyes al Vapor. Caminos de la Tecnología del Azúcar en Puerto Rico y el Caribe.* San Juan: La Editorial, Universidad de Puerto Rico.

Castellanos, Israel. 1929. *La Delincuencia Femenina en Cuba. Estadísticas Judiciales, Penitenciarias y Clínicas, Gráficas Criminológicas.* Havana: Imprenta Ojeda.

Dumoulin, John. 1974. "El primer Desarrollo del Movimiento Obrero y la Formación del Proletariado en el Sector Azucarero. Cruces 1886–1902." *Islas. Revista de la Universidad de Las Villas* 48:3–66.

Dumoulin, John. 1981. *Azúcar y lucha de clases 1917.* Havana: Editorial de Ciencias Sociales.

Dumoulin, John. 2000. "Evolución del Estado cubano, 1930–1958: La regulación de las relaciones laborales." *Temas. Cultura. Ideología. Sociedad* 22–23: 77–87.

Dye, Alan. 1998. *Cuban Sugar Production in the Age of Mass Production: Technology and the Economics of the Sugar Central, 1899–1929.* Stanford: Stanford University Press.

Ferrer, Ada. 1999. *Insurgent Cuba: Race, Nation, and Revolution, 1868–1898.* Chapel Hill: University of North Carolina Press.

Ferrer, Ada. 2002. "Raza, Región y Género en la Cuba Rebelde: Quintín Bandera y la Cuestión del Liderazgo Político." In *Espacios, Silencios y los Sentidos de la Libertad: Cuba entre 1878 y 1912*, edited by Fernando Martínez, Rebecca J. Scott, and Orlando García Martínez, 141–62. Havana: Ediciones Unión.

Figueras, Francisco. [1907] 1959. *Cuba y su Evolución Colonial.* Havana: Impr. Avisador Comercial [Havana: s.l.].

Fuente, Alejandro de la. 2002. "Mitos de 'Democracia Racial': Cuba, 1900–1912." In *Espacios, Silencios y los Sentidos de la Libertad: Cuba entre 1878 y 1912*, edited by Fernando Martínez, Rebecca J. Scott, and Orlando García Martínez, 235–69. Havana: Edición Unión.

Fuente, Alejandro de la. 2003. *A Nation for All: Race, Inequality, and Politics in Twentieth-Century Cuba.* Chapel Hill: University of North Carolina Press.

Fuentes Guerra, Jesús, and Armin Schwegler. 2004. *Lengua y Ritos del Palo Monte Mayombe. Dioses Cubanos y Sus Fuentes Africanas.* Madrid: Iberoamericana.

Funes Monzote, Reinaldo. 2001. "La Conquista de Camagüey Por el Azúcar, 1898–1926. El Impacto Ambiental de un Milagro Económico." *Tiempos de América* 8:3–28.

Funes Monzote, Reinaldo. 2008. *From Rainforest to Cane Field in Cuba: An Environmental History since 1492.* Chapel Hill: University of North Carolina Press.

García González, Armando, and Raquel Álvarez Peláez. 1999. *En Busca de la Raza Perfecta. Eugenesia e Higiene en Cuba (1898–1958).* Madrid: CSIC.

García Martínez, Orlando. 2001. "La Brigada de Cienfuegos: un Análisis Social de su Formación." In *Espacios, Silencios y los Sentidos de la Libertad: Cuba entre 1878 y 1912*, edited by Fernando Martínez, Rebecca J. Scott, and Orlando García Martínez, 163–92. Havana: Ediciones Unión.

Holt, Thomas. 2003. "The First New Nations." In *Race and Nation in Modern Latin*

America, edited by Nancy Appelbaum, Anne S. Macpherson, and Karin Alejandra Rosemblatt, 7–14. Chapel Hill: University of North Carolina Press.

Humboldt, Alexander von. 1991. *Reise in die Äquinoktial-Gegenden des Neuen Kontinents.* Edited by Ottmar Ette. Frankfurt am Main and Leipzig: Insel Verlag.

Iznaga, Diana. 1989. *Transculturación en Fernando Ortiz.* Havana: Editorial de Ciencias Sociales.

James Figarola, Joel. 1999. *Los sistemas Mágico-Religiosos Cubanos: Principios Rectores.* Caracas: UNESCO.

James Figarola, Joel, José Millet, and Alexis Alarcón. 1998. *El Vodú en Cuba.* Santiago de Cuba: Editorial Oriente.

Knight, Franklin W. 1985. "Jamaican Migrants and the Cuban Sugar Industry, 1900–1934." In *Between Slavery and Free Labor: The Spanish-Speaking Caribbean in the Nineteenth Century*, edited by Manuel Moreno Fraginals, Frank Moya Pons, and Stanley L. Engerman, 84–114. Baltimore: Johns Hopkins University Press.

Martí, José. [1893] 1975. "'Mi Raza' (Patria, 16 de Abril de 1893)." In *Obras Completas*, 2:298–300. Havana: Editorial de Ciencias Sociales.

Montejo, Esteban, and Miguel Barnet. 1966. *Biografía de un cimarrón.* México: Editorial Siglo Veintiuno.

Morales Carrión, Arturo. 1978. *Auge y Decadencia de la Trata Negrera en Puerto Rico (1820–1860).* San Juan: Centro de Estudios Avanzados de Puerto Rico y el Caribe and Instituto de Cultura Puertorriqueña.

Moreno Fraginals, Manuel, Frank Moya Pons, and Stanley L. Engerman. 1985. *Between Slavery and Free Labor: The Spanish-Speaking Caribbean in the Nineteenth Century.* Baltimore: Johns Hopkins University Press.

Moya Pons, Rafael Francisco. 2007. "Puerto Rico: The World's Second Largest Sugar Producer." In *History of the Caribbean*, edited by Rafael Francisco Moya Pons, 235–36. Princeton: Markus Wiener.

Naranjo Orovio, Consuelo. 1994. "La Población Española en Cuba, 1880–1953." In *Cuba la Perla de las Antillas. Actas de las I Jornadas sobre "Cuba y Su Historia,"* edited by Naranjo Orovio and Tomás Mallo Gutiérrez, 121–36. Aranjuez and Madrid: Doce Calles.

Naranjo Orovio, Consuelo, and Armando García González. 1995. *Racismo e Inmigración en Cuba en el Siglo XIX.* Madrid and Aranjuez: Doce Calles.

Naranjo Orovio, Consuelo, and Miguel Ángel Puig-Samper. 1998. "Delincuencia y Racismo en Cuba: Israel Castellanos Versus Fernando Ortiz." In *Ciencia y Facismo*, edited by Rafael Huertos and Carmen Ortiz, 12–23. Aranjuez: Ediciones Doce Calles.

Naranjo Orovio, Consuelo, and Miguel Ángel Puig-Samper. 2003. "Los caminos de la regeneración en Fernando Ortiz: su formación intelectual en España." *OP.CIT. Revista del Centro de Investigaciones Históricas*, Puerto Rico: 311–47.

National Archive of Cuba. 1837. *Miscelánea de Libros, leg. 692, Letra Q: Expediente Formado en Averiguación de un Baile de Tambor Verificado Por Cinco Negros de Propiedad de D Benito Rodríguez en la Jurisdicción de Güira de Melena.* Havana: ANC.

Ortiz, Fernando. 1906. *Los negros Brujos (Apuntes Para un Estudio de Etnología Criminal). Carta Prólogo del Dr. C. Lombroso.* Madrid: Librería de Fernando Fe.

Ortiz, Fernando. 1940. "El Fenómeno Social de la Transculturación y Su Importancia en Cuba." *Revista Bimestre Cubana. Havana* 46:273–78.

Palmié, Stefan. 2002a. *Wizards and Scientists: Explorations in Afro-Cuban Modernity and Tradition.* Durham: Duke University Press.

Palmié, Stephan. 2002b. "Genealogies of Morality: The Afro-Cuban Nganga as Wage Laborer, Slave, and Maroon." In *Wizards and Scientists: Explorations in Afro-Cuban Modernity and Tradition*, edited by Stephan Palmié, 159–200. Durham: Duke University Press.

Pérez de la Riva, Juan. 1979. *La República Neocolonial.* Havana: Editorial de Ciencias Sociales.

Portuondo Linares, Serafín. 2002. *Los Independientes de Color. Historia del Partido Independiente de Color.* Havana: Publicaciones del Ministerio de Educación.

Pruna, Pedro, and Armado García González. 1989. *Darwinismo y Sociedad en Cuba, Siglo XIX.* Madrid: Consejo Superior de Investigaciones Científicas.

Quiñones, Arcadio Díaz. 1999. "Fernando Ortiz y Allan Kardec: Espiritismo y Transculturación." *Catauro: Revista Cubana de Antropología* 1 (0): 14–31.

Rubiera Castillo, Daisy. 2000. *Reyita, Sencillamente. Testimonio de una Negra Cubana Nonagenaria.* Havana: Ediciones Verde Olivo.

Rubiera Castillo, Daisy, and Inés María Martiatu Terry. 2011. *Afrocubanas. Historia, Pensamiento y Prácticas Culturales.* Havana: Editorial Ciencias Sociales.

Santamaría García, Antonio. 2002. *Sin Azúcar No Hay país. La Industria Azucarera y la Economía Cubana (1919–1939).* Sevilla: Universidad de Sevilla, Escuela de Estudios Hispanoamericanos.

Santamaría García, Antonio. 2011. "Las islas españolas del azúcar en el Caribe (1760–1898). Grandes debates en perspectiva comparada." *América Latina en la Historia Económica* 35:149–76.

Sanz, Vicent, and Michael Zeuske. 2017. "Microhistoria de Esclavos y Esclavas." *Millars. Espai i Història* 42 (1): 9–21.

Sartorius, David. 2014. "'Long Live Spain! Death to Autonomy!': Liberalism and Slave Emancipation." In *Ever Faithful: Race, Loyalty, and the Ends of Empire in Spanish Cuba*, edited by David Sartorius, 158–86. Durham: Duke University Press.

Schmieder, Ulrike. 2018. "Periódicos Afrocubanos: La Independencia y el Distanciamiento de la Elite Afrocubana de Haití, África y la Esclavitud." In *Reshaping (G)local Dynamics of the Caribbean: Relaciones y Deconexiones—Relations and Disconnections—Relations et Déconnexions*, edited by Anja Bandau, Anne Brüske, and Natascha Ueckmann, 423–42. Heidelberg: Heidelberg University Publishing.

Scott, Rebecca J. 2000. *Slave Emancipation in Cuba: The Transition to Free Labor, 1860–1899.* Princeton: Princeton University Press.

Scott, Rebecca J. 2005. *Degrees of Freedom: Louisiana and Cuba after Slavery.* Cambridge, MA: Harvard University Press.

Scott, Rebecca J., and Michael Zeuske. 2004. "Le ‚Droit D'avoir Des Droits': Les Revendications des Ex-esclaves à Cuba (1872–1909)." *Annales HSS* 3:521–45.

Scully, Pamela, and Diana Paton. 2005. *Gender and Slave Emancipation in the Atlantic World*. Durham: Duke University Press.

Suárez y Romero, Anselmo. 1974. *Francisco, El Ingenio o las Delicias del Campo*. Havana: Editorial de Arte y Literatura.

Tomich, Dale W. 1988. "The 'Second Slavery': Bonded Labor and the Transformations of the Nineteenth-Century World Economy." In *Rethinking the Nineteenth Century: Contradictions and Movement*, edited by Francisco O. Ramírez, 103–17. New York: Greenwood Press.

Tomich, Dale W. 2004. *Through the Prism of Slavery: Labor, Capital, and World Economy*. Boulder: Rowman & Littlefield.

Tomich, Dale W. 2018. "The Second Slavery and World Capitalism: A Perspective for Historical Inquiry." *International Review of Social History* 63 (3): 149–64.

Tomich, Dale W., and Michael Zeuske, eds. 2008. *The Second Slavery: Mass Slavery, World-Economy, and Comparative Microhistories*. 2 vols. Binghamton: Fernand Braudel Center, Binghamton University.

Tomich, Dale W., and Reinlado Funes Monzote. 2002. "Naturaleza, Tecnología y Esclavitud en Cuba: Frontera Azucarera y Revolución Industrial, 1815–1870." In *Trabajo Libre y Trabajo Coactivo en Sociedades de Plantación*, edited by José Antonio Piqueras, 75–117. Madrid: Siglo XXI de España.

U.S. War Department. 1990. *Report on the Census of Cuba, 1899*. Washington, DC: Government Printing Office.

Vila Vilar, Enriqueta, and Luisa Vila Vilar. 1996. *Los Abolicionistas Españoles. Siglo 19*. Madrid: Ediciones de Cultura Hispánica.

Zanetti Lecuona, Oscar. 2012a. "Concentración Industrial." In *Esplendor y Decadencia del Azúcar en las Antillas Hispanas*, edited by Oscar Zanetti Lecuona, 30–40. Havana: Editorial de Ciencias Sociales.

Zanetti Lecuona, Oscar. 2012b. "El Régimen de Trabajo: Problemas y Soluciones." In *Esplendor y Decadencia del Azúcar en las Antillas Hispanas*, edited by Oscar Zanetti Lecuona, 40–52. Havana: Editorial de Ciencias Sociales.

Zanetti Lecuona, Oscar. 2012c. "La Gran Azucarera Imperial." In *Esplendor y Decadencia del Azúcar en las Antillas Hispanas*, edited by Oscar Zanetti Lecuona, 69–145. Havana: Editorial de Ciencias Sociales.

Zeuske, Michael. 1998. "El 'Cimarrón' y las Consecuencias de la Guerra del 95. Un Repaso de la Biografía de Esteban Montejo." *Revista de Indias* 58 (212): 65–84.

Zeuske, Michael. 1999. "Clientelas Regionales, Alianzas Interraciales y Poder Nacional en Torno a la 'Guerrita de Agosto' (1906)." *Islas e Imperios. Estudios de Historia de las Sociedades en el Mundo Colonial y Post-Colonial* 2:127–56.

Zeuske, Michael. 2002a. *Sklavereien, Emanzipationen und Atlantische Weltgeschichte. Essays über Mikrogeschichten, Sklaven, Globalisierungen und Rassismus*. Leipzig: Leipziger Universitätsverlag.

Zeuske, Michael. 2002b. "'Los Negros Hicimos la Independencia': Aspectos de la Movilización Afrocubana en un Hinterland Cubano—Cienfuegos entre Colonia y República." In *Espacios, Silencios y los Sentidos de la Libertad: Cuba Entre 1878 y 1912*, edited by Fernando Martínez Heredia, Rebecca J. Scott, and Orlando F. García Martínez, 193–234. Havana: Editorial de Ciencias Sociales.

Zeuske, Michael. 2002c. "Hidden Markers, Open Secrets: On Naming, Race Marking and Race Making in Cuba." *New West Indian Guide* 76 (3–4): 211–41.
Zeuske, Michael. 2004a. "De la 'Guerrita de Agosto' a la Derrota del Movimiento de los Veteranos: Raza, Política y Nación en la Primera República de Cuba." *OP.CIT. Revista del Centro de Investigaciones Históricas, Universidad de Puerto Rico* 15:59–99.
Zeuske, Michael 2004b. "Formation der Sklavenreligionen: Santería, Ifá-Orakel und Andere Reglas." In *Schwarze Karibik. Sklaven, Sklavereikultur und Emanzipation*, edited by Michael Zeuske, 287–310. Berlin: Rotpunktverlag.
Zeuske, Michael. 2005. "Two Stories of Gender and Slave Emancipation in Cienfuegos and Santa Clara, Central Cuba—Microhistorical Approaches to the Atlantic World." In *Gender and Slave Emancipation in the Atlantic World*, edited by Pamela Scully and Diana Paton, 181–98. Durham: Duke University Press.
Zeuske, Michael. 2008. "Humboldt, Esclavitud, Autonomismo y Emancipación en las Américas, 1791–1825." In *Alexander von Humboldt. Estancia en España y Viaje Americano*, edited by Mariano Cuesta Domingo and Sandra Rebok, 257–77, Madrid: Real Sociedad Geográfica/CSIC.
Zeuske, Michael. 2011a. "Slavery and Racism in Nineteenth-Century Cuba." In *Racism in the Modern World: Historical Perspectives on Cultural Transfer and Adaption*, edited by Manfred Berg and Simon Wendt, 105–21. New York and Oxford: Berghahn Books.
Zeuske, Michael. 2011b. "The Names of Slavery and Beyond: The Atlantic, the Americas and Cuba." In *The End of Slavery in Africa and the Americas: A Comparative Approach*, edited by Ulrike Schmieder, Katja Füllberg-Stolberg, and Michael Zeuske. Münster: LIT-Verlag.
Zeuske, Michael. 2013. "Legados de la Esclavitud y Afrodescendientes en Cuba." In *Afroamérica, Espacios e Identidades*, edited by Javier Laviña Gómez, Ricardo Piqueras Céspedes, and Cristina Mondejar Hidrobó. Barcelona: Icaria editorial.
Zeuske, Michael. 2014. "Postemancipación y Trabajo en Cuba." *Boletín Americanista Año LXIV* 1 (68): 77–99.
Zeuske, Michael. 2015a. *Sklavenhändler, Negreros und Atlantikkreolen. Eine Weltgeschichte des Sklavenhandels im Atlantischen Raum*. Berlin and Boston: De Gruyter Oldenbourg.
Zeuske, Michael. 2015b. "Doktoren und Sklaven. Sklavereiboom und Medizin als 'Kreolische Wissenschaft' auf Kuba." *Saeculum* 65 (1): 177–205.
Zeuske, Michael. 2016. "Francisco de Arango y Parreño: Representación (1811). Oder: Der 'Adam Smith der Plantagensklaverei in den Amerikas' und das Verhältnis von 'Rasse' und Klasse." In *Race and Sex: Eine Geschichte der Neuzeit. 49 Schlüsseltexte aus vier Jahrhunderten neu gelesen*, edited by Olaf Stieglitz and Jürgen Martschukat, 353–57. Berlin: Neofelis Verlag.
Zeuske, Michael. 2018. "Out of the Americas: Slave Traders and the Hidden Atlantic in the Nineteenth Century." *Atlantic Studies* 15 (1): 103–35.
Zeuske, Michael. 2021. "Humboldt in Venezuela and Cuba: The 'Second Slavery'." *German Life and Letters* 74 (3): 311–25.

Zeuske, Michael, and Norbert Finzsch. 2011. "What Came after Emancipation? A Micro-Historical Comparison between Cuba and the United States." In *Humanitarian Intervention and Changing Labor Relations: The Long-Term Consequences of the Abolition of the Slave Trade*, edited by Marcel van der Linden, 285–318. Leiden and Boston: Brill.

CHAPTER 17

Patterns of Work, Stratification, and Social Prestige in the Late Spanish Colonial Empire

Jochen Kemner

Over the course of the four centuries of Spanish colonial rule in the Americas, a social structure evolved that, to this day, shapes the social attitudes in most of the countries of the region. The aim of this chapter[1] is to examine the socio-structural traits that developed through a long-term historical process. The starting point of this investigation begins with the general phenomena proper to the Spanish American colonial societies, which will be studied by focusing on the last bastions of Spanish colonialism overseas, whose postcolonial legacies, especially those of the Caribbean, are examined in this book. A spotlight will be placed on the framework and mechanisms that established a strong correlation between certain forms of employment and occupations, on the one hand, and (ethno-racial) social status, on the other. One of the central ideas that will be developed is that social status was ascribed based on certain types of employment or ways of gaining a living, which were monopolized by an elite of European descent through exclusionary schemes that were often introduced and institutionalized through regulatory provisions. Social notions that implied a disdain for manual labor and marked hierarchization were consequently solidified. These demarcations were established, on the one hand, in line with gender divisions—a ubiquitous phenomenon during this time period and one certainly not limited to the colonial context—and, on the other hand, in accordance with ethnicized and racialized divisions, a widespread phenomenon both then and now in the Americas. The emphasis of this chapter will be on the latter form of social boundary making.

Related to these aspects of social stratification, personal domination and control over a workforce became another important mark of social distinction. This distinctive marker of Ibero-American colonialism evolved in the early phase of the conquest in agricultural estates built on exploitative labor practices such as the encomienda system. This closed social system, in which an overwhelmingly indigenous workforce was controlled through a system of mandatory services and debt peonage, became the source of enduring social attitudes (Kaltmeier 2016). In societies based on slave labor, the workforce, either acquired on the market or by descent, legally belonged to the owner. Absolute power over the workers' bodies was therefore built into society's configuration and set the foundation for patterns of social distinction and the formation of ties of belonging.

Socio-Structural Characteristics of Colonial Societies in Latin America and the Caribbean

When social historians began in the 1960s to study the social stratification in Spanish American colonial societies, which persisted in Cuba, Puerto Rico, and the Philippines until the end of the 19th century, they proposed a variety of theoretical concepts and models. Of course, and given that the ties connecting caste, class, and ethnic structures were not homogenous, social configurations did not evolve everywhere in the same manner but took on distinctive features as a result of particular spatial and temporal factors. Consequently, in colonial Latin America and the Caribbean, we find elements that relate to "castes," "estates," and "classes" as well as to "pigmentocratic" structures (Mörner 1967; Hoetink 1967; Lipschutz 1975).

At times, the accounts passed on by foreign travelers, who left testimonies of their journeys across the Americas, give the impression that the differences between the social groups were irreconcilable. The classic narrative presented in many of these accounts runs roughly as follows: Spaniards monopolized all the top positions in the colonial administration and wholesale trade and looked down on white creoles who, for their part, envied the privileges held by those born on the peninsula. What united these two groups of whites was their disdain for people of indigenous and African descent: those of African origin ("blacks") were branded brutes and savages; those of mixed-race personified promiscuity and illegitimate ancestry, since many were born out of wedlock. Indigenous people, for their part, were despised for their apparently passive and ignorant character. Those born in the Americas with mixed European and African/indigenous lineage were resentful toward whites, both criollos and those from the peninsula, who upheld their lineage-linked privileges and denied others equal treatment. Like whites, they scorned the black and indigenous population, above all those who had been born in Africa, for their "savage" culture. They displayed a sense of superiority on the basis of their European background, despite the fact that they were legally on the same level as freed blacks. Conversely, blacks, and especially Africans, disdained those of mixed-race, even though the whites seemed their natural opponents, responsible for their servitude and suppression. Adding to the equation the rivalries and hostilities among the diverse groups that were forcefully brought over from the African continent and the encounters between the different regional identities of the Spanish peninsula—including the persecution of those labeled as new Christian immigrants (Jews, Moriscos)—a picture of ever-present and superimposed conflicts emerges.

There are testimonial sources that substantiate this picture. However, the idea that American colonial societies were embroiled in constant internal turmoil contrasts with a macro-historical perspective that portrays the majority of the immense regions of the Spanish Empire as having been markedly tranquil and peaceful on a domestic level, at least in comparison with the religious wars and social conflicts that occurred in Europe's premodern period. The aforementioned social conflicts and tensions seldom erupted into violence. Slave or indigenous rebellions, like the one led by Túpac Amaru in the viceroyalty of Peru in 1780, were exceptional, and when they broke out, their impact was usually limited to a local context. Only the fugitive slave communities constituted a major problem for public security in rural zones that relied on forced labor. But runaway slaves endured severe persecution from slave hunters, and only a few *palenques* managed to sustain for a prolonged period of time their precarious freedom and resist destruction and re-enslavement (Franco 1973).

In general terms, it is fair to conclude that the social order of the Spanish American colonial societies was characterized by a hierarchical structure with marked social differences, which had the potential to generate serious conflicts. Nevertheless, these remained mainly below the surface. In this social configuration, origin and racial/ethnic adscription as well as patriarchal society's impositions were the principal factors responsible for social hierarchization. Until the age of 25, women were subject to the "parental authority" of the male household head, and after marriage, they were subject to their husband's authority. Only as single women or widows were they legally qualified to make decisions, sign contracts, and hold professions that allowed them to gain their own income. Primarily upper-class white women were affected by this patriarchal social order. They were nearly invisible in public life and were reduced to carrying out a role in the private sphere behind the walls of their household, as safeguards of family honor (Seed 1988; Potthast 2003).

Up until the end of the 18th century, the Spanish Antilles were demographically and socially more akin to continental Spanish American societies than to other European colonies in the Caribbean. In the neighboring French and English dominions, namely Saint Domingue, Jamaica, Martinique, and Barbados, the plantation economy had already left its mark through the imposition of monoculture cultivation and the mass importation of African slaves, who, on some islands, came to make up over 80 percent of the population (Heuman 1997). The Spanish American Empire also encompassed regions where forced labor was used, both in the Caribbean islands and on the continent. But the antagonism between white owners and black slaves was mitigated by intermediary social classes: Along the Río de la Plata, the fertile lands of the shores of the Pacific, and the Gulf of Mexico, where a plantation-based economy built upon slave labor was established, European immigration was not sufficient to meet the needs of the basic service sector in the cities and the craft professions. Most of these activities, therefore, were assumed by the free descendants of slaves, who also enlisted in the militia, defending the empire against foreign invaders and pirates. Last but not least, they were also valued as extramarital partners due to the scarcity of white women.

But the predominance of blacks and mixed-race individuals in these regions in manufacturing and the urban service sectors was not just the result of a lack of alternative labor but rather a symptom of the disdain for manual labor that united white criollos and Spaniards. In this way, "free men and women of color"[2] found an economic and social niche that offered access to earning a livelihood, but one that did not serve as a springboard for social mobility that could potentially question and transform the colonial order (Bowser 1972; Kemner 2010).

Unlike in the Philippines, where slavery never took on a central role in the organization of work and where other forms of coerced labor dominated (see Camba and Aguilar, this volume), at the end of the 18th century and the beginning of the 19th century in Cuba and at least some parishes in Puerto Rico like Ponce, Guayama, and Mayagüez, the social fabric changed notably: Following the Haitian Revolution (1791–1804), the circum-Caribbean region, including the Spanish Antilles and the North American Louisiana Territory, experienced a remarkable economic boom founded upon the expansion of the sugar industry, which would not have been possible without internal migration processes, technology and knowledge transfer, and the simultaneous abduction of hundreds of thousands of African forced workers (see Fradera; Pantojas García; Santamaría, all this volume), creating manifolded archipelagic connections among the islands and surrounding coastal areas. At the same time, with the loss of its continental dominions, the Spanish Empire was forced to content itself with and concentrate its energies on its hitherto outlying regions in the Caribbean and the Pacific. In this process of adaptation and reconfiguration of colonial relations, imperial interventions increased and control over the colonial population grew tighter.

It was at this point that the social confrontations on the Caribbean islands became more apparent. Criollo intellectuals like Francisco de Arango y Parreño and José Antonio Saco in Cuba emerged as the ideologues of a new spirit of social boundary drawing. Although African descendants' social position was not immediately affected, since their rights, obligations, and restrictions remained generally unaltered, a hostile discourse against the non-white population flared up, spawning stereotypes and negative ascriptions like vagrancy, laziness, and promiscuity. Both real and imagined rebellions and insubordinations gave form to threatening and frightening "Haitian" scenarios that led to the opinion that relying on slave labor was too dangerous. It should, therefore, be replaced by European migration, particularly free farmworkers, in order to "whiten" the population. Projects to rid the islands of their black population constituted part of this strategy (Naranjo Orovio and García González 1996). The situation in Cuba began to resemble that of Saint Domingue in the late 1700s. In that period, the economic positions acquired by some "*gens de couleur*," many of whom were the children of French fathers, were not directly altered, but legislative measures were introduced that were directed at limiting free Afro-descendants' liberties as a social class, reflecting an increasingly hostile and aggressive environment (Garrigus 1996). In Cuba, a similar repressive approach was adopted, particularly following the discovery of the alleged conspiracies led by slaves and free people of color in Havana in 1812 and in the Matanzas province in 1843/44 (Paquette 1988; García Rodríguez 2003).

The independence movements in the last remaining Spanish colonies in the Caribbean managed, to an extent, to unite criollos of both European and African descent. The rejection of metropolitan rule was the common denominator that transcended, in these special circumstances, racial barriers and suspicion. However, over the course of this conflict that lasted—with interruptions—for 30 years, new tensions emerged (Helg 1996; Ferrer 1999). In this way, the immanent legacy of the anticolonial struggle in the Caribbean was contradictory with respect to persisting racial stigmas. On the one hand, the experience of a joint resistance against Spain had the effect of preventing the imposition of segregationist racial rule when US-American authorities took control over both islands in 1899. Discriminatory regulations following the Jim Crow laws that had been implemented in various Southern states in the US after the end of Reconstruction and whose purpose was to establish a strict separation between whites and nonwhites in the public sphere did not gain traction in the Spanish Antilles. Particularly in 1890s Cuba, which was marked by the interracial alliances that were formed in the Second War of Independence, segregation was not compatible with the egalitarian and anti-racist discourse that leading figures of the Cuban Revolutionary Party like José Martí and Antonio Maceo advocated. Nonetheless, shortly after its first decade of independence, Cuba was the setting for one of the most infamous persecutions against people of African descent in the history of the Americas. The massacre of members and alleged sympathizers of the Partido Independiente de Color in 1912 in the eastern part of the island left more than 3,000 dead. After independence, racism and anti-racism perdured in a strained balance that shaped the configuration of Caribbean societies at the end of Spanish dominion and during the early 20th century (De la Fuente 2001; Bronfman 2004).

Work and Social Prestige

In contrast to descent and racial-ethnic belonging as hierarchization criteria in Spanish American colonial societies, economic class position tied to membership in a particular professional sector was, at first glance, of secondary importance in determining social standing. Neither the reputation that could be gained in exercising a certain profession nor the level of wealth that could be regarded as evidence of one's personal effort and capacities was enough to compensate for the inherent "defect" of belonging to an "inferior" ethnic and social stratum. This social order's conceptual and visual expression was captured by the famous caste charts, which portrayed a complex social system based on ethnic-racial classification and became particularly popular in New Spain in the 18th century (see Fisher and O'Hara 2009). That said, this did not mean that Spanish American colonial society discarded the necessity and advantages of implementing work restrictions—quite the opposite.

The extractivist colonial economic order in Spanish America was for centuries based on extorting manual work by means of various forms of coercive labor practices. Starting with the encomienda system, the adaptation of the mandatory *mita* services of the Inca Empire to fulfill the needs of the colonial mining industry, or resettlement practices, all these coercive practices were used to control the indigenous population's workforce. Later on, indigenous debt bondage and African enslavement were added (see Monteiro 2006). Spanish colonialism never contemplated the implementation of a system of coerced labor geared toward the white, European population, as was the case in the early English colonies' indentured servitude or in the French dominions' "*engages*." Spaniards arrived in the Americas not as religious refugees or to work the land but in the capacity of *hidalgos*, members of the Spanish lesser nobility, with the intention of enriching themselves through transatlantic commerce and, above all, the exploitation of natural resources overseas, always with the idea of returning to the mother country after having fulfilled their aspiration of acquiring wealth and social standing. The natural resources they profited from included land and minerals but also the native workforce and other laborers who were brought to the colonies with the sole purpose of being exploited.

This view of work had enduring consequences, both economically and culturally. On an economic level, access to an abundant supply of bonded labor prevented salaries from rising in the same way that they did in North America or Europe during the same period. The absence or limited nature of a free and dynamic labor market is considered by economic historians as a determining factor explaining the Great Divergence, the rift that opened between the development that took place in Europe and North America, where growth constraints were overcome, and the rest of the world that today is considered part of the Global South, which fell behind in competition as a consequence of lower rates of purchasing power (Pomeranz 2000; Allen, Murphy, and Schneider 2012).

On an intellectual and cultural level, the principal upshot of this labor model in the Spanish colonies was the spread and general adoption of an "aristocratic" view of work. To be employed in certain activities, not just in the large agricultural enterprises (plantations, haciendas) but also in mining, mills, and manufacturing (*obrajes*, clothing manufacturing, and in Cuba, above all, the tobacco industry), was associated with the stigma of forced labor and servitude. For free members of society, it was practically precluded to look for work in such professions. Only those who, due to their complexion and phenotype, could not escape being associated with (indigenous and African) indentured labor and the stigma it implied would work as salaried employees in these trades.

Spanish legislation reinforced this process of stigmatizing labor by prohibiting people employed in manual labor from holding municipal offices. By the end of the 18th century, when Charles III enacted the "honor and nobility of the mechanical trades" in 1783 by royal decree, the disastrous social consequences these discriminatory regulations had on the labor market were already manifest. The Crown's attempts to elevate the craft professions and impose new attitudes toward labor in its colonies were left unrealized. When, 20 years later, attempts were finally made to implement this ruling in Spain's overseas dominions, the Crown was met with fierce resistance from the local elites. To avoid protests, the Council of the Indies reconsidered and modified various aspects of the initial decree. As a result, even if tailoring, shoemaking, and carpentry professions were considered "honest and honorable" and theoretically offered access to municipal public careers, the council emphasized that the door should not be opened for these professional groups to "aspire to those distinctions for which they have always been at a disadvantage" (Konetzke 1953–62, 373). Included among these distinctions were entry into higher military orders, serving as state officials, and gaining access to higher education.

From the early days of colonial rule, these legal restrictions had a strongly ethnic tone. In the Caribbean and Pacific territories—which had until the early 19th century existed on the empire's margins and were characterized by low demographic density and white immigration—the majority of those who practiced manual trades were of non-European origin. This was precisely the demographic segment that was intentionally excluded from receiving Spanish society's highest honors. The Council of the Indies justified the ruling in these words:

> All these [castes] have vice in their origins and find themselves infected, unlike rightful Indians and blacks who are held to be vile, and since it is precisely these castes that practice blacksmithing, shoemaking and other mechanical trades that, if they were to be made aware of the referred to decree, they would think themselves freed from their original vice, which would occasion disturbances and harmful consequences for the State. (Konetzke 1953–62, 373)

In this manner, the craft professions remained activities viewed with open disdain by white criollos and Spanish immigrants. And, while the aspiration to obtain honorary distinctions and access to administrative, ecclesiastic, and military positions was not in itself a determining factor for the professional aspirations of the adolescent white youth, they shied away from searching for work in trades that did not correspond to their social status. They manifested an attitude that social scientists have termed a "fear of social downclassing" (Weber 1922; Bourdieu 1984).

The contempt for manual labor and the measures taken to preserve the distinction held by "superior trades" that granted certain privileges persisted, almost unaltered, until the end of Spanish colonial rule. Members of the criollo elite who were in favor of sovereignty and advocated for a national identity employed the same argumentation used by the Council of the Indies to explain, somewhat despairingly, why it was so difficult to convince middle- and lower-class whites to seek out work in the crafts and manual labor sectors. The 19th-century Cuban scholar José Antonio Saco cynically explained the predicament in this manner:

> One of the terrible evils that this wretched race [African slaves] has brought to our land is to have distanced the white population from the arts. Destined solely for mechanical work, they alone have been handed all the professions, as behooves their nature; and the masters who, from the beginning, were accustomed to treating slaves with disdain, soon began to see their occupations in the same light. . . . In such a deplorable situation, it was no longer an option that a white Cuban would dedicate himself to the arts, since the mere fact of taking them up suggested that he was renouncing the privileges afforded by his class: in this manner, everything became the exclusive patrimony of people of color, leaving only literary careers and two or three other activities considered meritorious to whites. (Saco [1858–59] 1962, 215–16)

Saco describes the situation as a vicious circle: Because the conquerors and colonizers had passed on manual labor to African laborers, the trades that slaves practiced fell into disrepute. As a result, people who wanted or needed to protect their social reputation did not seek work in these professions, despite the fact that practicing them could ensure them a decent income. This premise also explains why the Spanish Caribbean and the Philippines were never the destinations of major migration influxes of

European workers until well into the 19th century, despite various government incentives (Naranjo Orovio 2010). Due to the scarcity of white workers, the Cuban economy continued to depend on a non-European workforce, largely made up of bonded African and later Asian laborers, who were considered culturally and political unsuited for participating in the process of forming a sovereign, independent state and national identity. This deeply entrenched prejudice is one of the main reasons why members of the criollo elite did not throw themselves into the task of separating from Spain when in all the rest of the empire unrest erupted: without a white salaried working class in both the countryside and the cities, they did not see the possibility of constituting a united and sovereign people able to sustain nationhood.

Obviously, this does not imply that there were not white tailors, construction workers, and carpenters in the major Spanish Antillean cities. During the 19th century, authorities also increased coercive measures geared toward the white lower and middle classes, introducing codes against vagrants and loafers and obligating young men to sign apprentice contracts with master craftsmen when not being able to prove regular employment. Additionally, in many cases, everyday needs must have taken precedence over pride in maintaining social distinctions. As a result, it is difficult to determine, on the one hand, the extent to which white youth abstained from manual work and, on the other hand, whether in fact the superabundance of attorneys, lawyers, and those aspiring to public offices lamented by Saco and his contemporaries was actually a massive social phenomenon. Statistical data is scarce. But there are traces. For instance, population censuses undertaken in the major Cuban cities in the mid-19th century indicate an urban economy with strong rentier characteristics, which was reflected in the large number of people who reported no other income than living from "asset management," which could include real estate, land, or slaves.[3]

Mechanisms of Distinction and Social Exclusion

In spite of the inherent limitations of these demographic censuses, the information they provided about the adult population's professions make it possible to come close to determining who made up Spanish Antillean colonial society's upper class in the 19th century. This group was composed of wholesale merchants, property owners (land, real estate, slaves, etc.), government officials, and members of certain liberal professions like lawyers, notaries, and doctors. In the case of Cuba, the only place we avail of reliable data, around 50,000 men belonged to these professions in the mid-19th century (out of a population of nearly 1 million inhabitants). Within this group, 10 percent were of African descent. But those appeared principally as property owners, without providing evidence of the size and scale of their assets. If we exclude this ambivalent category and limit the group to the highest-esteemed and highest-earning professions (landowner, merchant, trade broker, government official, lawyer, doctor, attorney), there is practically no sign of the presence of black or mixed-race individuals (Iglesias 1982). How, then, were white criollos and peninsular Spaniards able to close ranks?

The white population's indifference or contempt toward "manual trades" was accompanied by exclusionary mechanisms that sought to ensure that members of their social class did not have to deal with competition in securing careers within the limited pool of distinguished professions and face the aspirations of social ascendance of the non-white population. This exclusion was strengthened and normatively reinforced thanks to marital prohibitions and restricted access to higher education.

While elementary education was in theory accessible to all of society's free sectors, the non-white sector was excluded from higher education and the few available university careers like medicine, theology, and jurisprudence. Since the first universities' foundation in the Spanish dominions, the laws stipulated that proof of "pure blood" was a necessary prerequisite for enrolling in institutions of higher learning. Originally exercised against converted Muslims and Jews in Spain, this concept was used in universities on American soil as a proto-racist mechanism to reject candidates of African origin.[4]

In the archives, petitions can be found in which parents requested special allowances so that their children who did not comply with this aforementioned condition were admitted to higher education facilities. But in spite of abounding suspicions that certain individuals were circumventing the law by using bribes, there is no evidence in the available sources that a considerable number of students "of color" gained admittance into the handful of higher education institutions of the time, even though the Council of Indies institutionalized in 1795 the possibility to purchase "Whiteness" and several petitions have been studied (Twinam 2015). Ambitious parents who sought advancement for their children were more likely to pursue the education of their offspring in Europe, as was the case for Pablo Lafargue, who was born in Santiago de Cuba to a mixed-raced French/Haitian/Jamaican family and later became the son-in-law of Karl Marx.

On the other hand, control over marital unions was a fundamental mechanism for intervening in social relationships and limiting the possibilities for upward mobility, as Ann Twinam has demonstrated in her classical examination on the "passing" mechanism and petitions to legitimize children born out of wedlock with racial/social inferiors in 18th-century Spanish America (Twinam 1999). Through marriage, families of different origin could be unified. It was presumably a gateway to call into question the separations established by social barriers. Unions that defied these norms not only affected the spouses at the time of their marriage but also other family members in the future. According to Spain's marital laws, parents as well as close relatives had the right to appeal a marriage if it could potentially harm the family's honor. The Pragmatic Sanction on marriage, ordered by Charles III in 1776 and enforced in the overseas territories two years later, established an enforceable legal basis for maintaining social exclusivity by means of severely restricting the freedom to enter into marriage. From this moment on, all those under the age of 25 seeking to wed had to provide proof of explicit paternal consent. Denial of consent was considered justified and valid if the marriage affected the honor of one of the families involved or the established social order. According to this ruling, adults theoretically had the freedom to marry whomever they pleased, with the exception of those who belonged to the aristocracy or military. Nonetheless, successive interpretations and amendments made by the viceroy of the Rio de la Plata government, the Council of the Indies, and finally the viceroy of New Spain modified the law to the point where it practically prohibited all marriages between whites and people "of color," unless the spouses-to-be had obtained special permission from the authorities. The royal decree of October 15, 1805, which established that no person of recognized noble birth and pure blood could enter into marriage with someone who was black, mixed-race, or from another caste, was interpreted in such a way that it legally established marital segregation between whites and non-whites in the Spanish colonies. In her study on interethnic relations in colonial Cuba, Verena Martínez-Alier (1974) shows through court records how the policy of preventing weddings between individuals of different social castes was fortified over the 19th century. The legalization of marriage bonds between whites and people of color was practically impossible up until the end of the colonial period. Thus, the overseas Spanish dominions' economic and social elite remained highly homogenous until the end of colonial rule and the beginning of the 20th century.

Authority over the Workforce

The feudal relationship of personal domination emerged from the early days of colonization as one of the principal markers of distinction among the inhabitants of Spanish America. The conquest's economic system was based on usurping and ruling over a territory in order to plunder its natural resources by means of exploiting the labor of others, whether autochthonous (indigenous) on the continent and/or imported (African) in the tropical coastal regions and the Antilles (Andreski 1967, 23–51). This model of wealth accumulation reached its height in the plantation economies of the 18th and 19th centuries, which were based on the exploitation of slaves brought from Africa. Manuel Moreno Fraginals (1978), Francisco A. Scarano (1984), and Dale Tomich and Michael Zeuske (2008) have demonstrated that the majority of the Caribbean's sugar mills were highly efficient and profitable, even in comparison to salaried labor, which became increasingly prevalent in other sectors of the global economy. Technically advanced, especially following the introduction of steam mills and trains, they were far from anachronistic in a world characterized by the progressive implementation of capitalist operating structures.

Nonetheless, this econometric evidence, which Robert W. Fogel and Stanley L. Engerman (1974) have similarly shown for the US's slaveholding South, does not imply that slave owning and, more generally, direct, personal, immediate, and continual control and power over other human beings as a mere source of labor were justified solely in economic terms following a model of rational choice theory. Alongside the thriving plantations of 300 or more workers that generated tremendous wealth, there also were a growing number of estates that carried enormous debts due to the elevated operating costs principally tied to the acquisition of unfree workers (see Moreno Fraginals 1978). Following the official ban on the transatlantic slave trade in 1820 and the subsequent rise in prices for acquiring enslaved people, it grew increasingly difficult for sugarcane plantation owners to recover the investments made in the purchase of slaves (Bergad, García, and Barcia 1995). However, the economic model of large-scale farming's expediency does not seem to have been questioned. To be an owner of land and slaves had a social value in and of itself, independent from the profitability of the undertaking a workforce was employed for.

Sales registered with notaries and wills also shed light on how socially entrenched slave ownership was in the major slave-owning societies. In

Cuba's case, the slavery system persisted well into the late 19th century, not just on a large scale in large agricultural enterprises, even though historians have proof of concentration processes due to the need for investment in more advanced technology (Moreno Fraginals 1978; Zeuske 2004). Nonetheless, to be a slave owner remained a widespread social phenomenon that extended far beyond the colonial economic elite. As a result of the devaluation of manual labor and scarce professional opportunities, a considerable share of households or families that would be considered middle or even lower middle class also owned slaves who worked for them. Often the salaries provided from these slaves, who were frequently hired out, constituted the main source of income for their masters, and, in some cases, the only one. Furthermore, a considerable percentage of small-scale slave owners were women, principally widows who depended on the returns that renting out their slaves provided for supporting themselves. But there were also thousands of people of African descent among these small-scale slave owners and even a high number of former African captives.[5]

The decision for acquiring and possessing slaves was undoubtedly in part justified by economic reasoning: it was an investment that would yield financial returns as well as alleviate one's own workload. But, on top of that, for members of a society who, because of their origin, social rank, or other attributes, were barred from social ascendency and could not aspire to enter into colonial society's upper-class ranks, owning slaves also encompassed a symbolic value that went beyond moral scruples: a person who dominates, who possesses another human being, automatically rises to another stratum in society and, according to slave-owning society's bipolar order, joins the ranks of those who can consider themselves to be superior to others. It is thus not surprising that the desire to enter into this privileged caste went beyond social group boundaries and even extended to those who in the past had suffered slavery in the flesh. In fact, the roots of this phenomenon extend back to the nature of wealth and social status in many African societies during the period of the slave trade, which were expressed through ruling over people, not owning land (Lovejoy 2011). As a result, economic utility and the symbolic, immaterial value of absolute, personal power over another's bonded labor went hand in hand in justifying the acquisition and ownership of slaves (Kemner 2010, 388–92, 412–15).

Legacies

The processes outlined in this chapter have, for centuries, marked the perception of work, the prestige associated with certain economic and professional activities, and, finally, a social structure based on personal domination in many Latin American societies. Decolonization and independence, the entry into the global capitalist system, the ban against forced labor systems, and the establishment of republican policy models that gave rise to the entire adult population's formal participation in politics in the 20th century—all of these factors undoubtedly disrupted this social order. However, they have yet to completely eradicate the traditions and structures inherited from the colonial system. The pronounced hierarchizations and privileges structuring the social order of Spain's overseas colonial territories today translate into high levels of economic inequality, as can be seen in Gini coefficient tables as well as in those case studies assembled in this volume dealing with contemporary social stratification in Cuba, Puerto Rico, and the Philippines. And these inequalities continue to include socio-racial connotations, even though most postcolonial republican successor states of the Spanish Empire had ceased to classify its citizens according to ethnic or racial origin, therefore complicating data collection and disaggregated sociodemographic analysis.[6]

New forms of (semi-)bonded labor persist subterraneously under formally free labor systems. Labor conditions often remain precarious, most of all for non-white populations. Right after Southeast Asia, Latin America is the region with the highest number of (female) domestic household workers in the world: in 2016, they numbered 16 million. Among them, 80 percent work in the informal labor market, without contracts, outside of the social system and in some cases receiving salaries that are low even for the minimal standards accorded to these workers (ILO 2016). Additionally, Latin American countries—particularly those in Central America, the Caribbean, and the Andean region—as well as the Philippines export migrants on a massive scale. These migrants overwhelmingly work in agricultural and domestic employment, often in precarious conditions, in Europe, North America, Japan, and the Arab Gulf countries.

Domestic employees (lacking both contracts and social security) are found in many Latin American homes, even in middle-class households. For young women with minimal education and without professional training, it remains the principal route of access to the labor market. This certainly is a consequence of the rise of the "care economy," inadequate state assistance to the elderly, and a relatively high rate of female participation in the workforce. Besides, domestic work is available and cheap. But certainly, this phenomenon can also be seen as a cultural colonial legacy. There is justified reason that the still widespread reliance on nonfamily domestic help way beyond the upper classes has to take into consideration extra-economic reasons as well. In simple words, to be able to delegate and externalize certain unpleasant tasks of daily life is still an indication of prestige and of belonging to a higher social class, even though one's own income may not indicate this positioning.

Furthermore, the employment structures in these services have maintained their colonial ethnic-phenotypic connotations: in the Caribbean and Latin America, the typical domestic employee continues to be predominantly dark skinned and of African or indigenous origin. Even in socialist Cuba, where José Martí's saying "Man is more than white, more than brown, more than black" (1893) came to form part of the official national character and where important advances have undeniably been achieved with respect to "racial" equality, until today, lawyers, doctors, university teachers, and self-employed persons tend to be light skinned, while among agricultural and factory workers, garbage collectors, and other basic services, the opposite is the case. The capitalist economic opening that allows for an increasing number of people to be (self-)employed in private enterprises tends to increase differences and has been criticized by intellectuals of African descent (Zurbano 2013).

In this manner, it is necessary to take note of the resurgence of the (post-)colonial legacies of social stratification along ethnicized or racialized employment structures, which, in Cuba, appeared to be in the process of being extirpated but which most likely only had been lying hidden (see Morín Nenoff, this volume). Of course, the means have changed in a postcolonial environment. Nowadays, access to higher education is universal, and there are no formal barriers for social advancement through the control of interethnic marriages. Contemporary tool kits are more subtle: they rely on stereotypes, prejudice, and access to informal networks, where the highly lucrative job opportunities are distributed among members of homogeneous social classes. In the end, these modern means of guaranteeing social exclusiveness nearly work as well as those employed in colonial times.

NOTES

1. I thank the editors for comments on an earlier version of this chapter. Also, I thank Rachel Barber for its translation.

2. "*Libres de color*" is one of the colonial period's terms for referring to free black and mixed-race individuals.

3. This is demonstrated, for example, in mid-19th century population censuses from cities like Havana, Matanzas, and Santiago de Cuba, which collected informa-

tion not only on residents' age and skin color but also on their work situation (see Comisión de Estadística 1847).

4. See "Real Cédula que excluye de las matrículas y grados de la Universidad a los mestizos, zambos, mulatos y cuarterones." Buen Retiro, 27 de septiembre de 1752. Reprinted in Konetzke (1953–62, 163).

5. In 1857, Cuba carried out their first and only count of slaves and their owners. According to this data, there were 372,511 slaves on the island. Slave owners, on the other hand, numbered 50,855. Considering that the free population had reached a total of 700,000 people at the time, the fact that 7 percent of the population were slave owners is not excessively high. However, taking into consideration the fact that there were generally five to six free people living in a home, we can conclude that one in three Cuban families still owned slaves in the mid-19th century. See Archivo Histórico Nacional de Cuba, sección Ultramar: Cuba, Gobierno, legajo 3.500, expediente 4 (1858). My own research in the eastern region of Santiago de Cuba includes information on nearly 2,000 archival records of free people of African descent buying and selling slaves between 1850 and 1880. See Kemner (2010, 292–303).

6. Only in recent years have several Latin American and Caribbean governments (re-)introduced self-identification based on ethnic/racial/geographical origin as a census category, a claim made by both civil society organizations and international bodies such as the United Nations and its Working Group of Experts on People of African Descent. They highlight the importance of data collection for assessing the disaggregated impact of poverty and inequality.

REFERENCES

Allen, Robert C., Tommy E. Murphy, and Eric B. Schneider. 2012. "The Colonial Origins of the Divergence in the Americas: A Labour Market Approach." *Journal of Economic History* 72 (4): 863–94.

Andreski, Stanislav. 1967. *Paratism and Subversion: The Case of Latin America*. New York: Pantheon Books.

Archivo Histórico Nacional de Cuba, sección Ultramar: Cuba, Gobierno, legajo 3.500, expediente 4 (1858). "Estado que Manifiesta el Número de Cédulas de Seguridad de Esclavos Urbanos y Rurales Espedidos [*sic*] en el Segundo Trimestre de 1857, con Distinción de Sexos."

Bergad, Laird W., Fe Iglesias García, and María del Carmen Barcia. 1995. *The Cuban Slave Market, 1790–1880*. Cambridge: Cambridge University Press.

Bourdieu, Pierre. 1984. *Distinction: A Social Critique of the Judgment of Taste*. Cambridge, MA: Harvard University Press.

Bowser, Frederick P. 1972. "Colonial Spanish America." In *Neither Slave nor Free: The Freed-Men of African Descent in the Slave Societies of the New World*, edited by David W. Cohen and Jack P. Greene, 19–58. Baltimore: Johns Hopkins University Press.

Bronfman, Alejandra. 2004. *Measures of Equality: Social Science, Citizenship, and Race in Cuba, 1902–1940*. Chapel Hill: University of North Carolina Press.

Comisión de Estadistica. 1847. *Cuadro Estadístico de la Siempre Fiel Isla de Cuba, Correspondiente al Año 1846*. Havana: Imprenta del Gobierno/Capitanía General.

De la Fuente, Alejandro. 2001. *A Nation for All: Race, Inequality, and Politics in Twentieth-Century Cuba*. Chapel Hill: University of North Carolina Press.

Ferrer, Ada. 1999. *Insurgent Cuba: Race, Nation, and Revolution, 1868–1898*. Chapel Hill: University of North Carolina Press.

Fisher, Andrew B., and Matthew D. O'Hara, eds. 2009. *Imperial Subjects: Race and Identity in Colonial Latin America*. Durham and London: Duke University Press.

Fogel, Robert W., and Stanley L. Engerman. 1974. *Time on the Cross: The Economics of American Negro Slavery*. New York: W. W. Norton.

Franco Ferran, José Luciano. 1973. *Los Palenques de los Negros Cimarrones*. Havana: Editorial Ciencias Sociales.

García Rodríguez, Gloria. 2003. *Conspiraciones y Revueltas. La Actividad Política de los Negros en Cuba (1790–1845)*. Santiago de Cuba: Editorial Oriente.

Garrigus, John D. 1996. "Colour, Class and Identity on the Eve of the Haitian Revolution: Saint Domingue's Free Colored Elite as 'Colons Américains.'" *Slavery & Abolition* 12 (1): 20–43.

Helg, Aline. 1996. *Our Rightful Share: The Afro-Cuban Struggle for Equality, 1886—1912*. Chapel Hill: University of North Carolina Press.

Heuman, Gad. 1997. "The Social Structure of the Slave Societies of the Caribbean." In *General History of the Caribbean, Vol. III: The Slave Societies*, edited by Franklin W. Knight, 138–68. London and Basingstoke: UNESCO/Macmillan.

Hoetink, Harry. 1967. *The Two Variants of Caribbean Race Relations: A Contribution to the Sociology of Segmented Societies*. Oxford: Oxford University Press.

Iglesias García, Fe. 1982. "Población y Clases Sociales en la Segunda Mitad del Siglo XIX." *Revista de la Biblioteca Nacional José Martí* 2:101–32.

International Labour Organization (ILO). 2016. *Políticas de Formalización del Trabajo Doméstico Remunerado en América Latina y el Caribe*. Lima: ILO Regional Office for Latin American and the Caribbean.

Kaltmeier, Olaf. 2016. *Konjunkturen der (De-)Kolonialisierung. Indigene Gemeinschaften, Hacienda und Staat in den Ecuadorianischen Anden von der Kolonialzeit bis Heute*. Transcript, Bielefeld.

Kemner, Jochen. 2010. *Dunkle Gestalten. Freie Farbige in Santiago de Cuba (1850–1886)*. Münster: Lit.

Konetzke, Richard, ed. 1953–1962. *Colección de Documentos Para la Historia de la Formación Social de Hispanoamérica*, 1493–1810. 3 vols. Madrid: Consejo Superior de Investigaciones Científicas.

Lipschutz, Alejandro. 1975. *El Problema Racial de la Conquista de América*. México: Siglo XXI.

Lovejoy, Paul. 2011. *Transformations in Slavery: A History of Slavery in Africa*. Cambridge: Cambridge University Press.

Martí, José. 1893. "Mi Raza." *Patria*, New York, April 16.

Martínez-Alier, Verena. 1974. *Marriage, Class and Colour in Nineteenth-Century Cuba*. Cambridge: Cambridge University Press.

Monteiro, John M. 2006. "Labor Systems." In *Cambridge Economic History of Latin America*, edited by Victor Bulmer-Thomas, 1:185–233. Cambridge: Cambridge University Press.

Moreno Fraginals, Manuel. 1978. *El Ingenio: Complejo Económico Social Cubano del Azúcar*. Havana: Editorial de Ciencias Sociales.

Mörner, Magnus. 1967. *Race Mixture in the History of Latin America*. Boston: Little Brown.

Naranjo Orovio, Consuelo. 2010. *Las Migraciones de España a Iberoamérica Desde la Independencia*. Madrid: Consejo Superior de Investigaciones Científicas.

Naranjo Orovio, Consuelo, and Armando García González, eds. 1996. *Racismo e Inmigración en Cuba en el Siglo XIX*. Aranjuez: Doce Calles.

Paquette, Robert L. 1988. *Sugar Is Made with Blood: The Conspiracy of La Escalera and the Conflict between Empires and Slavery in Cuba*. Middletown, CT: Wesleyan.

Pomeranz, Kenneth. 2000. *The Great Divergence: China, Europe, and the Making of the Modern World Economy*. Princeton: Princeton University Press.

Potthast, Barbara. 2003. *Von Müttern und Machos. Eine Geschichte der Frau in Lateinamerika*. Wuppertal: Peter Hammer.

Saco, José Antonio. [1858–59] 1962. "Memoria Sobre la Vagancia en la Isla de Cuba." In *Colección de Papeles Científicos, Históricos y Políticos y de Otros Ramos Sobre la Isla de Cuba*, 1:168–218. Havana: Dirección General de Cultura.

Scarano, Francisco A. 1984. *Sugar and Slavery in Puerto Rico: The Plantation Economy of Ponce, 1800–1850*. Madison: University of Wisconsin Press.

Seed, Patricia. 1988. *To Love, Honor, and Obey in Colonial Mexico*. Stanford: Stanford University Press.

Tomich, Dale W., and Michael Zeuske. 2008. *The Second Slavery: Mass Slavery, World-Economy, and Comparative Microhistories*. Binghamton: Binghamton University Press.

Twinam, Ann. 1999. *Public Lives, Private Secrets: Gender, Honor, Sexuality, and Illegitimacy in Colonial Spanish America*. Stanford: Stanford University Press.

Twinam, Ann. 2015. *Purchasing Whiteness: Pardos, Mulattos, and the Quest for Social Mobility in the Spanish Indies*. Stanford: Stanford University Press.

Weber, Max. 1922. *Wirtschaft und Gesellschaft. Vol. III: Grundriss der Sozialökonomik*. Tübingen: Mohr.

Zeuske, Michael. 2004. *Schwarze Karibik. Sklaven, Sklavereikultur und Emanzipation*. Zürich: Rotpunkt Verlag.

Zurbano, Roberto. 2013. "For Blacks in Cuba, the Revolution Hasn`t Begun." *New York Times*, March 23. https://www.nytimes.com/2013/03/24/opinion/sunday/for-blacks-in-cuba-the-revolution-hasnt-begun.html

CHAPTER 18

Lessons Learned

The Legacies of Spanish Colonialism

Hans-Jürgen Burchardt

In this volume, we propose an interdisciplinary, transregional, and systematic approach in order to address colonialism's influence on past and present societies. With this model, it is possible to comparatively trace the determinants of colonial rule in various different spatial-geographic, cultural, and socioeconomic contexts. This allows for an examination of whether the specific factors tied to the colonial experience continue to bear effects on current dynamics of development—and if so, to what extent they have been condensed into legacies. The historical and contemporary analyses of Cuba, Puerto Rico, and the Philippines presented in this volume offer a unique vision of each country and provide insight into the multileveled constellations of centuries-long Spanish domination, the period of strong US presence around the time of formal independence in 1898, as well as the three countries' current configurations of development.

This interdisciplinary approach as well as the local diversity present in the countries analyzed call for additional steps to be taken to distinguish general patterns as well as to identify the colonial trajectories that apply to each of the three cases under revision. First, therefore, this contribution outlines the historical and current development of each country using two dimensions extrapolated from research on colonial legacies: *political economy and authority* and the *hierarchization of difference*. In this way, it is possible to detect both overarching trends and the specific processes present in each country. Three synopses are presented that systematize and complement the existing studies as well as the analyses presented in this volume in a more detailed manner to demonstrate the aforementioned processes. Second, these synopses are compared, and the pathways of colonial and postcolonial development corresponding to the nature of the colonial legacies will be elucidated.

Finally, the results of this comparison are evaluated and discussed in light of present theoretical perspectives, leading to the formulation of an array of suggestions that hopefully can contribute to greater methodological and theoretical advances in postcolonial studies.

Cuba

Political Economy and Authority

Over the centuries, Cuba became the crown jewel of Spain's overseas territories. By 1560, Havana had established itself as a port city offering services on a global scale. Due to its central location, it quickly consolidated its position as the principal meeting point for the silver fleet coming and going from the Americas to the Spanish metropole, garnering its imperial status as a shipyard and trade center as well as a military stronghold. The island's forest reserve and the grasslands' livestock guaranteed provisions for the ships as well as for the local population.[1] Tobacco began being cultivated with greater intensity under the hacienda system.[2] After Britain's invasion and temporary occupation of Havana in 1762, free trade was increasingly tolerated in order to bolster the island's economic competitiveness among the surrounding plantation economies, the objective being to generate income that could be invested in military fortifications and protection measures against external threats. This in turn gave rise to large-scale land-grabbing by the new criollo elite, who were already engaged in international commerce and depended on sugarcane plantations worked by slaves. After Haiti's independence in 1804, Cuba became the powerhouse of Spanish sugar and, by 1830, the economically prosperous "Pearl of the Caribbean." By then, Cuba had in many respects surpassed Spain and was attracting a wide variety of migrants.

The plantation system was perfected, and it attained great economic efficiency. In general, the island's production relied heavily on labor regimes that operated using slavery, forced labor, and precarious working conditions. As a vital trade and administrative center with rural surroundings where the majority of the sugarcane plantations were located, Havana in particular benefited from these developments. At the same time, this geographic concentration gave rise to a wide gap in territorial development (see Santamaría García, this volume). The two wars of independence in 1868–78 and 1895–98 exacted an enormous cost in terms of human lives and also severely weakened the economy. Furthermore, Cuba came to depend almost entirely on the North American market and the exportation of a relatively undiversified number of agricultural products, especially sugar.

Following its occupation of the island in 1898, the US expanded Cuba's role as a producer and supplier of sugar through massive property acquisition and the modernization of the plantation economy, relying on cheap and precarious agriculture labor. Various diversification strategies were implemented in the 1930s and 1940s; however, they fizzled out and failed to enact the desired changes. Toward the end of the 1950s, Cuba found itself in a phase of decadence. Sugarcane production was becoming less efficient, the economy suffered from low levels of diversification, dependence on the US continued, and the island was seriously affected by high levels of unemployment and egregious disparities between rural and urban zones.

The Cuban Revolution of 1959 brought about a profound critical juncture: the state became the most important economic actor and eradicated nearly all market elements. The majority of foreign business—and later local business—was nationalized, and external commerce was abruptly forced to reposition itself in new arenas, converting the USSR into the new economic and political partner. Agrarian reforms led to the radical redistribution of land ownership, various industrialization campaigns were carried out, and socially compatible labor regimes were designed. In short order, the expansion of the welfare system and major training campaigns allowed Cuban workers to enjoy social assistance and capacity building on par with the benefits received by the European workforce (see Laguardia, this volume).

However, if another perspective is adopted, colonial continuities become apparent: the large properties of the colonial latifundio system—which were later modernized by the US—did not become decentralized: rather, they were converted into a state latifundio system with an even greater concentration density. Soon the Cuban state was the owner of four-fifths of cultivatable agricultural land. By expropriating the middle-class farmers, the revolution also dissolved one of the island's most productive internal sectors and eliminated all forms of a business culture geared toward local markets. Ultimately, Cuba also continued its traditional role of sugar exporter in the International Socialist Division of Labor (COMECON). Despite its efforts, the country was unable to diversify its domestic and external structure until the end of the 1980s. Its economic successes—and especially its social progress—were attained not by increased productivity and efficiency but instead through revenue received from COMECON's preferential pricing and credit.[3] According to Cuba's own declarations, the energy intensity of production increased, while work became decreasingly productive. The revolution's latent problem has always been state-run agriculture, which has never proven to be profitable, in spite of massive subsidies. Cuba is one of the world's most fertile regions; however, it currently must import around 80% of the food consumed on the island. As a result, Cuba diverts foreign exchange earnings away from strategic investment in development.

With the collapse of state socialism in 1989, Cuba quickly lost close to 90% of its external commerce, over half of its energy supply, and, consequently, a third of its gross domestic product (GDP) (Bell et al. 2017). The island plunged into a severe crisis that, still today, it has not managed to recover from. Nonetheless, the state was able to maintain its economic and social supremacy.[4] Remarkably, the government dealt with the crisis neither by mobilizing a highly qualified workforce nor by strengthening the national economy, particularly agriculture. Instead, it introduced strategies that drastically devalued local wages, especially in 1994, when it implemented a dual currency system with a highly overvalued foreign exchange rate. From that point on, the state has continued to depend on assets from a handful of isolated foreign (and lower-performing) currency sectors. Today, these include remittances,[5] tourism, agricultural products, nickel, and, for the past decade, international contracting of skilled workers (see Laguardia, this volume). Currently, local wages make up only a small part of household incomes. The country lacks a domestic economic foundation—characterized by managerial efficiency, productivity, and innovation—that would satisfy internal demand, despite the highly skilled population's potential. Instead, Cuba lives off of revenue based more on rents than on capitalist profit.

As for *political authority*, the first thing that needs to be mentioned is that since the early days of colonization, Cuba's settlements have been primarily concentrated in the Western part of the island, in Havana and its outskirts. Starting in the mid-18th century, this was where colonial power was situated, as well as where the bulk of production facilities and half the population were located. This territorial concentration generated a high degree of centralization on the island, which provoked geographic and political disparities, some of which are still in effect today. As a colony undergoing territorial expansion, the settlements farthest from the colonial center of power acquired a certain level of independence from the outset, which caused latent tension to develop with the center. In this manner, the Oriente, with its center in Santiago de Cuba, far away from Havana, was deeply integrated in Caribbean networks of economic, demographic, and cultural trade, a fact that is reflected in its inhabitants' idiosyncrasies to this day. The church only played a supporting role in colonization's early stages, given the fact that Cuba was a settlement colony, and it thus did not have to carry out a missionary mandate. It only held minimal economic and political sway, and its social power was primarily built on education.[6] Cuba, a property with strategic importance from an economic standpoint, had been governed by Spain in a centralized and authoritarian way for a long period of time; it was only after the first War of Independence in 1868–78 that feeble liberalization measures were introduced (such as the admittance of political parties and freedom of the press).

Following US occupation in 1898—and the implementation of the Platt Amendment to the Cuban Constitution, which guaranteed the US the right to intervene militarily—a bipartisan system was initially established in formally independent Cuba. This nominal independence was interrupted by subsequent US-American military interventions and replaced by two brutal dictatorships. Generally, in the postcolonial period, Cuban politics and the state were characterized by high levels of corruption, nepotism, *caudillismo*, authoritarianism, and repression. The economy and the state were tightly intertwined; furthermore, they were aligned with the economic and political interests of the US. The island was neither autonomous nor democratically governed. The democratic phases that existed led to dictatorships, and efforts to address social preoccupations were regularly blocked. Due to these frustrating experiences with democracy, the Cuban Revolution of 1959 had the immediate objective of fostering de facto social participation. In times of confrontation with the US—which, against international law, has in place an economic blockade on the island to this day—this policy turned more radical and oriented toward state socialism. Consequently, the economy and the state merged completely (Cuba had the highest level of state expenditure of all the socialist bloc countries), a single-party system was established, and the center of government power was composed of a small number of committees and a select group of individuals. In addition to legitimate results, the personalized credibility of the first generation of revolutionaries (most notably, Fidel Castro) served as a central source of legitimation. Neither the municipal reform of 1976, in which Cuba crowned itself the first Latin American country to break with colonially inherited territorial divisions (which expanded the state's potential operations and allowed for important steps to be taken to diminish geographical dissimilarities), nor the two popular votes—on the constitutional amendment of 1992 and the new constitution in 2019—diminished the state's economic and societal predominance.

Hierarchization of Difference

Cuba was the most important and largest colonial settlement in the Caribbean. By 1550, the indigenous population had been nearly completely eliminated due to imported diseases and massive enslavement. Later, the Cuban colony grew through mass migration from Europe and the subsequent "importation" of slaves, with a total of over 700,000 Africans abducted and brought to the island. The rise of the plantation economy at the end of the 18th century spurred another migration flow from Spain and Europe and, later, brought immigrant workers from China. At the end of the 19th century, nearly two-thirds of the population was white (see Gutiérrez and Iglesias, this volume). From colonization's beginnings, the social structure had a marked ethnic connotation. Through land distribution, marital laws, access to (higher) education, and requirements for professional and public positions, the white elite consolidated its political and economic supremacy and maintained a relatively high degree of homogeneity. While at the beginning, colonizers controlled the first haciendas, later the large latifundios and plantations were generally in the hands of criollos. This gave rise to a white criollo elite that soon controlled the island's land and initiated local development in tobacco and, later, coffee and sugar. Slavery wasn't abolished in Cuba until 1886.[7] Indeed, up until the Cuban Revolution of 1959, Cuba's social structure was essentially racist. However, the participation of segments of Cuba's black population in the liberation wars did somewhat palliate the ethnicization of the social structure at the end of colonialism. In Cuba, there has been a notable process of transculturation, wherein a national and cultural identity emerged in which the religious, cultural, and social influences of the people brought over from Africa continue to have an active presence today (Ortiz 1940). The country modernized economically and technically during the period of US-American rule, but a large proportion of the population, predominantly black, lived and worked in precarious and impoverished conditions. Ethnicity was one of the major markers of social inequality (see Morín, this volume).

The revolution ushered in significant socio-structural change that—in all the important areas like education, health, or work—depended on social and ethnic inclusion for its transformative success, primarily benefiting the most vulnerable sectors (often "non-whites" and women) of the Cuban population. In accordance with the regime's socialist tenets, wealth and income lost their central function in social standing; labor was completely decommercialized.[8] At the same time, compensatory transferences were implemented to try to reduce differences in territorial development. At first, for large sectors of Cuban society, the revolution brought about improvements in living conditions and significant upward mobility. Thanks to these policies, Cuba's "racial problem" was soon considered to have been resolved (Morales 2007). But the revolution's exemplary institutional anti-racism was not buttressed by cultural policies, by the possibility of any independent participation or organization, or through affirmative action; as a result, it was not widely accepted or adopted by society.[9] This not only affected the population's social practices but also manifested itself in Cuban social structure: not only in specific areas like politics or higher education but also in general, black Cubans remained underrepresented during the revolution.

The economic crisis that began in 1989 and the subsequent adjustment process once again had a dramatic impact on social structure. Although the government avoided all forms of social breakup, various dynamics caused breakdowns in the social equilibrium hitherto established. Multiple factors have combined to slowly erode the socialist social structure and have led to an inversion of the social pyramid (indeed, high-skilled work, which is for the most part state sponsored, has become devalued on a massive scale in comparison to unskilled work). The factors that have led to these outcomes are the introduction of a dual currency combined with a drastic drop in domestic revenue's purchasing power; the economic strategy of focusing on a limited number of foreign currency sectors geared toward the world market, such as tourism; remittances' growing economic importance; and the partial admission of private industry. One's livelihood is based not on one's qualifications or output. Instead, it is based on family ties abroad, working within the exchange sector, or possessing real estate (Galtés 2017). As a result, poverty and precariousness spread not from the margins but from the center. Additionally, the wage gap once again began to widen significantly: in the mid-1980s, Cuba had reached a Gini coefficient of 0.25; however, it was already at 0.40 by the turn of the millennium and has since increased (Laguardia, this volume). According to estimates, over a fourth of the population currently suffers income poverty, and territorial disparities have again taken hold (Espina 2012). Additionally, the reforms have been particularly harmful for the population's black sectors: they have less access to remittances, to lucrative sectors of foreign currency, and to marketable real estate. In this sense, Cuba's current social structure is once again marked by ethnic connotations (Hansing 2017; Núñez 2015).[10]

Puerto Rico

Political Economy and Authority

From a political-economy perspective, up until the end of the 18th century, Puerto Rico's importance was primarily strategic-military, for it protected the Spanish Empire's Atlantic and Caribbean trade routes. The island was a military bastion and supplier of wood and animal skins; it survived off of subsistence farming. The capital San Juan became a fortified administrative city, a Spanish Gibraltar in the Caribbean. After the Haitian Revolution, Puerto Rico's sugar and tobacco production and the plantation economy powered by slave labor also expanded at the beginning of the 19th century. By the mid-19th century, as many as 80,000 slaves had been abducted in Africa and taken to the island. Due to the geographic nature of the island, whose mountains impeded the unlimited expansion of sugarcane plantations, coffee was also cultivated in a hacienda system by rentiers and small farmers. Between 1849 and 1873, forced labor was introduced through vagrancy laws in order to gain access to the labor of the landless local indigenous population. In the 19th century, Puerto Rico's trade volume increased twentyfold and the island became an agricultural exporter. During the first half of the century, sugar dominated the market; in the second half of the century, the island became the fourth largest coffee exporter in the world. Toward the end of the Spanish colonial period, coffee was the principal economic activity, in which the landless population, day laborers, and freed slaves worked in abominable conditions under paternalistic labor regimes (Scarano 1994).

Starting at the time of the US occupation in 1898, sugar production was taken over by US-American companies, and Puerto Rico became, along with Cuba, one of the largest sugar producers in the world. The colonial agricultural production model—with its large-scale monoculture exportation—was upheld, and it expanded and modernized, similar to that of Cuba. Three decades after the turn of the 20th century, US-American businesses dominated nearly 80% of the production of export commodities (sugar, coffee, tobacco, fruit). Instead of hacienda owners and landless people, there were now American companies, represented by local managers, and a proletarianized mass of agricultural workers who earned wages significantly lower than those of other countries. Puerto Rico was marked by poverty and illiteracy and became the Caribbean's "poorhouse." In the 1920s, this led to a rise in migration, political protests, and, starting in the 1930s, the expansion of US-American social programs on the island (Dietz 1986).

Change in the global economy—and, above all, the new political situation following World War II—led the US to initiate profound structural changes in Puerto Rico. Tax exemption was utilized to launch low-paying factories into the global market; the so-called *maquiladoras* used unskilled labor to assemble industrial products or production parts for American exports. This transformation from a rural-agricultural to urban-industrial economic base significantly increased economic growth and improved working, educational, and living conditions for the population. However, the sectoral differentiation between work and production simultaneously increased social inequality (Sotomayor 2004). Additionally, the existing labor supply was unable to be sufficiently absorbed; as a result, an explosive rise in migration to the US occurred in the period between 1950 and 1970. The concurrent rise in economic dependence on the US also hindered the emergence of a productive national managerial class.

When this model became no longer internationally competitive due to the growing liberalization of global trade at the end of the 1970s, the US converted Puerto Rico into a tax haven with Section 936—in 1976—of the Internal Revenue Code. Billions of dollars in corporate earnings were temporarily deposited on the island, saving American companies from having to pay taxes and procuring Puerto Rico exorbitant proceeds through percentage shares.[11] In this manner, the island began to live almost exclusively off of external financial flows, which the state ensured and through which it financed itself, but which were unattached to any sphere of national production. Thus, a rent-based economy and a rentier state in its purest form emerged in Puerto Rico (see Pantojas, this volume). Following the termination of this special US fiscal regime in 2006, the island lost its production base: one consequence of the rent-based economy was major deindustrialization, and another was the massive devaluation of labor. In 2016, over 90% of the GDP was generated through property or cash holdings, and labor renumerations were marginal. As a result, Puerto Rico entered into a long-term depression and has been living off of debts, subsidies, and remittances ever since.[12] As Quiñones Pérez and Seda-Irizarry aptly summarize in this volume, today, Puerto Rico is built on a form of economy geared toward exportation and rents; it "consumes what it doesn't produce and produces what it doesn't consume."

Regarding *political authority*, it is important to note that Puerto Rico's first political elite came almost entirely from the Spanish upper class, and for a long period of time, it was financed exclusively through transfers from Mexico. It concentrated on the military base's operations and had little interest in domestic development or the island's population, the majority of whom lived in wretched conditions. The administration's military character impeded local society's civil sectors' access to politics for many years. It was only with the rise of agricultural exports beginning in the 18th century that the political constellation changed. In addition to the Spanish military administration on the island, there was a growing economic elite of criollo hacienda owners who required labor and demanded support from the state. This local elite wanted greater national autonomy, but they never sought political dominance.

After the US occupation in 1898, this elite became a diminished middle class composed of independent professionals and small business owners, while local sugar producers gained political influence and worked to align public policy with their demands. With the dawn of export-oriented industrialization in the 1950s, this economic elite changed their area of activity: they became factory owners and, later, financial agents, and they increasingly took on more public positions that guaranteed financial transfers from the state to the economy. At the same time, the majority of this group conserved their traditional culture originating from family, aristocratic, and conservative customs. To this day, the most important business groups are family-owned enterprises and can be identified by their surnames. There have yet to emerge active and independent local business initiatives on the island that are geared to the domestic market, which also generate employment, or a public policy that sustainably promotes national production (González 1991). In the wake of decolonization, Puerto Rico's economic and political elites saw themselves as the conveyors and agents—the bridgeheads—of US economic interests, in whose successes they fully shared. With Puerto Rico's transformation into a tax haven, the boundaries between state and economy completely blurred, and the economic elite received their income almost exclusively through public subsidies and rents. Pantojas-García (this volume) describes Puerto Rico as a "postcolonial colony" that has always been characterized by a dominant, absent, metropolitan elite; a weak corporate class; and a political rentier class that primarily makes its living through relations and transfers, first with Spain and later with the US. According to Quiñones Pérez and Seda-Irizarry (this volume), the reasons behind this multifaceted dependence relationship are to be found not only in the US but also through taking the role of the local elites into account.

Hierarchization of Difference

As was the case in the rest of the Caribbean, the Spanish colonizers eliminated almost the entire native population of the Borikén—or Borinquén—peoples in Puerto Rico. The forced work regime of the encomienda[13] that the *taíno* Indians were subjected to had a particularly deadly effect. Labor shortages were frequently remedied by using slaves of African origin. In 1530, African slaves made up 75% of the population, and by the end of the 18th century, freed and enslaved black people still constituted 60% of the population, the majority of whom lived in precarious conditions and were socially ostracized (see Denis-Rosario, this volume). Exclusionary and limited access to educational institutions, geographic segregation, and the racist denial of citizenship's rights and political participation further institutionalized the social structure's ethnic character.

These ethnic constellations shifted due to a rise in migration from Spain and various demographic developments. By the mid-19th century, half the population was white and a little less than a quarter was mixed-race. By 1869, the ratio of slaves in the population had dropped to 6%—due not only to the international abolition of slavery but also because of structural economic change in the direction of coffee production and the related development of domestic work. Ethnic inequalities did not lose their importance under US-American rule. Access to education, to desirable work, and to public service positions frequently remained inaccessible to blacks. In this sense, racism in Puerto Rico was and continues to be a relevant phenomenon, though less conspicuous in the present day (Godreau 2015).

Puerto Rico's social contrasts also have always been very pronounced: throughout the colonial period, the great majority of national wealth was concentrated within the small circle of the white elite. Although production and work regimes changed following the annexation of the island by the US, social differences in large part remained unaltered. Today, Puerto Rico is one of the most unequal countries in the world. According to statistics from 2016, Puerto Rico had a Gini coefficient of 0.54 and, as a result, one of the highest rates of inequality not just in Latin America but among all US territories (Instituto de Estadísticas de Puerto Rico 2018). These disparities had and continue to have strong gender, ethnic, and geographic connotations. Today, for example, over two-thirds of female heads of household and an even greater number of blacks are afflicted by poverty; furthermore, impoverishment is concentrated in rural zones (see Rivera Quiñones, this volume). It is also noteworthy that after more than four decades of massive state social support—which over a third of the population receives—the efforts to reduce social differences and dismantle poverty's foundations have proven unsuccessful. As a result, securing one's own (often meager) means of survival through transfers or rents is not just an elite privilege. Puerto Rico can be described as a "rentier society," a characteristic that permeates all areas of society and has certainly produced its own standard forms of conduct.

At the same time, toward the end of Spanish colonial rule in Puerto Rico, a unique cultural identity had developed, which today has an effect that transcends social strata and ethnic groups, is socially recognized and practiced, and, after US occupation, functions as a demarcation that separates Puerto Ricans from the Anglo-American economic and cultural sphere.[14] This autonomous identity—which has taken shape over many years and been productively strengthened in the sciences and the arts both on the island and in the diaspora—is, in a sense, a cultural counterweight to the island's extreme economic and political dependence on the US. This gives rise to a paradoxical and schizophrenic situation among the island's population: while economic stability and prosperity are only possible through contact with the US—often by means of migration—Puerto Ricans' identity is profoundly rooted in the island.

Philippines

Political Economy and Authority

With its location in Southeast Asia and its composition as a fragmented archipelago of around 7,260 islands speaking over 130 languages, the Philippines occupied a special position within the Spanish colonial empire. Originally, its colonization—a response to Portuguese expansion—was intended to secure Spanish influence in Asia and owed more from geostrategic interests than economic ones. Given that Spanish colonization was strongly connected to evangelization, the Catholic Church was from the beginning one of the most important actors in the colonization process. As a political project, the colony was also financed through Mexico for many years. Instead of instating a widespread colonization plan, Spain principally concentrated on Manila's metropolitan area, which was converted into a port, a supply depot, and a trade center. In this way, Manila soon emerged as a global hub and as one of the most important trade centers in Asia. Because the Spanish did not initially set up their own production sites, they predominately engaged in intermediate commerce, and Latin American silver was the economy's primary lubricant in the trade of Latin American, Asian, and, above all, Chinese products (like silk and porcelain). Using taxes and fees, the colonial administration participated in supplying a local workforce as well providing agricultural products to supply the ships. But it was not until the end of the 18th century that the colony became financially self-sustaining (Scott 1994).

The Spanish encomienda and hacienda systems were relatively slow in being established on the island, and their impact largely varied; both institutions were chiefly introduced through the assignment of lands that were subject to tax obligations. Land was not only granted to Catholic orders and members of the elite but also to loyal native clan leaders. As in other colonies, production was based on repressive forms of work like hereditary debt bondage, slavery, and forced labor—and the majority of agricultural workers lived in miserable conditions. The first labor regimes were also strongly personalized and paternalistic, ensuring support for the Crown not only from large local landowners but also through the political loyalty of the subaltern (see Camba and Aguilar, this volume).

After losing its continental Latin American colonies, Spain decided to allow greater foreign investment in the colony and attune commerce to the new global market, a move that clearly revitalized the Philippines' (agricultural) economy. Additionally, the state participated in the large-scale production of tobacco. The first exported products were sugar, tobacco, coffee, and hemp from Manila. Although the Philippines never attained agriculture efficiency of the same magnitude as the Caribbean, these policies served as a foundation for a focus on (agricultural) exports, which continues to be an important component of the archipelago's economy to this day. However, for Spain, the Philippines' exports always remained secondary (Legarda 1999).

With the US occupation, monocultural agricultural production intended for export (through the expropriation of the church's lands and other tactics) also spread in the Philippines; with Manila's hemp, coconuts, and sugar representing the exports of greatest importance in the US-American market. This orientation toward exports weakened the Philippines' food sovereignty and led it to begin importing food for domestic consumption. Another effect of this economic orientation was the strengthening of major local landowners' influence, though not the improvement in working conditions; rather, hacienda-based production led to labor regimes with semi-proletarian undertones (Borras 2001).

Starting in the mid-20th century, the Philippines, like Puerto Rico, also experienced a change in its economic structure. Agriculture consequently lost importance, while semi-industrial production and the service sector—for the most part oriented toward the global market—gained relevance. The dramatic loss of rural jobs spurred massive relocations to cities and urban service positions as well as emigration.[15] At the same time, the archipelago needed to import a considerable quantity of food to cover basic necessities: the Philippines became the largest importer of rice in the world. The new (often urban) economic sectors continue to be characterized by two factors. First, they are focused on the global market. The archipelago has yet to widely cultivate business activity oriented toward national production or public policy that would boost the local economy. Local economic activity is most visible in the privatized service area, which is not backed by the state. Family oligarchies control all the primary entry points to the market and secure lucrative rent-based revenues for themselves through monopolistic position. Second, the Philippines' labor regimes continue to be characterized by cheap, unskilled, and precarious labor—similar to that of the hacienda system (Sicat 2009).

In the field of *political authority*, prior to colonization, the Filipino archipelago was characterized by decentralized governmental frameworks with a high level of local autonomy. The Spanish, due to limited resources, were unable to institutionally penetrate the islands' extensive but highly decentralized local power structures. As a result, the Spanish concentrated on Manila as a center of colonial administration, trade, and power, which soon took on a position of prime importance for the Spanish Empire. Manila's distance in relation to the rest of the Philippines' vast series of islands was even greater than the distance between Havana and Cuba's interior. The "rest" of the Philippines constituted a separate world and, with a few exceptions, remained an uncontrollable periphery. For this reason, from the beginning of the island's colonization, the central administration depended heavily on the cooperation and co-optation of local indigenous communities, who were subject to taxes but were allowed to continue exercising their power.

Under this laissez-faire management style, the influence of large local landowners began to grow. Unlike in other colonies, landowners did not secure their economic success through access to the central state but instead fundamentally relied on their local base. Thus, from the beginning, a unique tension arose between the central state, the provincial governments, and the powerful family clan structures that continue to exert their influence today. Even the recentralization efforts of the Bourbon Reforms in the 18th century faced enormous resistance in the Philippines. More recently, Marcos's dictatorship launched a massive effort to reign in the provinces' influence in 1976. Nonetheless, in the wake of democratization, the provinces have regained significant stature. Put simply, the Filipino state cannot be understood without taking into account its polycentric structure.

Running parallel to this, under colonial rule, political influence and economic power merged (Simbulan 2005). Historically, the landlords first established a concentration of wealth and later secured access to political positions as well as decorations from the state. The hacienda's old paternalist labor relations gave rise to an extensive political network of nepotism, corruption, and the establishment of a spoils system. In this manner, many economically influential families in the Philippines secured their dominance in politics and within the state, regardless of whether the form of government in place was a dictatorship or a democracy (Hodder 2013; Tadem and Tadem 2016). Today, the most important economic sectors are disproportionately represented in parliament and the state through elected representatives and public servants. The Philippine Senate, for example, is a multimillionaires' club (see Melgar, this volume). Land ownership remains an important sector, but it is now complemented by other economic sectors like real estate, agriculture, light industry, services, and commerce. Due to a lack of basic public and social services, these sectors are provided by large private business conglomerates as well. In this way, the economic elite has managed to transform the state (which they control) and use its deficiencies to create private earnings for themselves. Also, given that they politically and economically monopolize almost all market access, they can prevent competition and capture the corresponding gains in the form of rents.

Hierarchization of Difference

The precolonial population in the Barangays was organized around local hierarchical clans and family structures, and subsistence farming remained a basic pillar of economic life. As a result, the population was familiar with both established hierarchies (headed by leaders) and indentured servitude, which was imposed as a punishment or used to cancel debts. With the imposition of colonization around 1570, the indigenous population was not entirely eliminated by imported diseases and mass slavery, as was the case in the Caribbean; instead, they were integrated into the stratified colonial society. The elite was made up of a very narrow stratum of Spaniards, the majority of whom were monks who soon became large landowners and played the important role of mediator for the colonized population.[16] Below these monks were the criollos, followed by the co-opted (and loyal) local leaders. During this same period, there was a significant flow of migrants from Asia (especially China). Since Europeans were definitively in the minority and could not guarantee the colonial power's personal security, these different migrant groups mixed relatively quickly, unlike in the Caribbean. This process produced, among other things, a prosperous class of Chinese-Filipino landowners and traders, the majority of whom were organized through family and clan structures and who also had experience with international markets and trade. In the 19th century, growing administrative demands opened access to education and careers for the native population, which laid the foundation for the rise of a relatively well-educated multiethnic urban class. At this point, a national and cultural identity took form that included elements from the native population as well as from the Spaniards, their descendants, and other migrant groups—and that increasingly called for national independence. The bottom of this social pyramid was made up mostly of the native farmers, the majority of whom lived in terrible conditions. The islands' Muslim minority was (and is) almost completely marginalized.

In the colonial social structure, social and political positions were relatively quickly determined by socioeconomic rather than ethnic factors. Following the US occupation, this trend has prevailed: for the large majority of the population today, the most important indicator of position within Philippine social structure is not ethnic or religious membership but geographic and social disparities. The top of the social pyramid is occupied by family dynasties who are interlaced with the state through many channels. Their wealth and influence were traditionally based on land titles[17] but now have come to include all lucrative economic sectors. At the extreme bottom of the pyramid is the quarter of the population who live below the poverty line. Three-quarters of impoverished people live and work in rural zones, and over 10% of them suffer from hunger (Bayudan-Dacuycuy and Lim 2014). Currently, the Philippines holds the highest rate of income inequality in Southeast Asia and the lowest rate of inequality reduction in the region since the 1990s (Jain-Chandra et al. 2016).

Lessons Learned I: Questions of Colonial Legacy

The synopses that summarize the social and historical studies of the three countries depicted show that the legacy of colonialism has exerted a strong influence in the two dimensions of *political economy and authority* and the *hierarchization of difference*. In short, *colonial legacies matter*! In what follows, these synopses will be analyzed with regard to the patterns of transnational and transregional colonial development paths.

Political Economy and Authority

Since the 16th century, Cuba, Puerto Rico, and the Philippines were designed following extractivist economic models, based increasingly on participation in international markets, agricultural exportations, and repressive labor regimes. Tobacco, coffee, and sugar constituted the most important agricultural products cultivated using single-crop agricultural production, with the aim of making them as productive as possible. Depending on the country and the product, different forms of production were developed. Coffee and tobacco were often cultivated by means of (half-)free producers, who faced restrictive purchasing conditions and were partly held captive by oppressive debt obligations. The Philippines also experimented with tobacco cultivation via large state companies. Beginning in the 19th century, slave-based, semi-industrialized sugar production emerged as a vitally important factor, proving an extraordinarily successful means of connecting the colonies—as well as the “mother country”—to the new and growing capitalist world market.[18] In the 19th century, Spain’s old silver empire was transformed into an empire of tropical exports (Fradera, this volume). It is interesting to note, however, that the plantations’ economic efficiency and operating rationality never extended to the colonies' other economic sectors.[19]

One of the principal reasons behind this was that the work ethic introduced into the colonies was in complete opposition to Western conceptions of work geared toward productivity. In the colonies, social status was primarily tied not to wealth or productivity but above all to heritage and familial pedigree. Paid labor was thoroughly disdained by the upper class, who considered it to be socially inferior and culturally objectionable.[20] This stigmatization of manual labor was adopted by essentially all the white members of colonial society and, as a result, by the elite. It was also institutionally sanctioned by colonial legislation: for example, for many years, working-class wage workers were barred from holding public office. As a result, the first production models that the Spanish brought to the New World—particularly the hacienda system—were concentrated not on work but rather on large latifundios and the exploitation of natural resources. Lower-class workers were used who could not be associated with the Spaniards' own rank: slaves, indigenous people, and imported Africans (slave labor was essentially considered to be just another raw material). The first work system, the encomienda, gained access to indigenous labor through forced work and debt peonage. It was a precursor to subsequent labor regimes of slave-based production and the Caribbean's plantation economies (Monteiro 2006; Wolf and Mintz 1977). Although by the 19th century work relations had become more differentiated in Spain's last three remaining colonies, unfree labor and forms of debt bondage, such as indentured servitude—and, later, the precarious work of day laborers—as well as other unprotected and low-paying forms of work, remained the principal labor models. With these models, one often could not make it to the end of the month, let alone amass any wealth.

This finding presents a new perspective on the three former colonies' current political-economic constellations: nonc of these countries have had a competitive local business class (based on efficiency, productivity, and innovation) that is aligned with the domestic market. Today, agriculture in these three countries has reached such levels of unproductiveness that they require large quantities of food imports to cover their populations' basic needs. The economic and political elite, instead of working to alleviate this food shortage, opt to exploit raw and natural resources and participate in the global market. They seek out strategies to generate rent through exports via the monopolization of the domestic market's supply structure or through financial speculation, which they pursue with relative flexibility and, frequently, success. Productivity and the workforce have not been (nor are) considered the principal source of value-added income. In the 19th century, the Spanish monarchy ensured economic stability using semi-industrial agricultural plantations geared toward the international market.

As for *political authority*, the most important objective of the late colonial state in Cuba, Puerto Rico, and the Philippines was to preserve its strict production and labor regime—as well as to ensure domestic order. Europe during this period was witnessing the expansion of liberalism's influence, the growth of political representation, and the rise of a new business class. The division between the economy and the state was clearly demarcated, and the modern, bourgeois state was consolidated. Meanwhile, in Spain's remaining colonies, an anti-liberal, hierarchical, and centralized form of government prevailed, effectively exercising colonial domination and merging statist and economic groups' interest. These colonial regimes' legal order and bureaucratic structures often manifested in the highest authorities' direct involvement and the simultaneous exclusion of wide swaths of the population. The most important forms of political influence and representation thus were not through institutionalized political representation but through direct, often personal, access to state leaders via nepotism, corruption, or lobbying. The exploitation of nature, repressive labor regimes, and a focus on exports meant that the state had little interest in increasing the economy's productivity and domestic revenue. Furthermore, social cohesion and political participation were not central to the state's functioning and, as a result, had little relevance as a source of legitimacy.

In these three cases, colonial regimes left behind a diverse colonial legacy, as the studies in this volume demonstrate. It is worth highlighting, however, the pivotal role of rent as an economic foundation. The features of this rent-based economy include a barely taxed revenue-producing monopoly, a flagrant lack of separation between economy and state, the merging of political and economic elites, and authoritarian tendencies combined with an executive with a strong individual presence and a spoils system that implicated many social groups. Capitalism's inherent move away from a specific sovereign (Foucault 1980) to the establishment of state government in the form of "*impersonal power*" (Gerstenberger 2007) never took root in these countries' social formations. Instead, the state transformed into a type of prey whose conquest and successful usurpation reflected not the interests of society as a whole but instead individual interests, whose goal was to access and extract rent (North and Clark 2018).

Hierarchization of Difference

Without a doubt, one of the most enduring of Spanish colonialism's legacies is the ethnicization of local social structures. In the early stages of colonization, the Habsburg monarchy was at its height in Europe and had installed a social organization based on state authority and a closed, inflexible education system. This supported a hierarchical organization of society that only allowed for limited social mobility. Social positions, power, and privileges were highly personalized, and they depended primarily on blood ties rather than on one's individual capabilities. In the New World, these configurations gave rise to marked ethnic distinction in the social structure, which in some regions even became a form of the caste system.[21] Given the multiple race-based distinctions—often rooted in external characteristics—many of these societies could be described as "pigmentocracies" (see Kemner, this volume): the highest positions in the political and economic sphere were reserved for whites, and the indigenous, mixed-race, and black populations occupied the lowest social positions or carried out work activities considered inferior, as denoted by skin color in a perfectly downward-sloping vertical structure. Not only was work and its classification highly hierarchized but since colonization's beginnings, work also had a particularly ethnic and racist connotation (Fisher and O'Hara 2009). For example, "whites" who economically depended on paid work preferred to own slaves and hire them out as temporary workers instead of working themselves. In contrast, if "free" workers who belonged to lower-ranked ethnic groups managed—by means of specializing in artisanal work—to find economic niches and reach a certain degree of economic prosperity, this rarely would lead to improvements in their social status.

Various forms of discrimination—such as upper-class women's complete incapacitation and their exclusion from higher education, incredibly strict marriage laws and a markedly patriarchal character that prohibited interethnic unions, and the exclusion of "non-whites" from influential professional fields like medicine and law—all worked to institutionally cement the social structure and stymie any form of social change. For a long time, the Spanish colonial elite (primarily state officials, merchants, landowners, slave owners, and self-employed professionals) exhibited a high degree of ethnic and social homogeneity (in this respect, the Philippines was an exception). This racist social hierarchy in colonial societies took form over the course of centuries.[22] One of the greatest achievements of postcolonial studies has been to bring ethnicization to the fore in the social analysis of social structure and to decode its numerous expressions (see, e.g., the analyses of Quijano 2000; Mignolo 2011).[23]

However, the contemporary analyses presented in this volume show that ethnicity's centrality to the social structure is waning. Instead, social and territorial disparities have gained increasing importance as one of the main markers of social inequalities. In Puerto Rico and the Philippines, poverty and difference are concentrated in rural areas in a manner relatively independent of ethnic belonging. Even in Cuba, where the re-ethnicization of society seems to be increasing, the principal motors behind this current dynamic are tied to socioeconomic factors.

In these recent configurations of inequality, the degradation of labor has a high impact not only on the extreme development gap between urban and rural zones but also on the inequality in access to the state for public services. One result of this is that wages tend to be relatively low and working conditions are generally subpar. Work more often fits the character of a coercive relationship because it is necessary for survival, and there is rarely an incentive for productivity.

In Cuba, this attitude toward work has transformed into a paradox, where all the prerequisites for social development on the basis of greater work output have been established, yet, nonetheless, political institutions have not done their part in incentivizing these outcomes. In Puerto Rico, a similar dynamic exists in a muted form, while in the Philippines, even more traditional labor regimes are in place—indeed, the archipelago is one of the countries in which modern forms of slavery and forced work continue to be widespread today (ILO 2017).[24]

Lessons Learned II: The Need for a *Material Turn* in Postcolonial Studies

The search for colonial legacies in Spain's last three overseas colonies has demonstrated that, especially in the field of *labor relations* and *state formation*, similar patterns can be found. This diagnosis offers interesting suggestions for postcolonial studies. The different facets of *labor relations* as they are found today in Cuba, Puerto Rico, or the Philippines are generally discussed under the blanket banner of socialism's economic inefficiency, the international division of labor, or capitalist exploitation. However, based on the comparison presented, it is argued that these constellations result not just from these aforementioned facets but also—or perhaps even in greater part—from the effects of colonial legacies, which are rooted in structures engendered by the predominance of economic rents. Postcolonial studies would perhaps do well to take note of this approach. It would help to conceptualize work from a postcolonial perspective that correlates to existing contributions (Chakrabarty 2000; Mezzadra 2011a) and move away from Eurocentric, Western notions of "normal labor relations." It is now common knowledge that capitalism's profits are generated not solely through free-contract labor and the commercialization of work but also through the social production of difference by use of the markers of race, nationality, geographic origin, and gender.[25] The question could be posed as to what extent colonial legacies have generated and continue to produce specific elite and work cultures, which have reinforced the central role of the pursuit of rent appropriation in social development, rather than capitalist aggregated value acquired through work.

This perspective on work also shines light on phenomena outside the work sphere because it allows us to better understand local power relations. In the Western narrative of modernity, the state and the economy, under democratic regulation, are the central determinants of social development. As a result, the citizenry's disposition plays an important role in representation, in demands, and in the concession of (social) rights. In developed capitalism, civil rights are—both subjectively and objectively speaking—strongly linked to work. In all Western countries, the right to hold a freely chosen and contractually negotiated job is linked to the status of citizenship rights (for the US, see Glenn 2004). But if work is not a central determinant of socialization, the granting of civil rights or the universal application of democracy follows other norms. For example, regarding Latin America's political culture and regimes, what are the consequences of 50% of the region's economically active population working for decades under unregulated labor conditions, gaining minimal salaries, and generating only 10% of the region's GDP (OIT 2015)? In other words, rights are largely irrelevant, both for society's reproduction in general and for the elite.[26] The new horizon of a research perspective on labor relations is of paramount importance not just for relational and contextualized analyses but also for future emancipatory politics. With this new perspective, postcolonial studies will regain its status as a pioneer.

The questions related to the Global South's *state configurations* have already been contextualized and illuminated in many different analyses from a postcolonial perspective (e.g., Coronil 2013; Mbembe 2001). Analyses are often centered on the field of discourse or the strengthening of the practice of *state formation* (Ferguson 2004). In doing so, the focus is often turned to the formation of the postcolonial state—and not always on clearly distinguishing between *state formation* and *nation building*. From the colonial legacies identified here, new approaches can be projected that allow postcolonial studies to further deepen its perception of the state. In this manner, the three country cases addressed in this volume display many characteristics of *rentier states*.[27] Unlike capitalist profit—which is generated from work optimization, the market, and competition and which is economically connected to the state—rents are the dominant form of economic surplus, which are appropriated through political mechanisms. They can—but do not have to—be reinvested. Their realization is not based on economic competition and, as a result, does not require investment in innovation (technology); instead, they are based on direct influence and political control. Coronil (2008, 19) succinctly summarized the governing formula for market economies: "the business of politics is business." In other words, the state establishes the main parameters for capitalist accumulation. In rentier states, on the other hand, the maxim "the business of business is politics" reigns supreme.

Research on rentier states, however, is strongly influenced by institutionalism and is frequently Eurocentric. Efforts to decentralize research and enrich the institutional field with new elements are limited. This opens a fruitful field of activity for postcolonial approaches, which not only allows for these same lacunae to be addressed but also promises productive paths for future research on the state. After all, the untangling of the interwoven threads involved in rent realization—as well as its state-level distribution—presents an empirically rich research field that allows for investigation into the concrete relations between the state, the economy, and society. Furthermore, it is capable of discovering both structural preconfigurations and relevant actors' precise patterns of action. In this way, not only is the black box of the state opened but the potential for insight into the different patterns of state practice on different levels is also presented. As such, the possibility for developing a contextualized understanding of power guided by a theoretical focus that moves beyond Western navel gazing is also presented.

Consequently, the definition of a new model of postcolonial society is put forward here: the "rentier society" (for more on the term, see Peters 2017, 2019). This term refers to a society with social formations that are characterized by intergenerational dependence on rents and that, on this basis, give rise to particularities that cannot be adequately captured by Western concepts nor, by extension, the bulk of knowledge generated within the social sciences. In rentier societies, the appropriation and distribution of rents frees economic actors from the capitalist structural restrictions of unlocking value through work and, at best, assigns subordinate significance to productivity gains and efficiency in social reproduction. Instead, economic success is founded on privileged access to the state and social spheres where rents are distributed. In the distribution process, the state often serves as the primary actor. Through the (unequal) distribution of rent-based revenue, social winners and losers are chosen. In this manner, a society's entire social stratification can be shaped. Especially among the winners, a negative relationship with work as well as an outward-looking focus are promoted. This is reflected in economic strategies as well as in education policy and consumption patterns. In general, these groups are frequently characterized by a specific culture and behavior that cannot be adequately captured through Western subjects' categories of understanding. So far, the concept of rentier societies has been principally applied to the Global South's oil-producing countries. The comparison of countries presented here points to a wider application of this approach, more closely tied to research on legacies and postcolonial studies. It is thus necessary to pay more attention to the local elite. According to the examples presented, the elite are close allies with the state and are marked by a particularly pronounced orientation toward rents and the foreign markets. However, the elite's organizational and cultural schemas, or "habitus," some of which derive from colonial family structures, have yet to be sufficiently researched.[28] A wider perspective—in which postcolonial studies no longer focus solely on the subaltern but also consider the elite—would methodologically and theoretically enrich our understanding of postcolonial societies. Furthermore, it would enrich general research on inequalities, which has thus far flagrantly neglected to consider studies on the elite.[29]

These diagnoses' emphasis on work, the state, the elite, and rents in this cross-country comparison highlights the importance that material conditions have for postcolonial societies' development. This indicates a clear direction forward for postcolonial studies: the adoption of a *material turn*. This recommendation is far from new (e.g., Mezzadra 2011b), but now it can be more fully developed. Until now, debates on the material or structural dimensions of postcolonial approaches have been predominated by Marxist critiques and proposals, signaling above all the fact that postcolonial approaches ignore capitalist structural restrictions (Dirlik 1994, 2002; Chibber 2013; for a general overview, see Sinha and Varma 2017). In some cases, these reproaches are rejected on the basis that Marxist theory is itself Eurocentric, universalistic, or nationalist; in others, attempts are made to integrate Marxist categories and economic and political dimensions into postcolonial analyses (such as Pradella 2017; Sanyal 2007; for a general overview, see Bartolovich and Lazarus 2002). However, this generally appears to be a tired debate that does not promise new perspectives.

An innovative approach would be to attempt to integrate structural dimensions in social analyses while avoiding untested axioms on capitalist constellations. Instead, the supposition of a capitalist socialization would become itself subject to empirical analysis. As mentioned earlier, in this context, the distinction between rent and capitalist profit is particularly useful. It is a question of two different forms of economic surplus that contribute to the configuration of structures, institutions, and models of collective action—each of which has very different limitations and dynamics. In an alternative, contextualized analysis of society, the objective would thus be to identify the central determinants of development in postcolonial countries *beyond* capital accumulation.[30]

This is undoubtedly a blasphemous proposal and will probably provoke fierce criticism from diverse theoretical positions. Nonetheless, there is no better area prepared to substantiate it than postcolonial studies, which has a wide knowledge base and a refined set of instruments to relativize Western approaches through methodological contextualization. It needs only to widen its approach with the introduction of a material dimension.

In light of the case studies presented here, the rentier theory seems particularly well positioned to offer an adequate theoretical framework for discussing socially determinant modes of socialization in postcolonial countries that go beyond capitalism. It is necessary to break with the limited Western view of the rentier theoretical approach—especially its neoclassical and institutionalist lineage. The aim is to get a closer look at the sociocultural impact of rents, as well as the accompanying formation of subjects' behavior patterns. On this point, many rentier theory approaches are vague or completely inadequate, while postcolonial studies has at its disposal a great wealth of knowledge and experience. Research on specific behavior patterns or the everyday marks left by rent seeking—as well as the significance it holds in different power constellations—opens a wide field in which postcolonial studies can address material practices without sacrificing a contextualized approach.[31]

Finally, the transregional comparison between Cuba, Puerto Rico, and the Philippines provides us with three insights. First, colonial legacies still have significant influence on postcolonial development. Colonial legacy matters. As such, postcolonial studies' accumulated knowledge should be an indispensable component of social analyses on the Global South. Second, the material dimension of development is highly significant in these countries. Postcolonial studies should therefore make use of its methodological tools and conduct relational social analyses. This means merging the analysis of socio-material and structural dimensions with the analysis of difference-based categories such as ethnicity, gender, religion, and other variables relevant in the contexts analyzed. Consequently, to move forward, a material turn is imperative to compensate for the relative neglect of the material component. The concepts and categories developed by and for theorizing rentier societies provide a promising starting point for such an endeavor. Third, the methodological focus and the systematization of the comparison presented here demonstrate that an investigation that is context sensitive can, in fact, break "the monoculture of modern science" (Santos 2007; see also Burchardt 2018; Dhawan et al. 2016; Santos 2010). This implies not the rejection of Western knowledge but instead its extension, finding complementary knowledge and pursuing new syntheses.

NOTES

1. The island's ecology was completely destroyed. By the turn of the 20th century, only 15% of the woods that had existed when the Spanish arrived remained (Funes 2010).

2. A hacienda was the equivalent of a latifundio, principally characterized by good access to land, water, labor, and markets. To retain workers, debt bondage was often established through salary advances, which could be inherited and, as a result, developed into a form of slavery. When there was a surplus of workers, labor agreements would be broken, and cheaper temporary workers were used. If market opportunities were poor, land was rented out. The hacienda constituted a relatively closed social system whose inhabitants had very little contact with the outside world. In addition to houses, it often included a chapel, a store, and other facilities similar to that of a small town, such as a post office, a prison, and a school. In this sense, for workers it presented a substitute to the old structure of their villages. In general, there tended to be an informal and strongly paternalistic relationship of dependence between the workers and the owner, the hacendado. The majority of the haciendas produced for exportation.

3. A large portion of this revenue could be characterized as international rents; that is, it was income that was unconnected to a job held or investment made on the part of the beneficiary. Of course, sugar production and exportation as well as other agricultural products and raw materials required a workforce and considerable investment. However, at the time, the international socialist market's preferential pricing was not based on the real cost of production but was instead politically determined. Prices were significantly higher than the real costs and were closer to

subsidies or unearned income. This phenomenon can also be found in the capitalist global market. For example, the cost of raw materials in the international market is currently calculated only in small measure in function of the real cost of production and labor; rather, it depends on other factors and, particularly, on speculation. In this case, the difference between the cost of production and the prices reached in the world market is used to generate a considerable portion of rents: for example, in oil production in the Arab nation-states, rents are calculated to reach between 80% to 90% (Ross 2012, 36).

4. Among other things, an interesting change in discourse emerged. Instead of the socialist paradigm, national identity was increasingly activated as an important source of legitimacy. According to this discourse, the Cuban Revolution guaranteed the island's independence for the first time in 500 years of foreign dominance.

5. Cuba has a large diaspora of around 2 million people, the majority of whom reside in the US and regularly send money to their relatives on the island. According to estimates, the average flow of remittances exceeds 3 billion dollars and, as a result, clearly exceeds foreign currency revenue gained through the exportation of goods (Triana 2017). Whites make up the great majority of remittance beneficiaries (Delgado 2016).

6. At the same time, with the massive immigration of African slaves in the 19th century, syncretized popular sects emerged (like Santería), which continue to make up an important part of Cuban culture.

7. For example, in the mid-19th century, ownership of slaves continued to be an everyday phenomenon. Kemner (this volume) has calculated based on census databases that in 1857 approximately one out of every three Cuban households owned slaves. This density is considerably higher than the slave-owning society of the antebellum American South.

8. In the 1980s, the state employed 95% of the total labor force: the salary gap between the highest and lowest salaries was 4.5 to 1 (Espina, Martín, and Núñez 2003).

9. This affects both external and domestic perceptions; for example, in the last census in 2012, nearly 65% of the Cuban population reported that they were white, while only 9% identified themselves as black. Given that nearly 50% of the population was black in the mid-19th century, these figures hardly reflect Cuba's current ethnic composition (see Zeuske's and Morín's contributions, this volume).

10. Fidel Castro also recognized racism's persistence in Cuba and that recent economic reforms have been particularly detrimental to black Cubans: "Notwithstanding the rights and guarantees attained for all citizens regardless of ethnicity or background, the Revolution has not attained similar success in its fight to eradicate differences in the social and economic status of the country's black population. Blacks do not live in the best houses, they still can be found carrying out the hardest and at times least compensated work, and fewer of them receive family remittances in foreign currency than their white compatriots" (Castro in Ramonet 2010, 261).

11. In 1996, Puerto Rico's earnings on foreign investment directly from the US was nearly 14%, ahead of both England and Canada, whose earnings through this type of investment generated 12% and 7% of the countries' respective earnings,

even though England's GDP was 26 times greater and Canada's was 13 times greater than the island's (Pantojas 2007).

12. Puerto Rico's domestic investment in 2017 was seven times lower than its consumption, while importations exceeded exportations by 10%. Over 80% of national consumption is imported, and US businesses on the island receive less than 15% of their production parts from national suppliers (Quiñones Pérez and Seda-Irizarry, this volume).

13. Under the encomienda system, the Spanish Crown granted land, along with the people who lived on it, to the conquistadors for them to oversee as fiduciaries. The feudal lords were responsible for the protection and catechism of the indigenous people who lived under their ward. Formally, the indigenous population was free and not property of the encomenderos, which is to say, they were not slaves. In practice, however, the encomienda, which was repeatedly redesigned, was in essence a regimen of forced, lifelong labor.

14. This is illustrated by a widespread rejection of the English language: after annexing the island in 1898, the US not only introduced the American school system (university) but also instated English as the official language in school and declared Spanish to be a primitive language. Today, however, Spanish continues to be the island's lingua franca among all sectors of the population, an expression of belonging and even subtle resistance.

15. This led to a massive labor exodus, which currently is primarily oriented toward *caregiving work* and largely made up by women. Remittances generated by this work constitute an important economic factor, making up at least 10% of the GDP.

16. The church's central position soon gave rise to a transculturated Christianity with independent local roots, which also had to be defended against the Islamized ethnic group from the Southern Philippines and the Sulu Sea.

17. Contrary to trends in the rest of the Southeast Asian region, concentration of land ownership in the Philippines rose between 1950 and 1991. The rate of 0.55 represents one of the highest in Southeast Asia. This asymmetrical distribution echoes Latin American conditions (You 2014).

18. One colony that stands out in this regard is Cuba, which became the world's principal sugarcane producer after the Haitian Revolution. For many years, the island had fertile land, easy access to maritime routes, rich reserves of wood to fuel the energy supply, and continuous access to slaves. In the mid-19th century, there were nearly half a million slaves in Cuba, the majority of whom worked in sugarcane plantations. Almost half the population was black.

19. The specific requirements for sugarcane cultivation and production required a strict division of labor, meticulously coordinated across numerous work stages with different skill requirements. This led to new hierarchization models in function of the different types of work, norms of social categorization, and discipline and control techniques. Based on North American cotton production, Beckert (2014) has demonstrated that slavery used in monoculture production and semi-industrial processing guaranteed the highest productivity and revenue margins. These semi-industrial production practices, experiences, and successes had an

impact on European centers and played a significant role in promoting the early stages of European industrialization—which, nonetheless, remains an unanalyzed phenomenon (Bortoluci and Jansen 2013).

20. For various historians, like Pomeranz (2000), the difference between North America's and South America's postcolonial development dynamics is in fact precisely due to this understanding of work, which prevented the rise of a free labor market driven by general economic demand. This resulted in limits on the increases in work productivity and economic growth. Since Andreski (1967), these differences have been frequently attributed to the first colonial rulers' different religious and cultural attitudes: while religious Puritan refugees in the US wanted to build a new world by the sweat of their own brow, Spaniards primarily sought out wealth through the extraction of raw materials by means of the exploitation of mainly non-Spanish laborers. In Mahoney's (2010) typology of various colonial frameworks, he also refers to the canon of values that the colonizers brought from Europe.

21. Referencing Franz Fanon, it is important to remember here that racism is a phenomenon not just limited to the elite but also actively practiced by the subaltern, in relation to those "below" as well as "above." Slave ownership was in this sense also a mark of social distinction that indicated inclusion to at least the lower middle class. This explains the occurrence of black slave owners (some of whom were themselves former slaves) who sought, in this way, to improve their social position.

22. The colonial legacy of ethnic discrimination's enduring strength is particularly evident in the Cuban experience, where over 50 years of exemplary institutional policies and concrete actions to combat racism have proven insufficient for dismantling society's racist schemas.

23. The emergence of national and cultural identities, which continues to have a legitimizing and mobilizing effect in these three countries' politics and societies, reveals the importance that ethnic and cultural identities have in processes of social change. According to the concept of *transculturation*, developed in Cuba by Fernando Ortiz (1940), or Bhaba's (1994) *hybridity*, while colonies suffered oppression and white domination at the hands of the colonizers, there was also a rich history of mutual influence, support, and synthesis between the colonial masters and other ethnic groups. In the Philippines, elements from the indigenous peoples and their organization models molded today's elite, while in Cuba and Puerto Rico, the fusion of different ethnic influences gave rise to their "national identity" (for Cuba, see Zeuske; for the Philippines, see Elizalde, this volume). This cooperation was—and continues to be—of central importance not just for decolonization but also later for various democratization and emancipation movements. The unique intellectual traditions that were established are germane to each country and have influenced artistic and scientific work in many areas.

24. Precarious and hierarchic work conditions seem to be a colonial legacy throughout Latin America. After Southeast Asia, for example, it is the region that employs the highest number of domestic workers. In 2016, 18 million caretakers made up 7% of the labor force, over 90% of whom were women and nearly 80% of whom were informally employed—that is, without a work contract, without health care, and poorly paid. Additionally, indigenous and black individuals are disproportionately represented in this group (OIT 2016).

25. For the case of the US (where, for Marx, the capitalist valuation of work was most advanced), see Lowe (1996).

26. O'Donnell (1999) attempted to capture this aspect of the theory of democracy with the concept *low-intensity citizenship*, i.e., a low level of civil, political, and social rights enforcement.

27. Since Hossein Mahdavy's introduction of this term in 1970, the rentier state has been ascribed various unappealing characteristics: the exacerbation of economic instability; low economic diversification; high level of external dependence and the economy's vulnerability to crisis; growing environmental pressures; the strengthening and stabilization of authoritarian power structures; the low level of transparency in public funds and unchecked corruption; the perpetuation of social disparity; and the rise of new social tensions. In this context, the state politically secured its power through a spoils system and other sociopolitical ways of parlaying power to allied groups (Ross 2012).

28. See Shore and Nugent's (2002) and Go's (2008) comparisons, which use the example of Puerto Rico and the Philippines to show how the local elite's colonial legacies have continued under US rule and are directly tied to rent generation and the strict employment conditions in agriculture.

29. See Appiah (1991), who indicated early on the need for postcolonial critiques to focus on nations' elite class.

30. Attempts to analytically address non-capitalist forms of sociation can be found, for example, in Hesketh (2016) from a Marxist perspective or in Gibson and Graham (2006) from a feminist perspective centered in reproduction.

31. In this context, postcolonial theories can also enter into the praxeological discussion, thus rebalancing the relationship between materiality and ideality (Reckwitz 2002). For the connection between rent theory and more recent praxeological action theories based in the example of violence, see, for example, Warnecke-Berger (2018).

REFERENCES

Andreski, Stanislav. 1967. *Parasitism and Subversion: The Case of Latin America*. New York: Pantheon Books.

Appiah, Kwame Anthony. 1991. "Is the Post- in Postmodernism the Post- in Postcolonial?" *Critical Inquiry* 17 (2): 336–57.

Bartolovich, Crystal, and Neil Lazarus. 2002. *Marxism, Modernity, and Postcolonial Studies*. Cambridge: Cambridge University Press.

Bayudan-Dacuycuy, Connie, and Joseph Lim. 2014. "Chronic and Transient Poverty and Vulnerability to Poverty in the Philippines: Evidence Using a Simple Spells Approach." *Social Indicators Research* 118 (1): 389–413.

Beckert, Sven. 2014. *Empire of Cotton: A Global History*. New York: Vintage Books.

Bell Lara, José, Tania Caram León, Dirk Kruijt, and Delia Luisa López García. 2017. *Cuba: Período Especial*. Havana: Editorial UH.

Bhabha, Homi. 1994. *The Location of Culture*. London: Routledge.

Borras, Saturnino, Jr. 2001. "State-Society Relations in Land Reform Implementation in the Philippines." *Development and Change* 32: 545–75.

Bortoluci, José H., and Robert S. Jansen. 2013. "Toward a Postcolonial Sociology:

The View from Latin America." In *Postcolonial Sociology*, edited by Julian Go, 199–229. Bingley: Emerald Group.

Burchardt, Hans-Jürgen. 2018. "How Spinoza and Elias Help to Decenter Our Understanding of Development—A Methodical Research Proposal on the Pluriverse." In *Constructing the Pluriverse: The Geopolitics of Knowledge*, edited by Bernd Reiter, 285–320. Durham: Duke University Press.

Chakrabarty, Dipesh. 2000. *Provincializing Europe: Postcolonial Thought and Historical Difference*. Princeton: Princeton University Press.

Chibber, Vivek. 2013. *Postcolonial Theory and the Specter of Capital*. London: Verso.

Coronil, Fernando. 2008. "It's the Oil, Stupid!!!" *ReVista. Harvard Review of Latin America* 8 (1): 19–20.

Coronil, Fernando. 2013. *El Estado Mágico. Naturaleza, Dinero y Modernidad en Venezuela*. Caracas: Editorial Alfa.

Delgado Vázquez, Denisse. 2016. *Efectos del Uso Diferenciado de las Remesas en la Desigualdad Social. Un Estudio en la Capital Cubana*. Buenos Aires: CLACSO. http://biblioteca.clacso.edu.ar/clacso/becas/20160401090229/denissedelgado.pdf

Dhawan, Nikita, Elisabeth Fink, Johanna Leinius, and Rirhandu Mageza-Barthel, eds. 2016. *Negotiating Normativity: Postcolonial Appropriations, Contestations, and Transformations*. Cham: Springer International.

Dietz, James L. 1986. *Economic History of Puerto Rico; Institutional Changes and Capitalist Development*. Princeton: Princeton University Press.

Dirlik, Arif. 1994. "The Postcolonial Aura: Third World Criticism in the Age of Global Capitalism." *Critical Inquiry* 20 (2): 328–56.

Dirlik, Arif. 2002. "Rethinking Colonialism: Globalization, Postcolonialism, and the Nation." *Interventions* 4 (3): 428–48.

Espina Prieto, Mayra. 2012. "La Política Social en Cuba: Nueva Reforma Económica." *Revista de Ciencias Sociales* 2012 (135–36): 227–36.

Espina Prieto, Mayra, Lucy Martín Posada, and Lilian Núñez Moreno. 2003. "Reajuste Económico y Cambios Socioestructurales." In *Los Cambios en la Estructura Socioclasista en Cuba*, edited by Manuel Menéndez Díaz, 10–50. Havana: Ed. de Ciencias Sociales.

Ferguson, James. 2004. "Power Topographies." In *A Companion to the Anthropology of Politics*, edited by David Nugent and Joan Vincent, 383–99. Malden: Blackwell.

Fisher, Andrew B., and Matthew D. O'Hara, eds. 2009. *Imperial Subjects: Race and Identity in Colonial Latin America*. Durham: Duke University Press.

Foucault, M. 1980. "Truth and Power." In *Michel Foucault: Power/Knowledge*, edited by Colin Gordon, 109–33. Brighton: Harvester.

Funes Monzote, Reinaldo. 2010. *De los Bosques a los Cañaverales*. Havana: Editorial de Ciencias Sociales.

Galtés Galeano, Indira. 2017. "Desigualdad de Ingresos en Cuba: ¿Qué Papel Juegan los Salarios?" In *Miradas a la Economía Cubana. Un Acercamiento a la "Actualización" Seis Años Después*, edited by Ricardo Torres Pérez and Dayma Echevarría León, 68–80. Havana: Ruth Casa Editorial.

Gerstenberger, Heide. 2007. *Impersonal Power: History and Theory of the Bourgeois State*. Leiden: Brill.

Gibson, Katherine, and Julie Graham. 2006. *The End of Capitalism (As We Knew It):*

A Feminist Critique of Political Economy. Minneapolis: University of Minnesota Press.

Glenn, Evelyn Nakano. 2004. *Unequal Freedom: How Race and Gender Shape American Citizenship and Labor*. Cambridge, MA: Harvard University Press.

Go, Julian. 2008. *American Empire and the Politics of Meaning: Elite Political Cultures in the Philippines and Puerto Rico during U.S. Colonialism*. Durham: Duke University Press.

Godreau, Isar P. 2015. *Scripts of Blackness: Race, Cultural Nationalism and US Colonialism in Puerto Rico*. Champaign: University of Illinois Press.

González Díaz, Emilio. 1991. *La Política de los Empresarios Puertorriqueños*. Río Piedras: Ediciones Huracán and Centro de Investigaciones Sociales.

Hansing, Katrin. 2017. "Race and Inequality in the New Cuba: Reasons, Dynamics, and Manifestations." *Social Research: An International Quarterly* 84 (2): 331–49.

Hesketh, Chris. 2016. "The Survival of Non-Capitalism." *Environment and Planning D: Society and Space* 34 (5): 877–94.

Hodder, Rupert. 2013. *High-Level Political Appointments in the Philippines: Patronage, Emotion, and Democracy*. Berlin: Springer Science & Business Media.

Instituto de Estadísticas de Puerto Rico. 2018. *Human Development Report for Puerto Rico*. San Juan: Instituto de Estadísticas de Puerto Rico.

International Labour Office (ILO). 2017. *Global Estimates of Modern Slavery. Methodology*. Genf: ILO. https://www.ilo.org/wcmsp5/groups/public/@ed_norm/@ipec/documents/publication/wcms_586127.pdf

Jain-Chandra, Sonali, Kalpana Tidiane Kinda, Shi Piao Kochhar, and Johanna Schauer. 2016. "Sharing the Growth Dividend: Analysis of Inequality in Asia." *IMF Working Paper* 16/48. Washington, DC: IMF Asia and Pacific Department.

Legarda, Benito, Jr. 1999. *After the Galleons: Foreign Trade, Economic Change and Entrepreneurship in the Nineteenth-Century Philippines*. Quezon City: Ateneo de Manila University Press.

Lowe, Lisa. 1996. *Immigrant Acts: On Asian American Cultural Politics*. Durham: Duke University Press.

Mahdavy, Hossein. 1970. "Patterns and Problems of Economic Development in Rentier States: The Case of Iran." In *Studies in the Economic History of the Middle East: From the Rise of Islam to the Present Day*, edited by M. A. Cook, 428–67. London: Oxford University Press.

Mahoney, James. 2010. *Colonialism and Postcolonial Development: Spanish America in Comparative Perspective*. Cambridge: Cambridge University Press.

Mbembe, Achille. 2001. *On the Postcolony*. Berkeley: University of California Press.

Mezzadra, Sandro. 2011a. "Bringing: How Many Histories of Labour? Towards a Theory of Postcolonial Capitalism." *Postcolonial Studies* 14 (2): 151–70.

Mezzadra, Sandro. 2011b. "Bringing Capital Back In: A Materialist Turn in Postcolonial Studies?" *Inter-Asia Cultural Studies* 12 (1): 154–64.

Mignolo, Walter D. 2011. *The Darker Side of Western Modernity: Global Futures, Decolonial Options*. Durham: Duke University Press.

Monteiro, John M. 2006. "Labor Systems." In *Cambridge Economic History of Latin America*, vol. 1, edited by Victor Bulmer-Thomas, John Coatsworth, and Roberto Cortes-Conde, 185–233. Cambridge: Cambridge University Press.

Morales, Esteban. 2007. *Desafíos de la Problemática Racial en Cuba*. Havana: Fundación Fernando Ortiz.
North, Liisa L., and Timothy D. Clark, eds. 2018. *Dominant Elites in Latin America*. Cham: Springer International.
Núñez González, Niurka. 2015. "Inequidades Raciales ante el Proceso de Actualización del Modelo Económico Cubano." In *Retos para la Equidad Social en el Proceso de Actualización del Modelo Económico Cubano*, edited by Zabala Argüelles, María del Carmen, Dayma Echevarriá León, Marta Rosa Muñoz Campos, and Geydis Elena Fundora Nevot, 135–46. Havana: Editorial de Ciencias Sociales.
O'Donnell, Guillermo. 1999. "On the State, Democratization, and Some Conceptual Problems: A Latin American View with Glances at Some Postcommunist Countries." In *Counterpoints: Selected Essays on Authoritarianism and Democratization*, edited by Guillermo O'Donnell, 133–57. Notre Dame: University of Notre Dame.
OIT. 2015. *Panorama Laboral 2015. América Latina Y El Caribe*. Lima: Organización Internacional del Trabajo, Oficina Regional para América Latina y el Caribe.
OIT. 2016. *Políticas de Formalización del Trabajo Doméstico Remunerado en América Latina y el Caribe*. Lima: Organización Internacional del Trabajo, Oficina Regional para América Latina y el Caribe. https://www.ilo.org/wcmsp5/groups/public/---americas/---ro-lima/documents/publication/wcms_480352.pdf
Ortiz, Fernando. 1940. "El Fenómeno Social de la Transculturación y su Importancia en Cuba." *Revista Bimestre Cubana* 46 (July–December): 273–78.
Pantojas García, Emilio. 2007. "'Federal Funds' and the Puerto Rican Economy: Myths and Realities." *CENTRO Journal* 19 (2): 207–23.
Peters, Stefan. 2017. "Beyond Curse and Blessing: Rentier Society in Venezuela." In *Contested Extractivism, Society and the State: Struggles over Mining and Land*, edited by Kristina Dietz and Bettina Engels, 45–68. London: Palgrave Macmillan.
Peters, Stefan. 2019. *Rentengesellschaften: Der Lateinamerikanische (Neo-)Extraktivismus im Transregionalen Vergleich*. Baden-Baden: Nomos.
Pomeranz, Kenneth. 2000. *The Great Divergence: China, Europe, and the Making of the Modern World Economy*. Princeton: Princeton University Press.
Pradella, Lucia. 2017. "Postcolonial Theory and the Making of the World Working Class." *Critical Sociology* 43 (4–5): 573–86.
Quijano, Aníbal. 2000. "Coloniality of Power." *Nepantla: Views from South* 1 (3): 533–74.
Ramonet, Ignacio. 2010. *Fidel Castro: Biografía a Dos Voces*. Madrid: Penguin Random House and Grupo Editorial España.
Reckwitz, Andreas. 2002. "Toward a Theory of Social Practices: A Development in Culturalist Theorising." *European Journal of Social Theory* 5 (2): 243–63.
Ross, Michael L. 2012. *The Oil Curse: How Petroleum Wealth Shapes the Development of Nations*. Princeton: Princeton University Press.
Santos, Boaventura de Sousa. 2007. "Beyond Abyssal Thinking: From Global Lines to Ecologies of Knowledges." *Review (Fernand Braudel Center)* 30 (1): 45–89.
Santos, Boaventura de Sousa. 2010. "From the Postmodern to the Postcolonial—

and Beyond Both." In *Decolonizing European Sociology: Transdisciplinary Approaches (Global Connections)*, edited by Encarnación Gutiérrez Rodríguez, Manuela Boatca, and Sergio Costa, 225–42. London: Routledge.
Sanyal, Kalyan. 2007. *Rethinking Capitalist Development: Primitive Accumulation, Governmentality and Post-Colonial Capitalism*. London: Routledge.
Scarano, Francisco A. 1994. *Puerto Rico, Cinco Siglos de Historia*. México: McGraw-Hill.
Scott, William Henry. 1994. *Barangay: Sixteenth-Century Philippine Culture and Society*. Quezon City: Ateneo University Press.
Shore, Cris, and Stephen Nugent, eds. 2002. *Elite Cultures: Anthropological Perspectives*. London: Routledge.
Sicat, Gerardo. 2009. "Labor Policies and Philippine Companies: Analysis of Survey Opinions." *Philippine Journal of Development* 36 (2): 1–46.
Simbulan, Dante. 2005. *The Modern Principalia: The Historical Evolution of the Philippine Ruling Oligarchy*. Quezon City: University of the Philippines Press.
Sinha, Subir, and Rashmi Varma. 2017. "Marxism and Postcolonial Theory: What's Left of the Debate?" *Critical Sociology* 43 (4–5): 545–58.
Sotomayor, Orlando. 2004. "Development and Income Distribution: The Case of Puerto Rico." *World Development* 32 (8): 1395–1406.
Tadem, Teresa S. Encarnacion, and Eduardo C. Tadem. 2016. "Political Dynasties in the Philippines: Persistent Patterns, Perennial Problems." *South East Asia Research* 24 (3): 328–40.
Triana Cordoví, Juan. 2017. "Economía Cubana 2016 y 2017: La Coyuntura y los Retos del Crecimiento." In *Miradas a la Economía Cubana. Un Acercamiento a la «Actualización» Seis Años Después*, edited by Ricardo Torres Pérez and Dayma Echevarría León, 37–48. Havana: Ruth Casa Editorial.
Warnecke-Berger, Hannes. 2018. *Politics and Violence in Central America*. London: Palgrave Macmillan.
Wolf, Eric R., and Sidney W. Mintz. 1977. "Haciendas and Plantations." In *Haciendas and Plantations in Latin American History*, edited by Robert G. Keith, 36–62. New York: Holmes & Meier.
You, Jong-sung. 2014. "Land Reform, Inequality, and Corruption: A Comparative Historical Study of Korea, Taiwan, and the Philippines." *Korean Journal of International Studies* 12 (1): 191–224.

Contributors

Maria Isabel B. Aguilar is a social science teacher at the Philippine Science High School Main Campus. She teaches Philippine history and civic engagement and leadership, which tackles and problematizes the various social issues plaguing the Philippines. She holds a BA in history and an MA in Philippine studies from the University of the Philippines Diliman.

Hans-Jürgen Burchardt is Director of the Maria Sibylla Merian Center of Latin American Advanced Studies (CALAS) and Chair of International and Intersocietal Relations at the University of Kassel. He has published extensively on North-South relations; ecological, labor, and social policy regimes from an international perspective; and theories of development and development politics, especially focusing on Latin America and the Caribbean (website: https://kassel-global.de/en).

Alvin Camba, Assistant Professor at the Korbel School of International Studies at the University of Denver and a research fellow at the Climate Policy Lab at Tufts University, studies Chinese investments in Southeast Asia. More information about his work can be found on his website (alvincamba.com).

Cristina Cielo is Professor-Researcher in the Department of Sociology and Gender Studies at the Latin American Faculty of Social Sciences—FLACSO Ecuador. She explores the subjective and political dimensions of inequalities, with a focus on affective ecologies and diverse economies in the Global South, including recent research on care work in extractive territories, changing university-society relations, and urban and popular economies and politics.

Milagros Denis-Rosario is Associate Professor of History at the Department of Africana and Puerto Rican/Latino Studies at Hunter College, New York. She holds a PhD in Latin American and Caribbean history from Howard University, an MA in Africana studies from Cornell University, and a BA in art history from the University of Puerto Rico. She just finished a book on the discourse of race and racist practices in Puerto Rican society, to be published by the State University of New York Press under the title *Drops of Inclusivity: Racial Formations and Meanings in Puerto Rican Society, 1898–1965*.

María Dolores Elizalde is Scientific Researcher at the Institute of History, Spanish National Research Council (CSIC) in Madrid, Spain. She received her PhD in history from the Universidad Complutense de Madrid. She has been a research scholar at the London School of Economics and Political Sciences (LSE) and visiting fellow at the Université de Paris 1-Sorbonne, the School of Oriental and African Studies (SOAS), University of London, and the School of Pacific and Asian Studies, University of Hawaii. She specializes in international history, colonial societies, and colonial and postcolonial processes in Asia and the Pacific with a particular interest in the Philippines.

Josep M. Fradera is Professor of Modern History at the Pompeu Fabra University in Barcelona. He has published extensively on the 19th-century economic, cultural, and political history of Catalonia, Spain, and its empire in America and the Philippines. His last book as sole author is *The Imperial Nation: Citizens and Subjects in the British, French, Spanish, and American Empire* (Princeton: Princeton University Press, 2018); more recently, he coedited with José María Portillo and Teresa Segura-García *Unexpected Voices in Imperial Parliaments* (London: Bloomsbury Academic, 2021).

Javiher Gutiérrez Forte is Coordinator of Activities for the Centro de Estudios Casa de Altos Estudios Don Fernando Ortiz and Assistant Professor of the Casa de Altos Estudios Don Fernando Ortiz of the Faculty of Philosophy and History. He graduated from the University of Havana with a degree in history and holds an MA in interdisciplinary studies on Latin America, the Caribbean, and Cuba. He works on the political and social history of Cuba, focusing on the history of Masonic lodges and their effect on the history of Cuba.

Janet Iglesias Cruz is Assistant Professor of the Casa de Altos Estudios Don Fernando Ortiz of the Faculty of Philosophy and History at the University of Havana. She graduated from this university with a degree in history and holds an MA in interdisciplinary studies on Latin America, the Caribbean, and Cuba. She was a scholarship holder for three consecutive years in the Banco Santander Program of Santiago de Compostela University. She works on the history of Spanish migrations to Cuba and was awarded "Anduriña" and "Galleguidad" prizes in 1998 and 1999, respectively, in the contests organized by the Xunta de Galicia, Spain.

Jochen Kemner, University of Kassel, is Managing Director of the Center for Advanced Latin American Studies in Humanities and Social Sciences (CALAS) in Guadalajara, Mexico. His research areas include Caribbean and Latin American history, slavery, social movements, history education, and global learning.

Jacqueline Laguardia Martinez is Lecturer at the Institute of International Relations at the University of the West Indies. She holds a PhD in economics from the University of Havana, where she worked as associate professor. She was research associate at the Cuban Institute for Cultural Research "Juan Marinello." She is a member of the Cátedra de Estudios del Caribe "Norman Girvan" at the University of Havana and the coordinator of the CLACSO Working Group on "Crisis, respuestas y alternativas en el Gran Caribe."

Johanna Leinius works as postdoctoral researcher in sociological theory at the University of Kassel, Germany. She holds a PhD in political science from Goethe-University Frankfurt, where she worked as a research associate at the Frankfurt Research Center for Postcolonial Studies, and a Master of Social Sciences (M.Soc.Sci.) from the University of Helsinki, Finland. Her research interests include social movement studies, postcolonial feminist theory, Latin American societies and the politics of post-extractivism. Her most recent book is *The Cosmopolitics of Solidarity: Social Movement Encounters across Difference* (Springer Nature, 2022).

Teresa R. Melgar is a comparative-historical sociologist with research interests in citizenship, democratization, participatory governance, social movements, development, and Latin America, particularly Brazil. She was a Fulbright Visiting Scholar at the Department of Sociology, University of California, Berkeley. She obtained her PhD in sociology from the University of Wisconsin–Madison and is currently Associate Professor of Sociology at the University of the Philippines Diliman, where she teaches graduate and undergraduate courses on political sociology, social theory, civil society, globalization, and development.

Jenny Morín Nenoff works as personal advisor to the secretary general of the German Academic Exchange Service (DAAD) in Bonn, Germany. She received her PhD in Latin American history from the University of Cologne. She specializes in history and political science with a particular interest in the socioeconomic transformation process in Cuba.

Emilio Pantojas-García is Senior Researcher and Director of the Institute of Caribbean Studies and Professor of Sociology at the University of Puerto Rico. He is the author of *Development Strategies as Ideology: Puerto Rico's Export-Led Industrialization Experience* (1990) and *Crónicas del Colapso: Economía Política y Sociedad de Puerto Rico en el Siglo Veintiuno* (2015; 3rd ed., 2019).

Argeo T. Quiñones Pérez obtained his ABD from the University of Massachusetts at Amherst in 1983, specializing in the areas of economic development, political economy, economic history, and macroeconomics. Since then he has been teaching in the Department of Economics, University of Puerto Rico, Río Piedras campus, while also serving as adviser of both labor unions and the president of the Planning Board. He is one of the major critical voices concerning the analysis of the economy of Puerto Rico, its crisis, adjustments, and alternatives, with more than a dozen articles about these topics, hundreds of radio programs, and dozens of public conferences.

Miguel A. Rivera Quiñones is Lecturer of Political Science at the University of Puerto Rico and Research Fellow at the Center of Social Research (CIS). He has been visiting research fellow at Princeton University and New York University. Prior to these appointments, Miguel taught at the International Relations Department and the Institute of Development Studies (IDS) at the University of Sussex.

Antonio Santamaría García is Researcher at the Institute of History, Centre of Human and Social Sciences, CSIC. He graduated with a degree in geography and history from the Complutense University (UCM) and received a doctorate in geography and history from the UCM (I. U. Ortega y Gasset), Spain. He has been a visiting professor at the Jaume I University of Castelló and at the University of Havana, as well as FPI scholar at the UCM, AEU professor in the Department of Economics at Carlos III University, and visiting fellow at St. Antony's College, University of Oxford. He is a member of the Research Group on Comparative Studies of the Caribbean and the Atlantic World and of the Working Group on the Caribbean within the framework of AHILA and of the Caribbean Studies Network.

Ian J. Seda-Irizarry is Associate Professor and Graduate Program Director at John Jay College, City University of New York, where he teaches courses on political economy, economic development, and history of economic thought. His research areas include the political economy of Puerto Rico and Marxist socioeconomic theory.

Michael Zeuske is Senior Research Professor at the Bonn Center for Dependency and Slavery Studies (BCDSS/University of Bonn) and Professor Emeritus of Iberian and Latin American History at the University of Cologne, Germany. In 2007, he was a research fellow at the Gilder Lehrman Center for the Study of Slavery, Resistance, and Abolition (Yale University, New Haven). He is a leading expert on Atlantic history and the history of the Caribbean, especially Cuba and Venezuela, and most known for his studies on global slavery, slave trade, and biographies of enslaved people.

Index